fine Cooking

fresh

fine Cooking fresh

350 Recipes that Celebrate the Seasons

From the Editors and Contributors of *Fine Cooking*

The Taunton Press

The Taunton Press
Inspiration for hands-on living®

The Taunton Press, Inc., 63 South Main Street, PO Box 5506, Newtown, CT 06470-5506
e-mail: tp@taunton.com

Indexer: Heidi Blough

Fine Cooking® is a trademark of The Taunton Press, Inc.,
registered in the U.S. Patent and Trademark Office.

Library of Congress Cataloging-in-Publication Data

Fine cooking fresh : 350 recipes that celebrate the seasons / editors and contributors of Fine cooking.
    p. cm.
 Includes index.
 ISBN 978-1-60085-109-4
 1. Cookery. I. Taunton Press. II. Taunton's fine cooking.
 TX714.F5654 2009
 641.5--dc22
                          2008042138

Printed in the United States of America
10 9 8 7 6 5 4 3 2 1

The following names/manufacturers appearing in *Fine Cooking Fresh* are trademarks:
Droste® cocoa powder, Old Bay® Seasoning, Pyrex®, Sutter Home® Moscato, Tabasco®, Total™ yogurt

Contents

Grilled Chicken Wings with
Asian-Style Barbecue Sauce *p. 4*

Small Bites & Cool Drinks

Grilled Chicken Wings

Serves four to six as an appetizer.

It's easy enough to double or triple this recipe. Just be sure to do the same with the sauce.

2 lb. chicken wings (about 10 whole wings), split into three segments at the wing joints (discard the wingtips or save for stock)
1 tsp. kosher salt
¼ tsp. freshly ground black pepper
Oil for the grill
1 recipe Asian-Style Barbecue Sauce (below)
2 scallions (both white and green parts), trimmed and thinly sliced

Heat a gas grill to medium high or prepare a medium-hot charcoal fire. Season the wings with the salt and pepper.

Rub the grill grate with oil. Grill the wings, covered on a gas grill or uncovered over a charcoal fire, flipping every couple of minutes, until they're browned and crisp and completely cooked through, about 20 minutes; if there are flare-ups, move the wings to another part of the grill. If the wings begin to burn at any point, reduce the heat to medium or transfer the wings to a cooler part of the grill.

As the wings are done, transfer them to a large bowl. Stir the sauce and toss with the wings. Arrange the wings on a platter, sprinkle with the scallions, and serve immediately.

Asian-Style Barbecue Sauce

Yields enough for 2 lb. wings.

¼ cup tomato ketchup
2 Tbs. soy sauce
1 Tbs. light brown sugar
1 Tbs. rice vinegar
2 scallions (both white and green parts), trimmed and thinly sliced
Large pinch crushed red pepper flakes

In a small bowl, whisk the ketchup, soy sauce, brown sugar, rice vinegar, scallions, and red pepper flakes.

Mojito

Serves one; recipe doubles or quadruples easily.

A hot summer day calls for a cool drink like this refreshing Cuban mint and lime cocktail (it's pronounced moh-HEE-toh). If your barware is particularly fragile, muddle the mint and sugar together in a mortar or other vessel and then transfer it to the serving glass.

6 large fresh spearmint leaves, plus 1 nice sprig for garnish
4 tsp. superfine sugar; more to taste
1 lime
Crushed ice as needed
2 oz. (¼ cup) light rum
Cold club soda as needed

In a tall, narrow (Collins) glass, mash the mint leaves into the sugar with a muddler or a similar tool (like the handle of a wooden spoon) until the leaves look crushed and the sugar starts to turn light green, about 30 seconds. Cut the lime into quarters. Squeeze the juice from all four quarters into the glass, dropping two of the squeezed quarters into the glass as you go. Stir with a teaspoon until the sugar dissolves into the lime juice. Fill the glass with crushed ice and pour the rum over the ice. Top off with club soda, stir well, garnish with the mint sprig, and serve right away.

Steamed Mussels with Lime & Cilantro

Serves four as a main course; eight as an appetizer.

This is a nice departure from the usual steamed mussels in wine. The jalapeño and chile sauce supply a little kick and the lime and cilantro give a boost of fresh flavor.

4 lb. mussels
2 Tbs. extra-virgin olive oil
1 medium carrot, peeled and cut into small dice
1 large fresh jalapeño, seeded and minced
2 cloves garlic, minced (about 1 Tbs.)
Finely grated zest and juice of 1 lime
½ cup dry white wine or white vermouth
½ cup heavy cream
⅓ cup loosely packed cilantro leaves and tender stems, coarsely chopped
½ to 1 tsp. Asian chile sauce, such as Sriracha, or other hot sauce (optional)
Kosher salt

Rinse the mussels in a colander under cold water, scrub the shells thoroughly, remove the tough, wiry beards, and discard any mussels with broken or gaping shells. While the mussels drain, heat the oil in a large, wide pot over medium-high heat. Add the carrot and jalapeño; sauté, stirring occasionally, until they begin to soften and lightly brown, about 2 minutes. Add the garlic and ½ tsp. of the lime zest and sauté until fragrant, 30 seconds. Pour in the wine and raise the heat to high. As soon as the wine boils, add the mussels and cover the pot. Steam the mussels, shaking the pot once or twice, until the shells open, 5 to 6 minutes.

Remove the pot from the heat. With a slotted spoon, transfer the mussels to a large bowl and keep warm. Return the pot with the cooking liquid to the heat, add the cream, and boil until the sauce reduces just a bit, 2 to 3 minutes. Add 1½ Tbs. of the lime juice, the cilantro, and the chile sauce, if using. Taste and add more lime juice and salt if needed. Ladle the mussels into wide, shallow bowls, pour some of the sauce over each portion, and serve immediately.

how to:

Buy and store mussels

Spotting the good ones: At the fish counter, use your eyes and your nose to guide you. Fresh mussels should look tightly closed or just slightly gaping open. If they're yawning wide, they're dead or close to it. Once you have them in hand, take a sniff. They should smell like the sea. If they're really fishy smelling, don't buy them.

Keeping them fresh: Shellfish will suffocate in plastic, so take mussels out of the bag as soon as you get home, put them in a bowl, cover with a wet towel, and refrigerate. Cook them as soon as possible, but if they were fresh to begin with, they should keep for two days.

Strawberry-Mint Tea Sparkling Punch

Yields about 3½ qt., about twenty 5-oz. punch-cup servings or twelve cocktail-size servings.

The beauty of serving this punch by the glass is that you can make a special concoction for each guest. Children will enjoy this tea with lemon-lime soda; adults might like a splash of Champagne or sparkling wine.

2 pt. fresh strawberries (about 1 lb.), cleaned, hulled, and halved
2 Tbs. plus ½ cup granulated sugar
2 Tbs. fresh lemon juice
⅛ tsp. (or a good pinch) kosher salt
2¼ cups water
6 regular-size mint tea bags (real tea with mint, not herbal tea), about ½ oz. total
6 cups cold water
1 liter (33.8 oz.) sparkling water, chilled
Mint sprigs for garnish (optional)
Whole fresh strawberries for garnish (optional)

Put the strawberries, 2 Tbs. of the sugar, the lemon juice, and salt in a food processor or blender. Process until it's a smooth purée, pour it into a container, and refrigerate until needed.

In a small saucepan, bring the 2¼ cups water to a gentle boil. Add the tea bags, remove from the heat, cover, and steep for 15 minutes.

Pour the remaining ½ cup sugar into a 3-qt. heatproof container (like a large Pyrex® liquid measure). Remove the tea bags from the hot water when they're finished steeping (don't squeeze them) and pour the tea over the sugar, stirring to dissolve the sugar. Add the 6 cups cold water and stir again. Chill until cold.

To serve, combine the strawberry purée with the mint tea and stir well to mix completely.

If serving in a punch bowl, put the strawberry-mint tea in the punch bowl and slowly add the sparkling water.

For individual servings, fill 10-oz. stemmed glasses (wine glasses work great) two-thirds of the way with the tea and top off with the sparkling water. Garnish with mint sprigs and a strawberry, if you like.

Grilled Bread with Garlic, Olive Oil, Prosciutto & Oranges

Yields about 24 toasts; serves eight.

The combination of salty ham and tart-sweet oranges is unexpectedly delicious, especially when the whole thing is bathed in a full-bodied, earthy extra-virgin olive oil.

1 loaf chewy, country-style bread
10 to 20 cloves garlic, peeled
4 to 5 oranges, peel and pith cut away, very thinly sliced, seeds removed
½ lb. prosciutto, preferably Parma, sliced paper-thin
Extra-virgin olive oil for drizzling

Prepare a wood or charcoal fire, or set a gas grill on high (you can also use a broiler). Wipe the grill rack clean and rub with oil.

Slice the bread a generous ¼ inch thick (cut the slices in half if they're large). When the coals are hot but no longer flaming, put the bread on the rack and grill until lightly browned, 1 to 2 minutes. Turn and grill the other side. Transfer to a plate or basket and cover to keep warm. Arrange the garlic cloves, oranges, and prosciutto on a platter and serve with the olive oil.

Each diner should rub a piece of toast with a garlic clove, drizzle the toast with olive oil, and add a slice each of orange and prosciutto.

Grilled Old Bay Shrimp with Lemony Horseradish Cocktail Sauce

Serves six as a starter; yields 2½ cups sauce.

Old Bay seasoning is a spice mix sold in grocery stores (look for the bright yellow tin). Serve these addictive shrimp with cold beer or sweet iced tea. Spread the shrimp out on newspapers and invite your guests to "peel and eat." The cocktail sauce will keep for a week, refrigerated.

FOR THE SAUCE:
2 cups tomato ketchup
Grated zest of 2 small lemons
Juice of both lemons (about 5 Tbs.)
4 heaping Tbs. prepared horseradish; more to taste
8 shakes Tabasco® or other hot sauce; more to taste
½ tsp. sea salt or kosher salt
Freshly ground pepper (optional)

FOR THE SHRIMP:
2 lb. jumbo shrimp in the shell (24 to 30 per lb.), thawed completely if frozen and blotted dry
¼ cup vegetable or olive oil
2 Tbs. Old Bay seasoning
½ cup salted butter, melted (optional)

In a medium bowl, combine the ketchup, lemon zest and juice, horseradish, Tabasco, salt, and pepper, if using. Taste and adjust the seasonings, adding more horseradish if you like. Refrigerate if not using right away.

Heat a gas grill to medium high or prepare a medium-hot charcoal fire. (If using charcoal, be sure the grate is hot, too.) Just before cooking, toss the shrimp in the oil to coat, sprinkle with the Old Bay, and toss to coat evenly (you can do this in a zip-top bag, if you like).

Put the shrimp on the grate directly over the heat and cook for 6 to 7 minutes, turning once halfway through. The shrimp are done when the shells are bright pink and the meat is opaque. Pile the shrimp on newspapers to peel and serve with the cocktail sauce, melted butter (if using), and lots of paper towels.

Prosciutto with Marinated Melon
Serves eight to ten.

This makes a lovely anti-pasto platter, and it would be perfect served with the Italian sparkling wine called Prosecco. The wine's ripe fruit, bubbles, and crisp acidity are just the right match for the salty, spicy, and tart flavors in this dish.

1 medium (4-lb.) ripe honeydew melon (or any kind of melon except watermelon)
Juice of ½ lime
½ tsp. crushed red pepper flakes
¼ tsp. kosher salt
4 fresh mint leaves, torn into small pieces
6 oz. paper-thin slices prosciutto di Parma or prosciutto San Danielle
1 Tbs. extra-virgin olive oil

Cut off the stem and blossom ends from the melon. Stand the melon on one cut end and slice off the remaining rind. Cut the melon in half lengthwise from stem to blossom end and scoop out the seeds. Halve each melon half, so that you have four long wedges. Slice the wedges crosswise about ¼ inch thick. Gently toss the melon in a bowl with the lime juice, red pepper flakes, salt, and half of the mint. Arrange on a platter, drape the prosciutto on top, and drizzle with the olive oil. Sprinkle with the remaining mint and serve immediately.

Cherry Tomatoes Stuffed with Mozzarella & Basil

Yields about 3 dozen hors d'oeuvre; serves ten to twelve as an appetizer.

This is a spin-off of the classic tomato, mozzarella, and basil salad, called Insalata Caprese. These little stuffed tomatoes deliver all the great flavors of that salad but in a much cuter package.

½ lb. fresh mozzarella, cut into tiny dice (to yield about 1¼ cups)
3 Tbs. extra-virgin olive oil
⅓ cup coarsely chopped fresh basil leaves
½ tsp. freshly grated lemon zest (from about a quarter of a lemon)
Kosher salt and freshly ground black pepper
1 pt. (about 18) cherry tomatoes, rinsed and stems removed

In a medium bowl, stir the cheese, oil, basil, zest, ½ tsp. salt, and ¼ tsp. pepper. Refrigerate for at least 2 hours and up to 4 hours before assembling.

When ready to assemble, slice each tomato in half (either direction is all right) and scoop out the insides with a melon baller or a teaspoon. Sprinkle lightly with salt. Invert onto a paper towel and let the tomatoes drain for 15 minutes.

Fill each tomato half with 1 scant tsp. of the cheese mixture. Arrange on a serving tray. Serve immediately or wrap and refrigerate for up to 2 hours.

how to:

Slice and mince basil

Fine shreds: Stack leaves atop one another and roll into a tight tube. (For smaller leaves, bunch as tightly together as possible before cutting.) Cut the rolled leaves using a single swift, smooth stroke for each slice. The width is up to you. This is known as a chiffonade.

Minced: Turn the chiffonade slices (keeping them together with a gentle pinch) and make a few perpendicular cuts as wide or as narrow as you like. Don't go back over the basil as you might when finely chopping parsley.

Baked Marinated Eggplant

Serves six to eight as part of an antipasto.

Italian eggplant are smaller and sweeter than globe eggplant. If you can't find them, the long, narrow Japanese variety is a good alternative. Like Italian eggplant, it has a dense flesh with fewer seeds and less water than the globe variety.

1½ lb. Italian eggplant
¼ cup olive oil
Kosher salt and freshly ground black pepper
2 Tbs. finely diced red onion
2 Tbs. red-wine vinegar
¼ cup extra-virgin olive oil
1 Tbs. chopped fresh mint

Heat the oven to 375°F. Cut away the eggplant stem and cut the eggplant lengthwise into ¼-inch slices. Brush the slices on both sides with the regular olive oil and sprinkle them with salt and pepper.

Pour enough water into two large rimmed baking sheets to just cover the bottoms. Arrange the eggplant slices side by side on each pan. Cover with foil and bake for 25 minutes. Remove the foil and bake until the eggplant has dried somewhat, 15 to 20 minutes. Take care during the second stage of the cooking to remove the eggplant before it sticks to the pan.

Transfer the cooked eggplant to a large serving platter. In a small bowl, combine the red onion and vinegar. Add a pinch of salt and pepper. Stir to dissolve the salt. Stir in the extra-virgin olive oil and mint. While the eggplant is still warm, spoon a little of the vinaigrette over each slice. Let stand for 30 minutes. Serve the eggplant at room temperature as part of an antipasto.

Lemongrass Lemonade

Yields about 4 cups.

Some supermarkets sell lemongrass in the fresh herb or exotic produce section, but your best bet is to head to an Asian grocery where the lemongrass is likely to be fresher. You need to peel away the fibrous outer lay of the stalk before bruising it lightly to release the aromatic oils.

1 cup granulated sugar
2 stalks lemongrass, bruised lightly with the side of a knife and cut into ½-inch pieces
3 cups water
1 cup fresh lemon juice (from about 3 large lemons)
½ cup fresh lime juice (from about 2 limes)
Pinch kosher salt
2 cups ice
1 lemon, thinly sliced
2 stalks lemongrass, cut into 4 swizzle sticks (optional)

In a small saucepan, combine the sugar, lemongrass pieces, and water, and bring to a boil, stirring to dissolve the sugar. Lower the heat and simmer for 20 minutes. Remove the syrup from the heat; let it sit for about 1 hour. Strain it into a glass pitcher. Just before serving, add the lemon juice, lime juice, and salt. Stir well and add the ice. Serve in tall glasses with more ice, garnished with the lemon slices and the lemongrass swizzle sticks.

Grilled Hoisin Chicken in Lettuce Cups

Serves six to eight as a starter; three as a main course.

These visually appealing and fun-to-eat hors d'oeuvres can also work as a light main course.

⅓ cup hoisin sauce
4 tsp. rice vinegar
1 Tbs. soy sauce
4 boneless, skinless chicken thighs (about 1½ lb.), untrimmed; rinsed and patted dry
Kosher salt
Very small inner leaves from 3 heads Boston lettuce (or larger leaves from 1 head Boston lettuce if serving as a main course), washed and dried
1 cup loosely packed torn fresh basil (about 20 large leaves)
1 cup loosely packed torn fresh mint (about 1¾-oz. bunch)
1 bunch scallions (whites and most of the greens), thinly sliced (about ½ cup)
½ cup coarsely chopped salted peanuts
1 fresh jalapeño or other small hot chile, very thinly sliced crosswise (optional)

Heat a grill to medium high. In a small bowl, whisk the hoisin sauce, rice vinegar, and soy sauce. In a larger bowl, season the chicken with 1 tsp. salt and 2 Tbs. of the hoisin mixture.

Grill the chicken thighs, covered, until well browned and beginning to blacken around the edges, about 5 minutes (rotate the chicken 90 degrees halfway through cooking for the most even cooking). Flip and continue to grill until cooked through (rotating again), about another 5 minutes. Let the chicken rest for 8 to 10 minutes and then chop into ¼- to ½-inch dice. Transfer the chopped chicken to a mixing bowl, add the remaining hoisin mixture, and toss to coat thoroughly.

Spoon the chicken into very small lettuce leaves, garnish with the basil, mint, scallions, peanuts, and jalapeño slices (if using). Arrange the filled leaves on a platter and serve.

Alternatively, to serve as a main course, put the chopped and dressed chicken in a serving bowl. Arrange larger lettuce leaves, basil, and mint separately on a platter and put the scallions, peanuts, and jalapeño slices (if using) in small serving bowls. To serve, have diners spoon the chicken onto the middle of a lettuce leaf, top with the herbs and condiments, and roll the edges of the lettuce leaves up and around the filling.

Cilantro-Lime Guacamole

Serves four to six as a dip.

Taste your guacamole as you're making it. Avocados can take a fair amount of lime juice and cilantro, but since both of these ingredients can vary in strength, it's a good idea to taste as you go.

2 medium-size ripe avocados
2 to 3 Tbs. fresh lime juice
¾ tsp. kosher salt
½ tsp. ground coriander
Pinch ground cumin
3 to 4 Tbs. chopped fresh cilantro
1 tsp. minced fresh jalapeño
Tortilla chips for serving

Halve the avocados, pit them, and scoop the flesh with a large spoon into a small mixing bowl. Sprinkle the lime juice over the avocados, add the salt, coriander, and cumin, and use a wooden spoon to break up the avocados, stirring until they're coarsely mashed. Stir in the cilantro and jalapeño. Transfer to a small serving bowl and serve with the tortilla chips.

Draping grilled vegetables such as zucchini, eggplant, and scallions over a cooling rack prevents them from steaming and becoming mushy.

Grilled Zucchini & Goat Cheese Roll-Ups

Yields 8 to 10 roll-ups.

You can make these ahead, refrigerate them, and broil them briefly before serving. Serve as part of an antipasto, with a first-course green salad, or as a side to grilled meat.

3 small zucchini
Olive oil
Kosher salt
3 oz. goat cheese, at room temperature
1 Tbs. finely chopped oil-packed sun-dried tomatoes, well drained
Heaping ½ tsp. fresh thyme, chopped
2 Tbs. freshly grated Parmigiano Reggiano

Heat a grill to high. Trim off both ends of the zucchini. Trim just a little off of the two long sides to even their shape; discard the trimmings. Cut the remaining zucchini into lengthwise strips, each about ¼ inch thick. Brush both sides of the strips with plenty of olive oil and season with a little salt. Put the slices on the hot grill at a 45-degree angle to the grates and grill, covered, until well browned and limp, 3 to 4 minutes per side. Check on the zucchini as they cook and gently move the slices around with tongs for even browning; don't overcook them. When done, drape them over a cooling rack to keep them from steaming as they cool. (The zucchini can be grilled up to a day ahead. They can stay at room temperature for a few hours, but refrigerate them for longer storage.)

In a bowl, combine the goat cheese with the sun-dried tomatoes, thyme, 1 tsp. olive oil, and ⅛ tsp. salt. Spread 1 heaping tsp. of the filling thinly over one side of each grilled zucchini strip (use a mini spatula or your fingers to spread). Roll up the zucchini (not too tightly; this is more like folding), and put them on a baking sheet lined with parchment or foil. Refrigerate if not using within an hour, but bring back to room temperature before broiling.

Heat the broiler. Sprinkle with a little of the grated Parmigiano and brown under the broiler, about 1 minute.

Feta & Olive Oil Dip

Yields about 1½ cups.

This spread, called chtipiti (pronounced SHTI-pity), is traditionally served as part of a Greek meze (the equivalent of Spanish tapas). Spread it on toasted or grilled bread, topped with roasted red peppers, if you like. Or serve it as a dip for raw vegetables.

½ lb. feta, roughly crumbled
¼ cup milk
¼ cup extra-virgin olive oil
Minced fresh jalapeño to taste
2 to 3 Tbs. cream cheese (optional)

In a blender, mix the feta with the milk until grainy. With the blender running, slowly pour in the olive oil and blend to a thick glossy cream. Stir in a little minced jalapeño to taste. To mellow the tang of the dip and get a creamier texture, mix in 2 to 3 Tbs. cream cheese.

tip: Because tahini, a key ingredient in hummus, contains no emulsifiers, it can separate. To remix the oil and solids, turn the container upside down.

Hummus with Mellow Garlic & Cumin

Yields about 3 cups.

If you have ever bought the Middle Eastern chickpea dip known as hummus at the supermarket, you will be delighted by how much better this fresh (and quick to make) hummus tastes. Tahini, a paste made of ground sesame seeds, is sold in cans and jars at specialty stores and at many supermarkets, usually in the international aisle. Serve hummus with pita bread or cucumber rounds or other vegetables for dipping.

⅓ cup plus 1 Tbs. extra-virgin olive oil
4 large cloves garlic, thinly sliced
2 tsp. ground cumin
2 15½-oz. cans chickpeas, drained and rinsed
3 Tbs. tahini
3 Tbs. fresh lemon juice; more to taste
1 Tbs. soy sauce
½ tsp. kosher salt; more as needed

Combine ⅓ cup of the oil with the garlic and cumin in a small saucepan. Set over medium-low heat and cook until the garlic softens, about 3 minutes from when you can hear the garlic bubbling quickly. Don't let the garlic brown. Take the pan off the heat and let cool completely.

Put the chickpeas, tahini, lemon juice, soy sauce, and salt in a food processor. Use a fork to fish the softened garlic out of the oil and transfer it to the processor (reserve the oil). Turn the machine on, let it run for about 20 seconds, and then start slowly pouring the cumin-flavored oil through the machine's feed tube. Be sure to scrape the pan with a rubber spatula to get all of the cumin and oil. Pour ¼ cup cool water down the tube. Stop the machine, scrape the sides of the bowl, and continue processing until the hummus is creamy and almost smooth. Season to taste with more salt and lemon juice, if you like. For best results, let the hummus sit at room temperature for an hour or two before serving so the flavors can meld. Or better yet, make it a day ahead, refrigerate it, return it to room temperature, and adjust the seasonings before serving. To serve, spread the hummus in a shallow dish and drizzle with the remaining 1 Tbs. oil. It keeps for about a week in the refrigerator.

Crunchy Roasted Pepitas

Yields 1 cup.

Pepitas—dark-green hulled pumpkin seeds—can be found at natural-foods and specialty food stores. These lightly spiced, brightly flavored pepitas are a great little nosh before a big meal.

1 cup large raw pepitas
1 tsp. olive oil
1½ tsp. ground coriander
¾ tsp. kosher salt
½ tsp. dried dill
¼ tsp. freshly ground black pepper
Pinch cayenne (optional)

Position a rack in the center of the oven and heat the oven to 325°F. Toss the seeds with the olive oil on a rimmed baking sheet large enough to hold them in a single layer. Spread in an even layer and roast the seeds in the oven, stirring occasionally, until golden, 13 to 15 minutes. Remove the pan from the oven and immediately toss the seeds with the coriander, salt, dill, pepper, and cayenne (if using). Let cool for 10 minutes. Transfer to a small serving dish or two and serve. (If you're working ahead, heat the pepitas for a minute or two in the oven before serving.)

Prosciutto-Wrapped Greens

Serves eight.

This little bite, with its contrasting flavors and textures (smooth, salty prosciutto versus crisp peppery greens) will surely stimulate your appetite. If the prosciutto is very long, cut each piece in half crosswise first.

3 Tbs. extra-virgin olive oil
2 tsp. red-wine vinegar
2 tsp. fresh lemon juice
½ tsp. Dijon mustard
¼ lb. mesclun or arugula, washed and spun dry
Kosher salt and freshly ground black pepper
2 Tbs. freshly grated Parmigiano Reggiano
12 thin slices prosciutto

In a small bowl, whisk the olive oil, vinegar, lemon juice, and mustard. Put the mesclun or arugula in a medium bowl and season with a generous pinch of salt and pepper. Add the Parmigiano to the greens and gently toss with just enough of the vinaigrette to coat the greens lightly. Taste for salt and pepper.

Set a slice of prosciutto on a work surface and put a small handful of greens at the narrow end of the meat. Squeeze the greens together and roll the prosciutto into a tight log. Cut the log into 2-inch pieces on the diagonal (two or three pieces, depending on the width of the prosciutto). Repeat with the remaining prosciutto and greens and serve.

Eggplant Caviar

Yields about 2 cups.

Slather eggplant caviar on little toasts or bread for a wonderful appetizer, or use it as a spread on sandwiches, or as a dip for vegetables. To save time, you can roast the garlic in the same oven as the eggplant; just check on it sooner, as the oven is very hot.

2 lb. eggplant (about 2 globe or 4 Italian)
Extra-virgin olive oil
Kosher salt
8 fresh thyme sprigs
30 cloves roasted garlic (2 large heads)
1 tsp. finely grated lemon zest
1 to 2 Tbs. fresh lemon juice
Freshly ground black pepper
1 Tbs. finely chopped fresh mint or parsley

Slice the eggplant in half lengthwise. Score the flesh deeply with a knife in a cross-hatch pattern. Press on the edges of the halves to open the cuts and sprinkle about ½ tsp. salt per half over the surface and into the cuts. Set aside, cut side up, for 30 minutes.

Heat the oven to 400°F. Line a baking sheet with parchment. Over the sink, gently squeeze the eggplant to extract the salty juice and wipe them dry with a paper towel. Brush each half thoroughly with olive oil and arrange, cut side down, on top of a sprig or two of thyme on the baking sheet. Roast until the eggplant collapses and becomes a deep brown color on the bottom, about 1 hour.

Let the eggplant and the garlic cool before handling, giving the eggplant at least 20 minutes.

Put the roasted eggplant on a cutting board and use a spoon to scrape the flesh from the skins. Squeeze each garlic clove gently at the untrimmed end to let the flesh squeeze out whole and add the flesh to the eggplant on the board. With a large knife, chop the eggplant and garlic together until they form a rough purée. Add the lemon zest, 1 Tbs. of the lemon juice, a generous (1½ to 2 Tbs.) drizzle of olive oil, ½ tsp. salt, and a few grinds of pepper. Chop and mix together thoroughly; taste and add more lemon juice, oil, or salt if needed. Transfer to a small serving bowl and fold in the mint or parsley. Refrigerate for up to 48 hours if you like; bring to room temperature before serving.

tip: Taste all dips after they've been refrigerated. They often need a little seasoning—a bit of lemon juice or salt—before serving.

Pico de Gallo

Yields about 1 1/2 cups.

This salsa is excellent on its own served with tortilla chips or used to garnish tacos or tortillas. Its fresh flavor comes through best when served within an hour of making.

1/4 cup coarsely chopped white onion
1/4 cup coarsely chopped fresh cilantro
3 fresh serranos or jalapeños, cored, seeded, and coarsely chopped
1 1/2 ripe medium tomatoes, finely chopped
Kosher salt and freshly ground black pepper

Put the onion, cilantro, and chiles in a food processor and pulse until very finely chopped. Transfer to a bowl and stir in the tomatoes. Season with about 1/2 tsp. salt and 1/4 tsp. pepper and serve.

Catalan Mushrooms with Garlic & Parsley

Serves six.

When these hot, garlicky, green-speckled mushrooms are put out on the table, they disappear in seconds. Simple to make with ingredients often on hand, they're also a delicious accompaniment to grilled chicken or steak, while leftovers are great on pizza or added to pasta sauce.

1 lb. medium white mushrooms, stems trimmed to 1/2 inch, and quartered
1/4 cup extra-virgin olive oil
1/4 cup finely chopped fresh flat-leaf parsley
2 Tbs. finely chopped fresh garlic
1 to 2 tsp. kosher salt or sea salt

Put the mushrooms in a large bowl of cold water to soak for 10 minutes. Rinse them well and then drain.

Heat a large sauté pan with a tight-fitting lid over medium heat. Add the drained mushrooms to the dry pan, cover immediately, and cook until all the moisture from the mushrooms is leached out, about 20 minutes. You'll know this has happened when you lift the lid for a peek and see the once-dry pan filled with liquid.

Remove the lid, raise the heat to medium high, and boil until the liquid evaporates and the mushrooms begin to sizzle in the dry pan but haven't browned; they'll have shrunk considerably and should be firm when poked with a fork. Lower the heat to medium and stir in 1 Tbs. of the olive oil, the parsley, and the garlic. Sauté, stirring frequently, until the garlic softens, another 3 to 4 minutes. Transfer the mushrooms to a serving bowl, stir in the remaining 3 Tbs. olive oil, and season liberally with salt to taste. Serve while hot.

Soups

Summer Vegetable Soup with Shrimp & Lemon *p. 18*

Summer Vegetable Soup with Shrimp & Lemon

Serves six to eight.

To save time as you cook, get the onion going while you prep the other vegetables. If you're not finished with the dicing and chopping, add just the chicken broth to stop the onion's sautéing while you finish up.

2 Tbs. olive oil
1 medium-large onion, finely diced
1 large clove garlic, finely chopped
1 qt. homemade or low-salt chicken broth
1 cup diced tomato
1 medium-large red bell pepper, cut into medium dice (about 1 cup)

2 small zucchini, cut into medium dice (about 2 cups)
1⅔ cups fresh or frozen corn kernels
1 lb. red potatoes, cut into medium dice (about 3 cups)
Kosher salt and freshly ground black pepper
½ lb. shrimp, peeled, deveined, and cut crosswise into ½-inch pieces if large; left whole if small
2 Tbs. chopped fresh herbs, such as basil, cilantro, parsley, or a mix
2 tsp. fresh lemon juice; more to taste

Heat the olive oil in a 4-qt. or larger Dutch oven or soup pot.

Add the onion and cook over medium heat, stirring occasionally, until softened, about 8 minutes. Add the garlic and cook, stirring, another minute or two, being careful not to let it brown. Add the broth, tomato, bell pepper, zucchini, corn, potatoes, and ½ tsp. salt. Simmer until the vegetables are tender, about 10 minutes. Add the shrimp and simmer until it just begins to turn pink, 1 to 2 minutes. Let the soup rest for 5 minutes (the shrimp will continue to cook off the heat) and then add the herbs and the lemon juice. Taste and season with salt and pepper and additional lemon juice if needed.

Puréed Corn Soup with Roasted Red Pepper Coulis

Serves four; yields ½ cup coulis.

Puréed soups can be deceptive. Although they may not look like much, they can offer an enormous intensity of flavor. This particular soup distills the essence of sweet corn and only gets better with every spoonful.

FOR THE COULIS:
1 small clove garlic
½ tsp. kosher salt
1 small red bell pepper, broiled until the skin is charred, peeled when cool, and seeded (for method, see p. 213)
1 tsp. extra-virgin olive oil
1½ tsp. balsamic vinegar
¼ tsp. red-wine vinegar
⅛ tsp. freshly ground black pepper
Pinch cayenne

FOR THE SOUP:
3 ears corn (to yield about 2¼ cups kernels)

8 sprigs fresh basil; more tiny leaves for garnish
10 sprigs fresh thyme
1 bay leaf
3 Tbs. unsalted butter
1 medium onion, sliced (to yield 1 cup)
Kosher salt
1 Tbs. minced fresh garlic

Make the coulis: Mash the garlic with ¼ tsp. salt in a mortar and pestle or with the side of a chef's knife to a fine paste. Put the garlic paste, red pepper, olive oil, balsamic vinegar, red-wine vinegar, black pepper, cayenne, and ¼ tsp. salt in a blender. Blend on high speed to a smooth purée.

Make the soup: Shuck the corn and rub off the silk. Stand one ear on a board or in a shallow bowl and with a knife, slice straight down the ear to remove the kernels. Turn the ear and repeat until all the kernels are removed. Scrape the dull side of the knife down the cob to extract the corn "milk." Put the cobs (broken in half, if necessary), basil, thyme, bay leaf, and 5 cups water in a large saucepan or a soup pot. Bring to a boil, reduce to a simmer, and cook uncovered for 15 minutes. Remove the cobs. Strain the broth and reserve it.

Melt the butter in a large, heavy saucepan set over medium heat. Add the onion and 2 tsp. salt, cover, and cook, stirring occasionally, until the onion is translucent, about 5 minutes; don't let it brown. Stir in the garlic and 2¼ cups of the corn kernels along with the corn milk. Add enough of the herb broth to cover the corn, bring to a simmer, and cook until the corn is very tender, 17 to 20 minutes. Purée the corn in batches in a blender and strain it through a fine sieve. If the soup is too thick, add a little more of the reserved broth.

Taste the soup and add salt if necessary. Serve warm, garnished with a swirl of the red pepper coulis and several tiny basil leaves.

Fresh Pea Soup

Serves four.

Fresh peas enjoy a short springtime run in most areas, so enjoy them while you can. This simple soup shows off their sweet freshness.

4 lb. fresh peas (to yield about 4 cups shucked)
2 Tbs. unsalted butter
1 small onion, chopped
3 cups homemade or low-salt chicken broth
1¼ tsp. kosher salt; more to taste
Freshly ground white pepper
4 tsp. crème fraîche
2 tsp. chopped fresh mint

Shuck the peas. In a large saucepan over medium heat, melt the butter. Add the onion and sauté until soft, 5 to 6 minutes. Try not to let it brown. Add the broth and salt, raise the heat, and bring the pot to a boil. Add the peas, cover, and return the pot to a boil. Lower the heat and simmer the peas until just cooked through, 2 to 5 minutes, depending on their size. Transfer the peas and some of the liquid to a blender and purée until smooth. Add the remaining liquid and blend again. Pass through a coarse strainer or food mill. Serve warm, topping each bowl with 1 tsp. of the crème fraîche and ½ tsp. of the chopped mint.

Two-Celery Soup

Serves eight to ten.

Celery, usually viewed as a work-horse in the kitchen, takes center stage in this simple, soothing soup. Punctuate its peppery flavor with the addition of a little celery root.

1 large bunch celery (about 1¾ lb.)
3 Tbs. olive oil
1 medium celery root (about 1¼ lb.), peeled and cut into small dice
2 large leeks (white and light green parts only), well rinsed and cut into small dice
1 large starchy potato, peeled and cut into small dice
2 qt. homemade or low-salt chicken broth
Juice of ½ lemon
Kosher salt and freshly ground black pepper
3 Tbs. chopped flat-leaf parsley
½ cup freshly grated Parmigiano Reggiano

Cut off the root and top of the celery. Rinse the celery well and dry. Reserve the leaves and wrap them in a moist paper towel. Peel the tough fibers from the outer ribs. Chop the ribs into small dice. (You should have about 4 cups.)

Heat the olive oil in a large pot over medium-high heat. Add the celery, celery root, leeks, and potato. Sauté for a few minutes until a strong celery aroma is released.

Pour in the chicken broth, bring to a boil, and simmer until all the vegetables are tender, 40 to 50 minutes. Add the lemon juice, salt, pepper, parsley, and reserved celery leaves. Sprinkle each serving with a little of the Parmigiano. Serve hot.

Escarole & Ham Soup with Fresh Peas & Tarragon

Serves six to eight.

2 Tbs. olive oil
1 medium-large yellow onion, cut into small dice
Kosher salt and freshly ground black pepper
1 qt. homemade or low-salt chicken broth
½ lb. carrots (2 to 3 medium), cut into ¼-inch coins (1 cup)
½ lb. escarole (about ½ medium head), coarsely chopped (about 4 cups)
½ lb. smoked ham, cut into ¼-inch dice (about 2 cups)
1 cup diced tomato (about 1 medium tomato)
½ lb. fresh or frozen peas (about 2 cups)
1 15½-oz. can white beans, rinsed and drained
1 Tbs. chopped fresh tarragon; more to taste
1 tsp. fresh lemon juice; more to taste

Heat the olive oil in a 6-qt. or larger Dutch oven or soup pot over medium heat. Add the onion, sprinkle with a little salt, and cook, stirring occasionally, until softened and a little browned, 6 to 8 minutes. Add the broth, carrots, escarole, ham, and tomato. Raise the heat to high and bring the broth to a boil; then reduce the heat to medium or medium low and simmer until the vegetables are barely tender, 5 to 10 minutes. Add the peas and beans, return the soup to a simmer, and cook until the vegetables are fully tender, about another 5 minutes. Let the soup rest for 5 minutes and then add the tarragon and lemon juice. Taste and adjust the seasonings with salt and pepper and additional tarragon and lemon, if you like.

Roasted Red Bell Pepper Soup with Star Anise

Serves three to four; yields 4½ cups.

This vibrant soup is also delicious served cold, and it can be garnished with a few cooked shrimp, a mound of crabmeat, or a bit of goat cheese.

2 Tbs. olive oil
2 onions (about ¾ lb. total), chopped
2 cloves garlic, chopped
½ cubic inch fresh ginger, peeled and chopped
1 medium carrot, peeled and chopped
1 qt. homemade or low-salt chicken broth
3 large red bell peppers, roasted, peeled, and seeded; juices reserved (for method, see p. 213)

1 whole star anise (or ¾ tsp. broken pieces)
½ tsp. kosher salt; more to taste
¼ tsp. freshly ground black pepper; more to taste
Small pinch cayenne
6 fresh basil leaves
Extra-virgin olive oil and sherry vinegar (optional)

Heat the olive oil in a 6-qt. soup pot over medium heat. Add the onions, garlic, ginger, and carrot and sauté until very soft but not browned, 15 to 20 minutes.

Add the broth and turn the heat to high. Add the roasted peppers and any reserved juices, along with the star anise, salt, pepper, and cayenne. As soon as the mixture comes to a boil, reduce the heat and simmer uncovered for 30 minutes. Stir occasionally.

Purée the soup in batches in a blender, with all the basil leaves going in the blender along with the first batch. Purée each batch of soup for at least 1 minute. Combine all the puréed soup in one container, taste, and add more salt and pepper to bring all the flavors into balance. (For a thinner soup, strain through a wide-mesh sieve.) Serve with a drizzle of extra-virgin olive oil and a splash of sherry vinegar, if you like.

Summer Corn Soup

Serves six; yields 6 to 7 cups.

You can get creative with the garnishes for this soup. Instead of (or in addition to) the sour cream and tomatoes, consider sautéed corn kernels, crème fraîche, snipped fresh chives, toasted pepitas, or a drizzle of basil oil.

5 to 6 large ears sweet corn, shucked, silks removed
Kosher salt
3 Tbs. olive oil or unsalted butter, or a combination
1 large onion, diced
4 cloves garlic, roughly chopped
½ cup diced celery
1 medium red potato (6 oz.), peeled and cut into 1-inch cubes
3 to 4 sprigs fresh marjoram, leaves stripped and chopped (1 Tbs. loosely packed leaves)
Freshly ground black pepper
Pinch cayenne
¼ cup sour cream, for garnish
½ cup finely diced fresh tomatoes, for garnish
¼ cup thinly sliced fresh basil, for garnish

Cut the kernels off the ears of corn by starting to cut halfway down the ear and slicing to the bottom, rotating the ear as you go; don't try to cut too close to the base of the kernels. Turn the ear over and repeat to remove all the kernels. You'll need 3½ to 4 cups of kernels for the soup.

Stand one cob on end in a pie plate or other shallow dish and use the back edge of the knife to scrape the cobs and extract as much "milk" and solids as you can. Set this raw corn purée aside.

Break the cobs in half and put them in a heavy 4-qt. pot. Add 6 cups water and 1 tsp. salt and bring to a boil over high heat. Reduce the heat to medium low, cover, and simmer for 30 minutes. Discard the cobs. Pour the liquid into a bowl and set aside.

Set the pot back over medium-high heat and add the oil or butter (or both). When it's hot, add the onion and sauté until translucent, about 3 minutes. Add the garlic and cook for 1 minute. Reduce the heat to medium, add the celery, sprinkle with salt, and stir. Cover the pot and cook, stirring occasionally, until the vegetables start to soften, 5 to 6 minutes; don't let them color. (If they start to brown before softening, reduce the heat.) Add the potatoes, marjoram, black pepper (about six turns of the grinder), and cayenne and stir to distribute the seasonings. Add the corn stock. Bring to a boil over medium-high heat, cover, lower the heat to medium low, and simmer until the vegetables are tender enough to purée, 20 to 30 minutes. Add most of the corn kernels, reserving about 1 cup. Simmer gently for another 10 minutes.

Purée the soup in batches in a blender (be careful to fill the blender no more than one-third full, vent the lid, and hold a towel over the lid while you turn it on). Put the puréed soup back in the pot. Taste for seasoning and add more salt or pepper if necessary. Add the reserved corn kernels and corn "milk," and simmer just long enough to take the raw edge off the corn, about 5 minutes. Serve hot, warm, or at room temperature, garnished with a small dollop of sour cream and the tomatoes and basil.

Roasted Carrot Soup

Serves four; yields about 1 qt.

A tablespoon of ginger gives a nice, throat-warming heat to this soup, which tastes best if it sits in the fridge several hours or overnight.

1 lb. carrots, peeled and cut into 3-inch lengths
1 Tbs. olive oil
1 Tbs. unsalted butter
½ medium onion, cut into medium dice (about ¾ cup)
1 large rib celery, cut into medium dice (about ½ cup)
1 Tbs. minced fresh ginger (from about ½-inch piece, peeled)
2 cups low-salt chicken broth
1 tsp. kosher salt
⅛ tsp. ground white pepper
Chopped fresh chives or chervil for garnish (optional)

Heat the oven to 375°F.

Put the carrots in a medium baking dish (11x7-inch, or any dish that will hold the carrots in a single layer without touching) and drizzle them with the olive oil. Toss them to coat well and roast, stirring once halfway through roasting, until they're tender, blistered, and lightly browned in a few places, about 1 hour.

Melt the butter in a medium (at least 3-qt.) heavy saucepan set over medium heat. Add the onion and cook until it's translucent and fragrant, 2 to 3 minutes. Stir in the celery and ginger and cook until the celery softens a bit and the onions start to brown, 4 to 5 minutes. Add the roasted carrots, chicken broth, salt, pepper, and 2 cups of water. Bring to a boil, reduce the heat to medium low, and cover. Cook at a lively simmer until the carrots are very tender, about 45 minutes. Turn off the heat and let the liquid cool somewhat (or completely).

Purée the soup in a blender in batches (fill the blender no more than one-third full, vent the lid, and hold a towel over the lid while you turn it on). If serving immediately, return the soup to the pot and reheat; garnish with the chives or chervil if you like. Otherwise, refrigerate for up to five days; reheat gently and taste for salt before serving.

Blender tips

Several of these soups require a blender to purée the ingredients. To keep your blender running smoothly and safely, follow these basic blender do's and don'ts.

1 Load liquids and soft ingredients first, solid ingredients last. Solids should be no larger than 1-inch chunks.

2 When you can, start slow and gradually build speed to lessen motor stress.

3 Immediately stop blending when ingredients jam.

4 Never wiggle the jar to jostle lodged ingredients when the blender is running.

5 To blend hot ingredients without splattering, vent the lid by removing the cap on the lid's fill hole (or if there is no cap, just open the lid slightly) and drape a thick dishtowel over the top. Add a minimal amount of liquid. Start at a low speed and increase gradually. (Ideally, let hot ingredients cool before blending.)

Chilled Beet Soup with Horseradish Sour Cream

Serves four; yields 4½ cups.

Roasting the beets—rather than boiling them—deepens their flavor and intensifies their sweetness. If you find golden beets at your market, by all means use them here. There's no need to drain the horseradish; the water in it will help thin the sour cream.

1½ lb. small or medium beets (about 2 bunches, trimmed), well scrubbed
4 cloves garlic, unpeeled
3 strips (3 inches long) orange zest
3 sprigs fresh thyme
Kosher salt and freshly ground white or black pepper
2 Tbs. extra-virgin olive oil
2½ cups low-salt chicken broth or water
2 tsp. honey
⅓ cup fresh orange juice
2 Tbs. red-wine vinegar
1 Tbs. prepared horseradish
½ cup sour cream
A few tsp. cream or water as needed
Fresh dill sprigs for garnish (optional)

Heat the oven to 375°F. Put the beets and garlic on a large sheet of heavy-duty aluminum foil. Scatter on the orange zest and thyme, season with salt and pepper, and drizzle with the olive oil. Fold up the sides of the foil and crimp to make a tight packet. Slide the foil packet onto a baking sheet and into the oven. Bake for 1 hour. Open the packet carefully (to avoid the steam) and check that the beets are tender by piercing one with the tip of a sharp knife. The knife should slide in easily; if it doesn't, reseal the package and continue baking. Set aside to cool for 15 to 20 minutes. Using paper towels, rub the skins off the beets and cut the beets into chunks. Peel the garlic cloves. Discard the thyme and orange zest, saving any juices collected in the foil.

Combine about one-third of the beet chunks, the garlic, and any collected juices in a blender. Add some of the chicken broth and the honey. Before turning on the blender vent the lid by removing the pop-out center if there is one, or just open the lid a bit, and drape a clean dishtowel over the vented lid. Blend to a smooth purée and transfer to a bowl. Continue in batches, puréeing all the beets. Stir in the orange juice and vinegar. Season to taste with salt and pepper. Cover and refrigerate to chill the soup thoroughly.

Meanwhile, stir the horseradish into the sour cream. If the sour cream is too stiff (it should be the consistency of lightly whipped cream), stir in a few teaspoons of cream or water to loosen it. Refrigerate until serving time. To serve, ladle the soup into cups or bowls and spoon a bit of the horseradish sour cream onto each serving. Garnish with fresh dill, if you like.

Yellow Tomato Gazpacho

Serves eight to ten; yields about 10 cups.

If you can't find Yellow Taxi tomatoes, substitute any truly ripe, in-season tomato.

FOR THE SOUP:
- **5 lb. Yellow Taxi tomatoes or other ripe yellow or red heirloom tomatoes, cored and cut into chunks**
- **3 cloves garlic**
- **1 seedless or regular cucumber (about ¾ lb.), peeled, seeded if necessary, and cut into large pieces**
- **1 medium yellow bell pepper, seeded and cut into large pieces**
- **1 small red onion, cut into large pieces**
- **½ small hot red chile (or to taste), seeded and cut into large pieces**
- **½ cup red-wine vinegar**
- **¾ cup extra-virgin olive oil**
- **Kosher salt and ground white pepper**

FOR THE GARNISH:
- **Avocado Salsa (at right)**
- **6 each red and yellow cherry tomatoes, cut in half**

Make the soup: Working in batches, purée the tomatoes, garlic, cucumber, yellow pepper, onion, chile, vinegar, and oil in a blender until smooth. Strain the mixture through a fine sieve into a bowl. Press on the solids with a wooden spoon to extract as much liquid as possible; discard the solids. Season to taste with salt and pepper. Refrigerate in an airtight container for at least 2 hours or up to two days.

To serve: Taste the soup and adjust the seasonings. Spoon 2 generous Tbs. of the avocado salsa in the center of each soup bowl. Pour or ladle the gazpacho over the salsa and garnish with the cherry tomato halves.

Avocado Salsa

Yields about 3 cups.

- **2 small ripe Hass avocados, cut into small dice**
- **1 small hot red chile, seeded and minced**
- **1 small red onion, cut into small dice**
- **1 red heirloom slicing tomato, seeded and diced**
- **1 Tbs. finely chopped fresh cilantro**
- **Juice of 1 lime**
- **¼ cup extra-virgin olive oil**
- **Kosher salt and freshly cracked black pepper**

In a medium bowl, stir the avocados, chile, onion, tomato, cilantro, lime juice, olive oil, and salt and pepper to taste. Refrigerate, covered, for at least 20 minutes and up to 3 hours before serving.

Creamy Asparagus Soup

Serves six to eight; yields 7 to 8 cups.

A rich vegetable stock, made from the dark green tops of leeks and the tough ends of asparagus, provides an underpinning of flavor for this smooth soup. It's delicious either warm or cold.

2 lb. asparagus
3½ Tbs. unsalted butter
2 small celery ribs, coarsely chopped (about 1 cup)
1 large yellow onion, coarsely chopped (about 2 cups)
1 large leek (white and green parts), halved lengthwise, thoroughly rinsed, and thinly sliced crosswise (keep dark-green parts separate from light-green and white parts)
8 whole peppercorns
5 sprigs flat-leaf parsley
2 sprigs thyme
Kosher salt
2 medium cloves garlic, chopped
1 large or 3 small red potatoes, peeled and cut into ½-inch dice
¼ cup heavy cream
Freshly ground white pepper

Snap off the tough ends of the asparagus, but don't discard them. Cut about 1½ inches of the tips off the asparagus spears and cut the spears crosswise in thirds; set the spears and tips aside separately.

Melt 1½ Tbs. of the butter in a 3-qt. saucepan over medium-low heat. Add the asparagus ends, half of the celery, the onion, and the dark-green parts of the leek. Cook uncovered, stirring occasionally, until the vegetables look very soft, about 30 minutes (if the vegetables show any sign of browning, reduce the heat to low). Add 6 cups cold water and the peppercorns, parsley, thyme, and ½ tsp. salt. Bring to a boil over high heat, reduce the heat to medium-low, cover, and simmer for 30 minutes to make a flavorful stock.

Meanwhile, bring a 2-qt. pot of salted water to a boil over high heat. Add the asparagus tips and cook until just tender, 2 to 3 minutes. Drain in a colander, shower with cold water to stop the cooking, and drain again.

In another 3-qt. (or larger) saucepan, melt the remaining 2 Tbs. butter over medium-low heat. Add the white and light-green sliced leek and the remaining celery and season with a generous pinch of salt. Cook, stirring occasionally, until the leeks look soft but not browned, 3 to 4 minutes. Add the garlic and cook for 1 minute more. Add the asparagus spears and the potato. Set a wire mesh strainer over the pot and pour in the stock from the other pot, discarding the solids. Stir well and bring to a boil over high heat. Reduce the heat to medium-low, cover, and cook at a lively simmer until the potatoes and asparagus are very tender, about 20 minutes. Turn off the heat and let cool slightly.

Purée the soup in a blender in batches (fill the blender no more than one-third full, vent the lid, and hold a towel over the lid while you turn it on). Return the puréed soup to the soup pot, add the cream, and stir well. Reheat the soup gently over medium-low heat. Season to taste with more salt and a large pinch of white pepper. Ladle the soup into bowls or soup plates and scatter in the asparagus tips, distributing them evenly among the servings.

Make it a menu

An elegant affair

Creamy Asparagus Soup *above*

Grilled Salmon with Wasabi-Ginger Mayonnaise *p. 122*

Raspberry & Blackberry Mousse *p. 186*

menu make-ahead

Make the mousse and the soup a day ahead, and cook the salmon, and perhaps a pot of rice pilaf too, once guests arrive.

Andalusian Gazpacho

Serves four; yields 4 cups.

If you like an absolutely smooth gazpacho, strain the soup. If not, purée it more coarsely so the soup is slightly chunky. Serve this cold soup as an appetizer on the first hot day of summer.

1½ lb. very ripe red tomatoes (about 4 large), cut into large pieces
1 large green bell pepper, seeded and coarsely chopped (to yield 2 cups)
2 cloves garlic, sliced
3-inch-long piece of baguette, sliced and dried overnight or lightly toasted until dry
½ cup good-quality extra-virgin olive oil
2 Tbs. sherry vinegar or red-wine vinegar; more to taste
2 tsp. kosher salt; more to taste
Freshly ground black pepper (optional)
1 cup peeled, diced cucumber, for garnish
1 cup diced onion, for garnish (optional)

Put the tomatoes, green pepper, garlic, bread, olive oil, vinegar, and salt in a food processor. Pulse until the ingredients begin to purée (if the bread is hard, it may bounce about and take a while to break down); continue processing until the mixture is as fine a purée as possible, 3 to 5 minutes.

Pass the soup through a fine sieve or strainer set over a large bowl, pressing until only solids remain in the sieve; discard the solids. Stir in ¼ to ½ cup water, or enough to give the soup the consistency of a thin milkshake. If you want a thicker soup, add less water, or none at all. Add more salt or vinegar to taste.

Cover and refrigerate until well chilled (or serve it immediately with a few ice cubes in each bowl).

Ladle the gazpacho into chilled bowls or cups. Grind fresh pepper on top, if you like, and pass bowls of diced cucumber and onion (if using) so people can garnish their own.

Creamy Roasted Garlic Soup with Sautéed Cauliflower & Fresh Herbs

Serves four.

In this rich, deeply flavored soup, the cauliflower acts almost as a garnish. Sautéed until well browned but retaining its crunch, it adds a nutty toastiness to the sweet garlic flavor of the soup.

FOR THE SOUP:
3 Tbs. extra-virgin olive oil
½ cup chopped onion
1 leek (white and light green parts only), chopped and well rinsed
2 large boiling potatoes, peeled and chopped
1 Tbs. fresh thyme, chopped
½ cup dry white wine
4 cups homemade or low-salt chicken or vegetable broth
4 heads garlic, roasted
Freshly ground black pepper

Parsnip & Carrot Soup with Ginger & Crème Fraîche

Serves six; yields 8½ cups.

Here the parsnip is paired with its more popular cousin, the carrot, in a simple and satisfying soup. A bright hit of fresh ginger is a perfect counterpoint to the mellow sweetness of the root vegetables. Freeze any leftover soup.

2 Tbs. canola or vegetable oil
2 medium onions, sliced
1 lb. parsnips, peeled and cut into 2-inch chunks
¾ lb. carrots, peeled and cut into 2-inch chunks
1½ qt. homemade or low-salt chicken or vegetable broth; more as needed
¼ cup grated fresh ginger
1 tsp. dried thyme
¼ tsp. freshly grated nutmeg
¼ cup sweet vermouth or other sweet white wine (optional)
Kosher salt and freshly ground black pepper
Crème fraîche or sour cream
A few sprigs of fresh thyme

In a large pot, heat the oil over medium heat. Put the onions into the pot, cover tightly, and cook gently until the onions are soft, about 5 minutes. Add the parsnips, carrots, and broth. Bring to a boil, cover the pot, reduce the heat, and let simmer until the vegetables are very soft, about 30 minutes. Strain the soup into a large bowl, reserving both the vegetables and the broth. Transfer the vegetables to a food processor and purée. Gradually add the broth to the purée until the mixture is loose enough to pour. Add the ginger, thyme, nutmeg, and vermouth (if using). If necessary, thin the soup with more broth. Season to taste with salt and pepper. Serve with a dollop of crème fraîche or sour cream and sprigs of thyme.

½ tsp. kosher salt; more to taste
¼ cup chopped fresh sorrel leaves or chives, or a combination

FOR THE CAULIFLOWER:
2 Tbs. olive oil
1 small head cauliflower (2 lb.), cut into small florets (about ½ inch at the widest point)

Make the soup: In a soup pot over low heat, sauté the onion and leek in 1 Tbs. of olive oil until very soft but not brown, about 10 minutes. Add the potatoes and thyme and cook another 1 minute. Turn the heat to medium high, add the wine, and let it reduce to just a few teaspoons, about 4 minutes. Add the broth; bring to a boil. Reduce the heat and simmer for 10 minutes. Add the garlic pulp and simmer until the potatoes are very soft, another 15 to 20 minutes.

Strain the soup, saving both the liquid and solids. In a blender or food processor, purée the solids in batches, using some liquid to help it blend, and pour the puréed solids back in the pot. When all the solids are puréed, add as much of the remaining liquid as necessary to get a consistency like heavy cream. Season to taste with salt and pepper.

Sauté the cauliflower: Heat 2 Tbs. oil in a large sauté pan over medium heat. Add the cauliflower florets and sauté. Once they begin to soften, after about 5 minutes, season with salt and pepper. Continue to sauté until the cauliflower is deep golden brown and tender but still firm, another 7 to 10 minutes.

To serve: Reheat the soup. Ladle it into individual bowls, add the cauliflower, and garnish with the sorrel or chives.

tip: Add a soup's final flourish—a drizzle of oil, a squeeze of lemon, a sprinkling of fresh herbs—just before serving to get the biggest boost of flavor.

Chilled Tomato Soup with Crab Salad

Serves four as a first course or light lunch.

The crab salad turns this soup into a meal. Make the soup close to serving time; chilling it for too long mutes the bright tomato flavors.

2 ears fresh corn
2 lb. ripe red or purple heirloom tomatoes (such as Stupice or Purple Cherokee)
3 Tbs. fresh lemon juice; more to taste
½ cup plus 1 Tbs. extra-virgin olive oil
Sea salt (preferably fleur de sel)
Freshly ground black pepper
½ lb. lump crabmeat, such as Dungeness, Maine, or blue
1 recipe Pistou (at right)

Grill the corn: Heat a gas grill to high or prepare a hot charcoal fire. Cut off the tip of the corn's husks (to make it easier to remove the husks once grilled). Grill the corn in the husk for 15 to 20 minutes, giving it a quarter turn every 5 minutes, keeping the grill covered (the kernels should be cooked but not charred). When it's cool enough to handle, remove all of the husk and silk. With a sharp knife, cut the kernels off the cobs. Set the kernels aside.

Make the soup: Core the tomatoes and cut them into chunks. Working in two batches, put half the tomatoes in a blender with 1 Tbs. of the lemon juice and ¼ cup of the olive oil in each batch. Season with a generous pinch of sea salt and black pepper, and blend on high speed until smooth. Strain through a fine sieve, pressing on the solids to force the liquid through the mesh; discard the solids. Taste and adjust the seasonings. Refrigerate until serving time.

Make the crab salad: Pick through the crabmeat for any bits of shell. Put it in a bowl along with 1 Tbs. lemon juice, 1 Tbs. olive oil, 1 tsp. sea salt, and black pepper to taste. Add the grilled corn kernels; mix thoroughly. Adjust the seasonings if needed.

Divide the soup among four chilled soup bowls. Spoon a mound of crab salad in the center of each serving. Stir the pistou and then drizzle it over the soup and crab. Serve at once.

Pistou

Yields about ¼ cup.

This classic basil purée is similar to Italian pesto but without the cheese and pine nuts. It adds herbaceous and earthy notes to the tomato soup.

1 medium clove garlic, peeled
¼ cup fresh basil leaves
Sea salt (preferably fleur de sel)
2 Tbs. extra-virgin olive oil

Put the garlic, basil, and a pinch of sea salt in a mortar and pound until puréed smoothly. (Alternatively, use a chef's knife to chop the basil very finely and to mash the garlic salt to a paste with the salt; then combine them in a small bowl.) Add the olive oil, mix, and let infuse at room temperature for 1 hour.

Rice noodles

Check out the Asian section of your grocery store and you'll probably see an array of cellophane packages filled with rice noodles of all shapes. These simple noodles have a subtle flavor and an appealing springy-chewy texture, with just a slight slipperiness. They add body to lots of Asian-inspired dishes including stir-fries, soups, curries, and salads.

What to buy: Also called "rice sticks," rice noodles come in various thicknesses: very thin ones ("rice vermicelli"); and flat, thicker ones that come in small, medium, and large widths, the widest being about the width of fettuccine. While vermicelli are often called for in salad recipes and the wider ones in stir-fries, the sizes are pretty much interchangeable.

Spicy Noodle Soup with Shrimp & Coconut Milk

Serves four.

Don't be intimidated by the long list of ingredients here—this soup comes together in under an hour. The end result is otherworldly: a bowl of rice noodles bathed in a silky, spicy coconut broth and capped with a crunchy, cooling garnish.

FOR THE SOUP BASE:
1 small onion, roughly chopped
One 2-inch piece fresh ginger, peeled and sliced into disks
5 cloves garlic, crushed
2 to 3 fresh serrano chiles, cored and roughly chopped
2 stalks lemongrass, trimmed and roughly sliced
1 Tbs. freshly ground coriander seeds
1 tsp. freshly ground cumin seeds
½ tsp. ground turmeric
¼ cup fish sauce
2 tsp. light brown sugar
2 Tbs. peanut or vegetable oil
Shells from the shrimp for the soup
2 cups low-salt chicken broth
3 cups water
1 can (14 oz.) coconut milk
¼ cup fresh lime juice
1 tsp. kosher salt

FOR THE SOUP:
6 to 7 oz. wide rice noodles
¼ seedless cucumber
1 cup mung bean sprouts, rinsed and dried
1 fresh chile (serrano, jalapeño, or Thai), cored and sliced into thin rounds (optional)
½ cup fresh cilantro leaves, roughly chopped or torn
½ cup fresh mint leaves, roughly chopped or torn
1 lb. shrimp (31-40 per lb.), shells removed and reserved; deveined
4 lime wedges

Make the soup base: Put the onion, ginger, garlic, chile, lemongrass, coriander, cumin, turmeric, fish sauce, and brown sugar in a food processor. Purée to make a paste, scraping down the sides as needed. Heat the oil in a heavy soup pot or Dutch oven over medium heat until hot but not smoking. Add the paste mixture and sauté, stirring often, until it softens, becomes very aromatic, and deepens in color, about 8 minutes. Stir in the shrimp shells and cook until they turn pink, about 2 minutes. Add the chicken broth, water, coconut milk, lime juice, and salt and bring to a boil. Lower the heat so that the broth simmers gently for 30 minutes. Strain the broth through a fine sieve into a clean pot and discard the solids. Season the broth to taste with salt, and return to a simmer.

While the soup base is simmering: Bring a large pot of water to a boil and then remove from the heat. Put the rice noodles in the water and let sit until tender, 5 to 10 minutes. Drain, rinse, and distribute among four large, shallow soup bowls.

Slice the cucumber into ¼-inch rounds, stack the rounds, and slice into thin matchsticks. Put the cucumber sticks in a medium bowl and toss with the bean sprouts, sliced chiles (if using), and herbs.

Just before serving, add the shrimp to the broth and gently simmer until they're just cooked through, about 3 minutes. Ladle the hot soup over the noodles. Arrange a mound of the cucumber and bean sprout mixture in the center of the bowl, top with a lime wedge, and serve immediately.

Chilled Curried Carrot Soup

Yields about 5 cups; serves four.

The ¾ tsp. of curry powder in this cold soup gives it a lovely fragrance and very mild heat. If you like things spicier, just add a bit more. Pepitas, available now at most supermarkets, are hulled green pumpkin seeds with a sweet flavor that comes alive when toasted.

2 Tbs. unsalted butter or vegetable oil
1 lb. carrots, peeled and thinly sliced
1 medium onion, chopped
1 large shallot, sliced
2 cloves garlic, chopped
1 heaping Tbs. minced fresh ginger
1 tsp. seeded and minced fresh serrano or
  jalapeño (about ½ a medium-size chile)
1 tsp. ground coriander
¾ tsp. Madras-style hot curry powder
Kosher salt
3 cups homemade or low-salt canned chicken
  broth, or water
½ cup coconut milk
1½ Tbs. fresh lime juice; more to taste
Freshly ground black or white pepper
Fresh cilantro leaves for garnish
Toasted pepitas or pine nuts for garnish

Heat the butter or oil in a wide soup pot over medium heat. Add the carrots, onion, and shallot and cook, stirring occasionally, until slightly softened, about 6 minutes. Add the garlic, ginger, chile, coriander, curry powder, and a generous pinch of salt. Cook until fragrant, another minute. Pour in the chicken broth, cover partially, and bring to a boil over high heat. Reduce the heat and simmer gently until the vegetables offer no resistance when mashed against the side of the pot with a wooden spoon, 25 to 35 minutes. Remove from the heat.

Ladle some solids and broth into a blender, taking care to fill the jar no more than two-thirds full. Before turning on the blender, vent the lid by removing the pop-out center if there is one, or just open the lid a bit. (Venting prevents the heat from building up inside the blender, which could cause hot soup to spew out all over the kitchen.) For extra precaution, drape a clean dishtowel over the vented lid as well. Purée the soup in batches if needed and then strain through a medium sieve. Stir in the coconut milk and lime juice; season to taste with salt and pepper. Chill thoroughly. Before serving, thin the soup gradually as needed with up to 1 cup of water and adjust the seasonings. Ladle the soup into bowls or cups. Garnish with a few cilantro leaves and the pepitas or pine nuts.

Miso Mushroom Soup

Serves two; may be doubled.

Fresh spinach leaves and scallions brighten up a bowl of soothing miso soup. You can make the soup with any type of miso, but darker types offer a richer, more savory flavor.

2 dried shiitake mushrooms,
  rinsed
½ cup baby spinach leaves
½ cup medium-diced silken tofu
2½ Tbs. miso (preferably red or
  brown)
2 Tbs. thinly sliced scallion
  greens
½ tsp. toasted sesame oil

In a medium saucepan, combine the mushrooms with 3 cups cold water. Bring to a boil over medium heat. Remove from the heat and use a fork or tongs to transfer the mushrooms to a cutting board. As soon as the mushrooms are cool enough to handle, trim off and discard the stems and slice the caps very thinly. Return the sliced mushrooms to the pan of water. Bring back to a simmer and then reduce the heat to low. Let the mushrooms steep for 15 minutes (the water needn't be simmering, but it's fine if it does). Taste one of the mushroom slices. If you like the texture, leave the mushrooms in; otherwise, fish them out and discard them.

Bring the mushroom broth to a simmer over medium heat. Add the spinach and tofu and simmer for 1 minute. Remove from the heat. In a small bowl, combine the miso with 2 Tbs. of the broth and mix well. Stir the thinned miso into the soup. Top each serving with 1 Tbs. of the scallion greens and ¼ tsp. of the sesame oil.

Pea & Spinach Soup with Coconut Milk

Yields 5½ cups soup; serves six.

Fresh peas are a must for this soup, but you don't need a ton of them. Spinach adds to the color and texture of the soup while letting the pea flavor come through.

- **2 large leeks (white parts plus the pale green), quartered and sliced to yield 2 cups (or 2 cups thinly sliced white onion)**
- **1 Tbs. unsalted butter**
- **2 Tbs. white basmati rice**
- **1 tsp. salt; more to taste**
- **2 tsp. curry powder**
- **4 sprigs fresh cilantro; more for garnish**
- **4 cups homemade Vegetable Stock (recipe at right) or low-salt canned vegetable or chicken broth**
- **1½ to 2 lb. peas, shucked (to yield 1½ to 2 cups)**
- **4 cups lightly packed coarsely chopped spinach leaves, any thick stems removed, well washed**
- **7 oz. coconut milk, about 1 cup**
- **Freshly ground white pepper to taste**

Soak the leeks in a bowl of cold water to remove any grit. Meanwhile, in a soup pot over medium heat, melt the butter and stir in the rice. Scoop the leeks from the water, shaking off excess, and add them to the pot along with the salt, curry powder, cilantro, and 1 cup of the stock. Cook over medium-low heat at a vigorous simmer for about 12 minutes, so the rice is almost done. Add the remaining 3 cups stock, the peas, and the spinach and bring to a boil. Boil for about 3 minutes. Turn off the heat and stir in the coconut milk. In a blender or a food processor, purée the soup in batches until smooth. Taste for salt, season with white pepper, and serve, garnished with fresh cilantro leaves. (If you prefer a soup with more texture, purée 1 cup and return it to the pot, season, garnish and serve.)

Vegetable Stock

Yields about 5½ cups.

This versatile stock would also be delicious in a risotto featuring peas.

- **Leek roots and 2 cups coarsely chopped leek greens (use the few inches of green nearest the root end, just beyond the whites), well rinsed**
- **2 cups parsley stems**
- **2 cups whole empty pea pods, well rinsed**
- **1 bay leaf**
- **1 or 2 sprigs thyme**
- **1 carrot, chopped**
- **1½ tsp. salt**
- **7 cups cold water**

Put all the ingredients in a stockpot. Bring to a boil, lower the heat, and simmer for 35 minutes. Strain.

tip: Peas are sweetest when cooked briefly. Look for bright-green, moist-looking, medium-size pods and use the shucked peas soon after purchasing.

Roasted Red Pepper & Tomato Gazpacho

Yields 5 cups; serves four.

Hearty and thick from chopped tomatoes, herbs, and roasted peppers (but not a speck of bread), this soup uses lemon juice instead of the traditional vinegar. It's almost as thick as a salsa; you can thin it with water if you like.

3 large red bell peppers, halved lengthwise and seeded

2 lb. ripe tomatoes (about 6 medium), peeled, seeded, and chopped (to yield about 3 cups)

2 cloves garlic, finely chopped

⅓ cup good-quality extra-virgin olive oil; more as needed

¼ cup fresh lemon juice (from 1 to 2 lemons); more to taste

4 scallions (white and green parts), finely chopped

1 cup peeled, seeded, very finely diced cucumber (from 1 small)

½ cup chopped mixed herbs, such as basil, chervil, parsley, thyme, marjoram, and tarragon

Salt and freshly ground pepper to taste

¼ cup crumbled goat cheese or ⅓ cup cooked tiny shrimp or larger shrimp cut into bite-size pieces (optional)

Roast the peppers: Set the broiler rack on the top rung and heat the broiler. Lightly oil a broiling pan. Set the pepper halves on the pan, cut side down, and flatten them with your palm. Broil until the skins blister and blacken, 10 to 15 minutes. Seal the peppers in a paper bag (or put them in a large bowl and cover it) so the peppers steam and the skins loosen.

When the peppers are cool enough to handle, peel away the blackened skin and discard it. (It helps to rinse your hands occasionally as you do this, but don't rinse the peppers or you'll dilute their flavor.)

Make the gazpacho: Put the peppers and tomatoes in a food processor and pulse to chop them finely (or use a knife). Put

them into a large mixing bowl and stir in the garlic. Gradually stir in the olive oil to incorporate it. Add the lemon juice, scallions, cucumber, and all but 2 tsp. of the herbs (reserve these for the goat cheese or shrimp; if you're not adding either of these garnishes, mix in all the herbs now). Taste, season the soup well with salt and pepper, taste again, and add more drops of olive oil or lemon juice, if you like. Cover and chill.

If using the goat cheese, put it in a bowl and sprinkle generously with olive oil, the reserved fresh herbs, and pepper to taste; toss gently with a rubber spatula. If using the shrimp, put it in a bowl, moisten with olive oil, and add the reserved fresh herbs and salt and pepper to taste; toss with a rubber spatula.

Taste the gazpacho again and adjust the seasonings if necessary. Serve in chilled soup bowls, garnished with either the goat cheese or shrimp (if using) or just a little spoonful of olive oil floating on top.

Puréed Eggplant Soup with Tomato Relish

Serves four; yields ¾ cup relish.

With no cream or other thickener, this soup is light bodied and intensely flavorful.

FOR THE SOUP:
4 Tbs. olive oil
1 lb. eggplant (1 medium eggplant), sliced in half lengthwise
Kosher salt and freshly ground black pepper
5 cups homemade or low-salt canned chicken broth
8 large sprigs fresh basil
12 stems fresh parsley
2 sprigs fresh thyme
1 large onion, sliced
1½ Tbs. minced fresh garlic

FOR THE RELISH:
2 tsp. extra-virgin olive oil; more for garnish
2 tsp. minced fresh garlic
¼ tsp. kosher salt
1 medium ripe tomato, peeled, seeded, and diced
½ tsp. sherry vinegar
2 Tbs. chopped fresh flat-leaf parsley

Make the soup: Heat the oven to 375°F. Spread 2 Tbs. of the oil on a rimmed baking sheet. Season the cut side of the eggplant with salt and pepper and put the halves face down on the pan. Roast until tender, about 40 minutes; a knife will enter the flesh easily. When cool enough to handle, scrape out the flesh with a spoon. Discard the skin.

Meanwhile, put the chicken broth, basil, parsley stems, and thyme in a large saucepan or a stockpot. Bring to a boil, reduce the heat, and simmer uncovered for 15 minutes. Strain the broth.

Heat the remaining 2 Tbs. olive oil in a large, heavy saucepan over medium heat. Add the onion and cook, stirring frequently, until golden and caramelized, about 20 minutes. Stir in ¾ tsp. salt and the garlic. Add 4 cups of the stock, bring to a boil, add the eggplant flesh, reduce to a simmer, and cook for 5 minutes.

Ladle the soup in batches in a blender, using about half as much broth as vegetables in each batch, until smooth. (Add additional broth only if needed to help the purée along.) Strain each batch through a fine-mesh sieve, pressing on the solids, into a clean soup pot. Thin the soup with any remaining broth, if necessary, so it has the consistency of heavy cream (you may not use all of the broth).

Make the relish: In a small pan, combine the oil, garlic, and salt. Heat over low until the garlic is tender but not colored, 3 to 4 minutes. Add the tomato and cook just until warm, about 2 minutes. Stir in the sherry vinegar, pepper, and parsley. Remove from the heat and serve within a few hours.

Taste the soup and add salt if needed. Serve warm, garnished with the relish and a drizzle of extra-virgin olive oil.

tip: Garnishes give puréed soups a visual lift. Try a spoonful of sour cream, a drizzle of peppery olive oil, or a handful of homemade croutons.

Barley Minestrone

Yields about 3 quarts.

This rendition of the classic Italian vegetable and bean soup uses barley instead of pasta. Simmering a piece of the rind from Parmigiano Reggiano in the soup is a traditional way of adding flavor. When you finish off a wedge of Parmigiano, just stash the rind in the freezer so you always have it on hand when you need it.

2 Tbs. extra-virgin olive oil
¼ cup finely diced pancetta (about 1 oz.)
2 cups large-diced Savoy cabbage
1 cup medium-diced yellow onion
1 cup sliced carrot (¼ inch thick)
¼ cup medium-diced celery
2 cloves garlic, minced
2 qt. homemade or low-salt canned chicken broth
1 14½-oz. can diced tomatoes, with their juices
½ cup pearl barley, rinsed
2 large sprigs fresh rosemary
2-inch-square Parmigiano Reggiano rind (optional)
Kosher salt
1 cup rinsed and drained canned kidney beans
Freshly ground black pepper
Freshly grated Parmigiano Reggiano for serving

Heat the oil in a heavy 6-qt. or larger pot over medium heat. Add the pancetta and cook, stirring frequently, until it becomes slightly golden, 2 to 3 minutes. Add the cabbage, onion, carrot, celery, and garlic. Cook, stirring frequently, until the vegetables begin to soften, about 6 minutes. Add the broth, the tomatoes with their juices, the barley, rosemary, Parmigiano rind (if using), ½ tsp. salt, and 1 cup water. Bring to a boil over high heat, and then reduce the heat to a simmer and cook until the barley and vegetables are tender, about 20 minutes. Discard the rosemary sprigs and Parmigiano rind. Stir in the beans and season to taste with salt and pepper. Serve sprinkled with the grated Parmigiano.

Purée of Sweet Potato & Ginger Soup with Apple-Mint Raita

Serves four to six.

Slices of fresh ginger are simmered with the soup base to gently infuse it with warmth and mellow sweetness. The raita is the perfect cooling counterpart. If you like heat, leave the ribs attached to the jalapeño half.

FOR THE SOUP:
2 Tbs. unsalted butter
1 medium yellow onion, roughly chopped
2 cloves garlic, minced
½-inch chunk (1 oz.) fresh ginger, peeled and thinly sliced
¼ tsp. ground cardamom
½ fresh jalapeño, seeds and ribs removed, and left whole
2 lb. sweet potatoes (about 4 medium), peeled and cut into 1-inch cubes
5½ cups homemade or low-salt canned chicken broth
1 tsp. kosher salt; more to taste
½ cup heavy cream (optional)
1 Tbs. fresh lime juice
1 Tbs. light brown sugar
Freshly ground white pepper

FOR THE RAITA:
½ cup plain nonfat or low-fat yogurt
½ firm, sweet apple, such as Gala or Pink Lady, peeled, cored, and finely diced
¼ cup chopped fresh mint
½ tsp. finely minced fresh jalapeño; more to taste
Kosher salt and freshly ground black pepper

Make the soup: Melt the butter in a soup pot over low heat. Cook the onion in the butter, stirring occasionally, until very soft but not browned, 10 to 13 minutes. Add the garlic, ginger, and cardamom and cook for another minute. Increase the heat to high

and add the jalapeño, sweet potatoes, 4 cups of the broth, and the salt. Bring to a boil, reduce the heat to medium low, cover, and simmer until the potatoes are very soft, 15 to 20 minutes.

In a blender, purée the soup in batches until very smooth. Rinse and dry the pot and return the puréed soup to it. Add the remaining broth and the cream (if using) and bring to a simmer over medium-low heat. Add the lime juice and brown sugar, and season with salt and white pepper to taste.

Make the raita: While the soup is simmering, combine the yogurt, apple, mint, and jalapeño in a small bowl. Season with salt and pepper to taste. Refrigerate until ready to serve.

To serve: Ladle the soup into individual bowls and add a dollop of the raita.

Grilled Yellow Tomato Bisque

Yields 8 cups; serves six.

This bisque can be made up to 2 days in advance. Although the yellow color is quite charming, red tomatoes can be substituted.

8 large, ripe yellow tomatoes (about 3½ lb. total)
1 Tbs. olive oil
1 medium-size red onion, chopped
1 qt. homemade or low-salt canned chicken broth
1 tsp. sugar
1 cup heavy cream
Kosher salt and freshly ground black pepper
¼ cup chopped fresh mint

Prepare a medium-hot grill fire. Put the whole tomatoes on the grate and grill, turning occasionally, until the skins crack and begin to blacken in some parts and the tomatoes soften—7 to 9 minutes over charcoal, 12 to 15 minutes on a gas grill. Take them off the grill, core them, and coarsely chop them.

Heat the olive oil in a large soup pot over medium-high heat. Add the onion and cook, stirring occasionally, until soft, about 7 minutes. Stir in the chopped tomatoes, chicken broth, and sugar. Increase the heat, bring to a boil, turn the heat to medium, and simmer until the soup is reduced by one-quarter, about 20 minutes. Let cool for 10 minutes.

In a blender, purée the soup in batches until smooth, 2 to 3 minutes per batch. Strain through a fine-mesh sieve, pressing on the solids, into a clean soup pot and bring to a simmer over medium heat. Turn off the heat and stir in the heavy cream. Taste and season with salt and pepper. To serve, ladle the soup into bowls and garnish with the chopped mint.

**White & Green Bean Salad
with Tomatoes & Basil** *p. 62*

Salads

Jícama, Avocado, Radish & Orange Salad with Cilantro

Serves six to eight.

Both jícama and radish give this salad a welcome crunch—jícama a sweet crunch and radish a peppery one.

4 oranges
1 tsp. cumin seeds
1 clove garlic
Kosher salt
5 Tbs. fresh lime juice; more to taste
Large pinch cayenne
¼ cup extra-virgin olive oil
1 small jícama (about 1¼ lb.)
8 small red radishes, cut into very thin round slices
5 scallions, dark green tops trimmed; cut diagonally into thin slices
Freshly ground black pepper
2 large ripe but firm avocados
1 cup packed fresh cilantro leaves

Finely grate 2 tsp. zest from the oranges and set aside. With a sharp paring knife, slice the ends off the oranges. Stand each orange on one of its cut ends and pare off the rest of the peel in strips, making sure to remove all of the pith. Working over a small bowl, carefully cut the orange segments away from the connective membrane. Squeeze the membranes over the bowl to get any remaining juice.

Put the cumin seeds in a small, dry skillet and toast over medium heat until slightly browned and aromatic, about 1 minute. Remove from the skillet and let cool. Grind the seeds to a fine powder in a mortar and pestle or an electric spice mill. Using a mortar and pestle or the flat side of a chef's knife, mash the garlic to a paste with a pinch of salt. Put the garlic paste and cumin powder in a small bowl (or keep it in the mortar) and whisk in the 2 tsp. orange zest, 3 Tbs. orange juice (from the bowl of orange segments), the lime juice, and the cayenne. Let the mixture sit for 5 to 10 minutes, and then whisk in the olive oil.

Meanwhile, peel the jícama and it cut into ⅛-inch-thick matchsticks 2 to 3 inches long. In a large bowl, combine the jícama, radishes, and scallions. Season with salt and pepper and toss with about two-thirds of the vinaigrette. Set aside for 5 to 10 minutes to let the flavors mingle.

Just before serving, thinly slice the avocados diagonally. Lay half of the avocado slices in a shallow bowl and season with salt and pepper. Drizzle some of the remaining vinaigrette on the avocado. Add the cilantro and orange segments to the jícama mixture and toss gently. Taste and adjust the seasoning with more salt, pepper, and lime juice if needed. Put the jícama salad on top of the sliced avocado and tuck the remaining slices of avocado into the salad. Season the top slices with salt and drizzle with the remaining vinaigrette. Serve immediately.

Grilled Corn Salad with Cherry Tomatoes, Arugula & Ricotta Salata

Serves six to eight as part of a buffet.

This summery side dish looks beautiful as part of an al fresco buffet. If served as a starter or one of only two sides, the salad serves four to six.

5 ears corn, unhusked
1 shallot, finely chopped
1 Tbs. Champagne vinegar or white-wine vinegar
2 Tbs. sherry vinegar
Kosher salt and freshly ground black pepper
⅓ cup extra-virgin olive oil
2 to 3 bunches arugula (about ½ lb.), stemmed, or ¼ lb. baby arugula
1 cup cherry tomatoes
2 oz. ricotta salata

Heat a gas grill to medium high or prepare a medium-hot charcoal fire. Remove the thick, outer leaves of the corn husk. Peel back the inner leaves, being careful to leave them attached to the cob. Remove as much of the corn silk as possible and then fold the inner leaves back over the corn. It's fine if some of the kernels show through gaps in the leaves.

Once the fire is hot, put the corn on the grate, cover the grill, and cook, flipping often, until the husk is very charred and some of the kernels are browned and feel cooked when pressed with a fingernail, 10 to 15 minutes. Set aside to cool.

Combine the shallot, Champagne or white-wine vinegar, and sherry vinegar in a medium bowl. Season with salt and pepper and let macerate for 20 minutes. Whisk in the oil. Taste and adjust the seasonings; set aside.

Meanwhile, wash and dry the arugula. Put it in a bowl, cover with a damp paper towel, and refrigerate.

Shuck the corn and wipe it off well, making sure no flecks of charred husk or corn silk cling to it. Cut the kernels off the cob and put them in a large salad bowl. Cut each cherry tomato in half from stem to tip and set aside (don't refrigerate).

Assemble the salad: Pour some of the the vinaigrette over the corn and toss well. Gently toss in the arugula and tomatoes, drizzle with the remaining vinaigrette, and season with a little salt and pepper. Crumble the ricotta salata over the salad and serve.

Bread Salad with Corn, Cherry Tomatoes & Basil

Serves four to six.

Stale bread is traditional for bread salad, but fresh bread toasted in a hot oven works really well—the outside gets crisp and the inside stays slightly chewy. Juicy tomatoes are key; if you can't find cherry tomatoes, use beefsteak tomatoes. (Grape tomatoes aren't juicy enough for this salad.) If your corn is exceptionally sweet and tender, you can skip the blanching step.

1 shallot, lobes separated and cut lengthwise into very thin slices
1 small clove garlic
Kosher salt to taste
2 Tbs. red-wine vinegar; more to taste
½ cup packed fresh basil leaves
½ loaf (8 oz.) rustic French or Italian peasant bread (choose a firm, chewy loaf, not an airy one), crusts trimmed and bread cut or torn into rough ½- to ¾-inch cubes
½ cup plus 2 Tbs. extra-virgin olive oil
3 cups corn kernels (from 4 to 6 ears)
12 oz. juicy cherry tomatoes, cut in half and lightly salted, or 2 small beefsteak tomatoes, cut into large dice and salted
Freshly ground black pepper to taste

Heat the oven to 400°F. Put the shallot slices in a small bowl filled with ice water. Using a mortar and pestle or the flat side of a chef's knife, mash the garlic to a paste with a pinch of salt. Put the paste in a small bowl (or keep it in the mortar, if using) and whisk in the vinegar. Bruise two of the basil leaves with the back of a knife to release some of their flavor. Add the leaves to the garlic.

Put the bread cubes on a baking sheet and toss with 2 Tbs. of the olive oil. Bake until the cubes are crisp and light golden brown outside but still soft inside, about 10 minutes. Set aside to cool.

Bring a small pot of water to a boil. Add the corn kernels and blanch for 1 minute. Drain and set aside.

Remove the two basil leaves from the garlic mixture and discard. Whisk the remaining ½ cup olive oil into the vinegar mixture. Drain the shallots. Put the corn kernels, shallots, and tomatoes in a large bowl. Season to taste with salt. Add the bread and toss with the vinaigrette. Taste again and season with salt and pepper. Let sit for at least 15 minutes but no longer than 30 minutes to let the bread absorb the juices. Taste again and, if needed, season with more salt, pepper, and vinegar. Just before serving, roughly chop the remaining basil and toss it with the salad.

how-to

See p. 217 to learn how to get fresh corn kernels off the cob.

tip: Never chill a tomato! Very cold temperatures destroy a tomato's flavor and ruin its texture, making it mealy.

Tomato & Fresh Green Bean Salad with Crisp Prosciutto

Serves six to eight.

Summer savory has a peppery flavor and pungent aroma. If you can't find it, substitute fresh thyme or marjoram.

6 medium, ripe red tomatoes, each cut into 6 wedges
Kosher salt
4 thin slices prosciutto (about 2 oz.)
12 oz. fresh green beans, trimmed and cut into 2-inch pieces
3 Tbs. chopped fresh summer savory, plus sprigs for garnish
2 cloves garlic, minced
2 Tbs. sherry vinegar
¼ cup extra-virgin olive oil
Freshly ground black pepper
1½ cups yellow and orange cherry tomatoes (or other bite-size tomatoes), halved

Heat the oven to 400°F. Put a large pot of salted water on to boil.

Put the tomato wedges in a colander set over a bowl. Sprinkle with 1 Tbs. salt, toss, and let stand for 30 minutes.

Slice the prosciutto crosswise into ½-inch strips. Arrange on a baking sheet in a single layer and bake until crisp and light golden, about 10 minutes. Set aside.

Meanwhile, when the water comes to a boil, add the beans and cook until tender, 4 to 6 minutes. Drain and let cool.

In a small bowl, whisk together the chopped savory, garlic, and vinegar. Whisk in the olive oil to blend. Season to taste with salt and pepper.

Combine the tomato wedges, cherry tomatoes, and green beans in a bowl. Add the vinaigrette, toss, and season with salt and pepper to taste. Transfer to a shallow serving bowl or platter, sprinkle with the prosciutto, and garnish with the savory sprigs. Serve immediately.

Traditional Caesar Salad

Serves four to six.

If you don't have a large mortar and pestle, you can easily mash the garlic to a paste with the flat side of a chef's knife. The dressing here is zesty and assertive and balances nicely with the cool, crisp romaine and salty Parmesan.

FOR THE CROUTONS:
3 Tbs. extra-virgin olive oil
1½ cups torn pieces from a baguette or other crusty bread
Coarse salt and freshly ground black pepper

FOR THE SALAD:
2 large heads romaine lettuce
2 small cloves garlic
Coarse salt
4 oil-packed anchovy fillets, rinsed and patted dry
1 egg yolk*
1 tsp. Dijon mustard
Juice from ½ lemon (about 4 tsp.)
Freshly ground black pepper
Dash of Tabasco or other hot sauce
¼ tsp. Worcestershire sauce
¼ cup extra-virgin olive oil
⅓ cup loosely packed flat-leaf parsley leaves
½ cup freshly grated Parmesan, preferably Parmigiano Reggiano

For the croutons, warm the oil in a medium skillet over medium low heat. Add the bread pieces, toss to coat, and cook, turning periodically, until golden on the outside but still tender inside, 12 to 15 minutes. Let them cool in one layer on paper towels. Season with salt and pepper to taste.

Remove the outer leaves of romaine until you reach the tightly packed heart (the leaves will be much paler); set the outer leaves aside for another use. Separate the leaves of the heart and slice them into pieces about 3 inches long (leave the smallest leaves whole) to yield a heaping 8 cups of loosely packed leaves. Rinse and dry very thoroughly.

Using a mortar and pestle or the flat side of a chef's knife, mash the garlic to a paste with a pinch of salt. Put the paste in a small bowl (or keep it in the mortar, if using). Add the anchovies, mashing with the pestle or a wooden spoon until they're broken down into bits. Add the yolk, working the mixture into a paste. Work in the mustard and then the lemon juice. Blend in a pinch of black pepper, the Tabasco, and the Worcestershire. Switch to a whisk and drizzle in the olive oil, whisking continuously until blended and creamy.

Put the lettuce, parsley, and croutons in a large bowl. Season with salt and pepper and toss. Add the dressing and toss to coat thoroughly. Sprinkle with 2 to 3 Tbs. of the Parmesan and toss again. Serve immediately with the remaining cheese on the side.

*If you're serving this salad to anyone with a compromised immune system, replace the raw egg yolk in the dressing with the yolk from a soft-boiled egg, or omit the egg yolk altogether.

the twist

New flavors and textures perk up a classic salad

A great spinach salad contains a variety of flavors and textures. This updated version adds basil for bright flavor, toasty tomatoes for color, and candied walnuts for a delicious crunch.

At a glance, you might not notice that the salad contains both baby spinach and fresh basil leaves, so the herb's flavor comes as a delightful surprise.

Candied Walnuts

Yields about 3 cups.

⅓ cup granulated sugar
2½ Tbs. brown sugar
½ tsp. kosher salt
½ tsp. ground cinnamon
Pinch cayenne
1 large egg white, at room temperature
½ lb. walnut halves

Heat the oven to 300°F. In a small bowl, mix both sugars with the salt, cinnamon, and cayenne. In a large bowl, whisk the egg white until frothy; whisk in 1 Tbs. water until combined. Add the walnuts and stir to coat. Sprinkle on the sugar mixture and stir to distribute evenly.

Line a rimmed baking sheet with a non-stick baking mat or parchment. Spread the sugared nuts in a single layer on the sheet. Bake for 15 minutes, stir the nuts, and continue baking until the nuts smell toasted and the sugar coating is caramelized, about another 15 minutes.

Let the nuts cool on the pan, separating them as they cool. When completely cool, transfer them to an airtight container. They'll keep for two weeks.

Spinach & Basil Salad with Tomatoes, Candied Walnuts & Warm Bacon Dressing

Serves four.

½ lb. baby spinach leaves, washed and dried
1 cup lightly packed fresh basil leaves, washed and dried
6 slices bacon
2 Tbs. white-wine vinegar
1 Tbs. Dijon mustard
⅓ cup plus 2 tsp. olive oil
Kosher salt and freshly ground black pepper
1 pint grape tomatoes, washed and dried
1½ tsp. dried herbes de Provence
½ tsp. dehydrated minced or granulated garlic
Candied Walnuts (see the recipe at left)

In a large salad bowl, toss the spinach and basil.

Cut each slice of bacon into thirds. Cook in a medium skillet over medium to medium-high heat, stirring occasionally, until crisp; drain on paper towels. Reserve 1 Tbs. of the bacon fat. Crumble the bacon into pieces.

In a medium metal bowl, whisk the vinegar with the mustard. Slowly whisk in ⅓ cup of the oil and then whisk in the 1 Tbs. bacon fat. Season to taste with salt and pepper. Set aside in a warm place.

Position an oven rack as close as possible to the broiler element. Put a heavy-duty rimmed baking sheet on the rack and heat the broiler to high. Toss the tomatoes with the remaining 2 tsp. olive oil, the herbes de Provence, dehydrated garlic, and ½ tsp. salt. Pour the tomatoes onto the hot pan and broil, stirring occasionally, until the skins are cracked and blistered and the flesh is warmed through, 4 to 5 minutes. Turn off the broiler. Transfer the tomatoes with a slotted spoon to the bowl with the salad dressing. Stir to coat and mix the seasonings into the dressing. Put the bowl in the oven to keep warm until ready to serve.

Just before serving, transfer the tomatoes from the dressing to another bowl with a slotted spoon. Whisk the dressing to recombine. Add half of the bacon to the greens. Drizzle the greens with 3 Tbs. of the dressing and toss lightly to coat. Add more dressing only if needed; don't over-ould dress the salad. Mound the greens on four salad plates. Garnish with the tomatoes, the remaining bacon, and some of the candied walnuts (you'll have leftovers for snacking). Serve immediately.

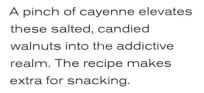

Tossed with garlic and herbs and then broiled, these sweet tomatoes add warmth and several layers of flavor to the salad.

A pinch of cayenne elevates these salted, candied walnuts into the addictive realm. The recipe makes extra for snacking.

Asparagus & Citrus Salad

Serves four.

This bright and simple salad tastes best with a fruity olive oil and good balsamic vinegar.

2 Tbs. finely chopped shallots
1 Tbs. good-quality balsamic vinegar
1 tsp. sherry vinegar
3 oranges, preferably blood oranges
2 to 3 Tbs. extra-virgin olive oil
1½ lb. asparagus, trimmed
Freshly ground black pepper (optional)

In a small bowl, combine the shallots with the vinegars and let the shallots macerate for at least 20 minutes. Meanwhile, finely grate the zest of one of the oranges (avoid the white pith). Add the zest to the shallots. Juice the zested orange to yield about ⅓ cup and add the juice to the shallots. Slowly pour in the olive oil, stirring to mix.

Bring a pot of salted water to a boil. Add the asparagus and simmer until just tender, about 4 minutes. Drain and spread the spears on paper towels to cool.

Cut off the ends of the remaining 2 oranges and peel them by running a sharp knife down the fruit vertically, following the contours. Slice the peeled orange horizontally into ¼-inch slices. Just before serving, toss the cooled asparagus with the vinaigrette. Arrange the spears and the orange slices on salad plates. Sprinkle with pepper, if you like, and serve immediately.

Arugula Salad with Nectarines & Fresh Raspberry Vinaigrette

Serves six.

This salad is delicious only if the fruit is good and ripe. Ripe peaches can easily stand in for the nectarines, so choose the fruit that looks, feels, and smells the best that day. You may have some leftover dressing, but it's delicious on other tossed green salads.

1 small shallot, minced
3 Tbs. raspberry vinegar
½ tsp. grated orange zest
1 Tbs. fresh orange juice
Kosher salt
2 ripe nectarines
6 Tbs. extra-virgin olive oil
Freshly ground black pepper
⅔ cup fresh raspberries
½ lb. baby arugula or 1 lb. arugula, stems trimmed; thoroughly washed, dried, and torn into bite-size pieces (to yield about 8 cups, loosely packed)

Combine the minced shallot with the raspberry vinegar, the orange zest, half the orange juice, and a pinch of salt; set aside. Halve the nectarines, remove the pits, and then slice the halves into ¼-inch wedges; toss them with the remaining orange juice and set aside. Gradually whisk the olive oil into the shallot and vinegar mixture and add a few grinds of black pepper. In a small bowl, very lightly mash the raspberries, allowing them to keep some of their original shape and then stir them gently into the vinaigrette. Just before serving, put the arugula in a large bowl and toss with half the dressing to coat the leaves lightly. Toss the nectarines in 1 Tbs. of the vinaigrette. Arrange the arugula on a platter or individual dishes, topping the greens with the nectarine slices. Drizzle with a bit more dressing and serve.

Mexican Melon Salad

Serves four.

A salad featuring melons makes a light and striking first course, especially good if what's to follow is on the heavy side. Using a regular honeydew and its orange-fleshed sibling makes the salad look very pretty, but it would still taste great with one variety. You can also make a salsa version of this salad by adding more lime juice and cutting the fruit into smaller pieces. The salsa makes a delicious accompaniment to grilled fish.

1½ cups peeled and diced
  jícama (about half a large
  jícama)
¾ cup diced very ripe papaya
1 fresh jalapeño, cored, seeded,
  and minced
1 tsp. dried red chile flakes
¼ cup fresh lime juice
¼ tsp. kosher salt
1 oz. crumbled feta cheese
½ cup loosely packed cilantro
  leaves, chopped coarse
8 thin wedges honeydew melon
8 thin wedges orange-fleshed
  honeydew melon

In a large bowl, combine the jícama, papaya, jalapeño, and chile flakes. Add the lime juice and salt; toss to coat. Crumble in the feta and add the cilantro. Divide the melon wedges among four plates and top with the jícama and papaya mixture.

tip: If you have leftover jícama, serve slices of it with a little salt and a wedge of lime as a refreshing appetizer.

Summer Squash Salad with Lemon, Capers & Parmesan

Serves six to eight.

An abundance of fresh herbs perks up this refreshing salad. Feel free to add a little basil, marjoram or other delicate herbs in addition to the chives and parsley.

1 clove garlic
Kosher salt
¼ cup fresh lemon juice
½ cup extra-virgin olive oil
1 lb. summer squash (yellow squash, zucchini, or a mix)
Freshly ground black pepper
4 cups loosely packed baby arugula
½ cup fresh flat-leaf parsley leaves
½ cup chopped chives, cut into ½-inch lengths
2 Tbs. capers, rinsed well
1 oz. (¼ cup) finely grated Parmigiano Reggiano; plus a chunk to shave for garnish

In a mortar or using the flat side of a chef's knife, mash the garlic to a paste with a pinch of salt. Put the paste in a small bowl (or keep it in the mortar, if using) and whisk in the lemon juice. Let sit for 5 to 10 minutes and then whisk in the olive oil.

Using a mandoline or a sharp chef's knife, cut the squash diagonally into very thin (¹⁄₁₆- to ⅛-inch) ovals. Put the squash in a medium bowl, season with salt and pepper, and gently toss with about two-thirds of the vinaigrette.

Combine the arugula, parsley, chives, and capers in a separate bowl, season with salt and pepper, and toss with just enough vinaigrette to lightly coat. Taste both the squash and herbs and adjust the seasoning with salt or pepper if necessary. Layer about a third of the squash in a shallow bowl or platter, scatter about a third of the arugula mixture on top, and sprinkle with a third of the grated Parmesan. Repeat the process with the remaining squash and arugula mixture, sprinkling each layer with grated Parmesan. For garnish, use a vegetable peeler to shave long strips of Parmesan onto the salad. Serve immediately.

Potato, Corn & Tomato Salad with Fresh Herbs

Serves six to eight; yields 8 cups.

This potato salad is lighter and brighter than most, making it a perfect match for grilled chicken or fish. Serve it on a bed of arugula or watercress, if you like.

2 lb. unpeeled firm boiling potatoes, brushed and trimmed of any blemishes
Kosher salt
¾ cup peanut or grapeseed oil
¼ cup finely chopped red onion
4 ears very fresh corn, shucked
¼ cup finely sliced fresh chives
½ tsp. finely chopped fresh rosemary
2 tsp. fine sea salt
½ tsp. freshly ground black pepper
¼ cup high-quality apple-cider vinegar
3 large firm but ripe tomatoes

Put the potatoes in a large pot of cold water, salt well (about 1 Tbs. per gallon), and set over high heat. Once the water reaches a boil, reduce the heat to a low simmer, cover, and cook the potatoes until they're just tender (test by piercing them with a thin skewer), 25 to 35 minutes, depending on size. Scoop the potatoes from the water and transfer to a cutting board; don't drain the water.

Meanwhile, when the potatoes are almost cooked, heat the oil over medium heat in a small, nonreactive skillet. Add the onion and simmer long enough to tenderize it and mellow its flavor, 1 to 2 minutes. Remove from the heat and keep warm.

Bring the potato water back to a boil over high heat, add the corn, and boil until just tender, 2 to 4 minutes. Transfer the corn to the cutting board; again, don't drain the water.

While the corn cooks, hold the potatoes with tongs or a clean dishtowel, quickly cut them into ½-inch dice, and put them in a large bowl. Sprinkle on the herbs, salt, pepper, cider vinegar, and the warm onion and oil; gently fold together. Cut the kernels from the corn cobs and fold them into the potatoes. Transfer the salad to a serving platter and refrigerate it until cool, about 1 hour.

Return the water to a boil and fill a bowl with ice water. Cut out the stems of the tomatoes and cut a shallow "x" in the base of each (this helps with peeling). Blanch the tomatoes in the boiling water until the skins begin to loosen, about 30 seconds. Immediately drop the tomatoes into the ice water to stop the cooking. Drain the tomatoes, peel them, cut them in half crosswise, and gently scoop out most of the juice and seeds. Cut the tomatoes into ½-inch pieces, cover, and set aside at room temperature.

To serve, transfer the salad to a shallow bowl; add the tomatoes. Toss gently, taste and adjust the seasonings if needed, and serve.

tip: Taking a little extra care with the preparation of the leaves not only makes this salad prettier, but also makes the overall eating experience even more enjoyable.

Tri-color Salad of Belgian Endive, Arugula & Radicchio with Shaved Parmesan

Serves six to eight.

Sea salt punches up the flavor of this take on a classic Italian salad; if you don't have any, consider buying some, as it's also a wonderful finish for grilled steak and seafood. Table salt won't do here; instead, use kosher salt as a substitute.

3 Tbs. fresh lemon juice
Sea salt
Freshly ground black pepper
5 Tbs. extra-virgin olive oil
¼ lb. baby arugula (about 3¾ cups of leaves)
¼ lb. radicchio
½ lb. Belgian endive
3 oz. Parmesan cheese, shaved with a vegetable peeler (about ¾ cup)

In a small bowl, whisk together the lemon juice, ¼ tsp. sea salt, and a few grinds of black pepper, and then whisk in the olive oil. Reserve the vinaigrette at room temperature until ready to use.

Wash the baby arugula and spin it dry. Place the arugula in a large bowl covered with a slightly damp towel and store in the refrigerator until ready to use.

With a paring knife, cut out the core from the radicchio in a cone shape. Pull the leaves from the head and tear them into fork-size petals, until you have about 3¼ cups. Add the radicchio to the arugula.

Trim and discard the brown root end of the endive but leave enough root to hold it together. Remove any bruised and discolored leaves. Beginning about ½ inch from the bottom, use a paring knife to remove the next layer of outer leaves. Continue moving up the endive, cutting every ½ inch to release more leaves as you travel toward the tip; the leaves will become smaller as you go. When you are an inch from the tip, cut the tip in half and toss it, along with the other leaves, into the bowl with the arugula and radicchio. Discard the remaining core.

Toss the salad with just enough of the vinaigrette to lightly coat the leaves; you will likely use it all. Season to taste with sea salt and freshly ground black pepper. Sprinkle the Parmesan shavings over the salad and serve.

Quick-Roasted Beet Slices

Serves four as a small side dish.

Aside from making a great bed for the salad, these roasted beets are also delicious on their own as a side dish.

1 lb. small or medium red or yellow beets (or a combination), scrubbed but not peeled
2 Tbs. extra-virgin olive oil
½ tsp. kosher salt
1 tsp. fresh thyme leaves

Heat the oven to 450°F. Cover two large rimmed baking sheets with parchment. Slice off the tops and bottoms of the beets and then slice the beets into rounds as thin as possible (⅛ inch thick is ideal). If your beets are large and tough, cut them in half first, lay them on their sides, and cut half-moons instead of rounds for safer cutting. Toss the slices well with the olive oil, salt, and thyme and spread them in one layer, with a little space between each, on the two baking sheets. Roast for 20 to 25 minutes, swapping the pans to opposite racks halfway through. The beets will be soft and shrunken, slightly glistening on top, and dark around the edges. The thinnest slices will be crisp and almost burned around the edges.

If making the beets well ahead of serving, wrap and refrigerate them for up to 2 days; allow them to warm up a bit at room temperature before using them in the salad. To reheat them as a side dish, spread the slices on a parchment-lined baking sheet and heat in a 350°F oven for about 5 minutes.

Frilly Lettuce Salad on a Bed of Beets with Lemon-Walnut Vinaigrette

Serves four

A mix of different-colored beets makes a very striking salad. Flavorwise, however, a single color will work just as well.

1 recipe Quick-Roasted Beet Slices (at right), at room temperature
2 Tbs. plus 1 tsp. Lemon-Walnut Vinaigrette (see recipe at right); more to taste
1½ oz. fresh goat cheese, crumbled into small pieces
¼ cup toasted walnuts, roughly chopped
2 cups torn frisée, washed and dried (from 1 large or 2 small heads)
1 cup tender watercress sprigs, washed and dried
¾ cup (about ¼ head) thinly sliced radicchio

Arrange equal portions of the roasted beet slices in one layer on four salad plates. Drizzle a scant 1 tsp. of the vinaigrette over the beets. Sprinkle the goat cheese over each plate of beets. Sprinkle all but 1 Tbs. of the walnuts over each of the four plates as well. In a small mixing bowl, combine the frisée, watercress, and radicchio. Drizzle 2 Tbs. of the vinaigrette over the greens and toss lightly. (Taste a piece of lettuce; if you want more dressing, toss just a small amount more with the greens, but don't overdress.) Divide the greens among the plates, lifting them out of the bowl and arranging them in a tall mound centered on top of the beets (some of the beets should be peeking out underneath). Sprinkle the remaining walnuts over each salad and serve right away.

Lemon-Walnut Vinaigrette

Yields a generous ⅓ cup.

This vinaigrette makes more than you'll need for the salad at left, but it keeps well and can be poured over warmed beets as a side dish or tossed with any other salad featuring hearty greens.

2 Tbs. walnut oil
2 Tbs. extra-virgin olive oil
1 Tbs. cider vinegar
1 tsp. finely grated lemon zest
2½ tsp. fresh lemon juice
1 Tbs. finely chopped toasted walnuts
1 tsp. fresh thyme leaves
¼ tsp. dry mustard
½ tsp. kosher salt
About 6 grinds black pepper

Measure all the ingredients into a small glass jar with a tight-fitting lid. Screw on the lid and shake the contents vigorously. The vinaigrette keeps in the refrigerator for a week. Bring to room temperature and shake vigorously again before using.

Frisée Salad with Roasted Beets & Orange Vinaigrette

Serves six to eight.

You may see frisée labeled as curly endive at the market. Mâche (also called lamb's lettuce) is a delicious alternative, and it's becoming much easier to find.

4 medium-size red or golden beets, tops sliced off, rinsed
2 shallots, minced
2 Tbs. sherry vinegar
Juice and grated zest of 1 orange
⅓ cup extra-virgin olive oil
Sea salt and freshly ground black pepper
10 oz. frisée (tough, bright-green outer leaves discarded), washed, dried, and torn
½ cup walnuts, toasted and lightly chopped

Heat the oven to 400°F. Put the beets in a small baking dish with 1 cup water. Cover with foil and roast until the beets are tender, 40 to 60 minutes. Meanwhile, in a small bowl, combine the minced shallots, sherry vinegar, orange juice, and orange zest. Whisk in the olive oil in a thin stream; season with salt and pepper. When the beets are cool, peel them and cut them into ½-inch dice. Toss with 1 to 2 Tbs. of the vinaigrette. Toss the frisée with some of the remaining vinaigrette (there may be a little vinaigrette left over). Divide the frisée evenly among salad plates, sprinkle with the beets and toasted walnuts, and serve.

Fresh Herb Salad

Serves three to four.

An herb salad, dressed lightly in the most basic vinaigrette, is a refreshing foil to rich cured meats and fish. Serve it over thin slices of gravlax, prime beef carpaccio, or prosciutto. You don't need to be so precise when measuring the herbs; the following is more like a guideline. But do use only tender herbs in perfect condition.

FOR THE VINAIGRETTE:
3 to 4 Tbs. fruity extra-virgin olive oil
1 Tbs. rice vinegar, aged sherry vinegar, or fresh lemon juice
Kosher salt and freshly ground pepper

FOR THE SALAD:
3 cups assorted, carefully picked herb leaves, well washed and dried; a good mix would include the following:
• 1 cup flat-leaf parsley leaves
• ½ cup basil leaves, larger ones cut into thin slices
• ¼ cup tarragon leaves, larger ones cut smaller
• ¼ cup chives, cut in 1-inch lengths
• ⅓ cup baby arugula leaves
• ⅓ cup chervil sprigs
• ¼ cup small cilantro sprigs

In a small bowl, whisk 3 Tbs. of the oil with the vinegar or lemon juice. Taste and add more oil if too acidic. Season with salt and pepper. Just before serving, toss the herbs in a scant amount of the vinaigrette, adding more if necessary; the leaves should just glisten.

Artichoke & Butter Lettuce Salad with Tarragon Vinaigrette

Serves six as a first course.

Fresh artichokes are really worth the effort of preparing them, and this salad shows them off beautifully. A great first course, the salad in larger portions also makes a nice lunch.

FOR THE VINAIGRETTE:
1½ Tbs. fresh lemon juice
1 large shallot, minced (to yield 3 Tbs.)
1 Tbs. Dijon mustard
4½ Tbs. extra-virgin olive oil
1½ tsp. minced fresh tarragon
Kosher salt and freshly ground black pepper

FOR THE SALAD:
Juice of 1 large lemon
4 large whole artichoke bottoms
2 heads butter lettuce, such as Bibb or Boston (about 6 oz. each), tough outer leaves removed, pale inner leaves washed and dried
3 hard-cooked eggs, quartered

Make the vinaigrette: In a small bowl, whisk the lemon juice, shallot, and mustard and then gradually whisk in the olive oil to create an emulsion. Add the tarragon; season to taste with salt and pepper. Refrigerate until serving time.

Make the salad: Bring a medium pot of salted water to a boil over high heat. Add the lemon juice and the prepared artichoke bottoms. To keep the artichokes from bobbing to the top, weight them with a pot lid that's smaller than the boiling pot. Keep the pot uncovered and adjust the heat to maintain a gentle simmer. Cook until the artichokes are tender when pierced with a knife, about 20 minutes. Drain upside down on paper towels until cool.

Tear the lettuce into bite-size pieces. Halve each artichoke bottom and cut each half into five or six wedges. Put the artichoke wedges in a salad bowl and add 2 Tbs. of the vinaigrette; toss to coat. Add the lettuce and the remaining dressing and toss gently. Arrange the salad on six plates and garnish with the egg wedges. Serve immediately.

tip: Choose artichokes that feel firm and heavy for their size, and use them within a day or two.

Mediterranean Carrot Salad

Serves four.

The look and texture of this salad are best when the carrots are cut into a thin julienne, a tedious task by hand but quick work if you have a mandoline or a Japanese slicer. You can also coarsely shred the carrots in a food processor or on a box grater and still get a tasty salad; it just won't hold up as well once it's dressed. Try this salad served alongside a hearty spring braise.

2 lb. carrots, peeled
¼ tsp. fennel seeds
¼ tsp. mustard seeds
¼ tsp. coriander seeds
⅛ tsp. cardamom seeds (from 1 or 2 pods)
2 cloves garlic
1 tsp. kosher salt
2 Tbs. fresh lemon juice
1 Tbs. sherry vinegar
⅛ tsp. cayenne
½ to ¾ cup extra-virgin olive oil
Freshly ground black pepper
¼ cup minced fresh chives, for garnish

Cut the carrots into a thin julienne, about 1/16 inch thick and about 2 inches long (or shred them with a coarse grater). Grind the fennel, mustard, coriander, and cardamom seeds in a spice grinder (or a coffee grinder used only for spices). In a mortar and pestle, smash the garlic with the salt to a paste. (Alternatively, smash the garlic on the cutting board with the side of a chef's knife. Sprinkle it with the salt and work it into a paste with a fork.) In a large bowl, combine the garlic paste, lemon juice, and vinegar. Whisk in the cayenne, the ground seeds, and the olive oil. Add the carrots and toss to coat. Let stand for at least 15 minutes and up to an hour. Taste and adjust seasonings, if necessary. Divide the salad among four plates, sprinkle with pepper, and garnish with the minced chives.

Cabbage Salad with Apples, Bacon & Walnuts

Serves six to eight.

You can make this salad with just red or green cabbage, but the contrast of colors looks great. Heated vinegar softens the cabbage's texture and helps the flavor penetrate. The components can be prepared up to 3 hours ahead and mixed at the last minute.

½ head green cabbage, cored and cut into thin strips
½ head red cabbage, cored and cut into thin strips
6 Tbs. sherry vinegar or red-wine vinegar
½ tsp. cumin seeds
Kosher salt and freshly ground black pepper
4 thick slices bacon, cooked until crisp and crumbled
1 small carrot, peeled and finely diced

1 sweet apple, such as Golden or Red Delicious, peeled and finely diced (toss with a little lemon juice to prevent browning, or cut just before adding to the salad)
3 Tbs. finely chopped flat-leaf parsley
3 Tbs. walnut pieces, lightly toasted
1 Tbs. sugar
2 Tbs. olive oil

Bring about 6 qt. water to a full boil. Fill a large bowl with ice water. Add the green cabbage to the boiling water and blanch it for 1 minute. With a slotted spoon, transfer the cabbage to the ice water to halt the cooking. Drain the cabbage well and set aside in another bowl. Repeat with the red cabbage, using the same pot of boiling water. Set the red cabbage aside in a second bowl (so its color doesn't bleed into the green cabbage).

In a small saucepan, bring the vinegar to a boil. Pour half the vinegar over the green cabbage and toss well; repeat with the red cabbage. Divide the cumin seeds between the two bowls of cabbage; season both with salt and pepper. Let the cabbage stand for about 20 minutes.

Drain the green cabbage and put it into a large mixing bowl.

Drain the red cabbage and toss it with the green cabbage. Add the bacon, carrot, apple, parsley, toasted walnuts, sugar, and olive oil. Toss several times, taste for seasoning, and add salt, pepper, or vinegar if needed.

Spinach & Cucumber Salad with Yogurt-Mint Dressing

Serves eight; yields ¾ cup dressing.

The refreshing flavors of mint and yogurt in this salad would be very welcome as part of a dinner featuring a spicy Indian or Thai curry.

2 Tbs. fresh lemon juice
1 tsp. honey
3 Tbs. Greek-style yogurt (like Total™) or whole-milk yogurt
5 Tbs. olive oil
2 Tbs. roughly chopped fresh mint
Kosher salt and freshly ground black pepper
8 cups lightly packed baby spinach leaves, washed and dried (8 oz.)
2 medium cucumbers, peeled, halved lengthwise, seeded, and sliced ⅛ inch thick (3 cups)
½ small red onion, halved lengthwise and sliced very thin (⅔ cup)

In a medium bowl, whisk the lemon juice and honey. In another bowl, whisk the yogurt and olive oil. Add the yogurt mixture to the lemon juice mixture in a thin stream, whisking constantly. Add the mint, ½ tsp. salt, and pepper to taste. Chill, covered, for up to 24 hours.

In a large bowl, combine the spinach, cucumbers, and onion. Season lightly with salt and pepper and add just enough dressing to moisten the ingredients. Toss to coat, divide among eight plates, and serve, passing any extra dressing at the table, if you like.

Spicy Cucumber Salad

Serves four; yields 2 cups.

This Thai salad is a traditional accompaniment to satay, but would also be welcome with all grilled meats, especially those with a little spice or heat.

2 medium-small cucumbers, peeled, seeded, and thinly sliced (2 cups)
2 medium shallots, thinly sliced (¼ cup)
6 to 8 fresh bird chiles or 4 to 6 fresh serrano chiles, cored, seeded, and minced (use more for a spicier relish)
3 Tbs. sugar
½ tsp. kosher salt
Juice of 2 limes (a scant ½ cup)
⅔ cup coarsely chopped fresh cilantro
2 Tbs. coarsely chopped unsalted dry-roasted peanuts

In a mixing bowl, combine all the ingredients except the peanuts. Toss gently and let stand for 15 minutes. Transfer to a serving bowl, sprinkle with the chopped peanuts, and serve.

Potato Salad with Lemon & Cilantro

Serves four to six.

This salad is easy to make and very fresh looking. The warm potatoes seem to temper the cilantro's flavor, so it's a good way to introduce newcomers to this bright, distinctly flavored herb.

2 lb. (6 to 8 medium) waxy potatoes, like Red Bliss, scrubbed
Kosher salt
½ cup extra-virgin olive oil
½ tsp. finely grated lemon zest
3 Tbs. fresh lemon juice
Freshly ground black pepper
½ cup lightly packed chopped fresh cilantro leaves (from about 20 large sprigs)
2 scallions (white and green parts), thinly sliced, or 1 shallot, minced

Put the potatoes in a large pot of salted water (about 1 Tbs. kosher salt). Bring to a boil and lower to a simmer. Cook, partially covered, until the potatoes are tender when pierced with a fork, about 25 minutes. Drain and let cool slightly. While the potatoes are still warm, slice them about ¼ inch thick (there's no need to peel, but discard any pieces of skin that come off on their own). Put half of the potatoes in a large serving bowl. In a small bowl, whisk the oil, lemon zest, lemon juice, 1 tsp. salt, and several grinds of pepper. Drizzle half of the dressing over the potatoes. Add the remaining potatoes to the bowl, drizzle on the rest of the dressing, and toss gently with a large rubber spatula to combine well. Add the cilantro and scallions and toss gently again. Taste and add more salt if needed. Serve warm or at room temperature.

Spinach Salad with Roasted Sweet Potatoes & Hot Cider-Bacon Vinaigrette

Serves four; yields ⅔ cup vinaigrette.

There are a few steps involved in making this hearty main-dish salad, but much of the work can be done ahead of the final assembly. Plus the intensely flavored vinaigrette that results makes it all worthwhile. For the absolute best flavor, use applewood-smoked slab bacon.

2 large sweet potatoes, peeled and cut into ½-inch cubes (about 4 cups)
2 Tbs. vegetable oil
1 tsp. chopped fresh rosemary leaves
1 tsp. chopped fresh thyme
¼ tsp. kosher salt
⅛ tsp. freshly ground black pepper
10 oz. spinach, well washed, dried, and stemmed

FOR THE VINAIGRETTE:
2 cups apple cider
½ lb. bacon, diced
Vegetable oil, as needed
2 Tbs. cider vinegar
¼ tsp. freshly ground black pepper

Roast the sweet potatoes: Heat the oven to 400°F. In a 9x13-inch pan, toss the sweet potato cubes with the oil, rosemary, thyme, salt, and pepper. Cover with foil and roast for 10 minutes. Remove the foil, shake the pan, and continue roasting until the potatoes are tender, about another 10 minutes. When roasted, keep warm. As the potatoes roast, prepare the vinaigrette.

Reduce the cider: In a heavy-based pan over high heat, bring the cider to a boil. When the cider has reduced by half (about 10 minutes), turn the heat to medium. When the cider has reduced by half again, turn the heat to low and begin to watch the cider closely; it can scorch easily at this point. When the reduction looks "gurgly," pour it into a Pyrex measuring cup; you should have ¼ cup. Set aside.

Cook the bacon: Sauté the bacon over medium-high heat until it's crisp and the fat is rendered, about 15 minutes. Remove the bacon with a slotted spoon to drain on a paper towels. (Reserve the sauté pan for rewarming the vinaigrette.) Pour the bacon fat into a Pyrex

measuring cup and add enough vegetable oil to bring the level to ½ cup.

Make the vinaigrette: Combine the reduced cider syrup, the cider vinegar, and pepper in a small bowl. Whisk in the warm bacon fat and oil, a few drops at a time. Set aside. When ready to serve, bring the vinaigrette to a simmer in the bacon pan.

Assemble the salad: Tear the spinach leaves into bite-size pieces and put them in a salad bowl. Pour the warm vinaigrette over the spinach and toss to coat. Add the sweet potatoes and toss gently. Portion the salad on individual plates and top with the crisp bacon from the vinaigrette recipe and a grinding of black pepper. Serve immediately.

tip: Drain cooked potatoes on a cooling rack set over or in the sink; they'll cool more quickly and won't get squashed (as often happens in the colander).

Creamy Potato Salad with Radishes, Lemon & Dill

Serves six; yields about 6 cups.

Instead of your usual classic potato salad, try this light and refreshing rendition. Thinly sliced celery, radishes, and a bit of tarragon add their delicate yet pronounced flavors, while a big hit of lemon zest brightens it all.

2 lb. unpeeled smallish red potatoes, scrubbed
Kosher salt
2 inner ribs celery and their tender leaves, finely chopped (about ½ cup)
¾ cup thinly sliced radishes (about 6 small radishes)
3 scallions (white and tender green parts), chopped
2 Tbs. chopped fresh dill
¼ cup heavy cream, well chilled
½ cup mayonnaise
1½ tsp. Dijon mustard
1½ Tbs. fresh lemon juice
2 tsp. grated lemon zest
Freshly ground pepper (black or white)

Put the potatoes in a medium saucepan, cover with cold water by an inch or two, add a large pinch of salt, and bring to a boil. Reduce the heat to medium, partially cover, and cook until the potatoes are tender, about 20 minutes. Test for doneness by spearing a potato with a thin metal skewer. It should penetrate easily into the center of the potato and then slide right out. If the skewer lifts the potato out of the pot when you withdraw it, continue cooking a little longer. Drain the potatoes and let them cool.

When the potatoes are at room temperature, cut them into ¾-inch chunks and put them in a mixing bowl. Add the celery, radishes, scallions, and dill and fold gently to distribute; set aside.

In a small bowl, whisk the cream until frothy but not at all stiffened. Whisk in the mayonnaise and mustard. Add the lemon juice and zest, ½ tsp. salt, and pepper to taste. Pour the dressing over the salad and fold it in with a rubber spatula. Taste for seasoning. Serve, or cover and chill for up to a day.

Minty Quinoa Tabbouleh

Yields about 8 cups.

Tabbouleh, a lemony Middle Eastern parsley and grain salad, is traditionally made with bulgur wheat. This version, fragrant from a touch of cumin and cinnamon, uses quinoa instead.

1½ cups quinoa
Kosher salt
1½ cups seeded and finely diced tomato (from about 1 large tomato)
1 cup finely chopped fresh flat-leaf parsley (from about 2 bunches)
1 cup peeled, seeded, and finely diced cucumber (about ¾ of a large cucumber)
½ cup thinly sliced scallion greens
½ cup extra-virgin olive oil; more to taste
6 Tbs. fresh lemon juice; more to taste
¼ tsp. ground cumin
⅛ tsp. ground cinnamon
½ cup finely chopped fresh mint

Rinse the quinoa well in a bowl of cool water and drain. Bring the quinoa, ½ tsp. salt, and 3 cups water to a boil in a medium saucepan over high heat. Cover, reduce the heat to medium low, and simmer until the water is absorbed and the quinoa is translucent and tender, 10 to 15 minutes. (The outer germ rings of the grain will remain chewy and white. Some germ rings may separate from the grains and will look like white squiggles.) Immediately fluff the quinoa with a fork and turn out onto a baking sheet to cool.

When cool, fluff the quinoa again and transfer to a large bowl. Add the tomato, parsley, cucumber, scallion, oil, lemon juice, cumin, cinnamon, and 1 tsp. salt. Toss well. Cover and refrigerate to let the flavors mingle, at least 2 hours or overnight.

Before serving, let sit at room temperature for 20 to 30 minutes. Stir in the mint. Taste and add more oil and lemon juice (you'll probably need at least 1 Tbs. of each), and more salt as needed.

Grilled Bell Pepper, Corn & Red Onion Salad with Blue Cheese Vinaigrette

Serves six; yields ¾ cup vinaigrette.

This is a substantial first-course salad, but it could easily be a vegetarian main dish by serving bigger portions (add a few spears of grilled asparagus, too). Leftover dressing is terrific on grilled steak. To grill the vegetables, follow the instructions on the facing page.

FOR THE VINAIGRETTE:
2 Tbs. sherry vinegar
7 Tbs. extra-virgin olive oil
¼ tsp. kosher salt; more to taste
Freshly ground black pepper
2 Tbs. crumbled soft-textured blue cheese, such as Gorgonzola or Roquefort
1 tsp. lightly chopped thyme leaves; more to taste
1 small ripe plum tomato, seeded and finely diced

FOR THE SALAD:
4 oz. arugula, tough stems removed, washed
1 red bell pepper, grilled
4 large portabella mushroom caps, grilled
1 large red onion, grilled
2 ears corn, grilled

Make the vinaigrette: In a small bowl with high sides, combine the vinegar, oil, salt, pepper, and blue cheese. Stir with a fork, mashing the blue cheese against the side of the bowl until it comes apart into the vinaigrette (it won't be completely emulsified and will look somewhat grainy; you can leave some cheese in small chunks). Add the thyme and diced tomato and stir vigorously. Taste and add more salt or thyme if you like.

Make the salad: Mound the arugula on six salad plates. Slice the peeled and seeded grilled pepper into ½-inch-wide strips. Slice the grilled portabella caps into ½-inch strips. Portion both vegetables evenly and put them in the center of the arugula in a loose pile. Break the grilled onion slices apart into rings and mound a few on top of the portabellas and peppers. Cut the corn off the cobs and sprinkle the kernels evenly over the six salads. Drizzle about 1½ Tbs. of the vinaigrette over each salad and serve. Save the extra vinaigrette for another use.

How to grill vegetables

Portabella mushrooms

To prepare: Wipe off any dirt with a damp paper towel. Cut or snap off the stem at the base. With a spoon, scrape out the dark gills on the underside of the cap and discard. Brush both sides of the mushroom cap with plenty of olive oil and season with kosher salt just before grilling.

To grill: Heat a gas grill to high. Put the mushrooms, stem side up on the grate. Grill the mushrooms for as long as they need to get very well browned (a lot of liquid will pool up in the cap), 5 to 8 minutes. When the cap is brown, turn it over and press down to gently push out as much liquid as possible. Grill for another 4 or 5 minutes until they're much thinner and drier.

Corn

To prepare: Shuck the corn, removing all the husk and silk. Lay each ear of corn on a 12-inch square of aluminum foil. Rub each ear with 1 tsp. butter and season all over with kosher salt and freshly ground black pepper. Tuck a sprig or two of fresh thyme or any other herb next to the corn and wrap the corn tightly in the foil.

To grill: Heat a gas grill to high. Put the foil-wrapped corn on the grate, cover, and cook, turning every 5 to 6 minutes, for 15 to 20 minutes. Remove from the grill and open the foil loosely. The corn should be blackened in places. If it isn't, rewrap it and return it to the grill for another 5 minutes. Let cool.

Onions

To prepare: Trim the ends, peel, and cut into ½-inch-thick slices. Thread the slices on thin metal skewers (poultry lacers work great) or soaked wooden skewers. Brush liberally with olive oil and season with kosher salt.

To grill: Heat a gas grill to high. Put the onion skewers on the grates and cook until the slices are well browned on both sides (they will have dark marks on them), about 15 minutes total. Turn one of the grill burners down to low and move the skewered slices to that area. Stack them loosely and leave them there for 10 minutes to finish cooking through. Alternatively, remove them from the grill and wrap them in foil to finish softening.

Bell peppers

To prepare: Leave whole.

To grill: Heat a gas grill to high. Put the peppers on the grate, cover, and cook until the skins are blackened on all sides, turning with tongs as needed, 3 to 4 minutes per side, or a total of 10 to 15 minutes. Wrap the peppers in foil or put them in a paper bag to cool completely. When cool, peel off the blackened skins and remove the stems and seeds, reserving the flesh and juices.

Asian Vinaigrette

Yields 1¼ cups.

This dressing is also delicious on grilled shrimp, seared steak, or warm salads, so you may want to double the batch; it will keep for a few days covered and refrigerated.

3 Tbs. minced ginger
1½ tsp. minced garlic
¼ cup chopped fresh cilantro
3 Tbs. dry sherry
¼ cup rice vinegar
⅓ cup fish sauce
2 Tbs. fresh lime juice
1 Tbs. honey
A few dashes hot sauce
  (optional)
Salt to taste
1 Tbs. toasted sesame oil
¼ cup peanut oil

Combine all the ingredients, except for the sesame and peanut oils, in a bowl. Whisk in one oil at a time. taste and add a bit more salt if you like.

Asparagus & Gingered Grapefruit Salad

Serves six.

All the components in this dramatic and delicious salad can be made ahead and then assembled at the last minute, making it perfect for a dinner party.

36 large or 42 medium spears asparagus (don't use pencil-thin spears)
Kosher salt
36 sections pink grapefruit (from 4 to 5 grapefruit)
¾ cup roughly chopped or sliced and smashed fresh ginger (from about 6 oz. ginger)
Grated zest of 4 small or 3 large limes
¾ cup tarragon vinegar
¾ cup sugar
1¼ cups Asian Vinaigrette (see recipe above)
3 scallions (whites only), thinly sliced at an angle
1 Tbs. toasted sesame seeds

Prepare the asparagus: Bring a large pot of salted water to a boil. Prepare an ice bath by filling a large bowl halfway with ice and adding cold water. Snap off the tough bottom part of each stem and lightly peel the asparagus from just below the tip down to the base. Parboil the asparagus until the stems just bend when lifted out of the water with tongs, about 3 minutes. Transfer immediately to the ice bath to stop the cooking and remove as soon as it's chilled; drain well. Refrigerate until about 15 minutes before you compose the salad so that the asparagus isn't served cold.

Make the ginger-lime glaze: Combine the ginger, lime zest, tarragon vinegar, and sugar in a nonreactive saucepan. Bring to a boil. Remove from the heat and let sit for 5 minutes to infuse the flavors. Bring back to a boil and repeat the process. Bring back to a boil for a third time, let cool to room temperature, strain through a coarse sieve, cover, and refrigerate.

Prepare the grapefruit: About an hour before serving, put the grapefruit sections into a bowl and cover with the ginger-lime glaze. Keep refrigerated.

Arrange the salad: Put the asparagus in a shallow container and cover it with a cup or so of the Asian Vinaigrette, saving enough to dress the bottom of each salad plate. Let the asparagus soak in the dressing for a couple of minutes. Meanwhile, cover the bottom of each of six large salad plates with some of the vinaigrette; use the back of a soupspoon to spread it evenly. Arrange a pile of six or seven asparagus spears in the center of each plate. Arrange three grapefruit sections on each side of the asparagus, fanning them out. Sprinkle the sliced scallions over the asparagus and sprinkle some of the sesame seeds over the whole salad (go lightly; you may have extra) and serve.

Forty Shades of Green Salad

Serves four.

This light, refreshing salad is named after a famous song about Ireland by Johnny Cash. It's a nice starter or side for spring menus.

FOR THE VINAIGRETTE:
3 Tbs. extra-virgin olive oil
1 Tbs. plus 1 tsp. fresh lime juice
1 tsp. honey
Big pinch of kosher salt
1 coarse grind of fresh pepper

FOR THE SALAD:
1 large head Boston lettuce, largest outer leaves and damaged leaves removed, washed, dried, and torn into bite-size pieces
¾ cup loosely packed fresh parsley leaves
1 large (or 1½ small) Belgian endive, damaged leaves removed, halved lengthwise, cored and thinly sliced crosswise (¼ inch)
2 to 3 scallions (white and light-green part only), very thinly sliced on the diagonal
1 small ripe but firm avocado

Make the vinaigrette: In a small bowl, combine all the vinaigrette ingredients and whisk until thoroughly emulsified (it will look creamy).

Make the salad: In a large mixing bowl, combine the lettuce, parsley, endive, and scallions. Gently toss the greens thoroughly with about 2 Tbs. of the vinaigrette. Mound the greens onto four salad plates (white looks nice), arranging any endive and parsley pieces that have fallen to the bottom of the bowl on top.

Cut the avocado in half and remove the pit. While in the skin, slice the halves crosswise in very thin half-moons (⅛ inch thick). Slide a large spoon between the skin and flesh to remove the slices from the skin.

With the flat side of a chef's knife, transfer the avocado halves to the mixing bowl, fan them out slightly, drizzle another 1 Tbs. of the vinaigrette over them, and gently toss just to coat, keeping the slices somewhat together. Arrange a little pile of avocado slices on one-quarter of the salad, propped up against the mound of leaves. Drizzle the whole salad with a tiny bit more vinaigrette and serve right away.

Romaine Hearts with Lemon Vinaigrette & Shaved Parmesan

Serves six.

The tangy lemon vinaigrette in this simple salad contrasts with the cool juiciness of the lettuce and the nutty saltiness of the shaved Parmesan.

1 medium shallot, minced
3 Tbs. fresh lemon juice
¼ tsp. sugar
Sea salt and freshly ground black pepper
3 small hearts of romaine or 3 heads of baby romaine
¼ cup extra-virgin olive oil
½ cup shaved Parmigiano Reggiano

In a medium bowl, combine the shallot, lemon juice, sugar, and ½ tsp. salt. Stir to dissolve the sugar and salt and then let the mixture sit for 15 minutes.

Meanwhile, cut off the root end of the romaine so that the leaves fall loose. Wash the leaves, spin them dry, and put them in a large bowl.

Slowly whisk the olive oil into the lemon juice mixture (you should have about ½ cup vinaigrette). Season with salt, if necessary, and a few grinds of pepper. (This vinaigrette can be made ahead; just whisk to recombine it before using. If you make it more than 2 hours ahead, cover, refrigerate, and bring it to room temperature before using.)

Toss the romaine with enough vinaigrette to lightly coat. Season the salad with salt and pepper to taste. Arrange the leaves on a large platter and sprinkle with the shaved Parmigiano Reggiano.

Grilled Corn & Tomato Salad with Basil Oil

Serves six to eight.

Some grilled bread would be delicious with
this end-of-summer salad.

2 ears sweet corn, husks removed
2 Tbs. extra-virgin olive oil
Kosher salt and freshly ground black pepper
3 to 4 large ripe beefsteak tomatoes
Basil Oil (see the recipe at right)
Small leaves of Dark Opal or Purple Ruffles
  basil, or gently torn larger ones, for
  garnish (optional)

Cut the corn cobs in half crosswise, put
them in a large bowl, and toss with the olive
oil, ½ tsp. salt, and ¼ tsp. pepper. Heat a
grill to medium-high. Grill the corn until the
tips of the kernels are nicely browned all
around, about 2 minutes on each of three
sides. Return the corn to the bowl with the
olive oil and toss again. When the ears are
cool enough to handle, place the flat end of a
cob on a cutting board so the cob is upright
and slice the kernels off with a sharp knife.
You should have about 1 cup kernels. Set
aside until ready to assemble.

Slice the tomatoes ½ inch thick and
generously season each slice with salt and
pepper. On serving plates, arrange one, two,
or three slices of tomato per person, depending on how big the tomatoes are. Scatter the
corn over the tomato slices. Drizzle basil oil
generously over each serving. Garnish with
fresh basil leaves, if using.

Other ways to savor basil's flavor

Basil oil

is perfect for when you want a hint of basil but don't want to overpower the flavors of summer's freshest corn or ripest tomatoes. Try:

* drizzling it over just-grilled bread
* tossing it with steamed green beans and sea salt
* pouring it over a cold summer soup, like gazpacho

Basil butter

is especially delicious made with sweet basil. Try:

* tossing it with cooked vegetables
* stirring it into hot pasta, polenta, or mashed potatoes
* melting it over grilled meats
* serving it softened, with bread

Basil Oil

Yields about 3/4 cup.

Blanching basil and chilling the oil keep the basil's color beautifully green.

2 cups tightly packed sweet basil leaves
1 cup mild olive oil, chilled
Kosher salt

Bring a pot of water to a boil. Have a bowl of ice water ready. Blanch the basil leaves in the boiling water for about 10 seconds. Remove them quickly with a strainer and dunk in the ice water, swishing them around to be sure they're all cold. Remove from the water and squeeze gently to remove the excess water.

Roughly chop the basil and put it in a blender. Add the oil and 1/2 tsp. salt; blend until the basil is puréed. The mixture will be very frothy. Let the purée settle for about 30 minutes. Strain through a cheesecloth-lined fine strainer, very gently pushing on the solids to extract the oil. Use immediately or refrigerate for up to a week. For the best flavor, let the oil come to room temperature before using.

Basil Butter

Yields 1/2 cup seasoned butter.

This butter lets you enjoy basil's wonderful flavor long after the last basil is harvested.

1/2 cup unsalted butter, softened at room
temperature
1/2 cup finely chopped sweet basil
1 tsp. minced garlic
1/2 tsp. freshly grated lemon zest
1/2 tsp. kosher salt
1/2 tsp. ground white pepper

In a bowl, combine the butter, basil, garlic, lemon zest, salt, and white pepper and mash with a spoon until well combined.

Use immediately or use plastic wrap to shape the basil butter into a log, tightening the ends as if it were a sausage. Refrigerate until very firm. Slice into 1/4-inch-thick coins and melt over just-off-the-grill chicken or pork cutlets, fish fillets, or vegetables. The butter will keep in the refrigerator for up to two weeks or in the freezer for a month. This recipe can easily be doubled.

Radish & Parsley Salad with Lemon

Serves two to three.

Crisp, peppery radishes make a delicious salad that's a welcome change from tossed greens. They taste best in spring, before summer's heat sets in, which makes them bitter. Try this salad with red globe, icicle, or watermelon radishes.

**10 medium or 12 small
  red radishes, scrubbed
3 large ribs celery, ends trimmed,
  peeled
1 cup tightly packed fresh
  flat-leaf parsley leaves
1 Tbs. fresh lemon juice; more
  to taste
¼ tsp. kosher salt; more to taste
2 Tbs. extra-virgin olive oil
Freshly ground black pepper**

Trim the root and stem ends of the radishes. Halve them lengthwise and then slice them ⅛ inch thick; you should have about 1½ cups. Slice the celery crosswise ⅛ inch thick. Combine the sliced radishes, sliced celery, and parsley leaves in a medium bowl. Add the lemon juice, salt, and olive oil; toss well. Add several generous grinds of black pepper, taste and adjust the seasonings, and serve.

White & Green Bean Salad with Tomatoes & Basil

Serves six to eight.

Emergo beans are especially wonderful in this colorful salad; they're creamy and mellow, with a rich, nutty flavor. Great Northern beans are also delicious. Whichever kind you use, try to buy them from a place with good turnover for the freshest beans.

**1 cup large dried white beans,
  such as Emergo or Great
  Northern, well rinsed (soaked
  and drained, if you like)
Several sprigs fresh thyme
1 large clove garlic, smashed
1 small yellow onion, cut in half
1 small carrot, cut into several
  pieces
Kosher salt
1 large shallot, finely chopped
2 salt-packed anchovies, filleted,
  (or 4 oil-packed anchovy
  fillets), rinsed, patted dry, and
  finely chopped
3 Tbs. red-wine vinegar
Freshly ground black pepper
½ cup extra-virgin olive oil
1 lb. cherry tomatoes, cut into
  quarters
1 lb. haricots verts or regular
  green beans, trimmed and cut
  into pieces if large
½ cup chopped fresh basil**

In a deep, heavy-based pot, cover the beans with 6 to 8 cups cold water. Add the thyme, garlic, onion, carrot, and 1 tsp. salt. Bring to a boil over high heat. Reduce the heat to a gentle simmer, skimming any foam that rises to the surface. Cover and cook until the beans are tender, about 90 minutes; let cool in the broth. (Refrigerate the beans in the broth if holding for more than a few hours; bring to room temperature before assembling the salad.)

In a large serving bowl, combine the shallot, anchovies, vinegar, ½ tsp. salt, and ¼ tsp. pepper. Whisk in the olive oil until well combined. Drain the white beans and add them and the tomatoes to the bowl. Toss until the vegetables are well coated with the dressing. Let stand at room temperature for 2 hours.

Cook the green beans in a large pot of boiling salted water until tender, about 5 minutes. Drain and spread on paper towels to cool. When ready to serve, add the cooled green beans and then the basil to the white beans, tossing well after each addition. Taste and add salt and pepper if needed.

Pink Bean Salad with Roasted Red Pepper & Fresh Herbs

Serves four to six.

Don't be dismayed at the length of this recipe list, as many of the ingredients are just spices measured from a jar or quickly chopped fresh herbs. This salad holds and packs well, making it perfect for a springtime picnic.

FOR THE BEANS:

1 cup dried pink beans (to yield about 3 cups cooked) or 1 29-oz. can pink beans
1½ tsp. kosher salt
½ large shallot or ¼ small onion
10 4-inch fresh cilantro stems

FOR THE RED PEPPER AND DRESSING:

1 medium red bell pepper
2 Tbs. minced fresh hot chile, such as jalapeño or serrano; more to taste
2 Tbs. minced shallot
2 tsp. minced garlic
2 tsp. sweet paprika
1 tsp. ground cumin
½ tsp. kosher salt
¼ tsp. freshly ground black pepper
1 tsp. finely grated lemon zest
¼ cup fresh lemon juice
¼ cup extra-virgin olive oil
½ cup chopped fresh cilantro
¼ cup chopped fresh flat-leaf parsley
2 Tbs. chopped fresh mint

Spread the dried beans on a baking sheet and feel for any stones. Rinse the beans well, put them in a large pot, cover by 3 to 4 inches of water, add the salt, shallot, and cilantro stems, and bring to a boil. Reduce the heat to a simmer, cover, and cook until the beans are very tender but not falling apart, 45 minutes to 1½ hours, longer if necessary. Start checking early because beans cook at different rates; if the water level gets low, add more water. When the beans are cooked, let them cool in their liquid for about 15 minutes and then drain. Transfer them to a large bowl and keep them warm. (If using canned beans, rinse and drain them well.)

While the beans are cooking, heat the broiler to high. Put the red pepper on a small foil-covered baking sheet and broil until the skin is completely charred, turning to char all sides. When the pepper is blackened, wrap it loosely in the foil and leave it to steam and cool. When cool enough to handle, pull out the core, scrape off all the skin, scrape out the seeds, and cut the flesh into ¼-inch dice. You should have about ½ cup.

Meanwhile, in a medium bowl, whisk the chile, shallot, garlic, paprika, cumin, salt, pepper, and lemon zest and juice. Let the mixture sit for at least 30 minutes so the shallots soften and the flavors marry.

Toss this dressing with the warm beans, using a rubber spatula to gently fold so the beans get well coated but not smashed. Let the beans sit for a few minutes and then toss a few more times. It may seem like too much liquid at first, but the beans will gradually absorb it all. Fold in the olive oil, roasted pepper, cilantro, parsley, and mint. Taste for seasoning and serve.

New Potato Salad with Spring Vegetables & Shrimp

Serves six.

This pretty salad would also taste delicious with seared scallops or cooked lobster or crab.

1 lb. medium or large shrimp, peeled and deveined
2½ lb. baby potatoes, halved if large
1 recipe Lemon-Chive Vinaigrette (see below)
½ cup ½-inch pieces of fresh green beans
½ cup fresh peas
½ cup diced celery
½ cup sliced radishes
4 scallions, trimmed and sliced
Salt and freshly ground black pepper
1 bunch watercress or 2 cups baby arugula, washed and stemmed
Lemon zest and chopped chives for garnish

Bring a large pan of salted water to a boil, add the shrimp, reduce the heat, and simmer just until the shrimp are opaque throughout, 2 to 3 minutes. Drain, dry on paper towels, and chill until you're ready to assemble the salad.

Put the potatoes in a large saucepan, cover with well-salted water, and bring to a boil. Reduce the heat and gently boil until tender, 8 to 15 minutes. Test by cutting and tasting a chunk to be sure it's fully cooked.

Drain the potatoes, and while they're still hot, add about three-quarters of the vinaigrette; toss to coat well. Let the potatoes stand for about 30 minutes so the dressing is absorbed.

Meanwhile, in a small saucepan, bring a few cups of salted water to a boil. Add the beans and boil for 1 minute. Add the peas; continue boiling for another 2 minutes, just until both vegetables are crisp-tender. Drain and immediately rinse in cold water to stop the cooking; drain very well.

When you're ready to serve the salad, toss the potatoes with the shrimp, peas, beans, celery, radishes, and scallions, and the remaining vinaigrette. Season well with salt and pepper. Arrange on plates with a bit of watercress or arugula and sprinkle with some lemon zest and chives.

Lemon-Chive Vinaigrette

Makes about 1 cup.

This would also be tasty on plain boiled potatoes, asparagus, or green beans.

1 tsp. grated lemon zest
¼ cup fresh lemon juice
2 Tbs. chopped fresh chives
1 clove garlic, minced
1 tsp. sugar
Salt and white pepper to taste
¾ cup vegetable oil

Put the lemon zest, lemon juice, chives, garlic, sugar, and a pinch of salt in a food processor, a blender, or a small bowl. Process (or whisk) until mixed. With the machine running or while whisking, slowly pour in the oil. Taste and adjust the seasoning with salt and pepper.

Arugula & Fried Mozzarella Salad with Tomato-Basil Vinaigrette

Serves four.

If you want to turn this salad into an even more filling dinner portion, serve it with your favorite sausage.

1 large (about 7 oz.) smoked mozzarella
1 large egg
Kosher salt and freshly ground black pepper
1 cup fine fresh breadcrumbs
1½ cups medium-diced fresh tomatoes
⅓ cup loosely packed basil leaves, roughly chopped
1 medium clove garlic, minced (about 1 tsp.)
¼ cup plus 3 Tbs. extra-virgin olive oil
2 tsp. balsamic vinegar
5 oz. baby arugula (about 6 cups loosely packed), washed and dried

Slice the mozzarella into eight slices and then again in half crosswise, so that you have 16 pieces of cheese. Whisk the egg in a medium bowl with a pinch of salt and pepper. Put the breadcrumbs in another medium bowl. Working with a few pieces at a time, dip the cheese in the egg, turning to coat all sides. Dredge the cheese in the breadcrumbs, pressing to help the crumbs adhere and cover the cheese as much as possible. Transfer the breaded cheese slices to a plate and refrigerate until ready to cook. You can prepare the cheese up to 1 hour ahead. Discard any leftover egg and crumbs.

In a small bowl, combine the tomatoes, basil, and garlic and season with ½ tsp. salt and a few grinds of pepper. Let the tomato mixture sit for 5 minutes and then add ¼ cup of the oil and the 2 tsp. vinegar.

Heat 1½ Tbs. of the oil in a 10-inch nonstick skillet over medium-high heat. Put half of the cheese in the pan and cook until the breadcrumbs turn golden, 30 to 60 seconds. Use two forks to turn the cheese and cook until the second side is golden, another 30 to 60 seconds. Transfer the cheese to a plate. Using the remaining 1½ Tbs. oil, repeat with the second batch of cheese.

Put the arugula in a large bowl. Stir the tomato mixture and toss it with the arugula. Taste and add salt and pepper as needed. Portion the salad among four plates. Arrange four pieces of cheese on top of each salad and serve immediately.

Grilled Salade Niçoise

Serves four.

This salad requires some work, but its array of hearty flavors makes it well worth the effort. Drizzling the vegetables with dressing as they come off the grill makes the salad even more flavorful because the dressing gets absorbed.

FOR THE DRESSING:
1 Tbs. minced anchovies (about 4 rinsed)
1 clove garlic, minced
2 Tbs. Dijon mustard
4 tsp. fresh lemon juice
½ cup extra-virgin olive oil
Salt and freshly ground black pepper to taste

FOR THE SALAD:
8 to 10 small red potatoes, halved or quartered, depending on size
1 large red onion, peeled and sliced ½ inch thick
2 plum tomatoes, halved
½ lb. green beans, trimmed
Extra-virgin olive oil
Coarse salt
1 to 1½ lb. fresh tuna

Freshly ground black pepper to taste
6 oz. Boston or Bibb lettuce
4 anchovy fillets, rinsed and patted dry
2 Tbs. drained capers
4 hard-cooked eggs, peeled and halved
¼ cup niçoise or other good-quality black olives
⅓ cup fresh basil leaves, cut in thin strips

Make the dressing: In a food processor, pulse the anchovies, garlic, mustard, and lemon juice until combined. With the machine running, slowly add the olive oil, a few drops at first, and then in a slow, steady stream. Season with salt and pepper.

Grill the salad: Prepare a charcoal fire or light a gas grill. Lightly coat the potatoes, onion, tomatoes, and beans with oil and sprinkle with salt. Lightly brush the tuna with oil and sprinkle with salt and a little freshly ground pepper. Put the potatoes over medium-low heat and cook until they're fork-tender and roasty

looking, turning occasionally to keep them from sticking, 30 to 35 minutes total. Put the onion, tomatoes, and green beans on a medium-high part of the grill. Grill the vegetables until they're lightly charred and tender, moving the ingredients around so they don't overcook. The onions will cook in 10 to 15 minutes, the tomatoes in 5 to 8 minutes, and the beans in 4 to 6 minutes. As the vegetables come off the grill, transfer them to a tray or a jelly-roll pan, drizzle with dressing, toss lightly, and cover with foil to keep warm.

Meanwhile, grill the tuna over medium-high heat until it's slightly pink in the center, about 6 minutes per side. Let it cool for a few minutes and slice.

Line four salad plates with the lettuce and arrange the grilled vegetables and tuna on top. Garnish with the anchovies, capers, eggs, and olives. Drizzle with a little more dressing, sprinkle with the basil, and serve.

Vietnamese Cool Noodle Salad with Stir-Fried Vegetables

Serves four.

This traditional Vietnamese noodle salad, called *bun*, translates into a perfect summer supper. The greens, garnishes, and noodles can be prepared hours in advance so that at serving time, you'll just have to stir-fry the vegetables.

FOR THE GREENS:
2 cups washed and shredded romaine, red, or green leaf lettuce
2 cups fresh, crisp bean sprouts
1½ cups peeled, seeded, and julienned cucumber
⅓ to ½ cup roughly chopped or small whole mint leaves
⅓ to ½ cup roughly chopped or small basil or Thai basil leaves

FOR THE GARNISHES:
2 Tbs. chopped roasted peanuts
Nuoc Cham (Vietnamese Dipping Sauce; see recipe at right)
12 sprigs cilantro

FOR THE NOODLES:
8 oz. dried rice vermicelli (the noodles are also called *bun*)

FOR THE TOPPING:
1 recipe Stir-Fried Vegetables (at right)

Prepare the greens and herbs: Divide the lettuce, bean sprouts, cucumber, mint, and basil among four large soup or pasta bowls. If working ahead of time, cover each bowl with damp paper towels and refrigerate.

Make the garnishes: Set peanuts aside. Make 1 recipe Nuoc Cham and refrigerate.

Make the noodles: Bring a medium potful of water to a rolling boil. Add the rice vermicelli and, stirring often, cook them until the strands are soft and white, but still resilient, 3 to 5 minutes. Don't be tempted to undercook them, as they must be fully cooked to absorb the flavors of the dish. Rinse them in a colander under cold water just until they are cool. Let the noodles drain in the colander for 30 minutes, and then set them aside for up to 2 hours, unrefrigerated.

Make the topping: Make the Stir-Fried Vegetables; the toppings can be served hot or slightly cooled.

Assemble the salad: Remove the bowls of greens from the refrigerator 20 to 30 minutes before serving. The greens and bowls should be cool, not cold. Fluff the noodles with your fingers and divide them among the prepared salad bowls. Put the Stir-Fried Vegetables on the noodles and garnish each bowl with the peanuts and cilantro. Pass the Nuoc Cham at the table; each diner should drizzle about 3 Tbs. over the salad and then toss the salad in the bowl a few times with two forks or chopsticks before eating.

Stir-Fried Vegetables

Serves four as a topping for the noodle salad.

The crisp tofu is delicious in this recipe, but you could substitute sliced, cooked chicken or cooked shrimp.

4 Tbs. vegetable oil
8 oz. firm tofu, drained and cut into rectangular strips about 1 inch wide
2 shallots, thinly sliced
6 dried black mushrooms, soaked in hot water for 30 minutes, drained, stemmed, and thinly sliced
2 cups sliced broccoli florets, blanched in boiling water and drained
1½ cups shredded green or Napa cabbage
1½ cups thinly sliced bok choy
2 Tbs. soy sauce; more or less to taste
½ red bell pepper, thinly sliced

Cook the tofu: Heat 2 Tbs. of the oil in a nonstick pan or skillet over medium heat. Add the tofu and stir-fry until nicely browned. Remove and drain on paper towels. When cool, cut tofu into bite-size pieces. Set aside.

Cook the vegetables: Heat the remaining oil in a 12-inch skillet or sauté pan over high heat. When the oil is very hot, add the shallots, constantly stirring until they become fragrant, about 20 seconds. Add the mushrooms and stir-fry for another 20 seconds. Add the broccoli, cabbage, and bok choy, stir for 30 seconds (the vegetables should be constantly sizzling) and add the red bell pepper. (If the pan gets too dry, sprinkle in 1 to 2 Tbs. water.)

Working quickly, create an open space in the middle of the pan by pushing the vegetables against the edges. Add the soy sauce to the open area. It should sizzle and caramelize slightly. Stir the vegetables with the soy sauce a few times and remove from the heat.

Toss the vegetables with the stir-fried tofu and top the Vietnamese Cool Noodle Salad with them.

Nuoc Cham (Vietnamese Dipping Sauce)

Yields 1½ cups.

Keep a jar of this Vietnamese Dipping Sauce in the refrigerator. It will last for a month.

1 clove garlic
2 to 3 Thai bird chiles (or 1 small jalapeño or serrano chile), cored, seeded, and minced; more or less to taste
½ tsp. chile paste; more or less to taste
⅔ cup hot water
¼ cup sugar
¼ cup fish sauce
2 Tbs. fresh lime juice
2 Tbs. shredded carrots (optional)

With a mortar and pestle, pound the garlic and fresh chiles into a paste (or mince them together with the side of a chef's knife). In a small bowl, combine this garlic and chile mixture with the chile paste, hot water, and sugar. Stir well. Add the fish sauce and lime juice and combine. Float the carrots on top (if using). Let sit for at least 15 minutes before using.

Pasta Salad with Spinach, Corn & Red Bell Pepper

Serves four.

You can prepare the components of this salad ahead, refrigerate, and assemble them just before serving; just let the pasta and vegetables come to room temperature before assembling.

FOR THE VINAIGRETTE:
⅓ cup fresh lemon juice
1 Tbs. whole-grain mustard
1 Tbs. finely chopped shallot
1½ tsp. honey
1 tsp. finely grated lemon zest
½ cup extra-virgin olive oil
2 Tbs. chopped fresh dill
2 Tbs. chopped fresh chives
¾ tsp. kosher salt
Freshly ground black pepper

FOR THE SALAD:
1 cup fresh corn kernels
½ lb. cavatappi or other short, curved pasta
1 Tbs. olive oil
3 oz. baby spinach leaves (about 4 cups), well washed and dried
1 small red bell pepper, stemmed, seeded, and very thinly sliced (about 1 cup)
½ small red onion, very thinly sliced
4 oz. crumbled feta cheese

Make the vinaigrette: Combine the lemon juice, mustard, shallot, honey, and zest in a medium bowl and set aside for 5 minutes to let the shallot's flavor mellow. Whisk in the oil. Stir in the herbs and season with the salt and pepper to taste.

Make the salad: Bring a large pot of well-salted water to a boil over high heat. Cook the corn until just crisp-tender, 2 to 3 minutes (see method box at right). Remove the corn and rinse under cold water to stop the cooking, drain well, and blot dry.

Bring the water back to a boil. Add the pasta and cook it until it is al dente. Drain it thoroughly and immediately pour it out onto a rimmed baking sheet to cool. Toss the pasta with the 1 Tbs. olive oil to prevent sticking.

In a large serving bowl, toss the pasta, corn, spinach, and bell pepper. Add enough of the vinaigrette to moisten the pasta. Add the cheese and most of the red onion. Let stand for 10 to 15 minutes. Taste, add more of the onion, the vinaigrette, salt, or pepper as needed, and serve.

An easy method for cooking peas and corn

To cook peas or corn kernels, put them in a strainer and dip the strainer in boiling water so that the vegetables are easy to fish out when they're done.

tip: Choose little zucchini over big. Smaller means firmer flesh that browns well without turning to mush.

The basic method for slicing and salting zucchini

Wash the zucchini well to remove any grit and dry them with paper towels. Trim off the ends and quarter the zucchini lengthwise. Slice off the top ¼ to ½ inch of the soft seed core by running a sharp knife down the length of each quarter; it's all right if some of the seeds remain. Arrange the zucchini, cut side up, on a baking sheet lined with paper towels. Sprinkle with kosher salt (about ½ tsp. per 1 lb. of zucchini) and set aside for 10 minutes. Blot the quarters dry with the paper towels.

Warm Couscous & Grilled Zucchini Salad with Grilled Shrimp

Serves four.

If you want to toss the shrimp in the salad, add a little more olive oil and orange juice to the salad.

3 small or 2 medium zucchini (about 1 lb.)
Kosher salt
2 tsp. ground cumin
2 tsp. packed light brown sugar
⅛ tsp. ground cinnamon
Pinch cayenne
Freshly ground black pepper
1 large red onion, sliced into ⅓-inch disks
4 to 5 Tbs. extra-virgin olive oil
1 lb. large shrimp, peeled and deveined
1¼ cups couscous
¼ cup chopped fresh cilantro
1 Tbs. finely grated orange zest
2 Tbs. fresh orange juice; more to taste

Slice and salt the zucchini following the instructions at left. Heat a gas grill to medium high or prepare a medium-hot charcoal fire. In a small bowl, mix the cumin, brown sugar, cinnamon, cayenne, 1 tsp. salt, and ¼ tsp. pepper. In a medium bowl, gently toss the zucchini quarters with 1 Tbs. olive oil and the spice mix.

Let sit for 10 minutes. Thread the onion on two thin skewers, brush both sides with 1 Tbs. olive oil, and sprinkle with a little salt. Skewer the shrimp on one or two skewers. Brush both sides with olive oil and season well with salt and pepper.

Meanwhile, bring 1½ cups water to a boil in a large saucepan. Stir in the couscous, 2 Tbs. olive oil, and ¾ tsp. salt. Cover, remove from the heat, and set aside.

Set the zucchini cut side down on the grill and cook, flipping occasionally until it browns and softens but doesn't turn mushy, 6 to 8 minutes. Return the zucchini to its original bowl and toss to pick up any spices clinging to it. Reduce the heat to medium (if using a charcoal grill, put on the lid and partially close air vents. Grill the shrimp, turning once, until just pink and cooked through, 2 to 3 minutes. Coarsely chop the zucchini and onions and stir them into the couscous, along with the cilantro, orange zest, and orange juice.

Taste for salt and pepper; add a little more orange juice to taste. Serve immediately with the shrimp.

Pasta Salad with Tomatoes, Green Beans, Peas & Pesto Vinaigrette

Serves four.

To streamline the assembly of this colorful salad, the vegetables and the pasta get cooked separately but in the same pot of boiling water.

FOR THE VINAIGRETTE:
1½ cups lightly packed fresh basil leaves
½ cup extra-virgin olive oil
½ cup fresh, finely grated Parmigiano Reggiano
3 Tbs. red- or white-wine vinegar
2 Tbs. fresh lemon juice
2 tsp. finely chopped garlic
½ tsp. finely grated lemon zest
¾ tsp. kosher salt
Freshly ground black pepper

FOR THE SALAD:
1 cup shelled fresh peas (from about 1 lb. pea pods)
1 lb. string beans (a mix of wax beans and green beans is nice), snapped into 2-inch lengths

½ lb. campanelle or other short, shaped pasta
1 Tbs. olive oil
½ pint cherry tomatoes, halved
2 Tbs. coarsely chopped olives
2 Tbs. toasted pine nuts

Make the vinaigrette: Put the basil, olive oil, Parmigiano, vinegar, lemon juice, garlic, and lemon zest in a blender. Blend until smooth. Season with salt and pepper to taste.

Make the salad: Bring a large pot of well-salted water to a boil over high heat. Cook the peas until just crisp-tender, 2 to 3 minutes. Remove the peas, rinse under cold water to stop the cooking, drain well, and blot dry.

Bring the water back to a boil. Add the green beans and cook until just crisp-tender, 4 to 6 minutes. Remove with a large slotted

spoon, rinse under cold water to stop the cooking, drain well, and pat dry.

Bring the water back to a boil. Add the pasta and cook it until it is al dente. Drain it thoroughly and immediately pour it out onto a rimmed baking sheet to cool. Toss the pasta with the 1 Tbs. olive oil to prevent sticking.

In a large serving bowl, toss together the pasta, peas, green beans, and tomatoes. Add enough of the vinaigrette to moisten the pasta. Add the olives and pine nuts, toss gently, and let stand for 10 or 15 minutes. Taste, add more of the vinaigrette, salt or pepper as needed, and serve.

VARIATION

Use this formula to create your own pasta salads:

- ½ lb. pasta
- 6 cups vegetables
- 1 cup vinaigrette

Add a burst of flavor with herbs, capers, olives, and scallions and round out the salad by tossing in a little diced mozzarella or crumbled feta or goat cheese.

Updated California Cobb Salad

Serves four to six.

This delicious salad was supposedly named in 1937 for Bob Cobb, the owner of the Brown Derby restaurant in Hollywood. As the story goes, Cobb was ravenous one night and threw together this salad, which a friend loved and named for him. This version tops it with a Balsamic Vinaigrette.

6 strips thickly sliced bacon
3 boneless, skinless chicken thighs, rinsed and patted dry with paper towels
Kosher salt and freshly ground black pepper
10 cups lightly packed mixed greens (a mix of iceberg lettuce, arugula, and radicchio is nice)
½ large red onion, thinly sliced
1 large tomato, cored, seeded, and chopped
1 large ripe avocado, peeled and thinly sliced
⅔ cup crumbled blue cheese, such as Roquefort
2 hard-cooked eggs, peeled and quartered lengthwise
1 large ear fresh corn, kernels sliced off (see p. 217 for instructions)
¼ cup chopped fresh flat-leaf parsley
1 cup Balsamic Vinaigrette dressing (see recipe below)

In a large skillet over medium heat, cook the bacon, turning once or twice, until evenly browned and fully crisped, about 7 minutes. Remove the pan from the heat and transfer the bacon to a plate lined with paper towels to drain and cool; reserve the skillet with the bacon drippings. Trim the chicken thighs of any excess fat and season with salt and pepper. Return the skillet with the drippings to medium-high heat. Carefully add the thighs and brown, turning once, until cooked through, about 4 minutes each side. Transfer the chicken to a plate to cool.

Toss the salad greens and onion in a large, shallow bowl. Cut the chicken into ½-inch slices and then into about ¾-inch-long pieces. Crumble the bacon. Arrange the chicken, bacon, tomato, avocado, blue cheese, quartered eggs, and corn in single-striped sections over the salad. At this point, you can cover the salad with a damp paper towel and plastic and refrigerate it for an hour or so. Just before serving, scatter the chopped parsley over the top. Sprinkle with salt and a few generous grinds of pepper.

Bring the salad to the table, drizzle with enough vinaigrette to lightly coat the ingredients, about ½ cup. Toss and serve immediately, passing the rest of the vinaigrette at the table.

VARIATIONS

- Use pancetta instead of bacon.

- Add fresh basil or mint leaves to the mixed greens.

- Replace the blue cheese with feta.

Balsamic Vinaigrette

Yields about 1 cup.

While this dressing tastes great with the Cobb salad, it's truly an all-purpose vinaigrette and would taste delicious on many kinds of salads.

3 Tbs. balsamic vinegar
2 tsp. Dijon mustard
1 small clove garlic, minced
1 tsp. kosher salt; more to taste
About 5 grinds black pepper; more to taste
¾ cup olive oil

In a small bowl, whisk together the vinegar, mustard, garlic, salt, and pepper. Whisking constantly, add the oil in a slow, steady stream until completely incorporated. Adjust the seasonings to taste.

VARIATION

- After whisking in the oil, add 1 Tbs. each sliced fresh chives and minced fresh basil.

Balsamic Portabella Salad with Goat Cheese

Serves four.

Serve this beautiful salad with toasted slices of sourdough bread rubbed with a garlic clove and the cut side of a tomato. The mushrooms also taste delicious grilled instead of broiled.

3 oil-packed anchovy fillets, drained
3 Tbs. balsamic vinegar
1½ Tbs. finely chopped shallots
3 tsp. Dijon mustard
1 tsp. dried marjoram
Kosher salt and freshly ground black pepper
½ cup extra-virgin olive oil
4 large portabella mushrooms (about 1 lb.)
4 oz. (6 cups loosely packed) mixed baby greens
1½ cups cherry tomatoes, halved
½ cup crumbled goat cheese (about 3 oz.)

Position a rack 4 inches from the broiler element and heat the broiler to high.

In a medium bowl, mash the anchovy fillets with a fork or a wooden spoon until they form a paste. Stir in the vinegar, shallots, mustard, marjoram, ¾ tsp. salt, and ⅛ tsp. pepper until well blended. Slowly whisk in the oil.

Wipe the mushrooms clean with a paper towel. Remove and discard the stems. Use a spoon to scrape out and discard the mushroom gills. Brush the mushroom caps with 4 Tbs. of the dressing and sprinkle with ¼ tsp. salt and ⅛ tsp. pepper. Set the caps, gill side up, on a rimmed baking sheet. Broil until the caps start to soften, 3 to 4 minutes. Flip them and continue to broil until they're well browned and tender, 3 to 4 minutes. Transfer the caps to a cutting board and cut into ¼-inch slices.

In a large bowl, combine the baby greens and cherry tomatoes; add 6 Tbs. of the dressing and toss well to coat. To serve, set equal portions of the greens and tomatoes on dinner plates and arrange the mushroom slices on top. Drizzle each salad with about 1 Tbs. of the remaining dressing. Sprinkle with the crumbled goat cheese and serve.

tip: Scraping the gills out of the portabella mushrooms gives them a cleaner flavor and a neater appearance.

Dressings

Bold

Caesar-Style Vinaigrette

Yields about ½ cup.

This dressing is best made in a food processor or blender.

- 1 Tbs. plus 1 tsp. freshly grated Parmigiano Reggiano
- 1 tsp. packed finely grated lemon zest
- 1 tsp. Dijon mustard
- 2 to 3 medium anchovy fillets
- 1 to 2 medium cloves garlic
- ¼ tsp. table salt
- ⅛ tsp. freshly ground black pepper
- 2 Tbs. fresh lemon juice
- 6 Tbs. good-quality extra-virgin olive oil

Put the cheese, lemon zest, mustard, anchovies, garlic, salt, pepper, and lemon juice in a food processor (or blender) and process until well blended. With the motor running, slowly pour in the olive oil and process until creamy and blended. Taste and adjust the seasonings. The vinaigrette will keep for a week in the refrigerator.

Sherry-Thyme Vinaigrette

Yields 1 cup.

Just a little bit of fresh thyme makes all the difference in this all-purpose vinaigrette. Refrigerate any extra dressing for up to three days.

- ¼ cup sherry vinegar
- ½ tsp. kosher salt
- 2 Tbs. finely chopped shallots
- ½ tsp. chopped fresh thyme
- ¾ cup extra-virgin olive oil
- Freshly ground black pepper

In a small bowl, whisk the vinegar, salt, shallots, and thyme. Add the olive oil in a slow stream, whisking to emulsify. Season to taste with pepper and more salt, if needed.

Black Olive & Mint Vinaigrette

Yields 2 cups.

The full flavors of this dressing work best with hearty greens such as curly endive or romaine. Another delicious way to use this vinaigrette is to drizzle it over slices of grilled lamb.

- 2 cloves garlic
- 1 Tbs. capers, rinsed
- ½ cup Kalamata or other good-quality black olives, pitted
- 3 shallots, thinly sliced
- 1 Tbs. grainy mustard
- 1 Tbs. chopped fresh marjoram (optional)
- 1 Tbs. chopped fresh mint
- ⅓ cup red-wine vinegar; more as needed
- 1 cup extra-virgin olive oil; more as needed
- Kosher salt and freshly ground black pepper

On a cutting board, mince together the garlic, capers, and olives. Transfer to a mixing bowl. Stir in the shallots, mustard, marjoram, mint, and vinegar. Mix in the olive oil with a fork to make a loose vinaigrette—it doesn't need to be emulsified. Season with salt and pepper. Taste and add more oil or vinegar if necessary.

A homemade vinaigrette is so much better than a bottled salad dressing and is just as delicious drizzled on a steak as tossed with a salad.

Lemony

Lemon Vinaigrette

Yields ³/₄ cup.

This all-purpose vinaigrette would taste just as lovely drizzled over steamed green beans or new potatoes as it does tossed with salad greens.

3 Tbs. fresh lemon juice
2 Tbs. mayonnaise or heavy cream
1 Tbs. minced shallots
³/₄ tsp. kosher salt
Freshly ground black pepper
¹/₂ cup canola oil

In a small bowl, combine the lemon juice, mayonnaise, shallots, salt, and pepper. Add the oil in a slow stream, whisking constantly until the vinaigrette is well blended.

Lemony Goat Cheese Dressing

Yields ³/₄ cup.

This thick dressing works especially well with baby spinach or romaine lettuce and garlicky croutons.

3 to 4 oz. soft fresh goat cheese
¹/₃ cup half-and-half; more as needed
1 tsp. finely grated lemon zest
¹/₄ tsp. kosher salt
¹/₄ tsp. freshly ground black pepper

In a small bowl, crumble the cheese and mash it with a fork until smooth. Add the half-and-half 1 Tbs. at a time, mixing and mashing the cheese with the fork. Stir in the lemon zest, salt, and pepper. Cover and refrigerate for up to 30 minutes. Stir before serving and thin with more half-and-half if needed.

Lemon-Chive Vinaigrette

Yields about 1 cup.

When snipping fresh chives, use a very sharp knife or kitchen scissors; otherwise you end up bruising this delicate herb.

1 tsp. grated lemon zest
¹/₄ cup fresh lemon juice
2 Tbs. chopped fresh chives
1 clove garlic, minced
1 tsp. sugar
Kosher salt and ground white pepper
³/₄ cup vegetable oil

Put all the ingredients except the oil in a food processor, a blender, or a small bowl. Process (or whisk) until mixed. With the machine running or while whisking, slowly pour in the oil. Taste and adjust the seasonings.

Lemon Poppyseed Dressing

Yields about 1 cup.

Poppyseeds add a little texture, color, and sweet flavor to a vinaigrette. To show this one off, try it over delicate lettuces or steamed new potatoes. It's also a great dressing for a chef's salad.

¹/₂ tsp. finely grated lemon zest
Juice of 1 lemon (about ¹/₄ cup)
2 Tbs. heavy cream
1 tsp. poppyseeds
1 tsp. minced shallot
³/₄ tsp. kosher salt; more to taste
About 5 grinds black pepper; more to taste
³/₄ cup canola oil

In a small bowl, whisk the lemon zest, lemon juice, cream, poppyseeds, shallot, salt, and pepper. Whisking constantly, add the oil in a slow, steady stream until completely incorporated. Adjust the seasonings to taste.

Creamy

Creamy Herb Dressing

Yields about 2 cups, enough for 12 portions of salad.

This recipe takes the basic ranch salad dressing one step further by incorporating a generous quantity of fresh herbs. Use a homemade mayonnaise if you like, but store-bought works quite well here.

¹/₄ small bunch dill, stems removed (about ¹/₄ cup loosely packed leaves)
¹/₄ bunch flat-leaf parsley, stems removed (about ³/₄ cup loosely packed leaves)
¹/₄ bunch thyme, stems removed (about 2 Tbs. loosely packed leaves)
¹/₂ bunch chives, coarsely chopped (¹/₃ cup)
³/₄ cup mayonnaise
¹/₂ cup buttermilk
2 Tbs. cider vinegar
¹/₂ tsp. kosher salt; more to taste
¹/₈ tsp. freshly ground black pepper
³/₄ tsp. hot sauce (such as Tabasco)

In a food processor, combine the dill, parsley, thyme, and chives with the mayonnaise; process until the herbs are chopped. With the motor running, slowly pour in the buttermilk and then add the vinegar, salt, pepper, and hot sauce. Taste and adjust the seasonings. Pour into a bottle or jar and refrigerate for up to two weeks.

Spinach, Goat Cheese
& Chive Quiche *p. 76*

Light Lunches

Spinach, Goat Cheese & Chive Quiche

Serves four to six.

Though the tart dough recipe at right is a winner, you could use store-bought pie dough in a pinch (but not the already-molded kind; it's not the right shape). Or use frozen puff pastry. Any dough you use must be partially baked (blind baked) before filling.

10 oz. fresh spinach, stemmed and washed
2 large eggs
2 large egg yolks
1½ cups heavy cream
Salt and freshly ground black pepper
½ cup semi-dry finely crumbled goat cheese, such as Bucheron
2 to 3 Tbs. finely snipped chives
1 Tbs. finely minced fresh thyme
⅓ cup freshly grated Parmigiano Reggiano
1 partially baked tart shell in a 10-inch porcelain quiche pan or a 10 ½- to 11-inch metal tart pan (see recipe at right)

In a large saucepan, bring 1 cup water to a boil. Add the spinach and cook until just wilted, 2 or 3 minutes. Drain and set aside. In a bowl, combine the eggs, yolks, and heavy cream. Season the mixture with salt and pepper and whisk until thoroughly blended. Add the finely crumbled goat cheese, chives, thyme, and Parmigiano Reggiano. Set aside.

Put the spinach in a kitchen towel and squeeze out all the moisture. Mince the spinach and add it to the egg mixture. Blend well.

Heat the oven to 375°F. Pour the spinach and egg mixture into a prepared, partially baked tart shell, being careful that it doesn't overflow. Put the tart on a baking sheet and bake until the filling is nicely puffed and browned, 40 to 50 minutes. Let cool for at least 15 to 20 minutes before serving.

Basic Tart Dough

Makes one 10- to 11-inch tart shell.

1½ cups all-purpose unbleached flour
¼ tsp. plus a pinch of salt
9 Tbs. unsalted butter, cut into small pieces and chilled
4 Tbs. ice water

Make the dough: In a food processor, combine the flour, salt, and butter. Using short pulses, process until the mixture resembles oatmeal. Add the ice water and pulse quickly until the mixture begins to come together around the blades. Transfer the mixture to a lightly floured surface and gather it into a ball with your hands. Gently flatten the ball into a smooth disk about 1½ inches thick and wrap it in plastic or foil. Refrigerate until firm enough to roll, at least 1 hour.

Roll and shape the shell: Roll the dough on a lightly floured surface into a circle about ⅛ inch thick. Roll the dough over your rolling pin and lift it over a 10½- or 11-inch tart pan with fluted edges. Unroll it loosely over the tart pan and gently press the dough into the pan without stretching it. Fold a bit of the excess dough inward to form a lip. Roll the rolling pin back and forth over the pan. Remove the severed dough from the outside of the pan. Unfold the lip of dough and press it down into the sides of the pan to form a double thickness. Prick the bottom of the shell all over with a fork, cover with aluminum foil, and freeze for at least 30 minutes and as long as overnight. At this point, the shell can also be wrapped and kept frozen for up to 2 weeks.

Partially bake the shell: Arrange a rack in the center of the oven and heat the oven to 425°F. Remove the foil, line the frozen shell with parchment or fresh foil, fill it with dried beans or pie weights, and put it on a baking sheet. Bake until the sides are set, about 12 minutes. Remove the parchment and weights and continue to bake until the dough is just beginning to brown lightly, another 6 to 8 minutes. Cool on a wire rack until needed.

Roasted Portabella & Garlic Sandwiches

Serves four.

In this recipe, the portabella is served whole, like a hamburger. If a whole cap doesn't fit on your bread, slice the cap on the diagonal, put the slices on the bread, top with cheese, and then broil.

1 head garlic, loose papery skins removed
1 tsp. plus 1 Tbs. olive oil
4 medium portabella mushrooms, stems removed, caps wiped clean
Coarse salt
2 medium shallots, finely chopped (to yield about ¼ cup)
1 clove garlic, finely chopped
1 tsp. chopped fresh thyme
1 Tbs. balsamic vinegar
Freshly ground black pepper
8 slices country-style bread, about ½ inch thick, or 4 good-quality rolls
⅔ cup grated Monterey Jack cheese
About 1 Tbs. chopped fresh parsley

Heat the oven to 450°F. Lay the garlic on a square of foil. Drizzle 1 tsp. of the olive oil over the top. Bring up the sides of the foil and wrap up the garlic. Roast until tender, about 40 minutes. Squeeze the garlic pulp into a small bowl and mash.

Rub the portabella caps all over with the 1 Tbs. olive oil and sprinkle with salt. Put them, gill side up, in an ovenproof pan. In a small bowl, combine the shallots, garlic, thyme, vinegar, and salt and pepper to taste. Sprinkle the mixture evenly over the portabellas. Roast (you can do this at the same time as the garlic) until the mushrooms are tender and browned, 20 to 30 minutes. Remove the portabellas from the oven and set the oven temperature to broil.

Toast the bread slices on both sides under the broiler. Spread each slice with some roasted garlic purée; sprinkle with salt and pepper. Top four of the slices with a portabella; put them on a baking sheet. Sprinkle the cheese over the portabellas and return them to the oven to melt the cheese. Top with the parsley and another bread slice to make a sandwich.

tip: Full-flavored spreads—such as those made with roasted garlic, sun-dried tomatoes, and olives—make all-vegetable sandwiches especially satisfying.

Goat Cheese Soufflé with Red Peppers & Chanterelles

Serves six.

Bucheron is an aged goat cheese with a white rind. If you can't find it, use a fresh, soft goat cheese.

1¼ cups heavy cream
1 small sprig fresh rosemary; more chopped rosemary for garnish
2 Tbs. extra-virgin olive oil
2 medium red bell peppers, cored, seeded, and finely chopped
1 medium shallot, finely chopped
1 cup finely chopped fresh chanterelle mushrooms (about 2 oz.)
Kosher salt and freshly ground black pepper
3 Tbs. unsalted butter; more for the soufflé dishes
3 Tbs. all-purpose flour
4 large egg yolks
1 cup (about 4 oz.) crumbled goat cheese (preferably Bucheron, rind trimmed)
6 large egg whites

Heat the oven to 400°F. Butter six 9- to 10-oz. soufflé dishes. In a small saucepan, heat the cream with the rosemary sprig over medium heat just until it boils. Remove from the heat and let steep for 10 minutes. Discard the rosemary sprig.

Heat the olive oil in a 10- to 12-inch skillet over medium heat. Add the red peppers and shallot. Sauté, stirring occasionally, until the vegetables begin to soften, about 6 minutes. Add the mushrooms and continue to sauté, stirring frequently, until everything is tender, 2 to 3 minutes. Season with salt and pepper; remove from the heat. Distribute the cooked vegetables evenly among the buttered dishes, covering the bottom of each dish.

Melt the butter in a medium saucepan over medium-low heat. When foamy, stir in the flour and cook over low heat, stirring constantly, for 2 to 3 minutes. Whisk in the heated cream. Add ½ tsp. salt (or to taste) and several grinds of pepper. Increase the heat to medium and whisk until the mixture bubbles and thickens. Remove from the heat. Whisk in the egg yolks one at a time until well blended. Stir in the cheese (the mixture needn't be completely smooth).

With a mixer, beat the egg whites in a large bowl with a pinch of salt on high speed until medium-stiff peaks form. Stir a small amount of the beaten egg whites into the cheese mixture to lighten it and then gently fold the cheese mixture into the remaining egg whites with a rubber spatula (it's fine to leave a few clumps of egg white). Divide the mixture evenly among the buttered dishes, covering the vegetables.

Lower the oven temperature to 375°F. Put the soufflés on a rimmed baking sheet and bake until golden and just slightly wobbly in the center, about 20 minutes. Sprinkle the soufflés with a bit of chopped rosemary and serve immediately.

Tomato & Mozzarella Omelet

Yields 1 omelet; serves one.

This recipe is easily multiplied. If you want to do that, combine all of the egg ingredients and ladle out ½ cup of beaten eggs per omelet.

2 large or extra-large eggs
1 Tbs. water
Kosher salt and freshly ground black pepper
5 leaves fresh basil, very thinly sliced (to yield 1 Tbs.)
2 tsp. olive oil
2 Tbs. finely chopped onion
½ tsp. finely chopped garlic
Kosher salt
¼ cup chopped and drained canned tomatoes
1 oil-packed sun-dried tomato, minced (to yield 1 tsp.)

Spring Vegetable & Potato Frittata

Serves four.

This frittata is a great make-ahead dinner. Let it cool to room temperature and refrigerate until ready to use. It can be warmed in the microwave or served at room temperature.

8 large eggs
¼ cup grated Parmigiano Reggiano (about ½ oz.)
3 Tbs. chopped fresh flat-leaf parsley
Kosher salt and freshly ground black pepper
⅛ tsp. cayenne
2 to 3 Tbs. extra-virgin olive oil
1 medium Yukon Gold potato (about ½ lb.), scrubbed and cut into ½-inch dice (about 1½ cups)
1 medium yellow onion, thinly sliced
½ lb. medium-thick asparagus, trimmed and cut on the diagonal into 1-inch pieces
3 cloves garlic, minced
6 oz. shredded sharp Cheddar (about 1¾ cups, lightly packed)

Several grinds freshly ground
  black pepper
1 tsp. unsalted butter
1 thin slice mozzarella, diced
1 Tbs. freshly grated Parmigiano
  Reggiano
1 Tbs. good-quality store-bought
  basil pesto

Whisk the eggs: In a medium
bowl, whisk together the eggs,
water, 2 pinches salt, and 4
grinds of pepper, until the yolks
and whites are well combined
but not foamy. Whisk in the basil.

Make the filling: In a medium
skillet over medium heat, heat
1 tsp. of the oil. Add the onion;
cook, stirring, for 2 minutes. Add
the garlic and 2 pinches of salt
and continue to cook until the
onion is tender and translucent,

about another 3 minutes. Raise
the heat to medium high. Cook,
stirring, until the onion is golden,
another 1 to 2 minutes. Stir in
the canned tomatoes; simmer
until the liquid has evaporated,
about 2 minutes. Add the sun-
dried tomatoes, several grinds of
black pepper, and a pinch of salt
if needed. You should have about
¼ cup filling; set aside 1 tsp. for
the garnish.

Cook the omelet: In an 8-inch
heavy-duty nonstick skillet over
medium-high heat, heat the remaining 1 tsp. of the oil. Add
the butter and swirl it to coat
the pan.
　Pour the eggs into the pan
and with a flexible, heatproof
spatula scramble the eggs gently

using small circular motions until
soft curds start to form, 30 to 50
seconds. As the mixture begins
to firm, spread it out in the pan.
Stop working the curds for about
30 seconds to let the omelet
begin to firm. Scatter the mozzarella and the Parmigiano over the
omelet, leaving a scant margin
around the omelet's edge. Add
the other filling ingredients and
use your spatula to press gently
to incorporate the filling into the
omelet.
　With the spatula, fold one-
third of the omelet over the
center like a business letter. Lift
the pan up and tilt it so that one-
third of the omelet hangs over
the pan's edge and touches the
plate. Using the spatula to help
support the omelet, turn the pan

completely over so that the omelet flips over itself as it slides
onto the plate. Garnish with the
pesto and the reserved 1 tsp. of
filling and serve.

In a medium bowl, whisk the
eggs, Parmigiano, parsley,
½ tsp. salt, ⅛ tsp. pepper, and
the cayenne.
　Heat 2 Tbs. of the oil in a
10-inch ovenproof nonstick skillet over medium-high heat. Add
the potato and ¼ tsp. salt and
cook, stirring occasionally, until
browned on several sides, 6 to
7 minutes. Transfer to a bowl
with a slotted spoon. Reduce
the heat to medium. If the pan is
dry, add the remaining 1 Tbs. oil.
Add the onion and cook, stirring
frequently, until it softens and
begins to brown, 4 to 5 minutes.
Stir in the asparagus, garlic,
¼ tsp. salt and ⅛ tsp. pepper.
Cook, stirring frequently, until
the asparagus is bright green
and crisp-tender, 3 to 4 minutes.
Lower the heat to medium low
and add the egg mixture and
the potatoes, stirring until the
ingredients are combined, 10 to
15 seconds. Add the Cheddar
and stir until well distributed.
Cook without stirring until the

eggs have almost set, 10 to
12 minutes. (The center may still
be loose but should be bubbling
a little; the sides should be set.)
Meanwhile, position an oven rack
6 inches from the broiler element
and heat the broiler to high.

　Transfer the skillet to the oven
and broil until the eggs have
set completely and the top of
the frittata is golden brown, 1 to
3 minutes. Let rest for 5 minutes.
Transfer to a cutting board, cut
into four wedges, and serve.

Grilled Vegetable Sandwiches

Yields four sandwiches.

These sandwiches are perfect for a picnic; the longer they sit (well wrapped in plastic wrap), the deeper their flavor becomes. That the bread softens a little from the spread is only a bonus.

2 medium zucchini, sliced lengthwise ¼ inch thick
2 medium yellow squash, sliced lengthwise ¼ inch thick
1 medium eggplant, sliced lengthwise ¼ inch thick
4 scallions, trimmed
4 medium portabella mushrooms, stems removed, caps wiped clean
Olive oil
Salt and freshly ground black pepper to taste
2 red peppers, roasted, peeled, and quartered
½ cup Sun-Dried Tomato & Olive Spread (see recipe at right)
4 6-inch lengths crusty French or Italian bread, sliced lengthwise
1 cup grated Asiago, provolone, or other sharp, dry cheese

Heat a gas grill to medium high. Brush the zucchini, squash, eggplant, scallions, and mushrooms lightly with olive oil and sprinkle with a little salt and pepper. Grill until tender (you can also broil the vegetables, if you prefer). Cut the mushrooms into thin slices.

If the bread is very thick, hollow it out slightly to make a pocket. Spread the Sun-Dried Tomato & Olive Spread liberally on each slice. Layer the vegetables, including the roasted peppers, on one-half of the bread, dividing them evenly among the four sandwiches. Pat the grated cheese on the other half and put the halves together.

Sun-Dried Tomato & Olive Spread

Yields ¾ cup.

This spread takes just minutes to make with the help of a food processor. You can find black-olive paste (labeled tapenade) in most supermarkets and in specialty food stores.

3 cloves garlic
½ cup coarsely chopped, oil-packed sun-dried tomatoes
3 Tbs. black-olive paste (tapenade)
¼ cup extra-virgin olive oil
2 Tbs. balsamic vinegar
1 scallion, minced
Salt and freshly ground black pepper to taste

In a food processor, mince the garlic. Add the tomatoes and olive paste and purée. Add the olive oil and vinegar and pulse to incorporate. Add the scallion, salt, and pepper; pulse until just combined. The spread will keep, covered and refrigerated, for a couple of weeks.

Corn Soufflé Puddings

Serves six.

The idea for a soufflé pudding—a sunken soufflé, unmolded and reheated in a puddle of cream—came from the late, great Richard Olney, a cookbook author and a superb cook. These have a delicate chive flavor, but you could also use thyme, summer savory, or basil. Soufflé puddings are a perfect dish for entertaining, as they can be made a day ahead and reheated just before serving.

1 cup milk
2 cups corn kernels (from about 3 ears; (see p. 217 for instructions on getting fresh corn kernals off the cob)
¼ cup unsalted butter; more for the ramekins
¼ cup all-purpose flour
3 large eggs, separated
1 tsp. coarse salt
2 or 3 grinds black pepper
1 Tbs. sliced fresh chives
½ cup heavy cream

Put the milk and 1¼ cups of the corn kernels in a blender. Blend until puréed. Strain the purée through a medium-fine sieve, using a rubber spatula to push through as much pulp as possible; you'll have about 1½ cups of purée.

In a heavy-based saucepan, melt the butter over low heat. Whisk in the flour and cook for a minute, still whisking. Slowly whisk in the corn purée and whisk over medium-low heat until the mixture becomes as thick as pudding, 3 to 5 minutes. Pour into a large bowl and let cool to room temperature.

Heat the oven to 400°F. Generously butter six 6-oz. ramekins.

When the soufflé base is cool, stir in the egg yolks, the remaining ¾ cup corn kernels, salt, pepper, and chives. In a clean, dry bowl, beat the egg whites until they form soft peaks. Working quickly, use a rubber spatula to gently stir half of the whites into the soufflé base and then fold in the rest. Fill the ramekins just over three-quarters full and set them in a baking dish large enough to hold all of them. Pour enough hot water into the baking dish to come halfway up the sides of the ramekins. Bake the puddings until they're puffed, set, and golden brown, about 30 minutes; rotate the pan once during baking.

Remove the puddings from the baking dish and let cool for about 15 minutes. Unmold the puddings by sliding a knife around the edge of each ramekin and gently inverting the pudding into the palm of your hand. Set the puddings browned side up in an oval gratin dish; they should be close but not touching. (For a more elegant presentation, you can put them in individual gratin dishes.) If you're not serving them right away, cover lightly with plastic and refrigerate for up to a day.

When ready to serve, heat the oven to 400°F. Pour the heavy cream over and around the puddings and heat them in the oven until the cream bubbles and the puddings repuff slightly, about 10 minutes.

how-to

See p. 217, to learn how to get fresh corn kernels off the cob.

Savory Tomato, Corn & Cheese Tart with Fresh Basil

Yields one tart; serves four for lunch or eight as an appetizer.

Once you try this pretty vegetable tart, go ahead and play with the elements to create your own version. Chopped, pitted olives, for instance, can be used in place of corn, and Parmigiano Reggiano for the cheese. The results will be very different but still delicious.

2 Tbs. olive oil
1 large white onion, thinly sliced
Kosher salt and freshly ground black pepper
2 cloves garlic, finely chopped
½ bunch basil, washed, dried, and coarsely chopped (to yield about ½ cup); plus 10 whole basil leaves
Kernels from 1 ear of corn (about 1 cup)
1 recipe Cornmeal Tart Dough (see the recipe at right)
1 large or 2 medium ripe tomatoes (about ¾ lb. total) cut into ⅓-inch slices, drained on paper towels
3 oz. Gruyère or Comté cheese, shredded
1 large egg yolk mixed with 1 tsp. milk or cream

Heat the olive oil in a sauté pan, preferably nonstick, over medium heat. Add the sliced onion and cook, stirring frequently, until lightly browned, about 10 minutes. Season with salt and pepper. Add the garlic, chopped basil, and corn and cook for 30 seconds. Transfer the mixture to a bowl and set aside to cool.

Position a rack in the middle of the oven and heat the oven to 375°F. Line a baking sheet, preferably one without sides, with parchment. (If your baking sheet has sides, flip it over and use the bottom.)

Roll the dough on a floured surface into a 15-inch round, lifting the dough with a metal spatula as you roll to be sure it isn't sticking. If it is, dust the surface with more flour. Transfer it by rolling it around the rolling pin and unrolling it on the lined baking sheet.

Spread the onion and corn mixture over the dough, leaving a 2-inch border bare. Arrange the tomatoes in a single layer over the onions and season them with salt and pepper. Sprinkle the cheese over the tomatoes. Lift the edges of the dough and fold them inward over the filling, pleating as you go, to create a folded-over border. (The look of the tart is rustic, so don't fret over the look of your pleats.) Pinch together any tears in the dough. Brush the egg yolk and milk mixture over the exposed crust.

Bake until the crust has browned and the cheese has melted, 35 to 45 minutes. Slide the tart off the parchment and onto a cooling rack. Let cool for 10 minutes. Stack the remaining 10 basil leaves and use a sharp knife to cut them into thin slivers. Cut the tart into wedges, sprinkle with the basil, and serve.

Cornmeal Tart Dough

Yields enough dough for one 11-inch tart; recipe can be easily doubled.

The texture of this dough makes it a little prone to tearing, especially as you fold it up and over a filling. If this happens, simply pinch the dough together and move on.

1¼ cups unbleached all-purpose flour
⅓ cup fine yellow cornmeal
1¼ tsp. table salt
1 tsp. sugar
6 Tbs. unsalted butter, cut into ½-inch pieces and chilled
3 Tbs. olive oil
¼ cup ice water

In a medium bowl, mix together the flour, cornmeal, salt, and sugar. Cut in the chilled butter using a stand mixer, a food processor, or a pastry blender until it's evenly distributed but still in large, visible pieces.

Add the olive oil and ice water and mix until the dough begins to come together. Gather the dough with your hands and shape it into a disk. Wrap the disk in plastic and refrigerate for at least 1 hour before using.

Fresh Spinach & Gruyère Pizza

Serves four as an appetizer.

This pizza dough is easy to handle, but you can certainly substitute purchased pizza dough in its place. If you want to omit the bacon in this recipe, increase the cheese just a bit.

FOR THE DOUGH:
1 tsp. active dry yeast
¼ tsp. sugar
½ cup warm water (100° to 120°F)
1½ cups unbleached all-purpose flour
½ tsp. salt
Olive oil for greasing the bowl

FOR THE PIZZA:
¼ lb. sliced smoked bacon or pancetta (about five ¼-inch-thick slices), cut in ½-inch pieces

Olive oil for brushing
¼ cup thinly sliced scallions (white and light green parts)
4 oz. coarsely grated Gruyère

FOR THE SALAD TOPPING:
2 tsp. red-wine vinegar
½ tsp. Dijon mustard
2 Tbs. olive oil
Kosher salt and freshly ground black pepper

¼ lb. loose baby spinach or ½ bunch tender young spinach, stemmed if needed, washed, and spun dry
1 hard-cooked egg, chopped

Make the dough: In a mixing bowl, dissolve the yeast and sugar in the water. Let rest until foamy, about 5 minutes. Add the flour and salt; mix until blended. Knead the dough on a very lightly floured surface until smooth and elastic, 5 to 10 minutes. Put it in a lightly oiled mixing bowl, cover loosely, and set in a warm place (70° to 80°F) until doubled in bulk, about 2 hours.

Make the pizza: Put a baking stone on the upper-middle rack of the oven and heat the oven to 475°F. In a small skillet over medium heat, brown the bacon. Drain on paper towels and set aside. On a heavily floured surface, flatten the dough ball. Roll the dough into a 12-inch round, lifting and stretching from underneath with the back of your hands. (If the dough resists, let it rest for a few minutes and then resume rolling.) The outside edges should be about ¼ inch thick, the center a bit thinner. Transfer the dough to a floured pizza paddle or the floured back of a baking sheet.

Brush the dough with the olive oil and sprinkle the scallions evenly to within ½ inch of the edge. Sprinkle on the cheese and the reserved bacon. Transfer the pizza onto the baking stone in the oven with a quick jerk of the paddle. Check the pizza after 2 or 3 minutes and deflate any giant bubbles if necessary.

Make the topping: While the pizza bakes, whisk together the vinegar, mustard, and olive oil; season with salt and pepper. When the edges of the crust are lightly browned and the cheese is bubbling, 10 to 12 minutes, return the pizza to the paddle or transfer it to a cutting board. Toss the spinach with the vinaigrette and pile it on the pizza. Sprinkle with the chopped egg, slice, and serve immediately.

Easy Pizza Dough

Yields four balls of dough for four individual 8-inch pizzas (1³⁄₄ lb. total).

Because the dough mixes together quickly in a food processor, you can have fresh pizza on the table in less than an hour. If you decide to make the dough ahead, follow the directions on the opposite page for proofing and storing.

1 package (2¼ tsp.) active dry yeast
1½ cups very warm water (110°F)
4 cups all-purpose flour; more for dusting
1½ tsp. salt
2 Tbs. olive oil

Make the dough: Dissolve the yeast in the warm water and set aside (a Pyrex 2-cup measure makes for easy pouring; be sure the cup isn't cold). Meanwhile, put the flour and salt in a food processor fitted with the steel blade; process briefly to mix. With the machine running, add the water-yeast mixture in a steady stream until the dough comes together (it will be very sticky). Turn the processor off and add the oil. Pulse a few times to mix in the oil.

Divide the dough: Scrape the soft dough out of the processor and onto a lightly floured surface. With lightly floured hands, quickly knead the dough into a mass, incorporating any bits of flour or dough from the processor bowl that weren't mixed in. Cut the dough into four equal pieces with a knife or a dough scraper. Roll each piece into a tight, smooth ball, kneading to push the air out. Put the dough balls on a lightly floured surface, cover them with a clean dishtowel, and let them rise until they almost double in size, about 45 minutes. Meanwhile, put a baking stone or unglazed terracotta tiles on the lowest rack of the oven and heat the oven to 500°F. (Ideally, let the stone or tiles heat in the oven for an hour before baking the pizza.)

Shape the dough: Put the ball of dough on a lightly floured wooden board. Sprinkle a little more flour on top of the ball. Using your fingertips, press the ball down into a flat cake about ½ inch thick.

Lift the dough and lay it over the back of the fist of one hand. Put your other fist under the dough, right next to your first fist. Now gently stretch the dough by moving your fists away from each other. Each time you do this stretch, rotate the dough. Continue stretching and rotating until the dough is thin, about ¼ inch, and measures about 9 inches across. Alternatively, use a rolling pin to roll out the dough thinly on a floured board. If you like a very thin pizza, roll the dough out to a 10-inch round.

Rub a bit of flour onto a wooden pizza peel (or the back of a baking sheet). Gently lift the stretched dough onto the floured peel. Top the pizza, scattering the ingredients around to within ½ inch of the border. (Use your own favorite toppings or choose one of the combinations listed on the opposite page.) Shake the peel (or baking sheet) gently back and forth to make sure the pizza isn't stuck. If it seems stuck, lift the edges up with a spatula and toss a bit of flour under the dough. Quickly slide the pizza onto the hot baking stone. Bake until the edges are golden, about 8 minutes. Using a peel, a wide spatula, or tongs, remove the pizza from the oven and serve.

tip: Be careful not to stretch pizza dough too thin, or it might tear. Also remember that the thinner the pizza, the less topping it can handle.

Make the dough ahead to have pizza whenever you want

For pizza tomorrow

If you want to bake the pizzas tomorrow, line a baking sheet with a floured dishtowel, put the dough balls on it, and cover them with plastic wrap, giving them room to expand (they'll almost double in size), and let them rise in the refrigerator overnight.

To use dough that has been refrigerated overnight, simply pull it out of the refrigerator about 15 minutes before shaping the dough into a pizza.

For pizza next week

To freeze the dough balls, dust each one generously with flour as soon as you've made it, and put each one in a separate zip-top bag. Freeze for up to a month.

It's best to transfer frozen dough from the freezer to the refrigerator the night before (or 10 to 12 hours before) you want to use it. But dough balls pulled straight from the freezer and left to warm up on the counter will be completely defrosted in about 1½ hours.

Ideas for topping your pizza

For some people, pizza isn't pizza without some red tomatoes peeking through mozzarella cheese. However, there are limitless flavor combinations to show off fresh, seasonal produce. Here are just a few. A drizzle of olive oil just before baking is a great addition to just about any pizza. (Unless noted otherwise, the ingredients go on before baking.)

- Roasted garlic, sliced oil-packed sun-dried tomatoes, crumbled goat cheese, a few capers, and a pinch of oregano. Drizzle with extra-virgin olive oil (photographed here).

- Sautéed onions, fresh sage leaves, grated pecorino, and grated Parmigiano Reggiano.

- Sliced scallions, crisped and chopped bacon, and grated Gruyere. Top cooked pizza with lightly dressed baby spinach garnished with chopped hard-cooked egg.

- Sautéed sliced asparagus, prosciutto, and grated fontina.

- Fresh ricotta, sliced roasted red peppers, fresh parsley, and grated Parmigiano Reggiano.

- Basil pesto, toasted pine nuts, and grated Parmigiano Reggiano.

- Sautéed leeks, chopped artichoke hearts, a bit of crushed tomatoes, and grated Parmigiano Reggiano.

- Sliced tomatoes, mozzarella, and fresh basil.

Pasta & Risotto

**Shells with Arugula, Feta &
Sun-Dried Tomatoes** *p. 94*

Fettuccine Primavera with Asparagus, Fava Beans & Peas

Serves six.

To peel fresh fava beans, cook them in boiling salted water until tender (1 to 2 minutes), rinse them with cold water, and then peel off the skin.

Kosher salt
1 lb. dried fettuccine
3 Tbs. extra-virgin olive oil
3 medium cloves garlic, very thinly sliced (about 1 Tbs.)
1 bunch fresh asparagus (¾ to 1 lb.), tough ends trimmed, spears cut crosswise into ¼-inch pieces and tips left whole
1 cup peeled fresh fava beans or frozen baby lima beans, thawed, rinsed, and peeled if desired
1 cup fresh or thawed frozen peas, rinsed
4 Tbs. unsalted butter, cut into 16 cubes
3 Tbs. thinly sliced fresh chives
3 Tbs. roughly chopped fresh chervil
1½ Tbs. chopped fresh tarragon
Freshly ground black pepper
1 lemon, cut into wedges
⅓ cup freshly grated Parmigiano-Reggiano

Bring a large pot of generously salted water to a boil and cook the fettuccine, stirring occasionally, until al dente, about 12 minutes.

Meanwhile, heat the olive oil in a large, wide pot, such as a Dutch oven, over medium heat. Add the garlic and cook until fragrant but not browned, about 1 minute. Add the asparagus and if using fresh fava beans or fresh peas, add them, too. Sprinkle with a pinch of salt. Cook the vegetables, stirring frequently, until barely tender, 3 to 4 minutes. If using thawed frozen lima beans and peas, add them and cook for 1 minute to warm through.

Reserve 1 cup of the pasta cooking water and then drain the fettuccine. Add the fettuccine to the vegetables, along with the butter, chives, chervil, tarragon, and ½ cup of the reserved pasta water. Toss. Season the pasta to taste with salt and pepper. The pasta should be moist, so add more of the pasta water as necessary. Serve immediately in warm bowls. Pass the lemon wedges and Parmigiano-Reggiano at the table, and invite diners to squeeze lemon juice and sprinkle cheese over their pasta.

How to Achieve Perfectly

Cooking pasta isn't difficult, but if you know a little about the science behind the cooking, you can help your pasta dishes really shine.

When you drop pasta into a pot of boiling water, starch granules on the surface of the pasta instantly swell up and then pop. The starch rushes out and suddenly the pasta's surface is sticky with this exuded starch. Eventually, most of this starch dissolves in the water and washes away. Here are a few tips that will help you manage these surface starches for perfectly cooked pasta.

Use plenty of water. This helps to prevent pasta from sticking together by quickly washing away the exuded starch. A big pot of water will also return to a boil faster after you've added the pasta.

Stir at the start. The first minute or two is the crucial period when the pasta surface is coated with sticky, glue-like starch. If you don't stir then,

Cavatelli with Arugula & Ricotta Salata

Serves four.

You can prep the ingredients for this dish in the time it takes for the pasta to boil, then just toss it together and serve. If you can't find ricotta salata, use feta and soak it for an hour in cold water before you use it.

¾ cup chopped imported black olives, such as Gaeta or Kalamata
5 Tbs. extra-virgin olive oil
1 Tbs. fresh lemon juice; more to taste
3 large cloves garlic, finely chopped
4½ tsp. fresh thyme
¼ tsp. cayenne; more to taste
Freshly ground black pepper
Kosher salt
1 lb. dried cavatelli or a similarly shaped pasta, such as castellane
1 large bunch arugula (about ½ lb.), rinsed, dried well, and coarsely chopped
1 cup (about 7 oz.) grated ricotta salata or feta

In a small bowl, whisk the olives, olive oil, lemon juice, garlic, thyme, cayenne, and black pepper to taste. Bring a large pot of well-salted water to a boil and cook the pasta until al dente. Drain the pasta well and return it to its pot. Add the arugula and the olive mixture, folding gently until the ingredients are combined. Let sit until the arugula has wilted, about 3 minutes. Sprinkle with the ricotta salata just before serving.

Cooked Pasta

the pasta can fuse together as it cooks.

Add salt, but not oil. A generous amount of salt in the water seasons the pasta internally as it absorbs liquid and swells. Pasta that's cooked in oily water won't stick together but it will become slippery and, as a result, the sauce will slide off the pasta rather than get absorbed.

Don't rinse. In addition to cooling the pasta too much, rinsing can wash off any re-maining surface starch, which at this point you don't want to do. Any surface starch that remains on the pasta is now beneficial: it can help to thicken your sauce slightly.

Toss hot pasta with hot sauce. As pasta cools, the swollen starches crystallize and become insoluble, which means the pasta can't absorb very well. So to help the pasta really soak up your flavorful sauce, be sure the sauce is warm and ready when the pasta is done.

Pasta Shells with Chickpeas, Fennel, Tomatoes & Prosciutto

Serves four.

Prosciutto can be salty, so taste it before you add the entire amount. You don't need to soak and boil dried chickpeas—canned chickpeas work just fine in this recipe.

4 salt-packed anchovies, boned and rinsed (or 8 oil-packed anchovy fillets)
16 large basil leaves, washed and thoroughly dried
4 large cloves garlic
5 Tbs. extra-virgin olive oil
Kosher salt
1 lb. medium-size ribbed pasta shells
1½ cups cooked, drained chickpeas
1 small bulb fresh fennel, trimmed and coarsely chopped (about 2 cups)
12 cherry tomatoes, cut into quarters
¼ lb. sliced prosciutto, cut into wide strips
Freshly ground black pepper
½ cup grated Parmigiano-Reggiano (optional)

Finely chop the anchovies, basil, and garlic and transfer to a small bowl. Whisk in the olive oil.

Bring a large pot of well-salted water to a boil and cook the shells. When the pasta is almost al dente, add the chickpeas to warm them. As soon as the pasta is al dente, drain it and the chickpeas well. Pour the anchovy mixture into the pot, add the pasta and chickpeas, and toss thoroughly with the fennel, tomatoes, and prosciutto. Season with pepper and let the pasta rest for 3 to 5 minutes, loosely covered. Toss with the grated Parmigiano, if using, and serve.

Fusilli with Fresh Spinach & Ricotta

Serves six.

Fusilli works best here, but a short, ridged pasta like penne rigate would also catch the sauce nicely.

Kosher salt
¾ to 1 lb. fresh spinach, stemmed, washed, and dried well
2 Tbs. extra-virgin olive oil
4 small scallions, thinly sliced
Freshly ground black pepper
1 cup ricotta cheese, preferably fresh
1 cup half-and-half or light cream
Pinch nutmeg (optional)
1 Tbs. unsalted butter
1 lb. dried fusilli
½ cup freshly grated Parmigiano-Reggiano

Bring a large pot of water to a boil; add about 1 Tbs. salt.

Stack several leaves of spinach at a time and cut them crosswise into ¼-inch strips. You should have about 8 packed cups of shredded spinach.

In a very large pan, heat the olive oil over medium-high heat. Add the scallions and cook, stirring, until softened, about 5 minutes. Stir the spinach and a pinch of salt and pepper into the pan. Cover and steam the spinach until it's wilted but still bright green, about 5 minutes, stirring as needed to cook the spinach evenly.

In a small bowl, stir the ricotta, half-and-half, and nutmeg, if using, until smooth. Stir the ricotta mixture and the butter into the spinach and season with salt and pepper. Reduce the heat to medium low and simmer for 5 minutes.

Meanwhile, cook the fusilli in the boiling water until al dente, about 12 minutes.

Reserve ½ cup of the pasta cooking water. Drain the fusilli well and return it to its pot over low heat. Add the spinach mixture and enough of the reserved cooking water to make a sauce that lightly coats the pasta. Toss thoroughly. Remove the pot from the heat and stir in the grated cheese. Transfer the pasta to a warm serving platter or individual bowls and serve.

tip: Stem spinach by folding the leaf and pulling down on the stem as you would a zipper.

Penne with Eggplant, Tomato & Basil

Serves four.

If you can get garden-fresh basil and ripe, farmers' market tomatoes, this pasta will really sing.

Kosher salt
¼ cup plus 2 Tbs. extra-virgin olive oil; more for drizzling
1 medium eggplant (1 lb.), cut into ¼-inch dice (about 6 cups)
1 small red onion, thinly sliced
¼ tsp. crushed red pepper flakes; more to taste
1¼ lb. tomatoes, seeded and cut into ½-inch chunks (about 2⅓ cups)
3 medium cloves garlic, finely chopped
1 cup roughly chopped fresh basil
¾ lb. dried penne rigate
½ cup coarsely grated Parmigiano-Reggiano or ricotta salata

Bring a large pot of well-salted water to a boil.

Heat ¼ cup of the oil in a 12-inch skillet over high heat until shimmering hot. Add the eggplant and a generous pinch of salt. Reduce the heat to medium high and cook, stirring occasionally, until the eggplant is tender and light golden brown, about 6 minutes. Transfer to a plate. Reduce the heat to medium, return the pan to the stove, and add the remaining 2 Tbs. oil, the onion, red pepper flakes, and a pinch of salt. Cook until the onion is tender and golden brown, about 6 minutes. Add the tomatoes and another pinch of salt, and cook until the tomatoes start to break down and form a sauce, about 3 minutes. Add the garlic and cook for 1 minute. Return the eggplant to the pan, add the basil, and cook for another 1 minute to let the flavors meld. Taste the sauce and add salt if needed.

Cook the penne in the boiling water until al dente. Reserve ¼ cup of the cooking water and drain the pasta. Put the penne in a large bowl and toss with the eggplant mixture. If the pasta needs a little more moisture, add a splash of the pasta water. Taste and add salt if needed. Put the pasta on a platter or divide among shallow bowls and finish with a drizzle of oil. Sprinkle the Parmigiano or ricotta salata on top and serve immediately.

Fettuccine with Arugula-Walnut Pesto

Serves four to six.

Walnut oil smooths out the peppery bite of the arugula, but you can omit it and just use more extra-virgin olive oil instead. A Caesar salad, served either with or after the pasta, is a good complement.

Kosher salt
¼ lb. arugula, washed and spun dry (about 3 lightly packed cups)
½ cup freshly grated Parmigiano-Reggiano; more for sprinkling
½ cup walnuts, toasted
2 Tbs. fresh lemon juice
1 clove garlic, smashed and peeled
½ cup extra-virgin olive oil
¼ cup walnut oil
1 lb. dried fettuccine

Bring a large pot of well-salted water to a boil over high heat.

Meanwhile, put the arugula, Parmigiano, walnuts, lemon juice, garlic, and 1 tsp. salt into a food processor, and process until the mixture is finely ground, 30 to 60 seconds. In a measuring cup, combine the olive oil and walnut oil. With the food processor running, drizzle the oil through the feed tube, and process the mixture until mostly smooth.

Cook the fettuccine in the boiling water until it's al dente, 6 to 8 minutes. Drain. In a medium bowl, toss the fettuccine with enough of the pesto to generously coat the pasta. Serve sprinkled with extra Parmigiano, if you like.

Stir-Fried Rice Noodles with Chicken, Mushrooms & Green Beans

Serves two.

This variation on pad thai (the most famous of all rice noodle stir-fries) features supermarket-friendly ingredients. Look for fish sauce and wide rice noodles, sometimes called rice sticks, in the Asian foods section.

¼ lb. wide (pad thai) rice noodles
¼ lb. green beans, cut on the diagonal into ¼-inch-thick slices (to yield 1 cup)
1 Tbs. vegetable oil
1 Tbs. minced garlic
1 boneless, skinless chicken breast half (6 to 7 oz.), cut in half lengthwise and then cut crosswise into ¼-inch slices (to yield ¾ cup)
½ tsp. kosher salt
2 Tbs. fish sauce
1 Tbs. minced fresh ginger
1 Tbs. granulated sugar
1 tsp. minced fresh red or green serrano chile
2 oz. white or cremini mushrooms, thinly sliced (to yield 1 cup)
1 Tbs. (or more) low-salt chicken broth or water, if needed
¼ cup roughly chopped fresh basil
2 Tbs. roughly chopped fresh mint leaves
1 lime, cut into wedges for serving

Submerge the rice noodles in a bowl of very warm (110°F) water and soak until they're pliable but still rather firm, about 30 minutes. (Meanwhile, you prep the rest of the ingredients.) Drain the noodles in a colander; there's no need to pat them dry.

Bring a small pot of salted water to a boil. Add the green beans and blanch until crisp-tender, 30 to 60 seconds. Drain in a colander and run under cold water to stop the cooking.

Once the noodles are drained, heat the oil in a large (12-inch) skillet or stir-fry pan over high heat until very hot. Add the garlic, stir, and immediately add the chicken. Season with the salt and stir-fry until the chicken is partially cooked, 1 to 2 minutes. Add the fish sauce, ginger, sugar, and chile and stir to combine. Add the mushrooms and stir-fry until they're limp, 1 to 2 minutes. Add the blanched green beans and noodles and stir-fry until the noodles are tender, about 1 minute. If they're too firm, add 1 Tbs. broth or water and stir-fry until the liquid is absorbed and the noodles are tender, about 1 minute. Transfer to a platter or plates, and garnish with the basil and mint. Serve immediately, with lime wedges on the side.

Farfalle with Fresh Tomato & Basil Sauce

Serves four to five.

This sauce is also great spooned over grilled shrimp, scallops, or whitefish. Or simply spread it on thick slices of grilled bread for a simple appetizer.

3 Tbs. extra-virgin olive oil
3 large cloves garlic, sliced as thinly as possible
2 lb. cherry tomatoes, rinsed and halved
Kosher salt and freshly ground black pepper
1 cup loosely packed fresh basil leaves (from about one small bunch), very thinly sliced
1 lb. dried farfalle
5 oz. ricotta salata, cut into ¼-inch dice (to yield about 1 cup); optional

In a 10- or 11-inch sauté pan, heat the oil and garlic over medium-low heat, stirring occasionally, until the garlic is softened but not browned, about 5 minutes. Add the tomatoes, 1 tsp. salt, and pepper to taste. Toss gently to coat and then raise the heat to medium. Simmer, stirring occasionally and adjusting the heat to maintain a lively but not too vigorous simmer, until the tomatoes have been reduced to a thick, pulpy sauce, 15 to 20 minutes. Remove from the heat. Sprinkle on the basil and stir to combine thoroughly.

While the sauce is cooking, bring a large pot of abundantly salted water to a vigorous boil and cook the pasta until al dente. Drain it well. Taste the sauce and adjust the seasonings if needed. Toss the pasta with three-quarters of the sauce and divide among individual serving bowls. Spoon a little of the remaining sauce over each serving and sprinkle on the cheese, if you like.

Make it
a menu

Supper on the back porch

Grilled Old Bay Shrimp with Lemony Horseradish Cocktail sauce p. 7

Farfalle with Fresh Tomato & Basil Sauce at left

Sangría Granita p. 188

Angel Hair Pasta with Lemon Cream Sauce

Serves four as a first course.

If you happen to have some grappa on hand, this fiery Italian spirit is a delicious alternative for the gin in this recipe.

Kosher salt
2 lemons
1 cup heavy cream
½ cup gin or grappa
12 oz. fresh angel hair pasta
Freshly ground black pepper
¼ cup chopped fresh flat-leaf parsley

Set a large pot of salted water over high heat and bring to a boil.

Meanwhile, finely grate the zest of one of the lemons; set aside. Cut a thick slice off both ends of the zested lemon to expose the flesh. Stand the fruit upright, then cutting from the top down, remove the peel, including all the white pith. Holding the fruit over a bowl to catch the juice, use a paring knife to cut along either side of each segment to free it from the membranes; let each segment fall into the bowl as you go. Once you've removed all the segments, squeeze any juice from the membranes into the bowl and then discard. Remove the seeds and set the segments aside in another small dish. Measure the juice in the bowl. Cut the remaining lemon in half and squeeze to obtain 2 Tbs. juice total.

In a 12-inch skillet over medium heat, combine the cream, gin or grappa, and lemon segments and bring just to a boil. Lower the heat and simmer until the cream thickens slightly, 5 to 8 minutes. Remove from the heat.

When the water boils, cook the pasta according to package directions until just al dente. Drain. Reheat the cream sauce over medium-low heat.

Add the lemon juice to the sauce, along with the drained pasta and half of the grated lemon zest. Toss the pasta in the warm sauce to coat thoroughly. Season to taste with salt and pepper. Serve in warmed pasta bowls. Sprinkle with the remaining lemon zest and the parsley.

Shells with Arugula, Feta & Sun-Dried Tomatoes

Serves four as a light main dish or eight to ten as a side dish.

If you can't find high-quality arugula (smallish leaves with no brown spots or large holes), use baby spinach instead.

Kosher salt
¼ lb. arugula, well washed and dried (stem and rip the leaves into smaller pieces if they're large)
6 oz. feta, crumbled
½ cup pitted kalamata olives (16 to 20), quartered
2 heaping Tbs. drained, thinly sliced oil-packed sun-dried tomatoes (or 8 sun-dried tomatoes, rehydrated in hot water and thinly sliced)
1 lb. dried small or medium shells or orecchiette
1 Tbs. red-wine vinegar
3 Tbs. olive oil
Freshly ground black pepper
10 fresh basil leaves, cut into thin strips

Bring a large pot of well-salted water to a boil. Put the arugula, feta, olives, and sun-dried tomatoes in a large bowl. Reserve or refrigerate until needed.

Cook the pasta in the boiling water until just tender. Meanwhile, add the vinegar and oil to the arugula salad, season liberally with salt and pepper, and toss well. Drain the pasta, add it to the salad, and toss. Check the seasonings and serve hot, warm, or at room temperature, adding the basil just before serving.

Pappardelle with Shrimp & Zucchini

Serves two to three.

This dish, in which the zucchini is sliced similarly to the shape of the pasta, is as pretty to look at as it is delicious to eat.

2 medium zucchini, washed and trimmed
6 Tbs. extra-virgin olive oil
¾ lb. large shrimp, peeled, deveined, rinsed, and patted dry
Kosher salt and freshly ground black pepper
2 cloves garlic, smashed and peeled
½ lb. dried pappardelle
¼ tsp. crushed red chile flakes
2 tsp. fresh lemon juice; more to taste
15 fresh basil leaves, torn into large pieces
2½ oz. thinly sliced prosciutto, cut crosswise into ½-inch-wide strips

Put a large pot of salted water on to boil.

Using a vegetable peeler (preferably a sharp, Y-shaped one), gently peel and discard the dark green skin of the zucchini. Pressing as hard as you can, continue to "peel" each zucchini lengthwise to make wide strips about ⅛ inch thick, rotating the zucchini as you go. Discard the squared-off seed cores.

Heat 1½ Tbs. of the oil in a large skillet over high heat. Add the shrimp, season with salt and pepper, and sauté until firm and pink, 2 to 3 minutes. Transfer the shrimp to a plate. Lower the heat to medium, add the remaining 4½ Tbs. oil and the garlic, and cook, swirling the pan, until the garlic browns and the oil is fragrant, 2 to 3 minutes.

Put the pasta in the boiling water.

Transfer all but 1 Tbs. of the oil from the skillet to a small bowl. Raise the heat under the skillet to high, add the chile flakes, and pile in the zucchini strips. Season with salt and pepper and sauté until the strips begin to soften (but don't let them turn mushy), 1 to 2 minutes. Discard the garlic cloves.

Finish cooking the pappardelle until it's just tender, about 5 minutes total. Drain and add to the shrimp, along with the zucchini, lemon juice, and reserved garlic oil. Toss gently. Stir in the basil and prosciutto, taste for salt and pepper, and serve immediately.

Bow-Tie Primavera

Serves four to six.

Because you cook the asparagus, peas, and spinach right in
the pasta cooking water with the
pasta, dinner comes together in
a snap. The tiniest bit of heavy
cream binds the flavors of this
vividly colored dish.

Kosher salt
**1 lb. dried bow-tie pasta
(farfalle)**
**¼ lb. asparagus, woody stem
ends snapped off; tips and
remaining stalk cut into
1-inch lengths**
1 cup frozen baby green peas
**10 oz. fresh spinach, stemmed
and washed**
2 cloves garlic, minced
2 Tbs. olive oil

**1 14½-oz. can diced tomatoes,
with their juices**
¼ cup heavy cream
**½ cup freshly grated Parmigiano
Reggiano; more for serving**
½ tsp. dried red chile flakes
Freshly ground black pepper

While preparing the ingredients,
bring 4 qt. water to a boil over
medium-high heat in a large pot.
Add 2 Tbs. salt and the pasta
to the boiling water. Cook the
pasta, stirring frequently, until it
starts to soften, about 7 minutes,
and then add the asparagus.
When the pasta and the asparagus are tender, add the peas and
spinach. Stir and simmer until
the spinach is wilted, about
30 seconds. Reserve ½ cup
of the pasta water and then drain
the pasta and vegetables.

Meanwhile, heat the garlic
and oil in a 10-inch skillet over
medium heat until the garlic
starts to sizzle and turn golden.
Add the tomatoes; cook until
they're thick enough to coat the
pasta, 4 to 5 minutes. Add the
cream; continue cooking until the
sauce is once again thick enough
to coat the pasta, 2 to 3 minutes.

After draining the pasta and
vegetables, return them to the
pot and add the creamy tomato
sauce, the reserved pasta cooking liquid if necessary, the Parmigiano, and chile flakes; toss
to coat. Taste and adjust the
seasonings. Serve, passing more
Parmigiano separately.

Orecchiette, Broccoli Raab & Anchovies

Serves four.

This is a classic orecchiette dish, delicious with dried pasta but even better if you can buy (or make) fresh.

Kosher salt
1 bunch broccoli raab, tough stems and outer leaves trimmed
¾ lb. orecchiette
3 whole salt-packed anchovies or 6 to 8 oil-cured anchovy fillets
¼ cup extra-virgin olive oil
1 large clove garlic, slightly crushed and peeled
Freshly ground black pepper

Bring a large pot of water to a boil. Add 1 Tbs. salt and the broccoli raab and boil until tender, 3 to 5 minutes. Remove the raab with a slotted spoon, reserving the boiling water, and run the raab under cold water to stop the cooking. Squeeze out as much of the water as possible and chop the raab coarsely. Set aside. Let the water return to a boil. Add the orecchiette and cook until tender.

Meanwhile, bone and rinse the anchovies if salt-packed or just rinse if oil-cured. Pat them dry, chop them, and set them aside. Heat 1 Tbs. of the oil in a large frying pan. Add the garlic clove and sauté until browned and fragrant; discard the clove. Add the anchovies and sauté 1 to 2 minutes, pressing with a wooden spoon to turn them into a paste.

When the pasta is cooked, drain it; add it to the pan along with the broccoli raab and remaining olive oil. Toss for about 1 minute to warm the ingredients and thoroughly coat the pasta. Serve immediately, drizzled with more olive oil, if desired, and seasoned with salt and pepper.

Cool Rice Noodle Salad with Ginger-Lime Dressing

Serves one.

While this recipe is for just one person, it can easily be doubled or tripled to serve more. Rice noodles, which you can easily find in the Asian section of the supermarket, cook up to a wonderful springy-chewy texture. They're great as part of a main-course Asian-inspired salad. You can vary the ingredients in this dish and it will still be light and refreshing. Bean sprouts or chopped mild onion will add some crunch; use one or both as well as——or in place of——the cucumber. Mint and cilantro are must-haves, but you could easily add a sprig of basil as well. Some chopped, unsalted and dry-roasted peanuts make a great garnish.

FOR THE DRESSING:
1 tsp. finely grated or very finely minced fresh ginger
1 to 2 tsp. minced fresh hot green chile, such as jalapeño or serrano
1 small clove garlic, minced
2 Tbs. fresh lime juice
1 Tbs. rice vinegar
1 Tbs. fish sauce
1½ tsp. sugar

FOR THE SALAD:
1 large or 2 smaller leaves of romaine or red leaf lettuce, chopped or torn into bite-size pieces
¼ cup thinly sliced seeded cucumber
¼ cup finely grated carrot
1 oz. thin rice vermicelli, cooked following the package directions and cooled (about 1 cup)
¼ to ½ cup fried tofu, sautéed shrimp, or leftover grilled chicken or flank steak, cooled
5 fresh mint leaves, torn
1 Tbs. coarsely chopped fresh cilantro

In a small bowl, mix the ginger, chile, garlic, lime juice, vinegar, fish sauce, and sugar. Taste and add more of any of the ingredients to get an assertive but tasty balance of flavors.

In a larger bowl, gently toss together the lettuce, cucumber, and carrot. Top with the cooked noodles, the tofu, fish or meat, and the herbs. Drizzle with the dressing and toss gently to combine.

Heat the oven to 450°F. Lightly coat a 9x13-inch (3-qt.) shallow baking dish or four individual baking dishes (about 2-cup capacity each) with olive oil. Bring a large pot of salted water to a boil. Add the asparagus and blanch until tender but with a slight bite, about 2 minutes. Scoop it from the water with a large slotted spoon, set it in a colander, and run it under cold water to preserve its green color. Drain well. Keep the water boiling for the pasta.

In a large skillet, heat the oil over medium heat. Add the scallions; sauté 1 minute to soften. Add the asparagus and sauté briefly, about 1 minute. Take the skillet off the heat and add half the zest, the lemon juice, thyme, salt, and pepper; mix well.

In a medium saucepan, heat the butter and flour over medium heat, whisking until smooth. Cook for 1 minute, whisking constantly, to cook away the raw taste of the flour. Add the milk and cook, whisking all the while, until it comes to a boil. Lower the heat a bit and cook until smooth and lightly thickened (about the consistency of heavy cream), 3 or 4 minutes.

Turn off the heat and add the mascarpone, the remaining lemon zest, and ½ cup of the Grana Padano or Parmigiano, whisking until the mixture is fairly smooth (there will be a slight grainy texture from the cheese). Season with the allspice, cayenne, salt, and pepper.

In a small bowl, combine the breadcrumbs and the remaining Grana Padano or Parmigiano. Season with salt and pepper and add a drizzle of olive oil. Mix well.

Return the cooking water to a full boil and cook the fettuccine, leaving it slightly underdone. Drain well. Return the fettuccine to the cooking pot. Add the mascarpone sauce, the pine nuts, and the asparagus with all its juices. Toss and taste for seasoning. Pour into the baking dish (or dishes) and sprinkle the breadcrumb mixture evenly over the top. Bake uncovered until bubbling and golden, 15 to 20 minutes. Serve immediately.

Baked Fettuccine & Asparagus with Lemon, Pine Nuts & Mascarpone

Serves four.

Although baked, this pasta dish still feels light due to the ample amount of lemon. Mascarpone is a rich Italian cream cheese; it usually comes in a plastic tub and is available at most supermarkets. Grana Padano is a hard Italian grating cheese similar to Parmigiano Reggiano but with a less bold flavor and a lower price. Bake this recipe in one large baking dish or in four individual ones.

2 Tbs. olive oil; more for the pan
2 lb. medium-thick asparagus, ends trimmed, cut in 1-inch pieces on an angle
8 scallions (whites and pale green parts), cut in thin rounds
Finely grated zest from 2 lemons
Juice from 1 large lemon (about ¼ cup)
A few sprigs fresh thyme or savory, leaves chopped
Kosher salt and freshly ground black pepper
1 Tbs. unsalted butter
1 Tbs. all-purpose flour
1 cup whole milk
1 cup mascarpone
1 cup grated Grana Padano or Parmigiano Reggiano
Generous pinch ground allspice
Small pinch cayenne
¾ cup fresh breadcrumbs
1 lb. fresh fettuccine
½ cup pine nuts, lightly toasted

Fettuccine with Artichokes, Hazelnuts & Cream

Serves four as a main course; eight as an appetizer.

The flavors and textures in this unusual pasta have to be tried to be believed. Although creamy, it doesn't feel heavy. A crisp salad before or after would round out the meal.

Kosher salt
2 Tbs. unsalted butter
2 Tbs. extra-virgin olive oil
1 small yellow onion, minced
4 large artichoke bottoms, halved, in lemon water
Freshly ground black pepper
1 cup homemade chicken broth (or equal parts water and low-salt chicken broth)
1 cup heavy cream
½ cup coarsely chopped toasted hazelnuts
2 Tbs. minced fresh flat-leaf parsley; more for garnish
1 lb. dried fettuccine

Put a large pot of salted water on to boil over high heat. Heat the butter and olive oil in a 12-inch skillet over moderately low heat. Add the onion and cook until softened, about 10 minutes.

Meanwhile, cut each artichoke bottom half into very thin wedges (about eight per half). Return the wedges to the lemon water. When the onion is soft, drain the artichokes and add them to the skillet. Season with salt and pepper; stir to coat. Cover and reduce the heat to low. Cook until the artichokes are tender, 20 to 30 minutes. Check occasionally to be sure they're not burning or sticking; adjust the heat accordingly and add a Tbs. or two of water if necessary to prevent burning. Add the broth, cream, hazelnuts, and 2 Tbs. parsley to the skillet and bring to a simmer over medium-high heat. Simmer until thickened slightly, 8 to 10 minutes. Taste and adjust the seasonings.

While the sauce is reducing, cook the pasta in the boiling water until al dente. Set aside 1 cup of the pasta water, drain the pasta, and return it to the warm pot. Add the sauce to the pasta and toss well. If the sauce is too thin, return the pot to medium heat and cook until the pasta absorbs most of it. If the pasta seems dry, moisten with some of the reserved pasta water. Serve immediately in warm bowls, garnishing each portion with a little more parsley.

Penne with Grilled Chicken, Portabellas & Scallions

Serves four.

Add the sliced portabellas and croutons at the last minute and toss gently so the mushrooms don't give a gray cast to the other elements in the dish.

5 fresh portabella mushrooms (4 to 5 inches in diameter), wiped clean, stems removed
1½ lb. boneless, skinless chicken breasts
16 thin scallions, trimmed
7 large ½-inch-thick slices Italian or French bread (if you're using a skinny loaf, cut on the diagonal for larger slices, or use more slices)
About ½ cup extra-virgin olive oil; more for brushing
Kosher salt and freshly ground black pepper
¼ cup finely chopped fresh flat-leaf parsley
3 large cloves garlic, finely chopped
½ lb. dried penne
Freshly grated Parmigiano Reggiano (optional)

Prepare a medium-hot charcoal fire or heat a gas grill for 20 minutes on high. Brush the mushrooms, chicken, scallions, and bread liberally with olive oil; season with salt and pepper. In a large bowl, stir the parsley, garlic, and 3 Tbs. of the olive oil. Grill the mushrooms until flattened and golden brown (15 to 25 minutes), the chicken until streaked golden brown and springy to the touch but still moist inside (10 to 12 minutes), the scallions until slightly blackened (about 5 minutes), and the bread until golden brown (about 5 minutes), turning everything as you grill.

Meanwhile, bring a large pot of well-salted water to a vigorous boil and add the pasta. Cook until al dente; drain, reserving about 1 cup of the pasta water for tossing with the pasta. Slice the grilled mushrooms and chicken thinly to about the same size as the penne; chop the scallions into ½-inch lengths. Crumble the toasted bread. Add the pasta, chicken, and scallions to the dressing in the bowl and toss. Add ¼ cup olive oil and about ½ cup of the reserved pasta water to moisten the pasta, using more or less water as needed. Finally, add the portabellas and the crumbled toasted bread. Season with salt and pepper. Serve with freshly grated Parmigiano, if you like.

Ditalini with Tomatoes, Capers & Lemon Oil

Serves eight to ten as a side dish; four as a light supper.

This is a simple version of the puttanesca sauce native to Naples, minus the anchovies. You'll have some lemon oil left over; use it in salads, salsas, or meat marinades.

Kosher salt
1 lemon
½ cup plus 1 Tbs. olive oil
2 cloves garlic, smashed
Large pinch crushed red chile flakes
1 14½-oz. can good-quality diced tomatoes, with their juices
2 heaping Tbs. drained capers, rinsed and roughly chopped
½ cup tightly packed pitted gaeta or kalamata olives, roughly chopped
1 lb. dried ditalini (or other small pasta)
Freshly ground black pepper
¼ cup thinly sliced chives

Bring a large pot of well-salted water to a boil. Using a peeler, gently skim wide strips of the zest from the lemon. Put the ½ cup olive oil in a small saucepan and set it over medium heat. When the oil is about 210°F (it should bubble lightly if you lower a strip of zest into it)——about 1 minute——add the strips of zest and then take the pot off the heat. When the oil is cool, strain it and set it aside.

Put a 10-inch skillet over medium-high heat. When the pan is hot, add the remaining 1 Tbs. olive oil; a few seconds later, add the garlic and chile flakes and cook for about 30 seconds, swirling the pan to keep them from burning. Carefully add the tomatoes, capers, and olives. Reduce the heat to medium low. Simmer until the sauce thickens and the tomatoes start to lose their form, 8 to 10 minutes. Reserve until needed.

Cook the ditalini in the boiling water until it's just tender, about 9 minutes. Drain the pasta and put it in a large bowl. Add the heated sauce and 2 Tbs. of the lemon oil and toss well (if you like a moister pasta, add more lemon oil). Taste and season well with salt and pepper. Serve hot, warm, or at room temperature, tossing in the chives just before serving.

Grilled Cherry Tomato Pasta with Crisp Breadcrumbs & Basil

Serves four to six as a light main dish or eight to ten as a side dish.

An array of differently colored tomatoes looks quite striking, but don't worry if you only have one or two colors; simply up their amounts and proceed as directed. While you can grill the tomatoes on a single skewer, sliding them onto two parallel skewers or one flat skewer makes them easier to turn.

2 cups red cherry tomatoes (about ¾ lb.)
2 cups yellow cherry tomatoes (about ¾ lb.)
2 cups orange cherry tomatoes (about ¾ lb.)
1 cup very coarse fresh breadcrumbs (made by processing a few slices of coarse bread or English muffins in the food processor)
6 Tbs. extra-virgin olive oil
Kosher salt and freshly ground black pepper
3½ to 4 Tbs. balsamic vinegar
1 lb. dried orecchiette
¾ cup roughly chopped basil leaves

Prepare a gas grill to high and a charcoal grill to medium hot.

Thread the tomatoes on two parallel skewers or one flat skewer.

Heat the oven to 375°F. Put the breadcrumbs on a rimmed baking sheet, drizzle with 2 Tbs. of the olive oil, and toss to distribute the oil evenly; season with salt and pepper. Bake in the middle of the oven, tossing occasionally, until the breadcrumbs turn golden brown, 8 to 10 minutes. Remove from the oven and let cool.

In a bowl, whisk the remaining 4 Tbs. olive oil with the balsamic vinegar. Season the vinaigrette to taste with salt and pepper.

Grill the skewered tomatoes, turning occasionally, until the skins darken and blacken in spots and begin to blister and shrivel, 5 to 7 minutes. Remove the tomatoes from the skewers and set aside.

Cook the orecchiette in boiling salted water until al dente. Drain and toss with the tomatoes and the vinaigrette, pour into a serving bowl, and garnish with the breadcrumbs and basil. Taste and season with more salt and pepper, if needed, and serve immediately.

Risotto with Spinach & Herb Pesto

Serves two as a main course.

This makes a generous amount of pesto, so use half and freeze the rest for another use or for the next time you make this risotto.

FOR THE PESTO:
¾ cup (densely packed) washed, dried, and stemmed spinach leaves
¼ cup mixed fresh flat-leaf parsley, cilantro, and tarragon leaves
¼ cup homemade or low-salt chicken broth, as needed

FOR THE RISOTTO:
3 cups homemade or low-salt chicken or vegetable broth; more if needed
3 Tbs. unsalted butter
1 cup arborio rice
½ cup diced onion
½ cup dry white wine
Kosher salt
2 Tbs. freshly grated Parmigiano Reggiano

Make the pesto: Put the spinach and herbs in a food processor or a blender. Process, adding a little broth to loosen if needed, until well combined. The pesto should resemble a very thick soup. Set aside.

Make the risotto: Bring the 3 cups broth to a boil; reduce to a simmer.

In a medium, heavy-gauge saucepan over medium-high heat, melt 2 Tbs. of the butter. Stir in the rice, toasting just until it starts to sizzle and pop, about 1 minute. It should not color. Add the onion, stirring constantly, and cook until translucent, 1 to 2 minutes. Stir in the wine. When almost all the liquid has disappeared, after about 1 minute, add just enough hot broth to cover the rice. Lower the heat to maintain a vigorous simmer; stir occasionally. When the broth is almost gone, again add enough broth to cover the rice, along with a pinch of salt. Check the risotto every 3 or 4 minutes, giving an occasional stir to make sure it isn't sticking to the bottom of the pan, adding just enough broth to cover the rice when the liquid has almost disappeared. Continue this way until the rice is just al dente, about 20 minutes total cooking time. Bite into a grain; you should see a white pin-dot in the center. Take the risotto off the heat.

Add the remaining 1 Tbs. butter. Stir in half of the pesto and the cheese, and stir vigorously for a few seconds. The risotto should be moist and creamy, not runny. Add more broth to loosen the risotto if you like, and more salt to taste, if needed. Serve immediately.

Artichoke Risotto with Lemon & Parsley

Serves six as an appetizer or a side dish; three as a main course.

The artichokes braise until tender in the same pot that will hold the risotto. This not only cuts back on the number of pots to clean, but more important, by the time the rice is cooked, the artichokes have all but melted, making the risotto exceedingly sumptuous.

4 large artichoke bottoms, halved, in lemon water
¼ cup extra-virgin olive oil
1½ cups thinly sliced leeks (white and pale green parts only), rinsed well and drained
1 large clove garlic, minced
Sea salt or kosher salt
5 to 6 cups homemade chicken broth (or equal parts low-salt broth and water); more as needed
1½ cups arborio rice
1 Tbs. minced fresh flat-leaf parsley
1 tsp. finely grated lemon zest
Freshly ground black pepper

Thinly slice each artichoke bottom half. Return the slices to the lemon water. Heat 2 Tbs. of the olive oil in a heavy, wide-based pot (like a Dutch oven) over medium-low heat. Add the leeks and garlic and cook, stirring occasionally, until the leeks are soft, about 10 minutes. Drain the artichokes and add them to the pot; season with salt and stir to coat. Cover and cook until the artichokes are tender, about 15 minutes, checking to be sure they're not burning (a little browning is good).

Meanwhile, put the broth in a medium saucepan and bring to a simmer. Adjust the heat to keep the broth at a bare simmer.

Add the rice to the artichokes and cook, stirring, for 2 minutes. Add enough broth to cover the rice and simmer gently, stirring often and adding more broth, ½ to ¾ cup at a time, when the previous addition has been absorbed. (You may not need to use all the broth, or you may need a little more.) After 18 to 20 minutes, when the rice is just al dente, cover the pot and remove it from the heat. Let stand for 3 minutes, uncover, and stir in the remaining 2 Tbs. olive oil, the parsley, lemon zest, and several grinds of pepper. Taste and adjust the seasonings, adding more broth to loosen the risotto if you like. Divide among warm bowls and serve immediately.

Contrary to popular belief, risotto doesn't need constant stirring; it's actually quite forgiving and weeknight-friendly.

Tortellini with Artichokes, Roasted Peppers & Olives
Serves four.

For an even fresher flavor, roast the peppers yourself and substitute a tablespoon of chopped fresh oregano for the dried.

- **6 Tbs. extra-virgin olive oil**
- **1 14-oz. can artichoke hearts, drained, quartered, and patted dry**
- **1 7-oz. jar roasted red peppers, drained, patted dry, and cut into ¼-inch slices**
- **1 lb. frozen cheese tortellini**
- **1 medium onion, thinly sliced**
- **1½ tsp. dried oregano**
- **12 cloves garlic, thinly sliced**
- **½ cup dry white wine**
- **½ cup kalamata olives, pitted and halved**
- **1 cup crumbled feta (about 4½ oz.)**

Put a large pot of salted water on to boil.

Heat 2 Tbs. of the oil in a large nonstick skillet over medium-high heat; add the artichoke hearts and the roasted peppers. Cook the vegetables, stirring occasionally, until they start to brown slightly, 4 to 5 minutes. Transfer to a bowl.

Put the tortellini in the boiling water and cook, stirring occasionally until tender, 7 to 8 minutes or as indicated on the package.

While the tortellini cook, heat 2 Tbs. of the oil in the same skillet used for the vegetables, and add the onion and oregano; cook, stirring occasionally, until the onion is light gold, 3 to 4 minutes. Stir in the remaining 2 Tbs. oil and the garlic; cook until the garlic is light gold, another 2 to 3 minutes. Add the wine, bring it to a boil and cook until reduced by about half, 1 to 2 minutes. If the tortellini aren't finished cooking, remove the skillet from the heat.

Drain the tortellini and add them to the skillet with the artichoke mixture and the olives; heat through, tossing over low heat until well mixed. Remove from the heat, stir in the feta, and serve.

Fettuccine with Tomatoes, Capers & Olives
Serves four.

This no-cook pasta sauce depends on juicy, flavorful tomatoes, making it a perfect recipe for late summer.

- **1½ lb. ripe tomatoes, peeled, seeded, and chopped**
- **4 cloves garlic, finely chopped**
- **1 lb. fettuccine**
- **¼ cup extra-virgin olive oil**
- **8 imported black olives, pitted and coarsely chopped**
- **8 imported green olives, preferably Cerignola olives, pitted and coarsely chopped**
- **2 Tbs. capers, rinsed; chopped if large**
- **3 Tbs. chopped flat-leaf parsley**
- **Salt and freshly ground black pepper to taste**

Toss the tomatoes and garlic together and drain them in a strainer while you continue with the recipe. Cook the fettuccine in a large pot of well-salted boiling water until al dente. Drain it well, return it to the pot, and toss it with the tomato mixture. Toss again with the olive oil, olives, capers, parsley, salt, and pepper. Let sit for 3 to 5 minutes to meld the flavors before serving.

Pasta with Peas, Arugula & Prosciutto

Serves four to six as a main course.

Sweet peas, salty prosciutto, and peppery arugula all go deliciously well together. Use a sharp vegetable peeler for the Parmigiano shavings.

- **1 lb. dried pasta, such as orecchiette or penne**
- **1 lb. arugula (about 4 small bunches)**
- **6 Tbs. unsalted butter**
- **3 cloves garlic, minced**
- **1 lb. fresh English peas, shelled, or 1 cup frozen peas, thawed**
- **Kosher salt and freshly ground black pepper**
- **3 Tbs. olive oil**
- **10 thin slices prosciutto, diced (6 to 7 oz.)**
- **2 Tbs. fresh lemon juice**
- **¼ cup freshly grated Parmigiano Reggiano; plus ¾ cup shavings for garnish**
- **2 Tbs. chopped fresh flat-leaf parsley for garnish**

Put a pot of water on to boil. Salt it well and boil the pasta following the package directions.

Meanwhile, trim, wash, and thoroughly dry the arugula; chop it coarsely and set aside. In a large saucepan over medium heat, melt 4 Tbs. of the butter. Add the garlic and sauté until barely golden, about 2 minutes. Add the peas and sauté until tender-crisp, another 3 to 4 minutes if using fresh or 1 minute if using thawed frozen. Season lightly with salt and pepper. With a slotted spoon, remove the peas and garlic from the pan and set aside. Leave as much liquid in the pan as possible and add the olive oil. Add the prosciutto and cook until very lightly browned, about 5 minutes. Add the arugula in batches, stirring and adding handfuls as it wilts. Add the lemon juice. Cook for only a few minutes, just until all the greens have wilted.

When the pasta is done, reserve 1 cup of the cooking water and drain the pasta. In a large bowl, toss the pasta with the peas, prosciutto, arugula, and grated Parmigiano, along with ½ cup of the reserved cooking water. Season with more ground pepper; toss. Taste and adjust the seasonings, if needed. If the pasta seems dry, toss with more of the reserved cooking water. To serve, garnish each portion with the parsley and the Parmigiano shavings.

tip: Choose arugula leaves based on what you plan to do with them. For salads, look for the smallest and mildest leaves. More mature leaves, which are a darker green and lobed, have a spicier flavor that is perfect for cooking.

garlic, remaining 6 Tbs. peanut oil, sesame oil, soy sauce, vinegar, sugar, and chile paste to the sesame seeds in the blender. Blend on high speed just until a thick, rough paste forms, 2 to 3 minutes. Stop blending when most of the seeds have broken up and been puréed. After the paste forms, it will begin to get oily if you continue to purée it, as the seeds begin to give off their oil. Refrigerate the purée (for up to a day).

Cook and dress the noodles: Bring a large pot of unsalted water to a rolling boil. Gently fluff the noodles and add them to the water, stirring. Return the water to a boil and cook the noodles for just 10 to 30 seconds. (These tiny fresh noodles don't need much cooking.) Drain the noodles immediately and cool them under cold running water. Drain well. Put the cold noodles in a bowl and toss with the peanut oil.

Assemble: When ready to dress the noodles, remove the purée from the refrigerator. Drain off any oil that has gathered on the top. Whisk about ¾ cup water into the purée to thin it and to reach a creamy consistency; the sauce will lighten in color and become emulsified; add more water as needed. Add the chopped cilantro to the sauce.

In a large bowl, toss the noodles with about half the dressing. Add the snow peas, red pepper, and daikon, and toss to combine (using your hands is easiest). Add more dressing, if you like. Put the noodles in a large serving bowl or on individual plates. Garnish with the cilantro leaves, chopped peanuts, and sliced scallions, or pass little bowls of the garnishes at the table.

Cold Sesame Noodles
Serves six as a main dish or eight to ten as a side dish.

Making the sesame purée at least several hours ahead lets the flavors marry beautifully—but whisk in the water just before assembling the dish.

FOR THE SESAME DRESSING:
¾ cup plus 1 Tbs. sesame seeds
7 Tbs. peanut oil
2 large shallots, sliced
1 large clove garlic, finely chopped
1 Tbs. toasted sesame oil
2 Tbs. soy sauce
¼ cup rice vinegar
¼ cup sugar
1 tsp. hot chile paste
¾ to 1 cup water
2 Tbs. chopped fresh cilantro leaves

FOR THE NOODLES:
12 oz. fresh Chinese egg noodles (also called wonton noodles)
3 Tbs. peanut oil
1 cup blanched snow peas, thinly sliced
1 red bell pepper, thinly sliced
1 cup thinly sliced daikon radish
1 cup fresh cilantro leaves
½ cup chopped peanuts
1 cup thinly sliced scallions

Make the dressing: Heat the oven to 350°F. Put the sesame seeds on a baking sheet and toast them in the oven until golden brown and fragrant, 15 to 20 minutes. Be careful not to overcook them. Put the toasted seeds in a blender.

In a skillet, heat 1 Tbs. of the peanut oil over medium-low heat. Sauté the shallots and garlic until softened, 3 to 5 minutes. Set aside to cool. Add the shallots,

Fettuccine Primavera

Serves six.

This quintessential springtime pasta includes lots and lots of fresh herbs, as well as leafy greens. The specific vegetables and herbs used are up to you; choose what looks best at the market.

Kosher salt
1 lb. fettuccine
2 Tbs. unsalted butter, cut into chunks
2 cloves garlic, minced
3 cups very thinly sliced mixed spring vegetables, such as asparagus (leave tips whole), baby carrots, baby leeks, baby turnips, baby zucchini, spring onions, and sugar snap peas
1 cup whole, shelled fresh or thawed frozen peas, baby lima beans (preferably peeled), or fava beans (peeled); or a mix of all
1 cup heavy cream
1 Tbs. thinly sliced lemon zest (remove zest with a vegetable peeler and thinly slice)
2 cups loosely packed pea shoots, watercress sprigs, or baby arugula
½ cup freshly grated Parmigiano Reggiano
½ cup roughly chopped mixed fresh herbs such as basil, chervil, chives, mint, parsley, and tarragon
¼ tsp. crushed red pepper flakes
Freshly ground black pepper
¼ cup toasted pine nuts

Bring a large pot of generously salted water to a boil and cook the fettuccine, stirring occasionally, until al dente, about 6 minutes. (While pasta is cooking, scoop out 1½ cups of pasta cooking water.)

Meanwhile, melt the butter in a 10-inch straight-sided sauté pan over medium heat. Add the garlic and cook until softened and fragrant but not browned, about 1 minute. Add 1 cup of the reserved pasta water. Add the sliced vegetables and peas or lima beans (if using fresh). Cover and simmer until the vegetables are just tender, about 3 minutes. Add the cream and lemon zest along with any fava beans or thawed, frozen peas or lima beans (if using). Bring to a simmer.

Drain the fettuccine and return it to its cooking pot. Toss with the vegetables and cream sauce, pea shoots (or watercress or arugula), Parmigiano, all but 1 Tbs. of the herbs, and the pepper flakes. Season to taste with salt and pepper. If necessary, adjust the consistency of the sauce with the reserved ½ cup pasta water; the sauce should generously coat the vegetables and pasta. Serve immediately, sprinkled with the remaining fresh herbs and the pine nuts.

Barley Risotto with Mushrooms & Gremolata

Serves four as a main course; six as a side dish or appetizer.

When cooked as a risotto, barley develops a rich and creamy consistency. The parsley, lemon, and garlic garnish is a fresh, simple accent to the risotto's nutty, robust flavors.

FOR THE GREMOLATA:
⅓ cup chopped fresh flat-leaf parsley
2 Tbs. grated lemon zest
1 Tbs. finely chopped garlic

FOR THE RISOTTO:
1 oz. dried porcini mushrooms, rinsed
1 cup hot water
2 Tbs. olive oil
1 lb. assorted fresh mushrooms, sliced ¼ inch thick
2 tsp. coarse salt; more to taste
Freshly ground black pepper
6 to 7 cups homemade or low-salt canned chicken or vegetable broth
3 Tbs. unsalted butter
1 small onion, finely chopped
2 cups pearled barley

Make the gremolata: In a small bowl, mix together the parsley, lemon zest, and garlic.

Make the risotto: Soak the porcini in the hot water for at least 30 minutes. Strain the liquid through a fine sieve and reserve. Chop the porcini into small pieces.

In a large sauté pan with straight sides, heat the oil over high heat until shimmering but not smoking. Sauté the sliced fresh mushrooms until they release some liquid and are browned, about 5 minutes. Stir in the porcini and the reserved liquid, scraping up any browned bits. Season to taste with salt and pepper. Transfer the mushrooms and liquid to a bowl.

In a saucepan, bring the broth to a boil, reduce the heat, partially cover, and hold at a simmer.

In the pan used for the mushrooms, melt the butter over medium heat. Add the onion and cook until tender and translucent, 8 to 10 minutes. Add 2 tsp. coarse salt and the barley, and stir until the grains are coated with butter. Add 1 cup of the hot broth, reduce the heat to low, and stir frequently until the broth is absorbed. Stir in another cup of broth. Once it's absorbed, add 1 more cup, stirring until it's also absorbed. Add 2 more cups and simmer the barley, stirring frequently, until it softens but isn't completely tender and the liquid is almost absorbed, about 10 minutes. Stir in the cooked mushrooms and their liquid and 1 to 2 more cups of broth. Simmer until the barley is tender, about 10 minutes more, stirring frequently and adding hot water or broth if needed.

The total cooking time for the barley can range from 30 to 60 minutes.

Stir in the gremolata and adjust the seasonings to taste. Serve hot.

Risotto with Peas, Mint & Lemon

Serves four as a main course or six as a side dish.

Fresh mint brightens the flavors of this simple rice dish. Do keep in mind that the better the quality of your chicken broth, the better tasting your risotto will be.

5 to 6 cups homemade or low-salt canned chicken broth
4 Tbs. unsalted butter
1 medium onion, cut into ¼-inch dice
Kosher salt
2 cups arborio rice (or other risotto rice)
½ cup dry white wine (like Pinot Grigio)
2 cups frozen peas
⅓ cup chopped fresh mint
2 Tbs. fresh lemon juice
1 Tbs. finely grated lemon zest
¼ cup freshly grated Parmigiano Reggiano; more for serving

Heat the chicken broth in a saucepan over medium-high heat until very hot and then reduce the heat to keep the broth hot. In another wide, heavy saucepan, melt 2 Tbs. of the butter over medium heat. Add the onion and a generous pinch of salt and sauté, stirring occasionally with a wooden spoon, until the onion softens and starts to turn lightly golden, 3 to 5 minutes. Add the rice and stir until the grains are well coated with butter and the edges become translucent, 1 to 2 minutes. Pour in the wine and stir until it's absorbed, about 1 minute. Add another generous pinch of salt and ladle enough of the hot broth into the pan to barely cover the rice, about 1 cup. Bring to a boil and then adjust the heat to maintain a lively simmer. Cook, stirring occasionally, until the broth has been mostly absorbed, 2 to 3 minutes. Continue adding broth in ½-cup increments, stirring and simmering, until it has been absorbed each time, at intervals of about 2 to 3 minutes.

After about 16 to 18 minutes, the rice should be creamy but still fairly firm. At this point, add the peas and another ½ cup broth. Continue to simmer and stir until the peas are just cooked and the rice is just tender to the tooth, another 3 to 4 minutes. Stir in another splash of broth if the risotto is too thick. Remove the pot from the heat and stir in the mint, lemon juice, lemon zest, the remaining 2 Tbs. butter, and the Parmigiano. Season with salt to taste. Serve the risotto immediately with a sprinkling of Parmigiano.

tip: Try experimenting with risotto rice varieties other than arborio, such as vialone nano and carnaroli.

Grilled Shiitakes with Mojo Oriental & Somen Noodles

Serves four as a light dinner.

A mojo is traditionally a boldly seasoned vinaigrette-type sauce, heated to infuse its flavors. Though usually associated with Caribbean and Latin American cuisine, this version deliciously incorporates Asian ingredients.

16 large shiitake caps, cut into quarters (or 32 smaller shiitake caps, cut in half)
¼ cup whole cumin seeds
½ tsp. Sichuan peppercorns (optional)
2 cups homemade or low-salt canned chicken broth
¼ cup toasted sesame oil
¼ cup honey
¼ cup soy sauce
¼ cup rice-wine vinegar
¼ cup minced fresh ginger
½ habanero chile, seeded

FOR THE SOMEN NOODLES:
8 oz. dried somen noodles (or dried capellini)
1 Tbs. toasted sesame oil
Minced garlic chives or chives for garnish (optional)
Black and white sesame seeds for garnish (optional)

Thread the shiitake caps on eight short wooden skewers. Arrange the skewers in a shallow, nonreactive pan.

To make the mojo, toast the cumin and peppercorns (if using) in a dry saucepan over medium-high heat until they're quite aromatic. Grind them in a spice or coffee grinder and return them to the pan. Add the broth, sesame oil, honey, soy sauce, vinegar, ginger, and habanero. Bring to a boil and reduce to a simmer.

After 5 minutes, remove the habanero; continue to simmer the sauce until it's reduced to 1½ cups, about another 10 minutes. Remove from the heat and strain the sauce through a fine sieve; let cool slightly. Pour the mojo over the shiitake skewers; let sit at room temperature for 30 minutes to 2 hours.

Light a grill or broiler. Remove the skewers from the mojo, letting any excess drip back into the pan. Transfer the mojo to a nonreactive saucepan and simmer until reduced to about ½ cup. Meanwhile, grill or broil the shiitakes until well-browned, 3 to 6 minutes.

Boil the somen noodles until just al dente (about 1 minute after the water comes back to a boil), drain well, and toss with the sesame oil. Mound the noodles in four shallow bowls, top with the grilled shiitake skewers, and drizzle with the reduced mojo.

Risotto with Corn, Tomatoes & Basil

Serves three as a main dish or six as a side dish.

Here's a risotto that's like eating summer in a bowl.

4 cups low-salt chicken broth
3 ears corn, shucked and cleaned of any silk
2 Tbs. unsalted butter or olive oil
1 shallot or small onion, minced
1 cup arborio rice (or other risotto rice)
⅓ cup dry white wine
1 cup chopped plum or cherry tomatoes
2 tsp. extra-virgin olive oil
3 Tbs. torn fresh basil leaves
Kosher salt and freshly ground black pepper
⅓ cup freshly grated Parmigiano Reggiano

Heat the broth in a pot or saucepan large enough to fit the corn over medium-low heat to just below a simmer. Simmer the corn in the broth for 4 minutes and transfer to a plate; reserve the broth and keep it hot. Using a chef's knife, slice the corn kernels off the cob into a large bowl (see instructions on p. 217); you should have about 1¼ cups.

In a heavy-based deep skillet or wide saucepan, melt the butter (or heat the oil) over medium heat. Add the shallot or onion and cook, stirring occasionally, until it's translucent, about 2 minutes. Add the rice and stir until the grains are well coated with butter or oil. Pour in the wine, stir, and cook until the wine is absorbed, about 1 minute.

Ladle in about 1½ cups of the hot broth, and cook, stirring occasionally, until absorbed, 3 to 5 minutes. Continue adding broth in ½-cup increments, stirring and simmering until it's absorbed each time, at intervals of about 3 to 5 minutes.

While the rice is simmering, combine the tomatoes, extra-virgin olive oil, and 2 Tbs. of the basil in a small bowl. Season with salt and pepper and set aside.

When the rice is just barely tender, after about 16 minutes, stir in the corn. Continue adding more stock and stirring until the rice is creamy but still firm to the tooth, 20 to 25 minutes total. Remove from the heat, fold in the Parmigiano and then the tomato-basil mixture. Top each serving with the remaining basil and serve immediately.

Luxurious Four-Cheese Macaroni & Cheese

Serves eight as a main course.

Kosher salt
3 cups whole milk
4 Tbs. unsalted butter
1 medium onion, finely diced (about 1 cup)
1 bay leaf
¼ cup all-purpose flour
Pinch freshly grated nutmeg
¼ tsp. Tabasco sauce; more to taste
Freshly ground black pepper
5 oz. Gruyère, coarsely grated (about
   1¾ cups lightly packed)
½ lb. blue cheese (such as Maytag Blue),
   crumbled (about 2 cups)
1 lb. dried penne rigate pasta
1 Tbs. finely grated lemon zest
11 oz. Monterey Jack, cut into ½-inch dice
   (2 cups)
½ cup chopped fresh flat-leaf parsley
2 Tbs. fresh thyme leaves
2½ oz. Parmigiano-Reggiano, freshly grated
   (scant 1 cup)
¾ cup fresh breadcrumbs

Heat the oven to 350°F. Put a large pot of well-salted water on to boil.

Heat the milk in a small saucepan over medium-low heat to just below a simmer. Remove from the heat and cover to keep hot. Melt the butter in a medium saucepan over medium-low heat. Add the onion and bay leaf. Cook, stirring occasionally, until the onion starts to soften, about 5 minutes. Add the flour and cook, stirring, for 2 minutes. Gradually whisk in the hot milk, bring to a simmer, and cook for 10 minutes, whisking frequently, until thickened and smooth. Season with 1 tsp. salt, the nutmeg, the Tabasco, and pepper to taste. Remove and discard the bay leaf. Stir in the Gruyère and blue cheese.

Cook the pasta in the boiling water to al dente, following the package directions. Drain well and return to the pot. Toss the lemon zest and half of the Monterey Jack into the pasta while it's still hot; add the cheese sauce and quickly toss to combine. Stir in the parsley and thyme and transfer half of the pasta to a large (3-qt.) shallow casserole or lasagna pan. Sprinkle with the remaining Monterey Jack and half of the Parmigiano; top with the remaining pasta. Sprinkle with the remaining Parmigiano and the breadcrumbs. Bake until bubbling and golden, 50 to 60 minutes. Let rest for 5 to 10 minutes before serving.

**Seared Scallops with Spicy Red
Pepper & Cilantro Sauce** *p. 118*

Seafood

Grilled Shrimp "Margarita" with Avocados & Garden Tomatoes

Serves four to six as an appetizer or light meal.

For a dish that includes lime, tequila, and salt, margarita glasses are an obvious and fun choice for serving.

1 lb. large shrimp in the shell (about 24), thawed completely if frozen and blotted dry
2 Tbs. olive oil
¼ cup good-quality tequila
¼ cup fresh lime juice
¼ cup fresh orange juice
2 Tbs. tomato ketchup
2 Tbs. green Tabasco or other jalapeño hot sauce
Kosher salt and freshly ground black pepper
2 cups diced ripe garden or heirloom tomatoes, drained (from about 3 medium tomatoes)
2 medium to large ripe avocados, peeled, pitted, and diced
1 bunch scallions (green tops only), thinly sliced
1 small white onion, finely diced (optional)
Lime wedges for garnish
Coarse sea salt (optional)
Saltine crackers

Heat a gas grill to medium high or prepare a medium-hot charcoal fire. (If using charcoal, be sure the grate is hot, too.) Put the shrimp in a large bowl and mix with the olive oil until well coated. Put the shrimp on the grate directly over the heat and grill until pink and almost cooked through, 4 to 5 minutes, turning once halfway through. Let cool completely.

An hour before serving, whisk together the tequila, lime juice, orange juice, ketchup, and green Tabasco. Peel and devein the shrimp, cut them into large pieces (about ½ inch), and toss with the tequila mixture. Cover and refrigerate for 1 hour. Just before serving, season the shrimp mixture with salt and pepper. (Alternatively, omit the kosher salt at this stage and sprinkle on a coarse sea salt like fleur de sel just before serving.) Gently fold in the tomatoes, avocados, and scallions, mixing well. Using a slotted spoon, portion the mixture into individual serving bowls or margarita glasses. Garnish with a sprinkling of onion (if using), a wedge of lime, and the optional sea salt. Serve immediately with the crackers.

Salt-Seared Snapper with Melon, Mint & Watercress Salad

Serves four as a first course.

Fish cooked with salt doesn't taste salty, just well seasoned. The salt helps keep the fish moist and allows you to cook it without adding fat to the pan. Shrimp makes a good substitute for the snapper.

2 cups loosely packed watercress leaves, well washed and dried
1½ cups diced cantaloupe or other melon, or a mix
1 cup loosely packed fresh mint leaves
1 tsp. kosher salt
½ lb. red snapper fillet, cut into four pieces
⅓ cup plus 1 Tbs. lemon juice
½ tsp. sugar

Portion the watercress, melon, and mint among four salad plates, reserving some of the watercress for a garnish.

In a frying pan, sprinkle the salt evenly over the surface of the pan and heat over high heat until very hot. Add the snapper and cook about 1 minute. Turn, add 3 Tbs. of the lemon juice, and cover the pan. Reduce the heat to low and cook until the fish is lightly browned, about another 2 minutes.

Dissolve the sugar in the remaining lemon juice. Divide the fish and pan juices among the plates and drizzle with the sweetened lemon juice. Garnish with the reserved watercress and serve.

Roasted Cod with Basil Pesto & Garlic Breadcrumbs

Serves four; pesto yields about 2/3 cup.

If you have the pesto already made and on hand—it keeps in the fridge for about three days and can be frozen as well—this dish comes together in minutes.

FOR THE PESTO:
4 cups lightly packed fresh basil leaves (from about 1 large bunch)
1/3 cup toasted pine nuts
1/4 cup lightly packed fresh flat-leaf parsley leaves
1 small clove garlic
Kosher salt and freshly ground black pepper
1/4 cup extra-virgin olive oil

FOR THE COD:
1 large ripe tomato, cored and very thinly sliced (about 1/8 inch)
Kosher salt and freshly ground black pepper
2 Tbs. extra-virgin olive oil
1 1/2 cups coarse fresh white breadcrumbs (from about 4 slices of bread, trimmed of crusts and pulsed in a food processor)
1 small clove garlic, minced
1 1/2 lb. cod or haddock, rinsed, patted dry, and cut into 4 even portions

Make the pesto: Put the basil, pine nuts, parsley, garlic, 1/2 tsp. salt, and 1/8 tsp. pepper in a food processor. With the machine on, slowly pour the olive oil into the feed tube and process, stopping to scrape the bowl as needed, until the mixture is very finely chopped and paste-like. Season to taste with salt, if you like. Keep covered in the refrigerator for up to three days.

To assemble the dish: Heat the oven to 450°F. Spread the tomato slices on a large plate and season with 1/4 tsp. salt and a few grinds of black pepper. Heat a large sauté pan over medium heat for 1 minute.

Pour in the olive oil, add the breadcrumbs, and season with 1/4 tsp. salt. Cook, stirring, until the breadcrumbs start to turn a light golden brown, about 4 minutes. Add the garlic and continue to cook, stirring, for another 1 minute. Transfer to a bowl.

Set the fish on a large rimmed baking sheet lined with foil. Season with salt and pepper. Divide the pesto evenly over the fish and top each with two or three tomato slices and the breadcrumbs. Roast until the fish is opaque on the sides and starts to flake, about 10 minutes. Serve immediately.

Don't rely on sight alone to choose the freshest fish. Ask to smell it before buying; good fish should not smell "fishy."

Flounder Fillets with Bacon, Red Onion & Citrus over Wilted Spinach

Serves four.

Serve the flounder with small boiled red potatoes, a salad, and good bread.

4 flounder fillets, 6 to 7 oz. each
2 oranges
2 grapefruit
8 slices lean bacon, diced into ¼-inch pieces
½ tsp. kosher salt
¼ tsp. ground white pepper
1 large or 2 medium red onions, sliced as thinly as possible
1 Tbs. chopped fresh tarragon
1 to 1¼ lb. fresh spinach, washed and drained

Trim the edges of the flounder to remove any traces of skin. Prepare the oranges and grapefruit by cutting away the rind and pith and then cutting the individual segments away from the membrane. Put into a bowl and set aside. Sauté the bacon slowly in a heavy skillet until golden and crisp, stirring occasionally. Drain on paper towels and set aside. Reserve the bacon fat for cooking the fish and spinach later.

Using the same heavy skillet, heat 2 Tbs. of the reserved bacon fat over high heat. Lightly season the fillets with salt and pepper and put them in the hot skillet. Sear well on one side, about 1 minute, and then turn them. Sprinkle the sliced onion around the fish. Add the fruit segments and their juices, the

bacon, and the tarragon. Cover with a tight-fitting lid. Remove from the heat and let steam for 5 to 6 minutes, depending on the thickness of the fillet.

Meanwhile, in another skillet, heat another 2 Tbs. of the reserved bacon fat over medium-high heat. (If you run out of bacon fat, supplement with vegetable oil.) Once the fat is hot, add the spinach. Toss it with a spatula just until the spinach is warm and has begun to wilt.

Portion the spinach onto warm plates. By this time, the flounder should be done. Lay the fillets on the spinach and arrange the fruit segments and onions over the fish. Spoon the bacon, tarragon, and pan juices over each portion.

Herb & Lemon Roasted Salmon on a Bed of Roasted Potatoes & Sautéed Greens

Serves six.

Celebrate the arrival of spring with this wonderful salmon dish. Although it may seem like there are a lot of steps, this one recipe takes care of the entire dinner. A couple of the elements can also be made ahead, and the recipe includes timing information. To highlight the lemon flavor, a little lemon oil gets drizzled on the salmon just before serving. Don't skip this step: It really pulls the flavors of the dish together.

FOR THE LEMON OIL:
½ cup good-quality extra-virgin olive oil
Finely grated zest of 1 lemon

FOR THE FISH, POTATOES, AND GREENS:
1½ cups olive oil, plus 2 Tbs. for sautéing the greens
3 Tbs. coarsely grated lemon zest
2 Tbs. chopped fresh flat-leaf parsley
2 Tbs. fresh thyme
2 Tbs. chopped garlic
6 skinless salmon fillets, 6 oz. each
2 lb. medium red or yellow potatoes (or 1 lb. each)
Kosher salt and coarsely ground black pepper
12 to 14 whole unpeeled cloves garlic, roasted
½ cup pine nuts, toasted
12 cups packed arugula, about 20 oz. (tough stems removed), or two 10-oz. bags spinach (stems removed), washed well and dried

Up to three days ahead, make the lemon oil: Combine the extra-virgin olive oil with the lemon zest. Cover and store in the refrigerator.

Up to one day ahead, marinate the salmon: Combine the olive oil, lemon zest, parsley, thyme, and the fresh chopped garlic. Preferably the night before or at least 1 hour before cooking, cover the salmon with about 1 cup of the marinade and refrigerate. Store the remaining marinade separately in the refrigerator.

An hour before serving, cook the potatoes: Heat the oven to 425°F. Slice the potatoes 3/16 inch thick. (Cut through the shortest width of the potato; discard the ends.) Make sure there are eight slices per person (48 slices total). Rub a rimmed baking sheet with a little oil. Lay eight potato slices in two slightly overlapping lines about 5 to 6 inches long and a total of 4 inches wide. Repeat with the remaining potatoes to make six separate beds for the salmon, spaced about an inch apart. Season the potatoes with plenty of salt and pepper and drizzle them with some of the remaining lemon-herb marinade. Cook until the potatoes are tender and beginning to turn golden brown, 30 to 35 minutes. Set the potatoes, still on the baking sheet, aside. Reduce the oven temperature to 400°F.

Meanwhile, coarsely chop the roasted garlic. Arrange the 2 Tbs. olive oil, roasted garlic, pine nuts, and washed greens next to the stove and put a large sauté pan on a burner. Take the salmon out of the refrigerator and let it come to room temperature.

About 20 minutes before serving, roast the salmon: Lift the salmon out of the marinade, letting excess oil drain off but leaving the herbs on the salmon undisturbed. Put a fillet on top of each bed of potatoes on the baking sheet. Season generously with salt and pepper. Put the pan in the oven and cook 12 to 14 minutes for medium-rare salmon or 16 minutes for medium. Set aside and let rest in a warm place before serving.

While the salmon is resting, heat the sauté pan over medium to medium high, add the olive oil, pine nuts, and chopped roasted garlic, and simmer for 1 minute. Add the arugula or spinach, season with salt and pepper, and cook until just wilted, 1 to 3 minutes, tossing with tongs constantly to mix the ingredients. (Add the greens in batches, if necessary; when the first batch wilts, add the next and toss.)

To serve: Using tongs, spread the arugula loosely on the bottom of each plate, almost in a ring. Carefully slide a spatula under one of the beds of potatoes, lift the potatoes and salmon together, and set them in the center of the plate over the greens. Drizzle a generous 1 tsp. lemon oil over all. Repeat with the remaining salmon. Serve immediately.

tip: Leftover lemon oil is excellent in vinaigrettes and delicious drizzled over steamed vegetables.

Scallops with Spinach, Lime & Candied Walnuts

Serves four to six.

Dry, untreated scallops retain less water and so brown better and have more flavor; ask before buying. This dish is delicious with Savoy spinach, a wrinkled variety with a great spring taste.

2 lb. sea scallops, preferably "dry" ones
1 lime
Extra-virgin olive oil
4 tsp. finely chopped garlic
1 tsp. finely chopped shallot
1 tsp. Dijon mustard
Kosher salt and freshly ground black pepper
¼ cup coarsely chopped walnuts
1 tsp. sugar
1½ lb. spinach leaves, preferably Savoy, well washed and dried

If the scallops still have a little muscle attached to the side, remove it. If the scallops are very large, cut them in half horizontally. Finely grate enough of the lime to get 1 tsp. of zest. In a bowl or zip-top bag large enough to hold the scallops, combine the zest, the juice from half of the lime, 1 Tbs. olive oil, 2 tsp. of the garlic, the shallot, the mustard, and a few grinds of pepper. Add the scallops, toss to coat, and refrigerate for 20 minutes and up to 1 hour.

Meanwhile, in a small nonstick pan over medium heat, cook the nuts and sugar, stirring, until the sugar melts and coats the nuts, about 2 minutes. Carefully transfer the hot nuts to a plate to cool.

Heat a large skillet over medium-high heat and brush it with a little oil. Remove the scallops from the marinade and pat them dry with paper towels. Season them with a little salt and sear them without moving them until nicely browned on one side, about 2 minutes. Flip them over and sear the other side. (Sear the scallops in batches, if necessary, to avoid crowding the pan.) Transfer the cooked scallops to a clean bowl. Return the pan to the hot stove without cleaning it. Squeeze the juice from the remaining lime half into the pan and scrape up any browned bits with a wooden spoon. Pour the juices and the browned bits over the scallops. Set the scallops aside and keep warm.

Wipe the pan clean. Add about ½ Tbs. olive oil to the pan and heat it over medium heat. Add the remaining garlic and cook until lightly browned. Add the spinach and stir briefly until wilted. Season to taste with salt and pepper.

To serve, divide the spinach among serving plates. Arrange a portion of the scallops with their accumulated juices on the spinach and top with the walnuts.

tip: Use high heat to sear fish. The golden-brown crust that results adds a ton of flavor and a great texture.

Swordfish with Red Pepper, Cucumber & Mint

Serves four.

The chopped vegetables that dress up this fish have a lively sweet-sour flavor. Great with swordfish, they can also be served with other fish, as well as grilled chicken or pork.

1 medium cucumber, peeled, seeded, and diced
Kosher salt
2 Tbs. olive oil
1 small onion, diced
2 cloves garlic, minced
1 large red bell pepper, roasted, peeled, seeded, and diced (for method, see p. 213)
1 Tbs. white-wine vinegar
1 tsp. sugar
Pinch cayenne
Pinch ground cinnamon
5 sprigs fresh mint, leaves chopped; more whole sprigs for garnish
2 Tbs. unsalted butter
4 swordfish steaks, about 4 oz. each

Toss the cucumber slices with about ½ tsp. salt and let drain in a colander for at least 20 minutes. In a large frying pan, heat the olive oil over medium-high heat. Toss in the onion and cook until it just starts to brown, about 10 minutes. Add the garlic and cook about another 1 minute. Stir in the cucumber and cook for 3 minutes. Stir in the roasted red bell pepper, vinegar, sugar, cayenne, cinnamon, and salt to taste. Cook until the liquid has evaporated, 3 to 5 minutes. Add the chopped mint leaves. Transfer to a bowl.

In the same frying pan, melt the butter over medium-high heat. Sprinkle the swordfish steaks with salt and put them in the pan. Cook until browned on one side, about 5 minutes. Turn the fish over and continue cooking until done, about 3 minutes longer. If there's excess oil in the pan, drain some of it off.

Transfer the fish to warm plates or a platter. Return the vegetable sauce to the pan to heat it through and to absorb the swordfish cooking juices. Spoon the cucumber sauce over the swordfish steaks and decorate with fresh mint leaves, if you like. Serve immediately.

Seared Scallops with Spicy Red Pepper & Cilantro Sauce
Serves two to three.

This is more like a flavorful coating than a sauce; you'll have just enough liquid to moisten the scallops as you roll them around in the pan. Be sure to buy "dry" scallops, which means that they haven't been soaked in a sodium solution.

FOR THE SCALLOPS:
1 lb. large "dry" sea scallops
2 Tbs. extra-virgin olive oil
Kosher salt and freshly ground black pepper

FOR THE SAUCE:
2 Tbs. extra-virgin olive oil
1 Tbs. minced garlic (2 large cloves)
1 fresh serrano chile or small jalapeño, cored, seeded, and minced
½ small red bell pepper, finely diced (about ⅓ cup)
1 Tbs. fresh lime juice
2 heaping Tbs. coarsely chopped cilantro
Kosher salt and freshly ground black pepper

Cook the scallops: If you feel any grit on the scallops, rinse them under cold water. Remove patches of tough muscle from the sides. Pat the scallops dry with paper towels.

Heat a 10- or 12-inch nonstick skillet over medium-high heat for 1 to 2 minutes. Pour in the oil and heat until quite hot. Pat the scallops dry once more and put them in the pan in a single, uncrowded layer. Season with salt and pepper and let sear undisturbed until one side is browned and crisp, 2 to 4 minutes. Using tongs, turn the scallops and sear until the second side is well browned and the scallops are almost firm to the touch, 2 to 4 minutes. Take the pan off the heat, transfer the scallops to a plate, and set them in a warm spot. Let the pan cool for a minute before you make the sauce.

Make the sauce: Return the pan to medium heat. Add the oil, garlic, and chile and sauté until fragrant, about 30 seconds. Add the bell pepper and sauté, stirring often, until the pepper is barely soft, about 1 minute. Add the lime juice and simmer to reduce slightly, 30 to 60 seconds. Stir in the cilantro. Reduce the heat to low and return the scallops and any accumulated juices to the pan. Gently roll the scallops around to coat them in the sauce and to warm them through. Taste for salt and pepper and serve immediately.

Stir-Fried Shrimp with Mango & Jalapeño-Mint-Ginger Sauce
Serves four.

You can omit the lettuce wrap for this dish and simply serve the shrimp with the garnishes.

2 lb. shrimp (26 to 30 per lb.), peeled, deveined, and rinsed
1 large bunch fresh mint, leaves picked
6 Tbs. seeded and chopped fresh jalapeños (4 to 6)
3 medium cloves garlic, thinly sliced
1 heaping Tbs. chopped fresh ginger
1 heaping Tbs. granulated sugar
6 Tbs. distilled white vinegar
1 Tbs. fish sauce (optional)
12 large leaves Boston lettuce or other soft lettuce
About 1 cup soybean sprouts or other fresh sprouts for garnish
About ½ cup fresh cilantro sprigs for garnish
1 large ripe mango, peeled and sliced, for garnish
2 Tbs. vegetable oil
Kosher salt and freshly ground black pepper

Dry the shrimp well with paper towels and set aside.

Measure a generous ½ cup mint leaves, somewhat loosely packed, and put them in a blender (or a mini food processor). Reserve the remaining mint leaves for garnish. To the blender, add the jalapeños, garlic, ginger, sugar, vinegar, and fish sauce (if using). Purée the ingredients until the mixture is smooth, scraping the sides once or twice, about 3 minutes. Set the dressing aside (or refrigerate it overnight; bring it to room temperature before using).

Arrange the lettuce leaves, sprouts, cilantro, mango, and reserved mint leaves on a platter; set aside.

Set a wok or large skillet over high heat and add the oil. When hot, add the shrimp, season with salt and pepper, and stir-fry until they're browned outside and opaque inside, 3 to 5 minutes; cut one in half to check. Transfer to a warm platter.

To serve, bring the platters of shrimp and of lettuce and garnishes to the table. Fill a lettuce leaf with some shrimp and spoon on about 1 tsp. of dressing. Add the garnishes, roll up the leaf, and eat.

Spice-Rubbed Tilapia with Tomatillo, Black Bean & Mango Salad

Serves four.

Tomatillos look like small green tomatoes surrounded by a papery husk. They're common in Mexican cooking, and their refreshing flavor is great either raw or cooked.

One 15-oz. can black beans, drained and rinsed
½ lb. tomatillos, papery covering discarded, fruit rinsed and cut into small dice
1 medium-size ripe mango, peeled, pitted, and cut into small dice
½ cup small-diced red onion
⅓ cup fresh lime juice
⅓ cup plus 2 Tbs. vegetable oil
¼ cup chopped fresh cilantro
Freshly ground black pepper
1½ tsp. chili powder
1 tsp. ground cumin
1 tsp. dried oregano
Kosher salt
4 skinless tilapia fillets (about 4 oz. each)

Put a heatproof serving platter on a rack in the center of the oven and heat the oven to 200°F.

In a medium bowl, combine the beans, tomatillos, mango, red onion, lime juice, ⅓ cup of the vegetable oil, cilantro, and a few grinds of black pepper; toss gently. Let the salad sit at room temperature while you cook the fish.

Mix ¼ tsp. black pepper with the chili powder, cumin, oregano, and 1 tsp. salt. Rub both sides of the tilapia fillets with the mixture.

In a large (12-inch) nonstick skillet, heat the remaining 2 Tbs. oil over medium-high heat until hot. Cook two of the tilapia fillets until lightly browned and the flesh is opaque and cooked through, about 2 minutes on each side. Transfer the fish to the platter in the oven to keep warm while you cook the remaining two fillets. Transfer the fillets

to the platter and spoon half of the salad on top. Serve with the remaining salad on the side.

Variations: For a different spice combination, try rubbing the fish with Old Bay seasoning. And for other salad combinations, try chickpeas or red beans in place of the black beans, and red tomato or cucumber in place of the tomatillo.

Make it a menu

Salmon Brochettes with Sliced Fennel Vinaigrette

Serves eight; yields 1 1/2 cups vinaigrette.

An arugula and red onion salad would make a nice complement to these brochettes. The vinaigrette can double as a salad dressing.

FOR THE FENNEL VINAIGRETTE:
1 clove garlic, peeled
2 anchovy fillets
1 Tbs. capers, rinsed
1 tsp. grainy mustard
2 shallots, thinly sliced
1/4 medium bulb fresh fennel, outer leaves removed, cored, and thinly sliced crosswise
1/2 tsp. fresh thyme
1/2 tsp. crushed fennel seeds
1/4 tsp. crushed red pepper flakes
1/3 cup fresh lemon juice; more as needed
1 cup extra-virgin olive oil
Kosher salt and freshly ground black pepper

FOR THE BROCHETTES:
One 4-lb. fresh skin-on salmon fillet
Kosher salt
Olive oil for brushing

Make the vinaigrette: Mince together the garlic, anchovies, and capers. Transfer to a bowl and add the mustard, shallots, fennel, thyme, fennel seeds, red pepper flakes, and lemon juice. Stir briefly. Mix in the olive oil with a fork. Season with salt and pepper. Taste the vinaigrette; it should be slightly acidic, so add more lemon juice if necessary. Let stand for at least 1 hour so the fennel softens and the flavors mingle.

Make the brochettes: Heat a gas grill to medium high or prepare a medium hot charcoal fire. Cut the salmon crosswise into 1-inch-wide strips, 3 to 4 oz. each. Thread the skewers through the salmon strips: starting at the tapered end, carefully pierce the flesh, pushing the skewer all the way through to the fat end until the point pokes through.

When the grill is just on the hot side of medium (you should be able to hold your hand just above the grate for 2 seconds), use tongs to clean the grate with a lightly oiled paper towel.

Season the salmon lightly with salt and brush lightly with olive oil. Put the brochettes on the grill, skin side down, keeping the exposed skewer ends away from the fire if using bamboo.

The salmon will cook quickly but not always at the same rate. Cook until the skin is crisp and it "releases" from the grill, 2 to 3 minutes. Turn the brochettes with tongs or a spatula and cook another 1 minute. If necessary, turn again and cook another 1 minute. The salmon is done when the flesh feels firm and almost begins to flake apart. Put the brochettes on a platter and drizzle immediately with the vinaigrette.

Sautéed Shrimp with Red Pepper, Carrot & Napa Slaw

Serves six as a light entrée; eight to ten as a side salad.

Seasoned rice vinegar is rice vinegar with added sweeteners and salt. Don't confuse it with plain rice vinegar or flavored varieties of seasoned rice vinegar. Look for a bottle that's labeled "original," "natural," or "plain seasoned."

3 Tbs. seasoned rice vinegar
5 tsp. granulated sugar
4 tsp. fish sauce
Kosher salt and freshly ground black pepper
1 small head Napa cabbage (about 1½ lb.), halved, cored, and sliced crosswise very thinly
2 medium carrots, peeled and grated
1 large red bell pepper, seeded and very thinly sliced
4 scallions (white and green parts), trimmed and thinly sliced on the diagonal
⅓ cup chopped lightly salted peanuts
2 Tbs. Asian sesame oil
2 lb. large or jumbo shrimp, peeled and deveined

In a small saucepan, combine the vinegar, sugar, fish sauce, and ⅛ tsp. salt; stir over low heat until the sugar dissolves. Set aside to cool slightly. In a large bowl, combine the cabbage, carrots, bell pepper, and scallions; toss well. Pour the vinegar mixture over the cabbage and mix well to combine. Toss in the peanuts. Let sit, stirring occasionally, for about 20 minutes.

In a large nonstick skillet, heat 1 Tbs. of the sesame oil over medium-high heat. Toss the shrimp with ½ tsp. salt and ¼ tsp. pepper. Put half the shrimp in the skillet and sauté until opaque throughout, about 3 minutes. Transfer the cooked shrimp to a clean bowl. Repeat with the remaining 1 Tbs. oil and the other half of the shrimp. Toss the shrimp into the slaw and serve.

Seared Tuna with Citrus, Tomato & Olive Sauce

Serves four.

To round out the meal, cook up a pot of couscous and add some sautéed zucchini to go alongside.

2 medium plum tomatoes
Kosher salt and freshly ground black pepper
2 medium navel oranges
1 medium lemon
2 Tbs. coriander seeds
1 Tbs. black peppercorns
4 tuna steaks, 1 inch thick (6 to 7 oz. each)
5 Tbs. extra-virgin olive oil
2 anchovy fillets, rinsed and patted dry
1 large clove garlic, minced
½ cup (about 18) pitted Kalamata olives

Cut each tomato into four wedges, cut out the cores, and remove the seeds and pulp. Slice the tomatoes lengthwise into ¼-inch strips. In a colander, toss them with ¼ tsp. salt and let them drain for 15 minutes.

Meanwhile, finely grate the zest of the lemon. Put the zest in a medium bowl. Working over the bowl, segment the oranges and the lemon: Slice the ends off the fruit with a small, sharp knife. Stand the fruit on one of its cut ends and slice off the skin in strips (try to get all the bitter white pith). Working over a bowl, cut the segments free from the membrane, letting each segment fall into the bowl as you go. Remove any seeds from the segments.

In a spice grinder or mortar and pestle (or with a meat mallet; put the spices in a zip-top bag), coarsely grind the coriander and peppercorns. Press the spices into both sides of the tuna steaks.

Gently heat 3 Tbs. of the oil in a 12-inch skillet over medium heat. Add the anchovies and mash them into the oil with the back of a spoon until nearly dissolved. Turn the heat to low, add the garlic, and cook until softened but not browned, 3 to 4 minutes. Remove from the heat. Add the drained tomato strips, the orange and lemon segments (with the zest and juice), and the olives to the pan. Toss very gently to warm through, being careful not to break up the citrus segments. Season to taste with salt and pepper. Transfer to a serving bowl and keep warm.

Wipe out the skillet, set it over medium-high heat, and pour in the remaining 2 Tbs. oil. Generously salt the tuna steaks on both sides. Working in batches if necessary, sear the steaks, pressing on them while cooking to help a crust develop, until golden brown, 2 to 3 minutes. Flip the tuna and continue to cook until golden brown, another 2 to 3 minutes for medium rare to medium. Transfer the tuna to dinner plates and serve with the warm citrus sauce.

Tuna & White Bean Salad with Arugula, Yellow Tomatoes & Olives

Serves four as a main course.

5 oz. (about 6 cups loosely packed) baby arugula
   leaves, washed and dried
1½ Tbs. balsamic vinegar
1½ Tbs. fresh lemon juice
1 clove garlic, finely chopped
½ cup plus 1 to 2 Tbs. extra-virgin olive oil
Kosher salt and freshly ground black pepper
4 tuna steaks (about 1½ inches thick), 4 to 6 oz. each
One 15½-oz. can Great Northern or cannellini beans,
   drained and rinsed
½ pt. yellow teardrop or grape tomatoes, halved
   lengthwise
½ cup green olives, pitted and roughly chopped
1 tsp. finely grated lemon zest

Put the arugula in a large bowl, cover with a damp paper towel, and refrigerate.

In a small bowl, whisk the balsamic vinegar with the lemon juice, garlic, and ½ cup of the oil. Season with salt and pepper.

Heat a 12-inch heavy skillet over medium-high heat. Brush the tuna generously with the remaining 1 to 2 Tbs. oil and season with salt and pepper. Cook the fish until the first side is browned, about 3 minutes. Flip and continue to cook until the second side is browned and the tuna is cooked to your liking, about another 3 minutes for medium rare. Transfer to a plate and keep warm.

In a medium bowl, combine the beans, tomatoes, olives, and lemon zest and toss with just enough of the dressing to coat, about 3 Tbs. Season generously with salt and pepper. Toss the arugula with just enough dressing to coat lightly, about 5 Tbs., and season with salt and pepper. Portion the arugula onto four plates and top with a mound of the bean mixture. Slice the tuna into ¼-inch slices and arrange on the arugula around the beans. Drizzle the tuna with a little of the remaining dressing and serve.

Grilled Salmon with Wasabi-Ginger Mayonnaise

Serves four.

You can usually find wasabi paste and powder in the Asian section of the supermarket and at Asian groceries. To turn powdered wasabi into paste, mix equal parts powder and tepid water and let stand for at least 15 minutes.

1½ limes
½ cup mayonnaise
1½ Tbs. wasabi paste; more to taste
2 tsp. finely grated fresh ginger
Kosher salt and freshly ground black
   pepper
Four 6-oz. skinless salmon fillets
Vegetable oil for the grill

Heat a gas grill to medium high or prepare a medium-hot charcoal fire (be sure the grill grate has been scrubbed clean with a wire brush).

Cut the half lime into four wedges and set aside. Finely grate the zest from the whole lime. Cut the zested lime in half and squeeze the juice from one half into a small bowl (save the other half for another use). In a medium bowl, combine 1 tsp. of the lime juice with the lime zest, mayonnaise, wasabi paste, ginger, and ¼ tsp. salt. Stir to combine. Taste and add more wasabi paste if you'd like a zippier flavor.

Run your finger along each salmon fillet to feel for tiny bones; use tweezers or needlenose pliers to pull out any that you find. Season the fillets lightly with salt and pepper. Spoon about 2 Tbs. of the mayonnaise mixture onto the salmon fillets and refrigerate the rest. With your hands, spread the mayonnaise in a thin layer over all sides of the fillets.

When the grill is ready, oil the grill grate using tongs and a paper towel dipped in oil. Grill the salmon until crisp and slightly charred on one side, about 4 minutes. Turn and continue to grill until the salmon is just cooked through, another 3 to 6 minutes. Serve the salmon topped with a dollop of the mayonnaise and a lime wedge on the side. Pass the remaining mayonnaise at the table.

Paprika Shrimp with Orange & Avocado Salsa

Serves six.

Serve this on a bed of saffron rice.

2 medium navel oranges
5 Tbs. extra-virgin olive oil
Kosher salt
1 ripe Hass avocado, cut into medium dice
⅓ cup thinly sliced scallions (from about 4 slender scallions, both white and green parts)
1 Tbs. fresh lime juice
2 tsp. sweet paprika, preferably Hungarian
½ tsp. ground cumin
1 tsp. Tabasco or other hot sauce
1½ lb. large shrimp (21 to 25 per lb.), peeled and deveined

Position an oven rack 4 inches from the broiler element and heat the broiler to high.

Segment the oranges: Slice the ends off one of the oranges with a small, sharp knife. Stand the orange on one of its cut ends and slice off the skin in strips, cutting below the bitter white pith. Working over a small bowl, cut the orange segments free from the membrane, letting each segment fall into the bowl as you go. Squeeze any remaining juice from the membranes into the bowl. Repeat with the other orange. Cut all of the orange segments in half crosswise and return them to the bowl.

Add 2 Tbs. of the olive oil, ¾ tsp. salt, the avocado, scallions, and lime juice to the oranges and toss gently to combine.

In a medium bowl, combine the remaining 3 Tbs. oil, 1 tsp. salt, the paprika, cumin, and Tabasco; stir well. Add the shrimp, tossing to coat. Arrange the shrimp on a foil-lined rimmed baking sheet. Broil until the shrimp are opaque and cooked through, about 4 minutes. Serve the shrimp with the salsa.

Buy shrimp by the count, not the size

The next time you buy shrimp, take a closer look at the label and you'll notice a set of numbers divided by a slash, like this: 21/25. This number, called the "count," tells you the size of the shrimp. The count refers to the number of individual shrimp in 1 pound. So for instance, when you buy 1 pound of 21/25 count shrimp, you can expect to get 21 to 25 shrimp. The smaller the numbers, the bigger the shrimp. Sometimes on big shrimp you'll see a count that looks like this: U/15 or U/10. This means there are "under 15" or "under 10" shrimp per pound.

When buying shrimp, the main advantage to using the count is that it's a reliable, consistent measure. Adjectives that describe the size, like "jumbo" or "large," aren't standardized. It's not uncommon to find a particular count—say 51/60s—labeled as "medium" in one store while another store just down the road calls them "small."

51/60 count

31/40 count

21/25 count

Shrimp shown actual size.

Sautéed Snapper with Broken Black-Olive Vinaigrette

Serves four.

⅓ cup coarsely chopped pitted Kalamata olives
⅓ cup plus 2 Tbs. extra-virgin olive oil
1½ Tbs. loosely packed finely grated lemon
   zest (from 1 large lemon)
1 Tbs. fresh lemon juice
1 small clove garlic, minced
⅛ tsp. crushed red pepper flakes
Kosher salt
4 skin-on snapper fillets, about 6 oz. each
⅓ cup all-purpose flour for dredging
5 oz. (5 cups loosely packed) baby arugula,
   washed and dried
4 lemon wedges for serving

Mix the olives, ⅓ cup of the oil, the lemon zest, lemon juice, garlic, and pepper flakes in a small bowl with a fork; the vinaigrette needn't emulsify. Season with salt to taste.

Pull out any bones in the fish with needle-nose pliers or tweezers. Season both sides of the fish with salt and dredge very lightly in the flour. Heat 2 Tbs. oil in a large nonstick skillet over medium heat. When hot, add two of the fillets, skin side up; cook until light golden brown, 4 to 5 minutes. With a thin slotted metal spatula, turn the fish and cook until the second side is lightly browned and the fish is cooked through, about 3 minutes. Transfer the fillets, skin side down, to a plate; cover to keep warm. Repeat with the remaining fillets.

Stir the vinaigrette, toss 1 to 2 Tbs. of it with the arugula to coat lightly, and portion the arugula among four plates. Lay the fish on top, spoon over the remaining vinaigrette, and serve with a wedge of lemon.

Tool tips

A nonstick skillet is perfect for sautéing fish fillets with no worries about sticking. A 12-inch pan will hold four fillets; two or three fillets work in an 8- or 10-inch pan. A thin, angled slotted spatula with a slightly curved lip is helpful for turning delicate fish.

Broiled Flounder with Parmesan "Caesar" Glaze

Serves four to six.

8 skinless flounder fillets, 4 to 5 oz. each
Kosher salt and freshly ground black pepper
⅓ cup good-quality mayonnaise
1½ oz. (½ cup) freshly grated Parmigiano-
  Reggiano, grated on the small holes of a
  box grater
1½ Tbs. loosely packed finely grated lemon
  zest (from 1 large lemon)
1 Tbs. fresh lemon juice
½ tsp. Worcestershire sauce
1 small clove garlic, minced
2 Tbs. coarsely chopped fresh flat-leaf
  parsley

Position a rack 4 inches from the broiler element and heat the broiler on high. Lightly season both sides of the fillets with salt and pepper. Set a fillet before you, skinned side up, and starting at the narrow end, roll up the fillet. Repeat with the remaining fillets.

Spray a broiler pan with nonstick cooking spray. Arrange the flounder rolls, seam side down, in the pan. Broil until the tops are lightly browned, 7 to 8 minutes. Meanwhile, whisk the mayonnaise, Parmesan, lemon zest and juice, Worcestershire, and garlic in a small bowl. Season with pepper to taste.

When the tops of the fillets are lightly browned, remove the fish from the broiler. Spread equal amounts of the mayonnaise mixture over the top of each fillet. Return to the broiler until the topping is golden brown and bubbling, 1½ to 2 minutes. Transfer the fillets to four dinner plates and sprinkle with the parsley. Serve immediately.

Baked Tilapia with Tarragon-Scallion Stuffing & Butter Sauce

Serves four.

6 Tbs. cold unsalted butter
¼ cup thinly sliced scallions (white
  and tender light green parts from
  about 4 scallions)
1 cup coarse fresh breadcrumbs
  (from a baguette or other crusty
  white loaf)
2 tsp. chopped fresh tarragon or
  ¾ tsp. crumbled dried tarragon
1 large egg, beaten
Kosher salt and freshly ground
  black pepper
4 tilapia fillets, about 6 oz. each
⅓ cup dry vermouth
⅓ cup homemade or low-salt
  chicken broth
2 tsp. Dijon mustard

Position a rack in the upper third of
the oven and heat the oven to 400°F.

Melt 4 Tbs. of the butter in a medium saucepan or skillet over medium-low heat. Lightly brush the inside of a 9x13-inch Pyrex baking dish with some of the melted butter. Transfer 1 Tbs. of the melted butter to a small dish and keep warm. Add the scallions to the remaining butter in the saucepan and cook, stirring, until softened, about 2 minutes.

In a medium bowl, mix the melted scallion butter with the breadcrumbs, tarragon, beaten egg, ¼ tsp. salt, and several grinds of pepper.

Lightly season the fillets on both sides with salt and pepper. Lay a fillet on a work surface with the pointed end facing you. Mound a quarter of the stuffing on the pointed half of the fillet. Fold the wide, split end of the fillet over and press firmly (but don't

squish) to cover the stuffing. Some stuffing will remain exposed. Put the stuffed fillet in the buttered baking dish. Repeat with the remaining fillets. Brush the tops of the fillets with the reserved 1 Tbs. melted butter. Pour the vermouth and chicken broth around, not over, the fillets.

Bake until the fish feels firm but flaky and the insides of the fillets look opaque when pierced with the tip of a sharp knife, 20 to 25 minutes. Using a thin, flexible slotted metal spatula, transfer the fillets to four dinner plates.

Add 1 Tbs. cold butter to the hot baking dish and whisk until the butter melts. Repeat with the remaining 1 Tbs. butter and the mustard. Season the sauce with salt and pepper and spoon over the fillets. Serve immediately.

Tandoori Chicken *p. 132*

Chicken, Beef & Pork

Roasted Cornish Game Hens with Tangerine-Herb Butter

Serves six.

Slipping butter under the skin is a great way to keep these game hens moist. After roasting, if the birds need additional crisping, run them under the broiler for just a few minutes.

6 Cornish game hens (about 1½ lb. each), neck and giblets removed and discarded or saved for stock, hens rinsed and patted dry
Kosher salt and freshly ground black pepper
⅓ cup fresh tangerine juice (from 1 or 2 tangerines)
½ cup unsalted butter, softened at room temperature
2 shallots, finely minced
2 Tbs. chopped fresh flat-leaf parsley; plus whole sprigs for serving
2 Tbs. snipped fresh chives
1 Tbs. chopped fresh oregano
2 Tbs. grated tangerine zest

Season the cavity of each hen with salt and pepper. In a small saucepan over medium-high heat, reduce the tangerine juice until 1 Tbs. remains. Remove from the heat. In a small skillet over medium heat, melt 1 Tbs. of the butter. Add the shallots and cook, stirring, until soft, about 2 minutes. Remove from the heat. In a small bowl, mash together the shallots, reduced tangerine juice, parsley, chives, oregano, tangerine zest, and 5 Tbs. of the butter just until combined. Add ¼ tsp. salt; season with pepper. Transfer to the freezer for 5 minutes to let the butter firm. (If not using right away, refrigerate for up to three days.)

Heat the oven to 425°F. Insert your fingertips at the wing end of one of the hen's breast and gently loosen the skin over the breast and around the legs, being careful not to tear it. Slip about 1 Tbs. of the tangerine butter under the skin, smearing it evenly over the breast and thighs. With kitchen twine, tie the legs together. Tuck the wings underneath. Repeat with each hen.

Arrange the hens breast side up on a wire rack set in a shallow roasting pan (or two). Melt the remaining 2 Tbs. butter and use half to brush over the hens. Season each hen with salt and pepper. Roast the hens for 20 minutes. Brush with the remaining melted butter. Continue to roast until the juices run clear when you prick the thickest part of the thigh and an instant-read thermometer inserted in the thigh registers 170°F, another 20 to 25 minutes. Transfer the hens to a platter, tent with foil, and let stand for 10 minutes. Serve with a few parsley sprigs next to each hen.

Broiled Coconut-Lime Chicken Thighs

Serves four.

This bake-broil method browns the thighs nicely and would work well with other marinades. Just be sure to keep an eye on the chicken as it broils so that it doesn't burn.

2 Tbs. minced fresh ginger
1 tsp. coriander seeds
Pinch turmeric
2 cloves garlic, minced
¼ tsp. cayenne
3 scallions (white and green parts), coarsely chopped
Grated zest of 1 lime
Juice of 2 limes
2 Tbs. soy sauce
1 Tbs. rice vinegar
⅓ cup coconut milk
¼ cup raw peanuts (salted are fine); plus 1 Tbs. coarsely chopped peanuts for garnish
¼ cup chopped fresh cilantro; plus sprigs for garnish
½ tsp. kosher salt
8 bone-in, skin-on chicken thighs, excess fat removed
Lime wedges for garnish

In a blender, purée the ginger, coriander seeds, turmeric, garlic, cayenne, scallions, lime zest, lime juice, soy sauce, vinegar, coconut milk, ¼ cup peanuts, chopped cilantro, and salt until smooth. Pour the marinade over the chicken thighs and mix well. Marinate for 1 to 2 hours in the refrigerator.

Position racks in the middle and top of the oven and heat the oven to 450°F. Line a rimmed baking sheet with foil. Arrange the chicken thighs, skin side up, in a single layer with space between. Bake the chicken in the middle of the oven for 15 minutes for small thighs, 20 minutes for larger thighs.

Turn on the broiler. Broil the thighs 5 to 6 inches from the heat source until the chicken is golden brown on the outside and firm to the touch, 10 to 15 minutes. Take care that they don't burn.

Arrange the chicken thighs on a platter and serve immediately, garnished with the chopped peanuts, cilantro sprigs, and lime wedges.

Quick Chicken Sauté with Asparagus, Cherry Tomatoes & Lemon Pan Sauce

Serves two.

This brightly flavored one-pan chicken dish comes together very quickly, thanks to a fast cooking method that includes cutting the chicken into chunks.

2 medium-size boneless, skinless chicken breast halves (¾ lb. total), cut into ¾-inch chunks
Kosher salt and freshly ground black pepper
2 Tbs. plus 2 tsp. olive oil
8 cherry tomatoes, halved
6 medium asparagus spears, ends trimmed, spears cut in half lengthwise and then into 2-inch pieces (or 8 skinny spears cut into 2-inch pieces)
3 large cloves garlic, thinly sliced
6 Tbs. water or homemade or low-salt chicken broth
3 Tbs. fresh lemon juice
2 Tbs. unsalted butter, cut into pieces
1 Tbs. minced fresh basil

Season the chicken with salt and pepper. Heat 1 Tbs. of the oil in a medium sauté pan over medium-high heat. Add the tomatoes and asparagus and cook, stirring occasionally, until the tomatoes have softened and the asparagus is golden brown around the edges, 2 to 3 minutes. Transfer to a medium bowl. Heat another 1 Tbs. oil in the pan and add the chicken. When the underside of the chicken has turned deep golden brown (about 1 minute), turn it with a metal spatula. Turn occasionally for even browning until almost cooked through, 3 to 5 minutes. Add the chicken to the bowl of vegetables.

Reduce the heat to medium and heat the remaining 2 tsp. oil in the pan. Add the garlic, cooking until golden brown, 1 to 2 minutes. Add the water or broth and the lemon juice, using a wooden spoon to scrape up any browned bits in the pan and blend them into the sauce. Simmer for 3 minutes. Reduce the heat to medium low and stir in the butter. Stir in the chicken, asparagus, tomatoes, any juices, and the basil. Season with salt and pepper to taste and serve immediately.

Sautéed Chicken & Snow Peas with Teriyaki Pan Sauce

Serves two.

Serve this fragrant sauté over fresh Asian egg noodles or rice noodles.

- 2 medium-size boneless, skinless chicken breast halves (¾ lb. total), cut into ¾-inch chunks
- Kosher salt and freshly ground black pepper
- 2 tsp. cornstarch
- ¼ cup water or homemade or low-salt chicken broth
- 2 Tbs. peanut oil or vegetable oil
- 5 oz. fresh snow peas, trimmed
- 1-inch chunk fresh ginger, peeled and cut into thin matchsticks (about 2 Tbs.)
- 1 clove garlic, minced
- ¼ cup sake or mirin (sweet rice wine)
- 3 Tbs. soy sauce
- 2 Tbs. rice vinegar
- 1 Tbs. honey
- 2 Tbs. crunchy bean sprouts or 2 Tbs. chopped fresh cilantro

Season the chicken with salt and pepper. In a small bowl, blend the cornstarch into the water or broth.

Heat 2 tsp. of the oil in a medium sauté pan over medium-high heat. Add the snow peas and cook, stirring frequently, until they're slightly browned and softened but still crisp, 2 to 3 minutes. Transfer to a medium bowl. Heat another 1 Tbs. oil in the pan and add the chicken. When the underside of the chicken has turned deep golden brown (about 1 minute), turn it with a metal spatula. Turn occasionally for even browning until almost cooked through, 3 to 5 minutes. Add the chicken to the bowl of peas.

Heat the remaining 1 tsp. oil in the pan. Add the ginger and cook until fragrant, about 1 minute. Reduce the heat to medium, add the garlic, and cook until fragrant, about 30 seconds. Add the sake (or mirin), soy sauce, vinegar, honey, and the cornstarch mixture. Use a wooden spoon to scrape up any browned bits in the pan and blend them into the sauce. Bring to a boil, reduce the heat to medium low, and toss the chicken and snow peas into the sauce. Season with salt and pepper to taste. Serve immediately, sprinkled with the sprouts or cilantro.

tip: When sautéing boneless chicken, cook until just barely opaque (slightly pink in the middle) so it doesn't dry out—it will continue to cook off the heat.

Chicken-Mesclun Salad with Hazelnut Dressing

Serves four.

You can use leftover roasted chicken pulled off the bone in place of the sautéed breasts. For variety, try crumbled Gorgonzola in place of the aged Gouda, replace the portabellas with chanterelles, or substitute spinach for the mesclun.

FOR THE DRESSING:
2 Tbs. red-wine vinegar
2 cloves garlic, chopped
1 shallot, chopped
1 tsp. Dijon mustard
⅓ cup extra-virgin olive oil
2 Tbs. hazelnut oil (or just use more olive oil)
1 tsp. chopped fresh thyme
2 tsp. chopped fresh basil
Kosher salt and freshly ground black pepper

FOR THE SALAD:
½ lb. mesclun mix
3 Tbs. olive oil
3 to 4 boneless, skinless chicken breast
   halves (1 lb. total)
2 large portabella mushrooms, thinly sliced
½ red onion, thinly sliced
½ cup grated aged Gouda
½ cup toasted chopped hazelnuts

Make the dressing: In a medium bowl, whisk together the vinegar, garlic, shallot, and mustard. Slowly whisk in the oils until emulsified. Add the herbs, season with salt and pepper, and mix well. Set aside.

Make the salad: Put the mesclun in a large mixing bowl; set aside. In a large sauté pan, heat 2 Tbs. of the olive oil over high heat until very hot. Add the chicken and sear well, 2 to 3 minutes per side. Reduce the heat to medium low and continue cooking until the chicken is done, 5 to 8 minutes, depending on thickness. Transfer the chicken to a cutting board, let rest 5 minutes, and slice thinly on the bias. Add the remaining 1 Tbs. oil to the sauté pan, turn the heat to medium high, and add the mushrooms and red onion. Sauté until tender, about 4 minutes. Reduce the heat to low, pour in the dressing, and just heat through. Pour the mushroom and onion mixture and about three-quarters of the liquid from the pan onto the greens and toss well to gently wilt them. Distribute the salad among four serving plates. Top with the sliced chicken, cheese, and hazelnuts. Drizzle the remainder of the dressing over the chicken and serve immediately.

Grilled Chicken Breasts with Sun-Dried & Fresh Tomato Salsa

Serves two.

A double dose of tomatoes lets you enjoy not only the sweet summery flavor of fresh tomatoes but also the deeper, more rich tones supplied by the sun-dried variety.

½ lb. small red and yellow
   cherry tomatoes, halved or
   quartered, depending on size
2 Tbs. chopped drained oil-
   packed sun-dried tomatoes
2 tsp. drained capers (roughly
   chopped if large)
½ tsp. finely chopped garlic
1 Tbs. sherry vinegar
2 tsp. lightly chopped fresh
   thyme leaves; plus sprigs for
   garnish, if you like
3 Tbs. plus 2 tsp. extra-virgin
   olive oil
Kosher salt and freshly ground
   black pepper
2 large (6 to 8 oz.) boneless,
   skinless chicken breast
   halves, tenderloins removed
   and reserved for another use;
   breasts butterflied

In a small bowl, combine the cherry tomatoes, sun-dried tomatoes, capers, garlic, sherry vinegar, 1 tsp. of the thyme, 3 Tbs. of the olive oil, ¼ tsp. salt, and a few grinds of pepper. Set aside, stirring occasionally to let the flavors combine.

Heat a gas grill to high. Put the chicken in a shallow nonreactive pan or plate. Rub the chicken all over with salt (about ½ tsp. for each piece of chicken), a few grinds of pepper, and the remaining 1 tsp. thyme. Drizzle ½ tsp. olive oil over each side of each piece of chicken and rub all over.

Lay the butterflied breasts on the hot grill grates and cook, covered, until the chicken has grill marks, 1½ minutes. With tongs, rotate the breasts 90 degrees (to get a crosshatch of grill marks) and continue grilling until grill marks form, another 1½ minutes. Flip the breasts and cook the second side in the same way but for a little less time, grilling for 1 minute in one direction and 1 minute in another, until cooked through.

Transfer the breasts immediately to two warm serving plates. Stir the tomato mixture and spoon equal amounts (it will be a generous portion) over each piece of chicken. Garnish with a sprig of thyme, if you like.

Tandoori Chicken

Serves four to six.

The red-orange color of tandoori chicken in Indian restaurants comes from food coloring in the marinade. You can buy this special tandoori coloring at Indian groceries or omit it; it won't affect the flavor. Serve the chicken with fragrant basmati rice.

FOR THE MARINADE:
One 2-inch piece ginger, peeled
4 large cloves garlic
¼ tsp. turmeric
1 tsp. chili powder
1½ tsp. kosher salt
½ tsp. cumin seeds, ground
¾ cup plain low-fat yogurt
1 Tbs. fresh lime juice
A few drops red food coloring or tandoori coloring (optional)

FOR THE CHICKEN:
2 to 3 lb. boneless, skinless chicken thighs and breasts
¼ cup melted butter or olive oil

FOR THE GARNISH:
½ mild onion, thinly sliced
½ cup chopped fresh cilantro leaves
1 or 2 fresh green chiles, thinly sliced
1 lime, cut in wedges

Make the marinade: In a blender or food processor, blend the ginger and garlic to a fine paste (you may need to add a little water to make a paste). Add the turmeric, chili powder, salt, cumin, yogurt, lime juice, and food coloring, if using; process until combined.

Prepare the chicken: Make a few slits in each piece and transfer to a nonreactive dish large enough for the pieces to lie flat. Pour the marinade over the chicken and stir to coat the chicken thoroughly. Seal with plastic, refrigerate, and marinate for at least 4 but no more than 12 hours, turning the chicken once.

Grill the chicken: Prepare a charcoal grill with an even layer of coals. While the grill is heating up, take the chicken out of the refrigerator. When the charcoal is red-hot, lay the chicken pieces on the grill about 2 inches apart. Baste with any remaining marinade. Cover the grill, leaving the vents half-open.

After about 5 minutes, remove the grill lid and turn over the chicken pieces; they should look slightly charred. Replace the lid and continue cooking for another 5 to 7 minutes. Uncover the chicken, baste it with the melted butter, turn it over, and leave it uncovered for the rest of the cooking time. Baste after 2 or 3 minutes and test for doneness: the meat should feel firm when you press it.

Transfer the chicken to a large platter. Arrange the onion, cilantro, chiles, and lime wedges over the chicken and seal the platter with foil. Let the chicken rest for 10 minutes to absorb the garnish flavors before serving.

Lemony Moroccan-Style Chicken Kebabs

Serves six.

Microwaving the lemons is a quick method for mimicking the flavor and texture of true preserved lemons.

FOR THE MARINADE:
2 lemons
6 cloves garlic, peeled
Two ⅛-inch-thick slices peeled fresh ginger
1 tsp. dried marjoram
1 tsp. ground coriander
1 tsp. ground cumin
½ tsp. ground turmeric
⅛ tsp. ground cinnamon
Pinch saffron threads
1 tsp. light brown sugar
2½ tsp. kosher salt
2 tsp. freshly ground black pepper
3 Tbs. olive oil

FOR THE KEBABS:
2½ lb. boneless, skinless chicken thighs, trimmed of excess fat and cut into 2-inch chunks
1 sweet onion (like Vidalia), cut into 1-inch pieces
1 red bell pepper, cut into 1-inch squares
1 yellow bell pepper, cut into 1-inch squares
2 Tbs. chopped fresh flat-leaf parsley for garnish

Grilled Chicken Breasts with Asian Dipping Sauce

Serves four; yields about 2 cups sauce.

Serve the sauce in four small (individual-size) bowls so everyone at the table has one within easy reach. If you have leftover sauce, use it to brush over grilled vegetables like onions or peppers to add an Asian twist.

FOR THE DIPPING SAUCE:
2 cloves garlic
¼ cup granulated sugar; more to taste
⅓ cup soy sauce
⅓ cup Asian fish sauce
⅓ cup fresh lime juice
**1 to 2 fresh serrano or jalapeño chiles,
    thinly sliced crosswise**
2 Tbs. chopped scallion greens
2 Tbs. chopped fresh cilantro leaves
2 Tbs. chopped fresh mint leaves
**¼ cup finely chopped unsalted dry-roasted
    peanuts**
½ to ¾ cup water; more as needed

FOR THE CHICKEN:
**4 large skinless, boneless chicken breast halves,
    rinsed and patted dry**
Kosher salt and freshly ground black pepper

Make the sauce: Finely chop the garlic on a cutting board. Sprinkle 1 Tbs. of the sugar over the garlic and repeatedly scrape the flat side of the knife over the garlic to mash it to a paste. Scrape the paste into a medium bowl. Add the remaining 3 Tbs. sugar, the soy sauce, fish sauce, and lime juice and whisk until the sugar is dissolved. Stir in the chiles, scallions, cilantro, mint, and peanuts. Stir in enough water to create a mellow but zesty sauce.

Grill the chicken: Heat a gas grill to medium high. Season the chicken breasts on both sides with salt and pepper. Grill the chicken, covered, until golden grill marks form, 4 to 6 minutes (for even cooking, rotate the chicken halfway through cooking each side). Flip the breasts and continue to cook, covered, until golden grill marks form and the chicken is cooked through, 4 to 6 minutes. Let rest on a cutting board for 5 minutes. Slice the chicken thinly on an angle and set on individual plates. Serve with the dipping sauce.

FOR THE YOGURT-LEMON SAUCE:
**1 seedless cucumber, cut into ½-inch
    dice**
½ cup chopped fresh cilantro
2 cups plain whole-milk yogurt
Kosher salt

Make the marinade: Cut four deep, lengthwise gashes, equally spaced, into each lemon. Put the lemons and garlic cloves in a small microwavable container. Cover and microwave on high until the lemons are soft and juice has exuded from them, about 4 minutes (If they're not soft, continue to microwave in 30-second intervals.) Strain the juice into a small container and let the lemons and garlic cool briefly. When the lemons are cool enough to handle, separate them into sections. Scrape the pulp and most of the white pith away with a spoon; discard. Put the scraped lemon peels, garlic, lemon juice, and remaining marinade ingredients in a blender. Purée to make a coarse, soft paste. Set aside 2 Tbs. to use for the yogurt sauce.

Marinate the chicken: Put the chicken in a 1-gallon zip-top bag; scrape in the remaining marinade. Massage the bag to coat all the chicken pieces and marinate for 1 to 2 hours in the refrigerator.

Grill the kebabs: Build a medium-hot charcoal fire or heat a gas grill to medium high. Dump the chicken into a bowl, but don't scrape off any excess marinade. Put the onion and peppers in the marinade bag and massage them to coat with the marinade (it's fine if the onion pieces break apart). Transfer to another bowl. Thread the chicken onto skewers, positioning a piece of onion and pepper between the pieces of chicken. If there's extra pepper or onion, thread them onto separate skewers, if you like.

When ready to grill, oil the grill grate. Grill the kebabs over direct heat (uncovered for charcoal; covered for gas), turning the skewers every 2 to 3 minutes until the chicken is firm and shows no redness when cut into, about 10 to 15 minutes. Check several pieces of chicken to be sure.

Make the sauce: Combine the reserved 2 Tbs. marinade with the cucumber, cilantro, yogurt, and 2 tsp. salt. Mix well. (Make the sauce no more than an hour before serving or it will become watery.)

To serve: Remove the chicken and vegetables from the skewers and serve them in a mound with the yogurt sauce on the side.

Thai Marinated Roast Chicken with Lemongrass-Peanut Pan Sauce

Serves four.

In this clever recipe, you marinate chicken pieces in a tangy mixture for up to 24 hours, but instead of discarding the marinade, you pour it into the roasting pan with the chicken, where it mingles with the drippings and reduces to become a flavorful sauce.

FOR THE CHICKEN:
2 bone-in, skin-on chicken breast halves
4 bone-in, skin-on chicken thighs
Kosher salt
5 large cloves garlic, peeled

FOR THE LEMONGRASS-PEANUT MARINADE:
¼ cup sliced and finely chopped fresh lemongrass (1 to 2 stalks, tough outer leaves removed)
¼ cup fresh lime juice (1 large lime)
½ cup coconut milk, well stirred
¼ cup fish sauce
¼ cup roughly chopped fresh cilantro
3 Tbs. packed light brown sugar
3 Tbs. creamy peanut butter
8 to 12 cloves garlic, peeled, or 4 to 5 shallots, peeled and cut in half (or a mix)

OPTIONAL GARNISH:
2 Tbs. finely chopped peanuts
Fresh cilantro, sprigs or chopped leaves

Prepare the chicken: Press down on the chicken breasts with the palm of your hand to flatten slightly (allowing rib cartilage to pop away or break in half). With a sharp knife, poke three or four slits in both sides of each piece of chicken to help the marinade penetrate. Put the chicken in a large nonreactive bowl. Toss with a scant teaspoon kosher salt. Crush the 5 garlic cloves, sprinkle with a little salt, and mince finely into a paste; you should have 1½ to 2 Tbs. Add to the chicken and coat the pieces roughly with the garlic paste.

Make the marinade: In a small bowl, combine the lemongrass, lime juice, coconut milk, fish sauce, cilantro, brown sugar, and peanut butter and whisk until thoroughly combined. Scrape into the bowl of chicken and toss to coat, using your hands to coat evenly. Toss in the 8 to 12 garlic cloves or the halved shallots and then press on the chicken to be sure the marinade has coated and surrounded all the pieces. Wrap the bowl well with plastic and refrigerate for at least 6 hours and up to 24 hours.

Cook the chicken: Up to an hour before roasting, remove the chicken from the refrigerator and pour the chicken and marinade (scraping the bowl) into one 10x15-inch or two 7x11-inch Pyrex baking dishes. Adjust the chicken so it's skin side up and the pieces are evenly spaced. Tuck the garlic or shallots under and around the chicken pieces. Let the chicken sit for at least 20 minutes or up to an hour to warm up so it will cook more evenly. Meanwhile, heat the oven to 400°F.

Put the chicken in the oven to roast. As it cooks, the marinade will bubble and begin to reduce. After 30 minutes, baste occasionally with the pan juices to help brown the skin and keep the chicken moist. The chicken is done when it turns deep brown and the pan juices have reduced (the sides of the pan will be very dark brown and look almost burned, and a paring knife will slide easily into a thigh), about 1 hour. The pan juices may separate, meaning the fat will be floating on top of the juices, which will be very thick.

Make a sauce from the pan drippings: Transfer the chicken pieces to a cutting board and tent with foil. Transfer the garlic cloves or shallots to a small bowl and reserve. Hold one end of the pan with a potholder and gently tilt the pan to let the juices run into one corner. With a large, shallow spoon, spoon off as much fat as possible but leave any savory juices and pan drippings behind (they may look clumpy). Add 2 Tbs. water to the pan (or 1 Tbs. to each of the two pans) and use a wooden spoon to scrape off enough of the baked-on pan drippings from the sides and bottom of the pan to form a slightly thickened, deeply colored, rich-looking sauce (you won't need to scrape the whole pan). Taste the sauce—if it's too intense, add a little more water; if it isn't flavorful enough, keep scraping and stirring. (Note: Make the pan sauce while the pan is still hot; if you get delayed, use hot water to make the sauce, or put the pan back in the oven briefly to warm it.)

Cut each chicken breast in half by centering a large chef's knife over it and then pushing down and slicing at the same time (the knife will cut right through the cartilage). Serve a thigh and half of a breast, with a few spoonfuls of sauce over all and a portion of the garlic or shallots, to each diner. Garnish with the peanuts and cilantro, if you like.

Grilled Flank Steak with Chimichurri Sauce

Serves three to four; yields about 2 cups sauce.

Chimichurri is an Argentinean garlic herb sauce. Serve any leftovers with sautéed chicken breasts, or fold into a potato salad for a little zip. The sauce will keep for several days, but the parsley will lose its bright green color.

FOR THE CHIMICHURRI SAUCE:
4 cloves garlic, peeled
1 tsp. kosher salt; more as needed
1 bunch fresh flat-leaf parsley, stemmed, and chopped (about 1½ cups, lightly packed)
1 tsp. dried oregano
1 small carrot, finely grated
½ tsp. freshly ground black pepper
½ tsp. crushed red pepper flakes
½ tsp. grated lemon zest
5 Tbs. white-wine vinegar or distilled white vinegar; more to taste
5 Tbs. cold water; more as needed
1 cup extra-virgin olive oil

FOR THE FLANK STEAK:
One 1½-lb. flank steak, trimmed of any excess fat and membrane
1 Tbs. extra-virgin oil
Kosher salt and freshly ground black pepper

Make the sauce: Finely chop the garlic on a cutting board. Sprinkle the salt over it and repeatedly scrape the flat side of the knife over the garlic to mash it to a paste. Scrape the garlic paste into a medium bowl. Add the parsley, oregano, carrot, pepper, red pepper flakes, and lemon zest and mix. Add the vinegar and water and mix again. Whisk in the oil. Taste and correct the seasonings, adding salt, vinegar, water, or red pepper flakes: the sauce should be highly seasoned.

Grill the steak: Heat a gas grill to high or prepare a hot charcoal fire (you should be able to hold your hand a couple of inches above the grate for 1 second). Rub both sides of the steak with the oil and season generously with salt and pepper.

Grill the steak for 8 minutes, flipping it a couple of times during cooking. If your grill has a hot spot, keep the thicker part of the steak over that area and the thinner, tapered end over any cooler area. It should be rare to medium rare at this point. Transfer the steak to a cutting board to rest for 2 to 3 minutes so the meat relaxes and the juices redistribute.

Slice the steak very thinly across the grain and on a 45-degree angle. Serve with the chimichurri sauce.

Make it a menu

A backyard barbecue

Strawberry-Mint Tea Sparkling Punch *p. 6*

Grilled Flank Steak with Chimichurri Sauce *at left*

Minty Quinoa Tabbouleh *p. 56*

Lemon Bars *p. 187*

Flank Steak with Chunky Tomato-Basil Vinaigrette

Serves four to six; yields 2 cups vinaigrette.

A chunky, colorful vinaigrette enlivens flank steak. The rub for the steak is a wet one; the oil in it helps spread the other flavors.

FOR THE VINAIGRETTE:
1¼ to 1½ lb. fresh ripe plum tomatoes, seeded and cut into ½-inch dice (2 cups)
1 large or 2 medium shallots, thinly sliced
¼ cup lightly packed chopped fresh basil
⅓ cup red-wine vinegar
¾ cup extra-virgin olive oil
¾ tsp. kosher salt; more to taste
Freshly ground black pepper

FOR THE STEAK:
2 Tbs. extra-virgin olive oil
2 medium cloves garlic, minced
2 Tbs. chopped fresh aromatic herbs (thyme, sage, rosemary, marjoram, or a mix)
1 Tbs. kosher salt
1 Tbs. ground black pepper
1½- to 2-lb. flank steak, trimmed of any excess fat and membrane

Make the vinaigrette: Toss all the vinaigrette ingredients together in a medium bowl, taking care not to rough up the tomatoes too much. You'll need to use a fair amount of salt to bring out the flavor of the tomatoes. The vinaigrette should have a slightly peppery bite. Set aside at room temperature until serving time.

Grill the steak: Mix the oil, garlic, herbs, salt, and pepper in a small bowl. Rub all over the steak and let sit for about 20 minutes at room temperature. Meanwhile, heat a gas grill to medium high (you should be able to hold your hand 2 inches above the grate for 3 to 4 seconds) or prepare a medium-hot charcoal fire. Grill until medium rare, 12 to 15 minutes, turning the steak every 3 to 4 minutes to ensure even cooking. The thickest part of the steak will register 135° to 140°F on an instant-read thermometer. Transfer the steak to a cutting board and let it rest for 3 to 5 minutes. Slice the flank steak straight down at ½-inch intervals for slices that are chewy yet juicy. (For more delicate slices of meat, slice at an angle into thinner pieces. These are easier to chew but dry out more quickly.) Portion the slices onto dinner plates, spoon on the vinaigrette, and serve.

Arugula's flavor ranges from mild to intense. Choose small, young leaves for the mildest flavor or larger leaves for a spicy kick.

Seared Beef Tenderloin with Sun-Dried Tomato Butter, Mushrooms & Arugula

Serves two.

If you can't get medallions, buy filet mignon (tenderloin steaks) and cut them in half to a ¹⁄₂-inch thickness.

3 oil-packed sun-dried tomato halves, drained and minced
4 Tbs. unsalted butter, well softened
¹⁄₄ tsp. sherry vinegar
Kosher salt and freshly ground black pepper
4 beef tenderloin medallions, ¹⁄₂ inch thick (³⁄₄ lb. total)
1 Tbs. olive oil
2 shallots, minced
¹⁄₄ lb. cremini mushrooms, stems trimmed and discarded; caps wiped clean and sliced about ¹⁄₄ inch thick
¹⁄₂ lb. arugula, trimmed, washed, and dried (or 10 oz. packaged baby arugula)

Mix the minced sun-dried tomatoes with 2 Tbs. of the butter and the vinegar. Season with a pinch or two of salt, wrap in plastic, and shape it into a 2-inch-long cylinder. Put in the freezer to firm.

Season the beef well on both sides with salt and pepper. In a large skillet, heat the olive oil over medium-high heat until quite hot. Sear the medallions until well browned on both sides and cooked to rare, about 2 minutes per side (or longer if you like your steak cooked more). Transfer to a plate and tent with foil to keep warm. Add the remaining 2 Tbs. butter to the pan. When it's foaming, add the shallots, cook for 30 seconds, and add the mushrooms and a good pinch of salt. Sauté until the mushrooms are well browned, 2 to 3 minutes. Add the arugula to the pan and toss with the mushrooms, cooking just until the leaves have wilted. Arrange the sautéed vegetables on dinner plates, top with the beef, and serve with a slice or two of the chilled butter on the meat.

Classic Grilled Hamburgers

Yields four 6-oz. burgers.

Ground chuck makes great burgers—it has a nice balance of fat and flavor. Try to get 85% lean ground chuck rather than 80% lean, which can cause grill flare-ups and shrinks more during cooking.

1½ lb. ground chuck
1 tsp. kosher salt
½ tsp. freshly ground black pepper
4 hamburger buns

If using charcoal, arrange the coals in an even layer and light one side so that the fire will "walk" across the coals and will be hotter on one side than the other. If using gas, set one burner to medium high and the other to medium low. When the grill is hot, clean the grate by rubbing it with a grill brush and a wadded-up oiled paper towel.

Meanwhile, put the ground beef in a mixing bowl; sprinkle with the salt and pepper. Mix gently and briefly to avoid overworking the meat. Shape the beef into four patties that are about 1 inch thick. (If you like thicker burgers, shape the patties ¼ inch thicker and grill the hamburgers a few minutes longer on each side for the same stages of doneness.)

When the first half of the fire has passed its peak intensity and the second half is still quite hot (you should be able to hold your hand 2 inches above this side of the grate for no longer than 2 seconds), grill the burgers to the doneness you like; for medium, grill about 5 minutes per side. Don't press on the burgers; you'll only press out the juices. Transfer the burgers to a plate and tent them with aluminum foil while you toast the hamburger buns briefly on the cooler side of the grill, cut side down. Serve with an array of toppings as suggested below.

For even better burgers, try these toppings

Each of these flavorful toppings yields enough to cover four burgers; all can be prepared ahead, too.

Tomato-Chipotle Ketchup

Purée one 12-oz. can plum tomatoes in a food processor; strain (discard the liquid), and set aside (or use a 12-oz. can of good-quality tomato purée). Sauté one small, thinly sliced onion in a little oil until translucent. Add 2 Tbs. brown sugar; cook for 2 minutes. Stir in the tomato purée, 2 tsp. tomato paste, 2 canned chipotle chiles (seeded and minced), 2 Tbs. cider vinegar, and 2 tsp. ground coriander. Simmer until thickened, about 25 minutes. Taste and adjust the seasonings and let cool.

Roasted Peppers & Goat Cheese

Grill or roast a red bell pepper until charred; seal in a bag or bowl to steam. Combine 1 Tbs. extra-virgin olive oil, 1 tsp. aged sherry vinegar, ½ tsp. kosher salt, ¼ tsp. freshly ground black pepper, and ⅛ tsp. crushed red pepper flakes. Peel and seed the pepper, separate the lobes at their natural clefts (or cut into wide strips), toss in the marinade, and let sit for about 20 minutes. Top each burger with a pepper slice or two and some goat cheese.

Bacon & Cheese

Brown eight slices good-quality bacon until crisp; drain on paper towels. Top each burger with a thin slice of good Cheddar and two bacon strips; move the burger to a cooler part of the grill and cover briefly so the cheese begins to melt.

Blue Cheese & Walnuts

Mince 1 clove garlic with a sprinkle of kosher salt and a pinch of black pepper; add 1 Tbs. chopped walnuts. Crumble 2 to 3 oz. blue cheese; mash in the garlic and nuts until well blended. Top each warm burger with a generous dollop.

Marinated Onions

Thinly slice a small red onion into rings. Add 2 Tbs. red-wine vinegar, 1 Tbs. extra-virgin olive oil, 2 tsp. kosher salt, 1 tsp. sugar, and a pinch red pepper flakes; toss to blend. Let marinate for at least 30 minutes.

Grilled Portabellas

Brush a large portabella mushroom with olive oil. Grill over a medium fire, turning, until the stem and cap are cooked through, 6 to 8 minutes; slice thinly. Drizzle the slices with extra-virgin olive oil and a few drops of balsamic vinegar, season with salt and pepper, and let marinate for 20 to 30 minutes.

Sun-Dried Tomatoes & Basil

Chop eight pieces of oil-packed or reconstituted sun-dried tomatoes; drain well. Combine with 1 Tbs. extra-virgin olive oil, 1 tsp. red-wine vinegar, a pinch of salt, freshly ground black pepper, and a few chopped fresh basil leaves. (If you're using oil-packed sun-dried tomatoes, use less olive oil.)

Prosciutto & Arugula

Top each burger with one slice of folded prosciutto, a pinch of ground black pepper, and an arugula leaf.

Grilled Pork Rib Chops with Fresh Herb Rub

Serves four.

The brown sugar and molasses brine helps keep the pork chops juicy and adds a subtle flavor.

FOR THE BRINE:
3½ cups water
¼ cup kosher salt
¼ cup dark brown sugar
1 Tbs. molasses
1 cup ice cubes
4 bone-in pork rib chops, ¾ to 1 inch thick (2½ to 3 lb. total)

FOR THE CHOPS:
1 Tbs. chopped garlic
1 Tbs. crushed fennel seeds
1 Tbs. finely chopped fresh sage
1 Tbs. finely chopped fresh rosemary
2 tsp. kosher salt
2 tsp. coarsely ground black pepper

Brine the chops: Pour the water into a large bowl or plastic tub. Add the salt, sugar, and molasses and stir until dissolved. Stir in the ice so the brine chills quickly. Add the pork chops, set a plate on top to keep them submerged, and cover the bowl. Refrigerate for at least 4 hours but no more than 6 hours (less for thin chops). Transfer the pork chops to paper towels, or wrap the chops in plastic and keep them refrigerated for up to two days.

Grill the chops: In a small food processor, combine the garlic, fennel seeds, sage, rosemary, salt, and pepper. Pulse several times to blend well. Lightly coat each chop on both sides with the herb rub.

Prepare a charcoal fire so there are thicker and thinner layers of coals for areas of varying heat. For a gas grill, set one side to medium high and the other side to low.

When the thicker area of coals is medium hot (you'll be able to hold your hand just above the grate for about 2 seconds), set the chops directly over them, or over the medium-high area on a gas grill. If flare-ups occur, move the chops momentarily to a cooler area. Sear the chops over the hotter area for about 1½ minutes per side and then use tongs to move them to the area that's less hot. Cover the grill and continue cooking until the chops are firm and their internal temperature reaches 145° to 150°F, another 3 to 4 minutes per side.

Transfer the chops to a clean platter and let them rest for 5 minutes so the juices redistribute and the chops finish cooking.

Hamburgers with Watercress & Roquefort Butter

Serves four.

Using watercress as opposed to say, iceberg lettuce, to top this rich blue-cheese burger adds a welcome peppery bite. Be sure to wash and dry the watercress well.

1½ lb. ground beef (preferably chuck)
Kosher salt and freshly ground black pepper
3 oz. Roquefort cheese, crumbled (a generous ⅓ cup)
2 Tbs. unsalted butter, softened at room temperature
4 hamburger buns or kaiser rolls, split
4 very thin slices red onion
1 cup loosely packed watercress sprigs, tough stems removed, well rinsed and dried

Heat the oven to 400°F. Season the beef with salt and pepper and shape it into four patties about 1 inch thick. Season both sides of each patty with salt and pepper.

In a small bowl, mix the Roquefort and butter with a rubber spatula.

Heat a large, heavy sauté pan over medium-high heat for 1 minute. Set the hamburgers in the pan, reduce the heat to medium, and cook until well browned on the first side, 4 to 5 minutes. Flip the burgers and cook to your liking: another 4 minutes for medium rare, or another 6 minutes for medium.

Meanwhile, toast the buns or rolls, split sides up, on a baking sheet in the oven until crusty and very light gold, 6 to 8 minutes. Spread each cut side of each bun with about 1 Tbs. of the Roquefort butter. Serve the hamburgers on the toasted buns, topped with the onion and watercress.

Orange-Chile Beef Stir-Fry

Serves two to three.

Irresistibly spicy sweet and ready in minutes, this fragrant stir-fry would be just as tasty with sliced chicken, pork, shrimp, or even a mix. Serve this over plain rice or—even better—jasmine rice.

1½ Tbs. soy sauce
2 tsp. cornstarch
½ cup homemade or low-salt chicken broth
1 Tbs. fresh orange juice
1 Tbs. dry sherry
½ tsp. finely grated orange zest
½ tsp. toasted sesame oil
2 Tbs. vegetable oil
1 heaping Tbs. minced fresh ginger
1 clove garlic, finely chopped
2 scallions (white and green parts), thinly sliced
½ tsp. Asian chile paste; more if you want it really spicy
½ lb. assorted vegetables, such as snow peas, red bell pepper, or broccoli, trimmed and thinly sliced or cut into small pieces
½ lb. boneless sirloin or beef strip steak (also called New York sirloin), thinly sliced
Cooked white rice for serving

In a small bowl, whisk 1 Tbs. of the soy sauce with the cornstarch until dissolved. Stir in the remaining soy sauce, the broth, orange juice, sherry, orange zest, and sesame oil. Heat the vegetable oil in a stir-fry pan or large skillet over medium-high to high heat. Add the ginger, garlic, scallions, and chile paste and stir-fry until fragrant, about 30 seconds. Add the vegetables and stir-fry until crisp-tender (if you're using some long-cooking vegetables like broccoli, add them before shorter-cooking ones to give them a head start). Add the sliced beef and stir-fry until just cooked through and the vegetables are tender. Stir the sauce mixture and pour it into the pan. Bring to a boil just to thicken. Serve the stir-fry over rice.

Thai Beef Salad with Mint & Cilantro

Serves two as a first course or a light main course, served with rice.

When you're in the mood for something refreshing and satisfying, nothing compares to a Thai salad, or *yam* (pronounced YUM).

FOR THE DRESSING:
1 small clove garlic
1 fresh hot red chile (like a red jalapeño), stemmed, cut in half crosswise (not seeded)
2 Tbs. fresh lime juice
1½ Tbs. fish sauce
2 Tbs. very thinly sliced lemongrass (from 2 stalks; remove the tough outer leaves and slice the tender white core)
1¼ tsp. light brown sugar
¼ tsp. red chile flakes

FOR THE STEAK:
½ Tbs. vegetable oil
1 1-inch-thick beef strip steak (also called New York strip), 9 to 10 oz.
¼ cup thinly sliced shallot rings (from about 2 medium shallots)
¼ cup loosely packed fresh mint leaves, roughly chopped
3 Tbs. roughly chopped cilantro leaves and stems
Iceberg lettuce leaves for serving

Make the dressing: Using a chef's knife, mince the garlic and one of the chile halves and then scrape them together against the cutting board with the flat side of the knife until they make a coarse paste (you can also do this in a mortar and pestle). Put the paste in a small bowl. Slice the remaining chile half into thin rings and add it to the paste, along with the lime juice, fish sauce, lemongrass, brown sugar, and red chile flakes. Stir well and set aside.

Cook the steak: Heat the oil in a medium skillet over medium-high heat. Sear the steak until it's well browned on one side, 5 to 6 minutes. Flip and cook until

the second side is dark brown and the meat is medium rare (touch the steak or cut into it to check), another 5 to 6 minutes. Transfer to a cutting board and let rest for 5 minutes. Slice the steak thinly and then cut into bite-size pieces.

In a medium bowl, combine the beef (and any accumulated juices), shallots, mint, and cilantro. Stir the dressing and pour it on top. Toss gently.

Transfer the beef to a platter and serve immediately with the lettuce leaves, or plate individual servings with a portion of beef cradled in a few lettuce leaves.

Don't be shy: Fresh herbs like mint and cilantro, and spices like ginger and garlic, give Asian salads their appeal.

Seared Rib-Eye with Montreal Spice Mix

Serves four.

Toasting the whole spices in a skillet opens up their flavors and aromas. Watch carefully so they don't burn.

1 Tbs. vegetable oil; more for the baking sheet
1 Tbs. finely chopped garlic (about 2 large cloves)
1 Tbs. finely chopped shallot (1 small)
½ tsp. black peppercorns, cracked
½ tsp. coriander seeds, cracked
½ tsp. garlic powder
¼ tsp. white peppercorns, cracked
¼ tsp. mustard seeds
Pinch crushed red pepper flakes
Kosher salt
4 rib-eye steaks, 1 inch thick (about 10 oz. each)

Heat the oven to 400°F.

Heat the oil in a small sauté pan over medium-high heat for 1 minute. Remove the pan from the heat, add the garlic and shallot, and let them soften, stirring occasionally, for 2 minutes. With a small spoon, transfer the garlic and shallot to a plate lined with paper towels, leaving the oil in the pan. Return the pan to medium heat and stir in the black peppercorns, coriander, garlic powder, white peppercorns, mustard seeds, red pepper, and ¼ tsp. salt. Cook, stirring frequently, until the spices are fragrant and the mustard seeds begin to pop, 2 to 4 minutes. Transfer to the plate with the garlic.

Turn on the exhaust fan. Line a rimmed baking sheet with foil and oil it lightly. Season the steaks with salt on both sides. Heat a heavy 12-inch skillet over high heat for about 3 minutes. Sear two of the steaks in the pan until they're well browned, about 2 minutes per side. Transfer the steaks to the baking sheet. Sear the remaining steaks in the same manner. Put the baking sheet with all four steaks in the oven. Cook for 5 minutes for medium rare, or to the doneness you prefer. Transfer the steaks to a platter, sprinkle with the spice mix, and cover loosely with foil. Let the meat rest for 5 minutes and then serve immediately.

Grilled Pork Tenderloin with Salsa Verde

Serves two to three.

One 1-lb. pork tenderloin
⅓ cup plus 1 Tbs. extra-virgin olive oil
¼ tsp. dried oregano
Kosher salt and freshly ground black pepper
1 cup packed fresh flat-leaf parsley leaves, washed and spun dry
¼ cup shelled walnuts
1 small clove garlic
2 Tbs. capers, drained
1 Tbs. fresh lemon juice
1 tsp. Dijon mustard
1 oil-packed anchovy fillet, rinsed and patted dry

Heat a gas grill to medium or prepare a medium-hot charcoal fire. Trim the pork of any excess fat and silverskin. Rub the pork with 1 Tbs. of the oil, the oregano, ½ tsp. salt, and ¼ tsp. pepper. Set the pork on the hottest part of the grill and close the lid. Grill, covered, turning once, until an instant-read thermometer inserted into the center of the pork registers 140° to 145°F, 15 to 20 minutes. Transfer to a clean cutting board and let rest for 5 minutes.

While the pork is on the grill, combine the remaining ⅓ cup oil, the parsley, walnuts, garlic, capers, lemon juice, mustard, and anchovy in a blender. Pulse the mixture until it forms a coarse paste, about five or six pulses. Slice the pork thinly and serve with the salsa verde spooned over it.

Make it a menu

An Italian shindig

Grilled Bread with Garlic, Olive Oil, Prosciutto & Oranges *p. 6*

Grilled Pork Tenderloin with Salsa Verde *at left*

Grilled Corn & Tomato Salad with Basil Oil *p. 60*

Gingery Plum Cake *p. 190*

Coriander-Rubbed Pork Chops with Orange Hoisin Sauce

Serves four.

Thicker pork chops are better at holding their juices during cooking, so it's worth your while to find a market that carries them or that will cut them to order for you. If you can only find 1-inch-thick chops, keep a close eye on them, as they'll cook through more quickly.

FOR THE SAUCE:
¼ cup hoisin sauce
2 Tbs. rice vinegar
**1½ tsp. frozen orange juice
    concentrate, thawed**

FOR THE PORK CHOPS:
**4 bone-in center-cut pork chops
    (1 to 1½ inches thick)**
¼ cup Asian sesame oil
3 Tbs. freshly cracked coriander seeds
1 Tbs. kosher salt
**1 Tbs. coarsely ground white or black
    pepper**
1 Tbs. olive oil

FOR THE SCALLIONS & PEPPER:
**6 scallions (white and light green
    parts), thinly sliced lengthwise into
    julienne strips**
**1 red bell pepper, cored, seeded,
    and thinly sliced lengthwise into
    julienne strips**
2 Tbs. chopped fresh ginger
3 Tbs. dry sherry
**Kosher salt and freshly ground
    white pepper**

Make the sauce: In a small bowl, mix the hoisin sauce, rice vinegar, and orange juice concentrate.

Cook the chops: Pat the chops dry with paper towels and rub both sides with 2 Tbs. of the sesame oil, the coriander, salt, and pepper. Heat the remaining 2 Tbs. sesame oil and the olive oil in a very large sauté pan over medium-high heat until hot but not smoking. (If you don't have a pan large enough to fit the chops without crowding, use two smaller pans, divide the sesame and olive oils between them, and cook two chops in each.) Cook the chops until well browned on one side, 3 to 5 minutes. Turn and cook the other side until the meat is done, 2 to 4 minutes. (If they start to burn, turn down the heat slightly.) To check for doneness, make a small cut near the bone and look inside—the pork should have a hint of pinkness. If it's still red, cook for another minute and check again. Transfer the chops to a plate, tent with foil, and let rest for 3 to 5 minutes before serving.

Make the garnish: Put the scallions, bell pepper, and ginger in the sauté pan over medium-high heat. (If you used two pans for the chops, use just one for the garnish.) Cook, stirring constantly, until crisp-tender, about 2 minutes. Add the sherry; cook for another 30 seconds. Brush each chop generously with the sauce, top with the vegetables, and serve.

Pork Tenderloin & Spinach Salad with Shallot Dressing

Serves four.

This salad is also terrific with chicken instead of pork. The shallots cook along with the pork, allowing you to mix the dressing in the pan.

FOR THE DRESSING:
3 Tbs. balsamic vinegar
1 tsp. Dijon mustard
2 cloves garlic, chopped
⅓ cup extra-virgin olive oil
1 tsp. chopped fresh rosemary
1 tsp. chopped fresh thyme
Kosher salt and freshly ground black pepper

FOR THE SALAD:
1 bunch spinach (about 10 oz.), stemmed and well washed and dried
1¼ lb. pork tenderloin, rinsed and patted dry
Kosher salt and freshly ground black pepper

1 Tbs. olive oil
6 whole shallots, peeled and quartered
½ cup dried cranberries
1 large ripe, firm pear, peeled, cored, and thinly sliced
½ cup toasted walnuts
8 very thin slices red onion (optional)

Make the dressing: In a medium bowl, whisk the vinegar, mustard, and garlic. Slowly whisk in the olive oil until the mixture is smooth and emulsified. Add the herbs, season with salt and pepper, and mix well. Set aside.

Make the salad: Heat the oven to 350°F. Put the spinach in a large bowl and set aside. Season the tenderloin with salt and pepper. In a large, ovenproof sauté pan, heat the olive oil over high until very hot, add the tenderloin, and sear well, about 2 minutes on all sides. Push the tenderloin

aside and add the shallots to the pan, shaking the pan to coat the shallots with the pan drippings. Put the pan in the oven and roast until the tenderloin is medium rare (135° to 140°F), 15 to 18 minutes, or to the doneness you prefer. Remove the pork from the pan and let it rest on a cutting board for 5 to 10 minutes. Slice it thinly on the bias.

Set the sauté pan over high heat, add the dressing, and bring it just to a boil, scraping the shallots and any pan drippings into the dressing. Pour the dressing over the spinach, add the cranberries and pear, and toss well. Use tongs to distribute the greens, cranberries, and pear slices evenly on four plates. Top with the pork slices and toasted walnuts. Garnish with red onion slices, if you like.

Pork Loin Chops with Fresh Sage, Parsley & Fennel Crust

Serves four.

Letting the meat "cure" while coated with a salted herb crust makes the pork really juicy and allows the flavors of the fresh herbs to penetrate the meat.

3 Tbs. loosely packed medium-finely chopped fresh sage
1 tsp. freshly ground fennel seeds
Grated zest of ½ lemon
1 tsp. kosher salt
Heaping ¼ tsp. freshly ground black pepper
6 Tbs. loosely packed medium-finely chopped fresh flat-leaf parsley
4 boneless pork loin chops (about 1 lb. total), ½ inch thick
¼ cup olive oil

Using your fingers, thoroughly mix the sage, fennel seeds, lemon zest, salt, and pepper in a shallow baking dish or pie pan. Mix in the parsley. Lightly press a chop into the herb mixture to coat one side. Turn it over and coat the other side. The goal

is a uniform and thin crust; you should be able to see the meat through the herbs. Repeat with the remaining chops. Stack the chops and wrap them tightly in plastic wrap. Refrigerate for at least 8 hours and up to 24 hours.

Heat the olive oil in a large (12-inch) skillet set over medium-high heat. When the first wisp of smoke rises from the oil, use tongs to carefully set the chops in the pan in a single layer. (If you need to do this in batches, add more oil to the pan for the second batch and let it get hot.) Cook until the herbs on the bottom turn very deep brown, about 3 minutes. Turn the chops over and cook until the other side is deep brown and the pork is cooked through, about 3 minutes. To test for doneness, press with your finger; the meat should be firm. Or cut into a chop; the meat should be very light rosy pink and still juicy; it continues to cook slightly as it rests. Transfer the chops to a warm platter and let them rest in a warm place for 5 minutes before serving.

Grilled Pork Tenderloin with Sweet Chili Glaze

Serves four to five.

While the glazed pork tastes great on its own, it's even better with a little fruit salsa on the plate (see the recipe at right). Be sure to buy pork tenderloins that haven't been treated or soaked in any kind of solution by the producer.

2 tsp. vegetable oil
2 tsp. chili powder
½ tsp. ground cumin
¼ cup frozen pineapple juice concentrate, thawed
2 pork tenderloins (about 2 lb. total), trimmed
Freshly ground black pepper
Spicy Fruit Salsa (see the recipe at right)

In a small saucepan, heat the oil, chili powder, and cumin over medium heat. When the mixture starts to sizzle and the spices are fragrant, add the pineapple concentrate. Simmer until the mixture reduces to about 2 Tbs. Set aside to cool slightly.

Rub the tenderloins all over with the glaze and then season with pepper.

Heat a gas grill, turning all the burners to high until the grill is fully heated, 10 to 15 minutes.

Put the pork on the hot grill grate. Close the lid and grill for 7 minutes. Turn the pork over, close the lid, and grill for another 6 minutes. Turn off the heat (keep the lid closed) and continue to cook the pork for another 5 minutes. At this point, an instant-read thermometer inserted into the middle of the thickest end of the tenderloin should read 145° to 150°F. (If not, close the lid and let the pork continue to roast in the residual grill heat.) Remove the pork from the grill and let it rest for 5 minutes before carving. Cut it across the grain into ½-inch slices and serve immediately topped with some of the fruit salsa, if you like.

Spicy Fruit Salsa

Serves four to five.

This salsa can accompany just about any grilled meat or fish and can be made with nearly any fruit singly or in a mix: peaches, nectarines, grapes, oranges, apricots, plums, pineapple, mangos, tomatoes, or avocados. You could also use fresh corn kernels, cooked and cooled first.

1½ cups fruit (see the note above), cut into small dice, or cooked corn kernels
¼ medium red onion, cut into small dice, or 2 scallions (white and light green parts), thinly sliced
¼ yellow or red bell pepper, cut into small dice
1 fresh jalapeño or other hot chile, cored, seeded, and minced
1 Tbs. minced fresh cilantro or flat-leaf parsley
2 Tbs. fresh lime juice or rice vinegar
½ tsp. ground cumin or chili powder (optional)
Kosher salt and freshly ground black pepper

Mix all the ingredients, including salt and pepper to taste, in a medium bowl. Let stand for 10 to 15 minutes to allow the flavors to blend.

Sides

**Roasted Baby Squash,
Carrots & Potatoes** *p. 148*

Roasted Baby Squash, Carrots & Potatoes

Yield varies.

Roasting a selection of baby vegetables practically guarantees there will be something offered that everyone likes. The amounts called for in the recipe list are per serving so you can buy and roast according to the number you plan to serve. Leftovers are delicious over soft polenta or with a green salad.

Baby pattypan squash, 2 to 3 per serving
Baby red and yellow potatoes, 2 to 3 per serving
Baby carrots, preferably with tops, 2 to 3 per serving
Extra-virgin olive oil
Kosher salt and freshly ground black pepper
Chopped fresh thyme or rosemary

Heat the oven to 450°F. Wash and dry the vegetables. Trim off any tips or stems that seem extra long, and halve any vegetables that seem a little large. Toss each type of vegetable separately in olive oil (just enough to coat), salt, pepper, and a little chopped thyme or rosemary. Spread the vegetables in a single layer on a rimmed baking sheet, keeping each type in a separate group so you can easily remove one if it cooks faster than the others. Roast in the center of the oven for 10 minutes. Use a spatula to flip and move the vegetables around, and then continue roasting for another 5 minutes. Pierce each type of vegetable with a fork to check for tenderness. If one type is tender, transfer it with a spatula to your serving bowl or platter, tent with aluminum foil, and continue roasting the other vegetables until they're tender, checking every 5 minutes. The longest-cooking vegetable—the potatoes—will take about 25 minutes total.

Broiled Asparagus & Orange Slices with Olive Oil & Shallots

Serves four as a side dish or three as a first course.

This pretty dish would go really well with a grilled steak, especially one that's been treated to a spice rub. The cooked orange slices—skin and all—are not only edible but also delicious and tender but with a snappy zing. Feel free to substitute lemon in place of the orange.

1 lb. asparagus, woody stem ends snapped off and discarded
2 Tbs. extra-virgin olive oil
Kosher salt and freshly ground black pepper
1 shallot, thinly sliced and separated into rings
4 very thin orange slices, cut into quarters
¼ tsp. finely grated orange zest

Position a rack as close to the broiling element as possible. Heat the broiler on high. In a bowl, toss the asparagus spears with the olive oil to coat and season with salt and pepper. Arrange the shallot slices in a thin layer on one side of a rimmed baking sheet or jellyroll pan. Put the asparagus in a single layer on top of them. Toss the orange slices with the leftover oil, salt, and pepper in the bowl you used for the asparagus. Arrange the slices in a single layer alongside the asparagus. Broil until the asparagus and the oranges just start to char, 5 to 8 minutes. Remove from the oven and sprinkle the asparagus with the orange zest. Arrange the asparagus, shallots, and oranges on a serving dish. Serve hot, warm, or at room temperature.

Sautéed Zucchini with Sun-Dried Tomatoes & Basil

Serves four as a side dish.

Two quick and easy steps give you the best-tasting, best-textured zucchini: Salting it well for about 10 minutes before cooking draws out some of the water; and cooking it over very high heat caramelizes the flesh before it has a chance to steam and get soggy.

3 small or 2 medium zucchini (about 1 lb.)
Kosher salt
3 Tbs. extra-virgin olive oil
2 cloves garlic, smashed and peeled
2 oil-packed sun-dried tomatoes, drained and finely diced
6 fresh basil leaves, torn into large pieces
Freshly ground black pepper
1 tsp. fresh lemon juice

Wash the zucchini well to remove any grit and dry them with paper towels; trim off the ends. Quarter each zucchini lengthwise.

Slice off the top ¼ to ½ inch of the soft seed core by running a sharp knife down the length of each quarter; it's fine if some of the seeds remain. Arrange the zucchini, cut side up, on a baking sheet lined with paper towels. Sprinkle with kosher salt (about ½ tsp. per 1 lb. of zucchini) and set aside for 10 minutes. Blot the quarters dry with paper towels and cut each on the diagonal into ¾-inch-thick diamonds.

Heat a large (12-inch) skillet over medium-high heat for 1 minute. Pour in 2 Tbs. of the oil. When the oil is hot, add the zucchini and garlic, and sauté, stirring occasionally, until the zucchini browns and softens enough that you can cut through it with the side of a fork, about 5 minutes. Take the pan off the heat, toss in the sun-dried tomatoes and basil, and season generously with salt and pepper. Drizzle with the lemon juice and the remaining 1 Tbs. oil and serve immediately.

Swiss Chard with Ginger & Peanuts

Serves four.

Swiss chard is a lot like spinach only sturdier. It takes well to all kinds of flavors; here it gets an Asian treatment.

2 lb. Swiss chard (about 2 bunches)
2 Tbs. extra-virgin olive oil
2 tsp. finely chopped garlic (about 4 cloves)
1 Tbs. minced fresh ginger
½ red bell pepper, cut into very thin strips
1 tsp. sugar
Kosher salt
Pinch dried red chile flakes
¼ cup unsalted roasted peanuts, coarsely chopped

Fill a clean sink or very large bowl with cold water and wash the Swiss chard to remove any grit. Transfer to paper towels and let dry for a couple of minutes (it's fine if a little water clings to the leaves).

Remove the thick part of each stem by cutting a V-shaped notch partway into the leaf. Split each leaf in half lengthwise by slicing down the center rib. Stack the halved leaves (in batches if necessary) and cut them in half crosswise to get 4- to 6-inch pieces.

Heat the oil in a large skillet over medium-high heat for 1 minute. Working in batches, pile the Swiss chard into the pan, turning and tossing gently until the leaves begin to wilt and turn glossy. Add a new batch of leaves as the previous batch wilts and makes room for more.

When all the chard is wilted, sprinkle in the garlic, ginger, red bell pepper, sugar, and a little salt and toss well. Lower the heat to medium low, cover, and cook for 4 minutes. Remove the lid, raise the heat to high, add the chile flakes, and continue to cook for 2 minutes so that much of the liquid evaporates; the leaves should be tender but not overly soft. Sprinkle with the peanuts and serve immediately.

Slow-Sautéed Asparagus with Pancetta

Serves four.

A longer, slower sauté eliminates the parboiling often called for in asparagus recipes. The asparagus becomes wonderfully browned and tender, with all of its flavor intact.

1½ oz. thinly sliced pancetta cut into strips (to yield about ¼ cup)
1 Tbs. olive oil
2 small cloves garlic, very thinly sliced
2 to 3 tsp. unsalted butter
1¾ lb. medium to large asparagus (28 to 32 spears), woody ends snapped off, stems peeled, rinsed, and drained
Kosher salt and freshly ground black pepper
Lemon wedges for serving

Put the pancetta and olive oil in a heavy 10-inch skillet and set over medium heat. Cook the pancetta, stirring frequently, until light brown and slightly crisp (don't let it fully crisp and harden), about 10 minutes. Remove from the heat and transfer the pancetta with a slotted spoon to drain on a plate lined with paper towels; leave the fat in the pan.

Set the skillet back over medium heat, add the garlic, and cook, stirring continually, until just starting to turn light gold, about 30 seconds. Transfer the garlic with the slotted spoon to drain with the pancetta. If less than 1 Tbs. fat remains in the pan, add enough olive oil to compensate. Melt the butter in the pan, add the asparagus, and season with salt and pepper. Sauté, stirring frequently, until the spears are light golden brown and tender (they won't brown evenly) with a slight edge of crispness, 20 to 30 minutes.

Transfer the spears to a serving platter, scatter the reserved pancetta and garlic over them, and serve with the lemon wedges.

Mushrooms & Spinach with Soppressata Crisps

Serves four to five.

What's nice about this dish is that the vegetables don't need to be cooked separately. Instead, they're added to the pan in succession, according to the amount of time each needs to cook.

1 oz. very thinly sliced hot soppressata or other spicy dried sausage, slices quartered (about ¼ cup or 8 slices ⅛ inch thick)
2 Tbs. extra-virgin olive oil; more for drizzling
15 oz. cremini mushrooms, halved if small or quartered or cut into sixths if very large (a scant 5 cups)
Kosher salt and freshly ground black pepper
5 medium scallions (white and green parts), trimmed and cut into 1-inch pieces (1½ cups)
2 medium cloves garlic, minced
5 oz. baby spinach (about 6 cups)

Put the soppressata in a large (preferably 12-inch) skillet over medium heat. Cook until crisp, 5 to 7 minutes. Transfer to a small plate lined with paper towels. Increase the heat to medium high and let the pan heat up for 1 minute. Pour in the oil and swirl to coat the pan. As soon as the oil is shimmering—but not smoking—add the mushrooms in an even layer. Season with salt and pepper and let cook undisturbed until the mushrooms begin to brown, about 3 minutes. Add the scallions and sauté, stirring as needed, until the mushrooms are golden brown and tender and the scallions are lightly browned in places and softened, another 6 to 7 minutes. If the vegetables seem to be cooking too fast or the pan bottom is starting to burn, lower the heat to medium. (Or, if using an electric stovetop, take the pan off the heat momentarily to let the pan cool.) Stir in the garlic and cook for another 30 seconds. Turn off the heat and add the spinach and crisped soppressata, flipping and stirring to blend and to wilt the spinach. Season to taste with salt and pepper, drizzle with a little olive oil, and serve immediately.

Japanese Eggplant with Sesame-Ginger Glaze

Serves four to six.

Slender Japanese eggplant work beautifully in this recipe, and they don't need to be salted in advance to remove bitterness. If you can't find them, cut a regular eggplant into half-inch rounds, salt generously, and let sit in a colander for half an hour. Pat dry and continue with the recipe.

1 Tbs. rice vinegar or cider vinegar
1 Tbs. soy sauce
1 Tbs. hoisin sauce (optional)
3 Tbs. toasted sesame oil
1 tsp. sugar
2 tsp. minced fresh ginger
3 cloves garlic, minced
8 small Japanese eggplant (about 4 oz. each), halved lengthwise
2 Tbs. oil
Kosher salt and freshly ground black pepper
2 scallions, minced

Heat a gas grill to medium or prepare a medium charcoal fire. Mix the vinegar, soy sauce, hoisin sauce (if using), sesame oil, sugar, ginger, and garlic in a small bowl. Brush the eggplant with oil and season with salt and pepper. Grill over medium heat, cut side down, about 5 minutes. Flip the eggplant and baste with some of the sesame-ginger glaze. Continue grilling until the flesh is quite soft and the eggplant is just starting to collapse. Remove from the grill and drizzle with more glaze. Top with the minced scallions and serve warm.

tip: When adding cured meats to a vegetable dish, take it easy on the added salt and taste as you go; the salt in these products varies.

Red Potato Slices Roasted with Lemon & Olives

Serves six.

Do eat the lemon slices (including any very tender rind) along with the potatoes for the best flavor.

2 lb. medium or large red potatoes (about 5 medium), scrubbed and sliced ¼ inch thick
3 Tbs. olive oil; more for the pan
1 lemon, very thinly sliced (discard the ends and seeds)
2 cloves garlic, minced
¼ cup chopped fresh flat-leaf parsley
1½ tsp. kosher salt
¼ tsp. freshly ground black pepper
⅓ cup pitted oil-cured olives

Position a rack in the center of the oven and heat the oven to 425°F.

Generously oil a large baking dish (a 9x13-inch size works well, or use an oval gratin dish). In a large bowl, combine the potatoes, the 3 Tbs. oil, lemon slices, garlic, parsley, salt, and pepper; toss well. Spread the potato mixture in the baking dish so the potatoes are evenly layered (it can be rustic looking). Roast, turning the potatoes with a spatula every 20 minutes, until most of the potatoes are crisp and golden and the lemon skins are shriveled and caramelized, about 1 hour. Scatter the olives over the potatoes for the last 3 to 5 minutes of cooking.

French-Style Potato Salad

Serves four.

Wine flavors are subtle but important in this salad, so use a wine you wouldn't mind drinking. White-wine vinegar will also work, giving you a result that's a little more tangy.

2 lb. Yukon Gold potatoes, scrubbed but not peeled
1⅓ cups dry white wine (or ½ cup white-wine vinegar)
Salt and freshly ground white pepper to taste
½ cup extra-virgin olive oil
1 Tbs. minced shallot
⅔ cup chopped scallions

Boil the whole unpeeled potatoes in generously salted water until fork-tender, 20 to 30 minutes, depending on size. As soon as you can handle the potatoes but while they're still warm, slice them just under ½ inch thick with a very sharp knife.

In a small saucepan over medium heat, boil the wine until it's reduced by half. (If using vinegar, don't cook it.) Sprinkle the salt, pepper, and hot reduced wine (or the vinegar) over the warm potatoes; toss gently. Add the olive oil, tossing just until combined, and then add the shallots and scallions. Taste and adjust the seasonings. Serve at room temperature.

VARIATIONS

One of the wonderful things about this quick and easy potato salad is that you can vary it endlessly (below are a few favorites). Follow the basic recipe at left; just omit the scallions and substitute one of these combinations:

- Chopped tomato, diced crisped bacon, and hard-cooked egg
- Chopped anchovies and sliced roasted red peppers
- Chopped olives, minced garlic, and cubed chicken or turkey
- Lemon juice, caviar, crème fraîche, and snipped chives
- Paprika, capers, and smoked salmon (to avoid cooking the salmon, don't add it until the salad is at room temperature)

Potato Cakes with Chives & Sour Cream

Yields four cakes.

These are essentially seasoned mashed potatoes shaped into cakes and pan-fried until they've developed a delicious crusty exterior. They can be shaped into patties up to a day before frying. Serve with bacon and eggs or alongside roasted meats. Of course, you can skip the frying and just serve the chive-mashed potatoes as is.

**1 lb. Yukon Gold potatoes,
    peeled**
Kosher salt
**¼ cup packed finely grated
    Asiago cheese (1 oz.)**
5 Tbs. extra-virgin olive oil
**3 Tbs. sour cream; more for
    serving**
**¼ tsp. freshly ground black
    pepper**
**¼ cup thinly sliced chives; more
    for serving**

Put the potatoes and 1 tsp. salt in a medium saucepan and add water to cover by about ½ inch. Cover and bring to a boil over high heat. Uncover, reduce the heat to prevent a boilover, and boil until the potatoes are tender when pierced with a fork, 20 to 25 minutes.

Drain the potatoes and pass them through a ricer or food mill back into the saucepan (or mash them as smoothly as possible with a hand masher). Add the cheese, 3 Tbs. of the olive oil, the sour cream, pepper, and ½ tsp. salt; mix thoroughly. Add the chives and stir until well mixed. Taste and add more salt and pepper, if necessary. Divide the potato mixture into quarters and shape each into a squat patty about ¾ inch thick. (If making ahead, put the patties on a plate or tray in a single layer, cover with plastic, and refrigerate.)

Heat the remaining 2 Tbs. oil in a 10-inch nonstick pan over medium-high heat. When the oil is hot, set the cakes in the pan so they aren't touching. Cook until a deep brown crust forms, 2 to 3 minutes, and then turn and brown the other side, another 2 to 3 minutes (the cooking time will be a bit longer if the patties are chilled). Serve immediately, topped with a dab of sour cream and a sprinkle of chives.

Warm Potatoes with Basil Vinaigrette

Serves four; yields about ¾ cup vinaigrette.

Though this dressing can be whisked by hand, a food processor renders it a wonderful shade of green.

1¾ lb. small red potatoes, scrubbed
½ cup packed fresh basil leaves
1 small clove garlic
3 Tbs. red-wine vinegar
1 Tbs. Dijon mustard
¾ tsp. kosher salt
Freshly ground black pepper
⅔ cup canola oil

Steam the potatoes over boiling water until tender when pierced with a paring knife, about 15 minutes. (Alternatively, boil them in well-salted water until tender. Drain them and return them to the pot in which they were cooked and set over low heat for a few seconds to dry them.)

In a food processor, combine the basil, garlic, vinegar, mustard, salt, and pepper. With the motor running, gradually add the oil until completely incorporated.

When the potatoes are cool enough to handle, halve or quarter them, depending on their size. Put them in a serving bowl and drizzle with about ½ cup of the vinaigrette. Serve warm with extra vinaigrette on the side, if you like.

Olive Oil Mashed Potatoes

Serves four.

The parsley and olive oil make these mashed potatoes feel light and lovely. To keep the parsley fresh-tasting and green, add it just before serving.

2 lb. Yukon Gold potatoes, peeled and cut into 2-inch cubes
2 Tbs. kosher salt; more for seasoning
½ cup extra-virgin olive oil
½ cup potato cooking water or milk; more as needed
Freshly ground black pepper
¼ cup chopped fresh flat-leaf parsley

Put a large pot of water on high heat. Add the potatoes and salt and bring to a boil. Boil just until a skewer or knife can easily penetrate the center of the potatoes, 20 to 30 minutes.

When the potatoes are done, reserve about 1 cup of the cooking water. Drain the potatoes and return them to the pot in which they were cooked. Mash them with a potato masher. With a wooden spoon, stir in the olive oil. Add some of the cooking water or milk until you reach the consistency you like. Season generously with salt and several grinds of black pepper.

Just before serving, check the consistency of the potatoes and add a little more of the cooking water if they need loosening. Mix in the parsley. Taste and adjust the seasonings.

Green Beans with Mushrooms, Cream & Toasted Breadcrumbs

Serves four.

Here's a green bean recipe for those still-chilly spring nights.

FOR THE BREADCRUMBS:
1 cup coarse fresh breadcrumbs
¼ cup olive oil
Freshly ground black pepper

FOR THE GREEN BEANS:
4 Tbs. unsalted butter
½ lb. white or cremini mushrooms, quartered
1 small onion, finely diced (about ½ cup)
1 tsp. kosher salt
3 medium cloves garlic, minced
10 oz. fresh green beans, trimmed
¾ tsp. freshly ground black pepper
1½ cups homemade or low-salt chicken broth or water, or a combination
½ cup heavy or whipping cream

Make the breadcrumbs: Heat the oven to 375°F. Toss the breadcrumbs in a bowl with the olive oil and pepper. Spread them on a baking sheet and toast until golden, stirring occasionally, about 10 minutes.

Cook the beans: Melt the butter in a large skillet over medium heat. Add the mushrooms and onion. Increase the heat to high to reheat the pan and then drop the heat back to medium. When the mushrooms are slightly golden, add the salt. Sauté until the mushrooms are deep golden, about 5 minutes. Add the garlic, green beans, and pepper.

Add the broth or water and simmer, stirring occasionally, until the liquid has reduced by about three-quarters and the beans are fork-tender and fully cooked (taste one to check), about 20 minutes.

Add the cream and simmer until the sauce is reduced to a very thick consistency, about 10 minutes. Serve the beans and sauce topped with the toasted breadcrumbs.

Simply Delicious Green Beans

Serves four as a side dish.

To really enjoy the fresh flavor of green beans, cook them just until tender (don't undercook or overcook) and dress them simply with your best olive oil and plenty of sea salt. Then, if you feel like gussying up the dish, toss in a flavorful extra or two—a little creamy goat cheese, quartered pitted olives, shredded endive or radicchio, toasted nuts, quartered cherry tomatoes—while the beans are still warm.

1 lb. fresh, tender green beans
1½ Tbs. good-quality extra-virgin olive oil
¼ teaspoon fleur de sel or other medium-grain sea salt; more to taste

Bring a pot of water to boil over high heat. Rinse the beans and trim their stems. Boil the beans just until tender, 4 to 5 minutes for regular green beans, less for extra-thin filet beans. Drain well. Spread the beans on a platter or shallow serving dish. If there is still water clinging to them, let them dry briefly. While the beans are still hot, drizzle with the olive oil. Toss gently with your hands or two serving forks, turning the beans until they're evenly coated with oil. Sprinkle with sea salt, toss, and serve warm.

Southwestern Squash Sauté

Serves four to six as a side dish.

This sauté is an especially good partner to grilled fish, chicken, or pork. With the addition of some cheese and a sliver of ripe avocado, you get a wonderful filling for quesadillas and soft tacos.

3 Tbs. olive oil
1 medium onion, diced
Kosher salt
1 medium red bell pepper, diced
3 small or 2 medium zucchini or
**   summer squash (about 1 lb.),**
**   cut in medium (⅓-inch) dice**
1 large ear fresh corn, kernels
**   cut from the cob**
2 cloves garlic, minced
1 large or 2 small fresh hot
**   chiles (such as serrano or**
**   jalapeño), seeded and minced,**
**   or 1 mild green chile (such as**
**   poblano or Anaheim), roasted,**
**   peeled, seeded, and diced**
Freshly ground black pepper
½ tsp. ground cumin
¼ tsp. chili powder (optional)
1 to 2 Tbs. roughly chopped
**   fresh cilantro**
½ lime

Set a large skillet over medium-high heat. When hot, add 2 Tbs. of the oil and let it heat. Add the onion, season with a little salt, and sauté until translucent, about 2 minutes. Add the diced red pepper and a little more salt and sauté for another 1 to 2 minutes. Transfer the pepper and onion to a bowl or plate. Turn the heat to high, add 1 Tbs. more of the oil and the squash. Season with salt and sauté for 3 or 4 minutes, stirring only occasionally, so that it begins to brown lightly and the flesh turns slightly translucent and is pleasantly tender (don't overcook; it should still be toothy, not mushy). Put the peppers and onions back in the pan, add the corn, garlic, and chiles, season again with salt, and sauté for another few minutes. Season with a few grinds of pepper, the cumin, and the chili powder (if using). Toss in the cilantro, squeeze the lime over all, toss, and serve.

If you can, buy corn from a farmers' market or roadside vegetable stand; it will be fresher and taste sweeter. Store the ears in the refrigerator until you use them.

Sweet Corn Relish with Avocado, Jalapeño & Cilantro

Serves four.

Spoon a generous amount of this relish on top of grilled fish or chicken breasts. Add a simple green salad and you have a delicious warm-weather meal.

Kernels from 3 large ears corn (about 2½ cups)
1 small red onion (about 6 oz.), cut into ⅛-inch dice
½ fresh jalapeño, cored, seeded, and minced
3 Tbs. fresh lime juice; more to taste
1 tsp. Champagne vinegar or white-wine vinegar
Kosher salt
½ ripe avocado, pitted
⅓ cup chopped fresh cilantro
3 Tbs. olive oil

Bring a small pot of water to a boil. Add the corn kernels and blanch for 1 minute. Drain and set aside.

In a medium bowl, combine the red onion, jalapeño, lime juice, vinegar, and a generous pinch of salt.

Dice the avocado: Use a paring knife to carefully make ¼-inch thick slices through the flesh without piercing the skin. Rotate the avocado 90 degrees and slice again, to create ¼-inch squares. With the avocado in the palm of your hand, slide a large metal spoon between the skin and flesh and gently scoop out the squares.

Add the avocado pieces, corn kernels, and cilantro to the onion mixture. Add the olive oil and another pinch of salt and stir gently. Season to taste, adding more salt or lime juice as needed.

Overnight Coleslaw with Mustard Seed

Yields 11 cups.

Making your own coleslaw is quite easy, and the results taste so much fresher than store-bought. For the best flavor and texture, make the coleslaw the day before you plan to serve it.

1 head green cabbage, cored and thinly sliced
2 carrots, peeled and grated
1 medium white onion, diced
1 cup white-wine vinegar
¾ cup canola oil
½ cup honey
1 Tbs. fresh lemon juice
2 Tbs. mustard seeds
1 Tbs. kosher salt
½ tsp. freshly ground black pepper

In a large mixing bowl, combine the cabbage, carrots, and onion.

In a saucepan over medium heat, mix the vinegar, oil, honey, lemon juice, mustard seeds, salt, and pepper. Bring to a boil, stirring often. Take the dressing off the heat; immediately pour it over the vegetables. Toss well, cover, and refrigerate for at least 6 hours (overnight is best) before serving.

tip: Slightly bitter vegetables like broccoli and mustard greens really take to the robust flavorings used in Asian cooking.

Spicy Asian-Roasted Broccoli & Snap Peas

Serves four.

If you have trouble finding fresh Thai chiles (also called bird chiles), try using the same amount of the dried version.

5 cups broccoli florets (from about 2 broccoli crowns)

3 cups (about 12 oz.) fresh sugar snap peas, trimmed

6 to 8 red or orange fresh Thai chiles, stems trimmed

3 Tbs. extra-virgin olive oil

2 Tbs. plus 1 tsp. toasted sesame oil

1 tsp. kosher salt

2 Tbs. fresh cilantro leaves, chopped

1½ Tbs. light-colored (white or yellow) miso

1 Tbs. honey

2 tsp. sambal oelek (Asian chile paste)

1 tsp. finely grated orange zest

1 tsp. grated fresh ginger

1 clove garlic, minced

Position a rack in the center of the oven and heat the oven to 450°F.

Put the broccoli, peas, and chiles in a large bowl; toss with 2 Tbs. of the olive oil and 2 Tbs. of the sesame oil. Sprinkle with salt and toss again. Transfer the vegetables to a 10x15-inch Pyrex dish and roast, stirring once, until the peas are lightly browned and the broccoli tops are quite dark in spots, about 22 minutes.

Meanwhile, in a small bowl, whisk the remaining 1 Tbs. olive oil, 1 tsp. sesame oil, cilantro, miso, honey, sambal oelek, orange zest, ginger, and garlic. Pour the mixture over the roasted vegetables and toss to coat. Remove the chiles (or leave them in for color but warn diners not to eat them). Serve immediately.

Spicy Mustard Greens with Asian Noodles

Serves four.

With the beef, this recipe can also act as a light main dish. Leave the beef out, and it's a perfect side for grilled fish or seared chicken. The spicy-sweet heat of fresh ginger combines with the peppery bite of mustard greens to make a very warming dish. If you can't find somen noodles, use another type of Asian noodle or angel hair pasta.

Salt
4 oz. somen noodles
2 tsp. peanut oil
¼ cup vegetable oil
6 oz. cremini mushrooms, thickly sliced
3 Tbs. minced fresh ginger, divided
2 cloves garlic, minced
¼ tsp. dried red pepper flakes
2 cups low-salt chicken broth
8 oz. stemmed mustard greens, coarsely chopped (to yield about 8 cups), thoroughly washed
6 oz. marbled beef (such as a small sirloin, rib-eye, or skirt steak), very thinly sliced and tossed in 1 tsp. peanut oil
2 Tbs. soy sauce
2 tsp. balsamic vinegar
2 Tbs. toasted sesame seeds

In a 4-qt. low-sided soup pot or Dutch oven, bring 2 qt. water to a boil. Add ½ Tbs. salt and the somen noodles. Cook just 3 minutes, and then drain in a colander and rinse under cold water until cool. Drain well and toss with 2 tsp. peanut oil in a medium bowl. Set aside. These can sit for 30 minutes.

In the same pot (or another similar one), heat the vegetable oil over medium heat and sauté the mushrooms until softened and beginning to brown, 4 to 6 minutes. Add half of the ginger, the garlic, the red pepper flakes, and a little of the broth, stirring constantly to scrape up browned bits from the bottom of the pan. Add the rest of the broth and the mustard greens. Bring to a boil, stirring to wilt the greens, and cover. Reduce the heat and simmer about 8 minutes. (Check the texture of the greens; they shouldn't be tough, but they can still have a little toothiness.) Uncover, shut off the heat, and add the thinly sliced beef, soy sauce, vinegar, and the remaining ginger. Stir well.

Using tongs, portion the noodles into shallow serving bowls, putting them to one side. Use tongs to portion some of the greens and beef into each bowl next to the noodles. Spoon some broth from the pan (the meat will finish cooking in it) over all and sprinkle with sesame seeds.

Seared Asparagus with Lemon & Parmesan Curls

Serves four.

Although you can choose to keep the asparagus whole in this dish, it sears better when the spears are cut in half.

¼ tsp. grated lemon zest
1 tsp. fresh lemon juice
2½ Tbs. extra-virgin olive oil
1 lb. large asparagus (about 16 spears), woody ends snapped off, spears peeled and cut in half crosswise
1 clove garlic, peeled and smashed
1 large shallot, cut into ¼-inch disks
Pinch dried red chile flakes
Kosher salt and freshly ground black pepper
¼ cup water; more if needed
10 shavings (2 inches long; use a vegetable peeler) Parmigiano Reggiano

Combine the lemon zest, lemon juice, and ½ Tbs. of the olive oil in a small bowl; set aside. Turn on the exhaust fan and heat a heavy 12-inch skillet or large wok over high heat for 2 minutes. When the pan is hot, pour in the remaining 2 Tbs. olive oil, and a few seconds later, add the asparagus, garlic, shallot, and chile flakes. Season well with salt and pepper. Cook, shaking the pan often, until the asparagus begins to brown and starts to shrivel slightly, 3 to 4 minutes. Reduce the heat to medium low, carefully add the water (it will steam), and cover the pan with the lid ajar. Cook until the asparagus is just tender, 3 to 4 minutes. (If the water evaporates before the asparagus is done, add more, 1 Tbs. at a time.) Drizzle the lemon mixture over the asparagus. Season to taste with salt and pepper. Transfer the asparagus to a small serving dish and top with the Parmesan curls. Serve immediately.

Green & Wax Beans with Brown Butter

Serves four.

The distinctly nutty taste of the brown butter is enhanced by toasted pine nuts.

¼ cup pine nuts
2 Tbs. unsalted butter
½ lb. green beans, ends snapped, cut into 2-inch lengths
½ lb. wax beans, ends snapped, cut into 2-inch lengths
1 small shallot, diced fine
2 Tbs. lemon juice
1 tsp. grated lemon zest
2 tsp. chopped fresh thyme (or 1 tsp. dried)
Salt and freshly ground black pepper to taste

In a small, dry skillet, toast the pine nuts over medium heat, shaking the pan occasionally, until the nuts are fragrant and lightly browned, about 5 minutes. Set aside.

In a large skillet, melt the butter over medium heat until it begins to brown and smell nutty. Be careful: If the butter cooks too long, it will burn; if it isn't cooked long enough, it will lack the deep flavor it needs. Add the beans and shallot, tossing to coat, and cook for 2 to 3 minutes. Add the lemon juice, cover the pan, and cook for 4 to 6 minutes. Do not overcook. Remove the pan from the heat. Toss in the grated lemon zest and thyme. Season with salt and pepper to taste, sprinkle with the toasted pine nuts, and serve.

Braised Asparagus & Cipolline Onions with Pancetta & Balsamic Butter Glaze

Serves three to four.

Cipolline onions have a sweet, delicate flavor that's especially welcome in braises. Shaped like flying saucers, these tiny onions hail from Italy but are becoming a common sight in produce departments here. If you can't find them, substitute shallots as the recipe directs.

1 lb. medium or thick asparagus
2 tsp. balsamic vinegar
2 tsp. fresh lemon juice
1 tsp. Dijon mustard
1 tsp. honey
2 Tbs. extra-virgin olive oil
1½ oz. thinly sliced pancetta, cut into slivers (about ⅓ cup)
1 Tbs. plus 1 tsp. unsalted butter
5 oz. small cipolline onions (about 6) or large shallots (about 6), halved and peeled (quartered if very large)
Kosher salt
⅓ cup homemade or low-salt canned chicken broth

Cut off the tough ends of the asparagus so that all the spears are about 6 to 7 inches long; you should have about 10 oz. trimmed asparagus. Combine the balsamic vinegar, lemon juice, Dijon, and honey in a small bowl; set aside. Heat 1 Tbs. of the oil in a 10-inch straight-sided sauté pan over medium-high heat. Add the pancetta strips and cook, stirring frequently, until browned and crisp, 2 to 3 minutes (don't let them burn). Take the pan off the heat and transfer the pancetta to a plate, leaving behind as much fat as possible.

Return the pan to medium-high heat, add 1 Tbs. of the butter to the fat in the pan, and swirl to melt (there will be browned bits on the bottom of the pan). Add the onions and a pinch of salt and sauté until nicely browned on all sides and beginning to soften, 2 to 3 minutes. Take the pan off the heat and transfer the onions to another plate.

Return the pan to medium-high heat and add the remaining 1 Tbs. olive oil, the asparagus, and ¼ tsp. salt. Toss well with tongs. Cook without stirring until the bottoms of the spears are nicely browned, 3 to 4 minutes. Toss and turn over, and cook for another 1 to 2 minutes to lightly brown another side. Return the onions to the pan, stir, and pour in the chicken broth. Immediately cover the pan and simmer until the liquid is almost completely reduced, about 3 minutes.

Uncover, add the balsamic and Dijon mixture, stir to coat thoroughly, and cook for a few seconds until it has a glazy consistency. Add the remaining 1 tsp. butter and toss to melt and combine, scraping up any browned bits in the pan with a heatproof spatula or a wooden spoon. Toss in the crisped pancetta. Serve right away as individual servings or pour and scrape the contents of the pan onto a small platter and serve family-style.

Spanish Braised Spinach with Chickpeas

Serves six.

This side dish is quite hearty, and so would balance nicely with a light piece of flaky white fish, such as pan-fried cod, halibut, or sea bass.

3 Tbs. olive oil
3 slices bacon (about 2 oz.)
6 cloves garlic, 3 whole and 3 chopped medium fine
6 slices (¼ inch thick) baguette or crusty country bread (about 1½ oz. total)
½ tsp. ground cumin
¼ tsp. paprika
20 oz. fresh spinach, stemmed, washed, drained, and coarsely chopped
1 can (15½ oz.) chickpeas, rinsed and drained
Kosher salt and freshly ground black pepper
1 Tbs. sherry vinegar or another wine vinegar

In a large, straight-sided skillet, heat the olive oil over medium heat and add the bacon. Cook, flipping occasionally, until the bacon is golden and crisp, 6 to 8 minutes. Transfer to a plate lined with paper towels. Add the 3 whole cloves of garlic and the bread to the pan and sauté until the garlic is tender and golden and the bread is deep golden brown on both sides, 4 to 5 minutes. Using tongs or a slotted spoon, transfer the whole garlic cloves and four of the toasts to a mortar (or a small food processor). Set aside the remaining two slices of toast on a paper towel.

To the same skillet, add the 3 cloves chopped garlic, the cumin, and the paprika. Cook, stirring, until fragrant and the garlic begins to brown, 15 to 30 seconds. Increase the heat to medium high and immediately begin adding the spinach in batches, stirring to wilt. When all the spinach is in the pan, add the chickpeas, 1 cup water, 1 tsp. salt, and several grinds of black pepper. Bring to a simmer.

Meanwhile, mash the bread slices and garlic in the mortar or process in the processor (don't mash the two reserved bread slices) with the vinegar and 1 to 2 Tbs. water until puréed.

Stir the mashed bread mixture into the spinach, lower the heat to medium, and simmer until the liquid has reduced almost completely but the spinach is still moist, about 10 minutes. Crumble the bacon and stir it in. Taste and add more salt or vinegar if needed. Crumble the reserved toast over the spinach. Serve hot or warm.

tip: Don't be fooled by spinach. What may look like too much to start with will reduce tremendously when cooked.

1 lb. broccoli
3 Tbs. low-salt canned chicken
   broth, or water
½ tsp. cornstarch
2 Tbs. oyster sauce
1½ tsp. toasted sesame oil
2 Tbs. peanut or vegetable oil
4 cloves garlic, sliced
1-inch piece fresh ginger, peeled,
   cut into quarter-size coins,
   and smashed with the side of
   a knife
1 fresh red chile, thinly sliced
   (optional)

Separate the broccoli florets from the stems. Pare the stems with a paring knife or vegetable peeler and cut them into ¼-inch slices on the diagonal. Separate the floret clusters into smaller florets (1 inch wide) and halve them lengthwise if large. The pieces need to be small to cook quickly, but not so small that they risk getting overcooked.

In a small bowl, stir together the broth and cornstarch until the cornstarch dissolves. Add the oyster sauce and toasted sesame oil and stir to blend.

Heat a large wok (or high-sided skillet) over high heat. When hot, add the peanut oil and swirl to coat. When the oil is hot, add the garlic, ginger, and chile (if using) and stir-fry for 15 seconds to release the garlic's fragrance. Be careful not to let the garlic burn. Add the broccoli stems and florets and stir-fry until crisp-tender, about 3 minutes, adding water 1 to 2 Tbs. at a time, as needed, to prevent burning. Add the oyster sauce mixture and stir-fry for about 30 seconds to allow the cornstarch to thicken the sauce slightly. Immediately transfer to a warm platter and serve.

tip: When buying broccoli, look for compact, tightly closed florets and thin-skinned stems that are on the slender side. And don't forget to use the stem, too; just pare it well to remove its tough outer layer.

Stir-Fried Broccoli with Oyster Sauce

Serves three to four.

The key to stir-frying raw broccoli so it turns out crisp yet tender is to cut it into very small pieces. Serve the broccoli along with some steamed rice to soak up the delicious sauce.

Grilled Asparagus with Fresh Tarragon Mayonnaise

Serves four; yields about ²/₃ cup mayonnaise.

Here's the best way to eat these asparagus spears: with your fingers, dragging them through the mayonnaise. The tarragon mayonnaise is delicious with boiled asparagus, too.

1 large egg yolk, at room temperature*
½ cup extra-virgin olive oil; more for grilling
2 tsp. minced shallot
2 tsp. minced fresh flat-leaf parsley
1 tsp. minced fresh tarragon
1½ tsp. fresh lemon juice; more to taste
Kosher salt
1½ lb. asparagus, trimmed

Make the mayonnaise: Put the egg yolk in a small bowl. Add a few drops of lukewarm water and whisk well. Begin adding the olive oil in a very thin stream, whisking constantly. When the sauce thickens and forms a creamy emulsion, you can add the oil a little faster. Whisk in the shallot, parsley, tarragon, and lemon juice. Season with ½ tsp. salt or more to taste. If needed, whisk in a few drops of water to loosen the mayonnaise until it's spoonable, not stiff.

Cook the asparagus: Bring a large pot of salted water to a boil over high heat. Add the asparagus and blanch for 1 minute for small spears, or 1½ minutes for medium spears. Transfer the asparagus with tongs to a bowl of ice water. When cool, lift the spears out of the ice water and thoroughly pat dry.

Prepare a hot charcoal fire or gas grill. Put the spears on a rimmed baking sheet or platter. Drizzle with 1 Tbs. olive oil, season with a generous pinch of salt, and toss with your hands to coat the spears evenly.

Position the grill grate as close to the coals or heat source as possible. Heat the grate and then arrange the asparagus on the grate directly over the heat with all the tips pointing in the same direction. (Be sure to arrange the asparagus perpendicular to the bars so the spears don't fall through.) Grill, turning the spears once with tongs, until they're blistered and lightly charred in spots, about 3 minutes total. Transfer to a platter and serve immediately, passing the mayonnaise separately.

*If you're serving this dish to anyone with a compromised immune system, replace the raw egg yolk with a pasteurized egg product.

Fava Beans with Prosciutto, Mint & Garlic

Serves two.

A pound and a half of fava bean pods will only yield a scant cup of beans, so this recipe is designed to serve two people. If you want to double the recipe, you can use a cup of shelled fresh peas in place of the extra cup of favas if you like, since peas pair well with these flavors, too.

2 Tbs. extra-virgin olive oil
2 Tbs. minced prosciutto
1 tsp. minced garlic
1½ lb. fresh fava beans in the pod, shelled, parboiled, and peeled to yield 1 scant cup of favas
½ tsp. coarse salt; more to taste
½ tsp. balsamic vinegar
8 large mint leaves, finely chopped (to yield 2 to 3 tsp.)

In a medium skillet, heat the olive oil over medium heat. Add the prosciutto and sauté for 1 minute. Add the garlic and sauté, stirring constantly, until it's very fragrant and just beginning to turn brown, another 1 to 2 minutes. Add the fava beans, season with the salt, and sauté until the favas are heated and coated well with the pan contents, another 2 minutes. (Some of the beans will begin to turn a lighter color.) Add the balsamic vinegar, turn off the heat, and stir to coat. Add the mint and stir to combine and wilt it. Taste for salt; depending on the saltiness of your prosciutto, you might want to add more.

tip: Pasta side dishes are best served warm or at room temperature. Chilling mutes the flavors and softens the texture.

Tiny Pasta with Zucchini & Peppers

Serves six as a side dish.

If you can't find the tiny, round acini di pepe, you can use tubettini or rice-shaped orzo.

Kosher salt
1¼ cups dried acini di pepe (or other small) pasta
3 Tbs. olive oil
1 medium carrot, cut into small dice
1 small onion, cut into small dice
2 cloves garlic, minced
¾ cup diced red or yellow bell peppers, or a combination
1 medium zucchini, cut into small dice
¼ cup dry white wine; more as needed
3 Tbs. chopped fresh flat-leaf parsley
1 Tbs. chopped fresh oregano leaves (optional)
¼ cup grated Romano
Freshly ground black pepper

Bring a large pot of well-salted water to a vigorous boil and add the pasta. Cook until al dente; drain and rinse briefly under cool water. Return it to the pot, toss with 1 Tbs. olive oil, and set aside. You can do this up to a day ahead; if so, cover and refrigerate.

Heat a large frying pan over medium-high heat. Pour in the remaining oil, let it get hot, and then add the carrot and onion. Sauté over medium heat until the onion is soft and translucent, about 8 minutes. Turn the heat to high. Add the garlic, peppers, and zucchini, season with a little salt, and sauté for another 5 minutes. Don't let the garlic burn. The zucchini and peppers should be soft but not mushy. Add the wine and cook over medium heat, scraping up any browned bits stuck to the bottom of the pan.

Add the pasta and sauté over high heat, jerking the pan frequently so the ingredients mix well. If the pasta sticks, add a little more wine. When the pasta is heated through, remove the pan from the heat. Gently stir in the parsley, oregano (if using), and Romano. Season with pepper and additional salt if necessary and serve.

Orzo with Shiitakes, Caramelized Onions & Spinach

Serves eight to ten as a side dish; four as a light supper or lunch.

It may seem unlikely at first glance, but tiny orzo pairs wonderfully with Asian flavors. This recipe makes a lot, so it's a perfect side for a dinner party, but you can easily cut it in half.

Kosher salt
3 Tbs. soy sauce
1 Tbs. rice vinegar
1 tsp. toasted sesame oil
5 Tbs. peanut oil
2 cloves garlic, smashed
1 Tbs. grated fresh ginger
Pinch dried red chile flakes
6 oz. fresh shiitake mushrooms, stemmed, cleaned, and thinly sliced
2 Tbs. dry sherry (or dry white wine)
Freshly ground black pepper
1 large yellow onion, finely diced
10 oz. spinach, stemmed, washed, and coarsely chopped
1 lb. dried orzo
2 scallions (white and green parts), thinly sliced
1 tsp. toasted sesame seeds (optional)
1 lime, cut into small wedges

Bring a large pot of well-salted water to a boil. In a small bowl, whisk the soy sauce, rice vinegar, sesame oil, and 2 Tbs. of the peanut oil.

Set a large skillet or wok over medium-high heat. When the pan is hot, pour in 1½ Tbs. of the peanut oil and, after a few seconds, add the garlic, ginger, and chile flakes. Stir for 20 seconds, making sure that the garlic doesn't burn. Add the mushrooms and stir-fry until they soften, 2 to 3 minutes. Add the sherry or wine and cook for another 30 seconds. Season with salt and pepper and transfer the mixture to a bowl. Reduce the heat to medium, heat the remaining 1½ Tbs. peanut oil in the pan, and add the onion. Season with salt and then sauté, stirring often, until the onion is soft and slightly caramelized, 9 to 10 minutes. Add the spinach, cover the pan, and steam, shaking the pan occasionally, until the spinach wilts, about 3 minutes. Remove and discard the garlic from the mushrooms, put the mushrooms back in the pan, and toss. Remove from the heat and season lightly with salt and pepper. Reserve until needed.

Cook the orzo in the boiling water until it's just tender, about 9 minutes. Drain it well and put it in a large bowl. Add the mushroom mixture, soy vinaigrette, scallions, and sesame seeds (if using) and toss. Taste and season. Serve hot, warm, or at room temperature, with lime wedges to squeeze over the pasta.

Butternut squash on the grill

Though grilling season may be coming to a close, there's still time to try grilling butternut squash. Boil ³⁄₄-inch wedges (or 1-inch pieces for kebabs) in well-salted water until just shy of tender, 7 to 8 minutes. Drain and cool under cold water. Toss with olive oil, season with salt and pepper, and grill (skewered if you like) until browned and tender, about 5 minutes.

If you're grilling a marinated main course, like chicken or steak, reserve some of the marinade before it comes in contact with the meat and brush it onto the squash before grilling.

Or try this quick and bright treatment: Before grilling toss the par-boiled squash with oil, a little ground cumin, and a decent amount of salt. When the squash comes off the grill, squeeze some lime juice over it and sprinkle with chopped fresh cilantro. You'll have a perfect dish (great with steak as well as Mexican fare) for one of the last warm nights of the season.

Butternut Squash & Potato Gratin with Walnut Crust

Serves nine.

So simple and so deliciously sweet and creamy with a contrasting nutty topping, this gratin is guaranteed to become a favorite.

**1 butternut squash (about 2 lb.),
  peeled**
**2 Idaho potatoes (about 1¼ lb. total),
  peeled**
**Kosher salt and freshly ground black
  pepper**
6 Tbs. grated Parmigiano-Reggiano
1 cup heavy cream
½ cup finely chopped walnuts
**½ cup fresh breadcrumbs, combined
  with 2 Tbs. melted unsalted butter**

Heat the oven to 350°F. Grease an 8x8-inch (2-qt.) glass or ceramic baking dish. Cut the squash in half lengthwise and scrape out the seeds and fibers. Slice the squash and potatoes about ⅛ inch thick (use a mandoline if you have one).

Line the bottom of the baking dish with a layer of squash (overlapping slightly), season lightly with salt and pepper, sprinkle with a little of the Parmigiano, and drizzle with a little of the cream. Cover with a layer of potato slices, season with salt, pepper, cheese, and cream. Repeat with the remaining squash and potatoes until the dish is full, ending with a top layer of squash, seasoned and topped with any remaining cheese and cream. (You may have extra squash.) Press down lightly to distribute the cream and compact the layers. The last layer of squash should be just sitting in the cream, but not covered by it. Cover the dish with foil and bake until the vegetables feel tender when poked with a thin, sharp knife (check the middle layer), about 1 hour and 10 minutes.

Combine the walnuts and buttered breadcrumbs. Remove the gratin from the oven, sprinkle with the breadcrumb mixture, and bake until the top is lightly browned, 5 to 10 minutes. Let sit in a warm place for 20 minutes before serving so that liquids will set and tighten the gratin. Cut into nine squares and serve.

Baking butternut squash in this gratin could hardly be easier—it's truly a "slice-and-bake" dish.

Roasting halves of squash gives you a deeply flavored yet soft flesh that's perfect for puréeing.

Ways to use roasted squash

Layer roasted butternut squash in a lasagna with wilted spinach or chard, feta, and a vibrant tomato sauce. Use it sparingly throughout, or make one entire layer of butternut squash.

Purée roasted butternut squash with spices like cumin, coriander, ginger, or curry. Add a squeeze of orange juice and a little grated zest for a flavorful side dish.

Mash the flesh with plenty of butter and a little goat cheese for an alternative to mashed potatoes.

Flavor risotto with roasted butternut squash; finish with sautéed slivered sage leaves as a garnish.

Purée roasted squash with cream, chicken broth, and a little vinegar for a pasta sauce.

Make a simple soup: Cook onions with curry powder until soft, add chicken broth and roasted squash, and purée.

Fill ravioli with roasted butternut squash mixed with a little cream and Parmigiano-Reggiano.

Roasted butternut squash halves

Roasting butternut softens its flesh while concentrating its flavor. (It can also eliminate the need to peel the squash before cooking it.)

To roast halves, cut the squash lengthwise, scoop out the seeds, and scrape out the strings. Rub the cut surfaces with oil, season generously with salt and pepper, and roast at 400°F on a foil-lined baking sheet, cut side up, until deeply browned and very tender, about 80 minutes. Let cool before using in other recipes (see the boxes at left for ideas), or cover and refrigerate for up to two days. One 2-lb. squash will yield about 1¾ cups roasted chunks or 1⅓ cups mashed.

Slow-Roasted Tomatoes

The secret to delicious roasted tomatoes is not to undercook them. Roast the tomatoes (halved on a heavy-duty baking sheet) until they are a deep, rich brown and very collapsed. You can certainly use this method on less-than-ripe tomatoes—and they will taste better after roasting—but if you start with really meaty, juicy-ripe tomatoes, the end result will be out of this world.

Ready for the oven.

Slow-Roasted Summer Tomatoes

Yields about 24 tomato halves.

For best results, it's important to use a heavy-duty rimmed baking sheet; thin pans could cause burning. Also, pack the sheet full of tomatoes; if it's not full, expect the tomatoes to cook more quickly.

3 Tbs. plus 1 cup extra-virgin olive oil
4½ to 5 lb. medium-large ripe beefsteak tomatoes (about 12), stemmed but not cored
Kosher salt
Granulated sugar
Scant 1 Tbs. balsamic vinegar
3 to 4 cloves garlic, very thinly sliced
2 Tbs. fresh thyme leaves

Heat the oven to 350°F. Line a 12x17-inch rimmed baking sheet or two 9x12-inch rimmed baking sheets with foil. (Don't use unrimmed sheets or the oil and juices will spill out; instead, use several shallow gratin dishes.) If you have parchment, put a sheet on top of the foil. Coat the pan or pans with 3 Tbs. of the olive oil.

Cut the tomatoes in half through the equator (not through the stem). Arrange the halves, cut side up, on the baking sheet, turning to coat their bottoms with some of the oil. Sprinkle a pinch each of salt and sugar over each half, and drizzle each with a few drops of balsamic vinegar. Arrange the garlic over the halves and top with a generous sprinkling of thyme. Pour the remaining 1 cup olive oil over and around the tomato halves.

Roast in the center of the oven until the tomatoes are concentrated, dark reddish brown (with deep browning around the edges and in places on the pan) and quite collapsed (at least half their original height; they will collapse more as they cool), about 3 hours for very ripe, fleshy tomatoes, about 4 hours for tomatoes that are less ripe or that have a high water content. (Check on the tomatoes frequently after the first 1½ hours. If they're browning too quickly, reduce the oven temperature.)

Let cool for at least 10 to 15 minutes and then serve warm or at room temperature. Be sure to re-serve the tomato oil (keep refrigerated for up to a week) to use on its own or in a vinaigrette.

To store the tomatoes, refrigerate for up to a week or freeze for up to a couple of months. They'll continue to release juice during storage.

Quicker-cooking variation: Remove the seeds and gelatinous pulp (poke them out with your fingers) before roasting. These tomatoes cook more quickly (sometimes in as little as 2 hours) but yield a slightly flatter, less meaty—but perfectly pleasant—result.

Plum tomato variation: Substitute plum tomatoes, cut in half through the stem end and seeded. The roasting time will be 1½ to 2 hours. Roasted plum tomato halves hold together particularly well; layer them in a terrine or roll them up, stuffed with goat cheese and basil, as an appetizer.

After 3 hours.

Braised Carrots, Red Onions & Bell Peppers with Ginger, Lime & Cilantro

Serves three to four.

This colorful dish goes well with just about everything. For the deepest flavor, be patient when browning vegetables; let them sit in the pan undisturbed until they develop color on one side and then turn them over.

¾ lb. fresh young carrots, preferably with the tops on
1 Tbs. fresh lime juice
1 tsp. freshly grated lime zest
1 tsp. light brown sugar
2 Tbs. extra-virgin olive oil
1 Tbs. unsalted butter
Kosher salt
4 oz. yellow bell pepper (about 1 small, cored and seeded), cut lengthwise into ½-inch strips
4 oz. red onion (about 1 small), cut into ½-inch-wide strips
1 piece fresh ginger, 2x¾ inches, cut into thin matchsticks (a scant ¼ cup)
½ small fresh jalapeño, cored but not seeded, cut crosswise into slices about ¼ inch thick
⅓ cup plus 2 Tbs. homemade or low-salt canned chicken broth
¼ cup loosely packed chopped fresh cilantro

Trim the tops and tails from the carrots and peel them; you should have about 8 oz. trimmed carrots. Cut them in half crosswise and then cut the thicker end in half lengthwise to get pieces of about the same width, no more than ¾ inch (the length can vary). In a small bowl, combine the lime juice, lime zest, and brown sugar; set aside.

Heat 1 Tbs. of the olive oil and 2 tsp. of the butter in a 10-inch straight-sided sauté pan over medium-high heat. When the milk solids in the butter are just beginning to turn a nutty brown, add the carrots and ¼ tsp. salt. Toss well with tongs and then arrange the carrots in one layer. Cook without stirring until the bottoms are nicely browned, 3 to 4 minutes. Toss and turn over, and cook for another 2 minutes to lightly brown another side. Transfer the carrots to a plate with tongs.

Heat the remaining 1 Tbs. olive oil in the pan. Add the bell pepper, red onion, and a pinch of salt and sauté until browned, 3 to 5 minutes. Add the ginger and jalapeño, toss, and sauté for another minute. Return the carrots to the pan, stir, and pour in the chicken broth. Immediately cover the pan and simmer until the liquid is almost completely reduced, about 2 minutes.

Uncover the pan, remove it from the heat, and add the lime juice mixture, the remaining 1 tsp. butter, and the cilantro. Toss to combine well, scraping any browned bits from the bottom of the pan with a heatproof spatula or a wooden spoon. Serve right away as individual servings or pour and scrape the contents of the pan onto a small platter and serve family-style.

tip: When buying carrots, choose young, slim ones with their bright, leafy greens still attached. They will be more tender and flavorful than older, already-trimmed ones.

Ginger-Glazed Carrots

Serves four to six.

Fresh ginger and carrots are natural companions, and cilantro gives this dish an added boost. For a simple dinner, serve these carrots with pan-fried fish and a wedge of lime.

1½ lb. carrots (about 8), peeled and trimmed
About ⅔ cup water
2 Tbs. unsalted butter
1 tsp. sugar
1 tsp. kosher salt; more as needed
2 tsp. minced fresh ginger
1½ Tbs. chopped fresh cilantro (optional)

Cut the carrots in half lengthwise. Holding your knife at a sharp angle, cut the carrot halves into 1-inch lengths, measured point to point, to make diamond shapes (see instructions on p. 178). Put them in a 10- to 12-inch sauté pan (they should be almost in a single layer) and add water to come halfway up their sides. Add the butter, sugar, and salt and bring to a boil over high heat. Cover the pan with the lid slightly askew, reduce the heat to medium high, and cook at a steady boil, shaking the pan occasionally, until the carrots are tender but not soft (a paring knife should enter a carrot with just a little resistance), 7 to 9 minutes. Uncover, stir in the ginger, and continue to boil until the liquid evaporates to create a syrup. Shake the pan and roll the pieces around to evenly glaze the carrots. Add a pinch more salt if needed, toss with the cilantro (if using), and serve.

Cauliflower & Green Beans with Indian Spices

Serves four to six.

This is a great side for grilled lamb. It can also work as a light vegetarian supper served with basmati rice.

½ tsp. cumin seeds
½ tsp. yellow mustard seeds
2 Tbs. olive oil; more if needed
1 small yellow onion, cut into medium dice (about ½ cup)
1 small head cauliflower (1¼ to 1½ lb.), trimmed and cut into ½- to 1-inch florets (about 3 cups)
8 oz. green beans, trimmed and snapped into 1- to 1½-inch pieces (about 2 cups)
1 large carrot, peeled and chopped into small (about ⅜-inch) pieces
Kosher salt and freshly ground black pepper
2 cloves garlic, minced
1 tsp. finely minced fresh ginger
Large pinch crushed red pepper flakes

Toast the cumin and mustard seeds in a large (preferably 12-inch) dry skillet over medium-low heat, stirring occasionally, until very fragrant, 4 to 5 minutes; don't let them burn. Immediately transfer to a small bowl. Put the skillet back on medium-high heat for 1 minute. Pour in the oil and swirl to coat the pan. As soon as the oil is shimmering—but not smoking—add the onion and stir to coat with the oil. After about 30 seconds, add the cauliflower, green beans, and carrot in an even layer across the pan. Season with salt and pepper and let cook undisturbed until the vegetables have begun to brown, 2 to 3 minutes. Sauté, stirring occasionally, until the cauliflower is nicely browned, 5 to 7 minutes. If the pan bottom gets too dry and starts to burn, add a scant Tbs. olive oil. Reduce the heat to medium and continue to sauté until the cauliflower is tender, another 2 to 3 minutes. (Cut through a floret with the edge of the metal spatula; the floret should slice in half without crumbling.) Stir in the garlic, ginger, toasted cumin and mustard seeds, and chile flakes. Cook for another minute to blend the flavors. Season to taste with salt and pepper and serve immediately.

Roasted Carrots & Parsnips with Shallot & Herb Butter

Serves two to three.

Although carrots and parsnips may seem better suited to winter, this colorful rendition feels bright and vibrant, thanks to an abundance of fresh herbs.

5 large carrots (about 1 lb.), peeled
4 large parsnips (about 1 lb.), peeled
3 Tbs. extra-virgin olive oil
1½ tsp. kosher salt
½ tsp. freshly ground black pepper
¼ cup unsalted butter, softened at room temperature
2 Tbs. minced shallot
2 Tbs. finely chopped fresh chives
1½ tsp. finely chopped fresh rosemary
1½ tsp. chopped fresh thyme
1 clove garlic, minced

Position a rack in the center of the oven and heat the oven to 450°F.

Cut the carrots and parsnips into 2x¼-inch matchsticks. Put them in a large bowl; toss with the oil. Sprinkle with the salt and pepper and toss again. Transfer the vegetables to a 10x15-inch Pyrex dish and roast, stirring every 15 minutes, until the vegetables are nicely browned, 40 to 45 minutes.

Meanwhile, combine the butter, shallot, chives, rosemary, thyme, and garlic in a small bowl and stir well. Add the butter to the roasted vegetables and toss to coat. Serve immediately.

Fennel & Red Onion with Arugula

Serves four.

If you can't find baby arugula, larger leaves are fine. Just discard any large stems, tear the leaves into bite-size pieces, and be sure they're washed well.

2 cups loosely packed baby arugula
2½ Tbs. olive oil
1 medium-large bulb fennel, cored and cut into ¼-inch thick slices (to yield about 2 cups)
1 cup ⅛- to ¼-inch-thick half-moon slices red onion
Kosher salt and freshly ground black pepper
1 large clove garlic, minced
¼ cup orange juice, preferably fresh
4 kalamata olives, pitted and coarsely chopped

Scatter the arugula in a wide, shallow serving bowl. Heat a large (preferably 12-inch) skillet over medium-high heat for 1 minute. Pour in 2 Tbs. of the oil and swirl to coat the pan. As soon as the oil is shimmering—but not smoking—add the fennel and onion in an even layer. Season with salt and pepper and let the vegetables cook undisturbed until they have begun to brown, about 2 minutes. Stir occasionally until the fennel and onion are tender and deep golden brown in places, about another 5 minutes. If the vegetables seem to be cooking too fast or the bottom of the pan is starting to burn, lower the heat to medium. (If using an electric stovetop, take the pan off the burner momentarily to let the pan cool.) Clear a space in the center of the pan and add the remaining ½ Tbs. oil and then the garlic. Let cook until the garlic is fragrant, about 30 seconds. Add the orange juice and stir to combine with the vegetables. Pour the mixture over the arugula and toss to combine and to wilt the arugula. Season to taste with salt and pepper, sprinkle with the chopped olives, and serve immediately.

Eggplant & Tomato Gratin with Mint, Feta & Kalamata Olives

Serves six to eight as a side dish; four as a main dish.

Because the purple skin of the eggplant looks pretty in a gratin, it's nice to leave it on. But since it can also get tough, you may want to partially peel the vegetable as suggested in the recipe. For a change of pace, try this gratin in four individual dishes rather than one large one.

FOR THE EGGPLANT:
2 lb. eggplant
2½ Tbs. olive oil
½ tsp. coarse salt

FOR THE ONIONS:
2 Tbs. olive oil
2 medium onions (14 oz. total), thinly sliced
2 cloves garlic, minced

TO ASSEMBLE THE GRATIN:
1¼ lb. ripe red tomatoes, cored and cut into ¼-inch slices
¼ cup plus 1 Tbs. chopped fresh mint
6 oz. (1 cup) crumbled feta cheese
⅓ cup pitted and quartered kalamata olives
Coarse salt
Freshly ground black pepper to taste
1½ Tbs. plus 1 tsp. olive oil
⅓ cup fresh breadcrumbs
1 tsp. olive oil
⅓ cup chopped toasted pine nuts

Cut and cook the eggplant:
Trim the ends from the eggplant and, using a vegetable peeler, peel off ½-inch strips of skin along the length of the eggplant every ½ inch or so (or leave the eggplant unpeeled, if you like). Cut the eggplant crosswise into ⅜-inch slices and cut the widest slices in half.

Heat the oven to 450°F. Cover two baking sheets with parchment. Lightly brush the parchment with olive oil. Arrange the eggplant slices in one layer on the parchment, brush them with the remaining oil, and season with the ½ tsp. salt. Roast until the slices are lightly browned and somewhat shrunken, 25 minutes, rotating the pans once after 12 minutes. Let cool. Reduce the oven temperature to 375°F.

Cook the onions: In a medium skillet, heat the olive oil over medium heat. Add the onions and sauté, stirring frequently, until limp and golden brown, about 20 minutes. Reduce the heat to medium low if they're browning too quickly. Add the garlic and sauté until soft and fragrant, 1 to 2 minutes. Spread the onions and garlic evenly in the bottom of an oiled 2-qt. shallow gratin dish (preferably oval). Let cool.

Assemble the gratin: Put the tomato slices on a shallow plate to drain for a few minutes and then discard the collected juices. Sprinkle 1 Tbs. of the mint over the onions. Starting at one end of the baking dish, lay a row of slightly overlapping tomato slices across the width of the dish; sprinkle with some of the mint and some of the feta. Next, lay a row of eggplant slices against the tomatoes (overlapping the first row by two-thirds). Sprinkle again with mint and feta. Repeat with alternating rows of tomato and eggplant slices, seasoning each as you go, and occasionally pushing the rows back. Tuck the quartered kalamata olives randomly between tomato and eggplant slices.

When the gratin is full, sprinkle the vegetables with about ½ tsp. salt and any remaining mint and feta. Season lightly with pepper, drizzle with the 1½ Tbs. olive oil. Thoroughly combine the 1 tsp. olive oil with the breadcrumbs and pine nuts, and sprinkle this mixture over the gratin. Cook until well-browned all over and the juices have bubbled for a while and reduced considerably, 65 to 70 minutes. Let cool for at least 15 minutes before serving.

tip: While peeling roasted peppers, don't rinse them or you'll lose some of that great smoky flavor.

Roasted Bell Pepper Antipasto

Serves six to eight as part of an antipasto.

This simple dish looks stunning as part of a buffet. After roasting the peppers, you can cover and refrigerate them for up to 3 days before assembling the dish.

4 bell peppers, preferably a mix of yellow, orange, and red
1 tsp. finely chopped fresh chives; more to taste
1 tsp. finely chopped fresh parsley; more to taste
1 tsp. finely chopped garlic
2 tsp. small capers, rinsed and drained
Good-quality extra-virgin olive oil
Kosher salt to taste

Position an oven rack to 6 to 7 inches below the broiler element and heat the broiler. Put the whole peppers on a baking sheet and broil until the skins are blistered and blackened, about 7 to 8 minutes. Turn carefully with tongs to expose an uncooked side and broil again until black-ened. Repeat until the peppers are charred on all sides. Transfer them to a large bowl, cover the bowl with a dinner plate, and let the peppers steam for at least 15 to 20 minutes or until cool.

Working over the bowl to catch the juices, peel the skin off a pepper, pull out the stem and seed cluster, and separate the pepper into wide strips. Strip away any remaining seeds and trim off any white membrane. Layer the slices in a container and repeat with the remaining peppers. Strain the collected juices over the peppers.

About a half hour before serving, arrange the roasted peppers on a dish. Sprinkle with the chopped chives, parsley, garlic, and capers. Scatter more chopped herbs over the top, drizzle with good olive oil, and season with just a little coarse salt, remembering that the capers can be salty.

Classic Glazed Carrots

Serves four to six.

For the glaze, you can use brown sugar instead of white, but in that case, omit the herbs.

1½ lb. carrots (about 8), peeled and trimmed
About 1 cup water
2 Tbs. unsalted butter
1 Tbs. sugar
1 tsp. kosher salt; more as needed
1½ Tbs. chopped fresh flat-leaf parsley, chervil, or chives (optional)

Cut the carrots in half lengthwise. Holding your knife at a sharp angle, cut the carrot halves into 2-inch lengths to make diamond shapes; try to make all the pieces the same size so they cook evenly. Put the carrots in a 10- to 12-inch sauté pan (they should be almost in a single layer) and add enough water to come halfway up their sides. Add the butter, sugar, and salt, and bring to a boil over high heat. Cover the pan with the lid slightly askew, reduce the heat to medium high, and cook at a steady boil, shaking the pan occasionally, until the carrots are tender but not soft (a paring knife should enter a carrot with just a little resistance), 12 to 14 minutes. Uncover and continue to boil until the liquid evaporates and forms a syrup. Shake the pan and roll the pieces around to evenly glaze the carrots. Taste and add a pinch more salt if necessary. Toss with the fresh herbs, (if using) and serve.

how-to

See p. 178 to learn how to cut a carrot four ways.

Grilled Corn on the Cob with Lime-Cayenne Butter

Serves 8 to 10.

This tart and spicy butter offers a nice contrast to the sweet, smoky flavors of the grilled corn. While a charcoal fire creates the best flavors, the butter will enhance corn cooked on a gas grill, too.

8 Tbs. unsalted butter
Juice of 1 lime
1 tsp. coarse salt
½ tsp. cayenne
8 to 10 ears corn

Melt the butter in a small saucepan and stir in the lime juice, salt, and cayenne. Keep warm.

Peel off all but one or two layers of the corn husks. Pull the remaining husks down, but not off, and remove the bulk of the silks (the rest will come off easily after they char). Pull up the husks; it's okay if some kernels peek through.

Prepare a hot charcoal fire or heat a gas grill to high. Put the corn on the grate while the coals are still red-hot. (Cover a gas grill.)

Grill the corn, turning often, until the outer layer of husk is completely charred. Depending on your fire, this could take from around 5 to 10 minutes. You can push the corn to a cooler spot if you're grilling other things for your meal, or transfer the grilled corn to a platter and keep it warm in the charred husks.

Just before serving, peel off the husk and brush away any remaining silks. Brown the kernels on the grill briefly, turning the corn frequently to develop a roasty color and a little additional smoke flavor, about 1 minute. (If the corn spends too long on the grill without the protection of the husk, the kernels will become dry and a bit chewy.)

Brush the warm cayenne butter on the hot grilled corn and serve immediately.

Sautéed Swiss Chard

Serves four.

Swiss chard cooks up similarly to spinach but has a lot more personality. On its own, it's plenty satisfying (and goes especially well with grilled lamb), but the versatile vegetable readily takes to other flavorings, such as the additions at right.

2 lb. Swiss chard (from about 2 bunches), well rinsed of grit
2 Tbs. extra-virgin olive oil
2 tsp. finely chopped garlic (from about 4 cloves)
Kosher salt
Pinch crushed red chile flakes

Transfer the wet chard to paper towels and let dry for a couple of minutes (it's fine if a little water clings to the leaves).

Remove the thick part of each stem by cutting a V-shaped notch partway into the leaf.

Split each leaf in half lengthwise by slicing down the center rib. Stack the halved leaves (in batches if necessary) and cut them in half crosswise to get 4- to 6-inch pieces.

Heat the oil in a large skillet over medium-high heat for 1 minute. Working in batches, pile the Swiss chard into the pan, turning and tossing gently until the leaves begin to wilt and turn glossy. Add a new batch of leaves as the previous batch wilts and makes room for more.

When all the chard is wilted, sprinkle in the garlic and a little salt and toss well. Lower the heat to medium low, cover, and cook for 4 minutes. Remove the lid, raise the heat to high, add the chile flakes, and continue to cook for 2 minutes so that much of the liquid evaporates; the leaves should be tender but not overly soft. Serve immediately.

Sautéed Swiss Chard with Gremolata (Lemon-Garlic)

Yields about 3 Tbs. gremolata.

Gremolata, classically sprinkled on ossobuco, goes extremely well with assertive chard.

2 tsp. finely grated lemon zest (from about 1 lemon)
1 small clove garlic, very finely chopped
2 Tbs. minced fresh flat-leaf parsley
1 recipe Sautéed Swiss Chard (at left)

Combine the lemon zest, garlic, and parsley in a bowl. Make the basic Sautéed Swiss Chard, add the mixture at the end, toss, and serve immediately.

Sautéed Swiss Chard with Sun-Dried Tomatoes & Feta

Yields about ⅔ cup topping.

To make this a main dish, toss the chard and the sun-dried tomato mixture with cooked pasta.

6 oil-packed sun-dried tomato halves, drained and cut into thin strips
⅓ cup feta cheese, crumbled
½ tsp. lightly chopped fresh thyme leaves
1 recipe Sautéed Swiss Chard (at left)

Combine the sun-dried tomatoes, feta, and thyme in a bowl. Make the basic Sautéed Swiss Chard, add the sun-dried tomato mixture at the end, toss, and serve immediately.

Grilled Zucchini with Lemon-Balsamic Vinaigrette

Serves four.

This quick-to-make zucchini dish goes with just about everything. If you don't have fresh thyme available, you can leave it out and still have a tasty side.

3 small or 2 medium zucchini (about 1 lb.)
Kosher salt
2 Tbs. plus 1 tsp. extra-virgin olive oil
1 Tbs. balsamic vinegar
½ tsp. chopped fresh thyme
½ tsp. finely grated lemon zest
Freshly ground black pepper
3 Tbs. freshly grated Parmigiano Reggiano

Slice and salt the zucchini.
Heat a gas grill to medium high or prepare a medium-hot charcoal fire. In a small bowl, whisk 2 Tbs. of the oil, the vinegar, thyme, lemon zest, ¼ tsp. salt, and ⅛ tsp. pepper.

Toss the zucchini with the remaining 1 tsp. olive oil. Set the zucchini cut side down on the grill and cook (if using a gas grill, keep the lid closed), flipping occasionally, until it browns and softens but doesn't turn mushy, 6 to 8 minutes. Cut the zucchini into 3-inch pieces and put in a medium bowl. Whisk the vinaigrette again and drizzle over the zucchini. Sprinkle on the Parmigiano, toss well, adjust the seasonings to taste, and serve immediately.

Fresh Peas with Sesame Seeds, Scallions & Cilantro

Serves two to three.

When spring arrives, indulge in fresh peas. A mix of white and black sesame seeds adds drama, but one kind is fine.

2 lb. fresh peas, shucked, to yield 2 cups
2 scallions (white and light green parts), cut into slivers
1 Tbs. chopped fresh cilantro
1 tsp. toasted sesame oil
Kosher salt to taste
2 tsp. sesame seeds, toasted

Cook the peas in salted water until just tender, 2 to 3 minutes. Drain and transfer to a medium serving bowl. Add the scallions, cilantro, and sesame oil and toss gently. Season to taste with salt. Sprinkle with sesame seeds and serve immediately.

Great Techniques

Four ways to cut a carrot

Carrots are one of the most fun vegetables to work with because of the many ways you can cut them. When cooking carrots, such as in braising and glazing recipes, you can use just about any cut you want, as long as the pieces are about the same size and shape, which helps them cook evenly. It's easier to accomplish this if you start with whole carrots that are all about the same width, and if they're more cylindrical than conical; carrots with wide tops and thin tips are tricky to cut evenly. Keep in mind that the thicker and larger cuts will take longer to cook.

Oval slices

Cut the carrot into ¼-inch oval slices with a sharp diagonal cut (on the bias).

Diamonds

Cut the carrot in half lengthwise. Cut the halves into 1- or 2-inch lengths (measured point to point) with a sharp diagonal cut.

Roll cuts

Trim the tip of the carrot with a sharp diagonal cut. Roll the carrot 180 degrees and cut off a 1-inch piece, keeping your knife at the same diagonal angle as the original cut. Continue to roll and cut the carrot in this way. If the carrot widens dramatically toward the top, adjust the knife angle and carrot length so that the pieces are all about the same size.

Half-moons

Cut the carrot in half lengthwise. Cut each half into ¼-inch slices with a sharp diagonal cut.

How to string a pea pod

Sugar snap peas and snow peas have tough, stringlike fibers running along their top seams. It won't hurt you to eat them, but why would you want to when they're so simple to remove? Here's how:

Using your fingernails or the tips of your fingers, snap off the stem end of the pea pod toward the top seam, leaving the stringy part attached. The partially disconnected end will act as your "zipper pull."

Pull the disconnected stem end to remove the string, much as you would unzip a zipper. If the string breaks before you've removed it all, repeat the process using the blossom end of the pea pod.

Mandoline tricks & tips

If you love vegetables and do a lot of slicing, a mandoline might be perfect for you. Here's how to best use one:

- Set the mandoline lengthwise in front of you so that you're pushing forward, not sideways.

- Use a sweeping motion from the top to the bottom of the "runway."

- Keep the pressure constant. Don't bear down or let up midway as the food hits the blade.

- For blades that are oriented to hit the food straight on rather than on an angle, use a gentle back-and-forth sawing motion to slice high-moisture foods that are apt to squish, compress, or collapse under pressure, such as tomatoes, citrus, kiwi, eggplant, and bell peppers.

- For thin or thick julienne, the less mass that has to pass through the blades, the less wedged in (and stuck) the food is likely to get. For example, choose small to medium potatoes for french fries.

- Very dense vegetables, such as winter squash and sweet potatoes, can be difficult to slice, especially into julienne or french-fry cuts. Use your chef's knife on these vegetables instead.

- Lightly grease the runway with cooking spray if it feels sticky.

- For round fruits or vegetables, such as potatoes, oranges, or beets, use a knife to cut off a portion to make a flat edge or, if necessary, cut in half and then slice them cut side down.

- Never be tempted to use a mandoline without a guard.

A mandoline comes in handy when making...

caramelized onions

cucumber salad

eggplant Parmesan

french fries

potato gratin

julienned (matchstick) vegetables for salads or stir-fries

paper-thin slices of carrots, cucumbers, onion, fennel, or melon for salads or hors d'oeuvres

perfect planks of zucchini for grilling

onion rings

crinkle-cut roasted potatoes

crinkle-cut pickled vegetables

Slice an avocado before peeling it

It's usually easier to slice or dice a ripe avocado before removing its skin. Cut the avocado in half lengthwise and remove the pit (whack it with the blade of a chef's knife and pull the pit out). Using a paring knife, cut the avocado diagonally into ¼-inch (or wider) slices, without piercing the skin. (If a dice is your goal, make a second set of diagonal slices perpendicular to the first.) To remove the sliced or diced avocado from its skin, hold the avocado in the palm of your hand and, using a large spoon, carefully scoop out the slices.

Mashing garlic to a paste

Mashing garlic is easy with a mortar and pestle, but if you don't have one (or don't want to dirty one), just use your chef's knife. Here's how: Trim off the ends of the garlic cloves and slice the cloves in half lengthwise. Turn the cloves flat side down on the cutting board. Lay the side of the blade of a chef's knife on each clove and smash down with the heel of your palm. Sprinkle the garlic with kosher salt and chop coarsely. Pile the chopped garlic on one side of the board. Tilt the knife at a 30-degree angle to the board and drag it over the garlic, scraping it across the surface of the board. Pile up the garlic again, sprinkle lightly with salt, and scrape again. Repeat once or twice until the garlic is a smooth paste.

Desserts

Chocolate Strawberry Shortcakes *p. 182*

Chocolate Strawberry Shortcakes

Serves nine.

Chocolate jazzes up this traditional strawberry dessert. Made with cocoa and semisweet chocolate, the shortcakes have an intense flavor close to that of a brownie, but also a light, flaky texture.

FOR THE BISCUITS:
2¼ cups unbleached all-purpose flour
¼ cup plus 3 Tbs. Dutch-processed cocoa powder, such as Droste®
¼ cup sugar; plus about 3 Tbs. for sprinkling
1½ Tbs. baking powder
¾ tsp. table salt
9 Tbs. cold unsalted butter, cut into small pieces
6½ oz. semisweet chocolate, grated or finely chopped (the food processor works well); more for garnish
1¼ cups heavy cream; plus about 3 Tbs. for brushing
1½ tsp. pure vanilla extract

FOR THE STRAWBERRIES:
5 cups ⅛-inch-thick strawberry slices (from about 3 pints)
1 to 3 Tbs. sugar, depending on the sweetness of the berries

FOR THE WHIPPED CREAM:
1½ cups heavy cream
2 Tbs. sugar
¾ tsp. pure vanilla extract

Make the biscuits: Line a heavy baking sheet with parchment. Sift the flour, cocoa powder, sugar, baking powder, and salt into a large bowl. Toss with a fork to combine. Cut the butter into the dry ingredients with a pastry cutter or a fork until the largest pieces of butter are the size of peas. Add the grated chocolate and toss to combine. Combine the cream and vanilla in a liquid measure. Make a well in the center of the flour mixture and pour the cream into the well. Mix with a fork until the dough is evenly moistened and just combined; it should look shaggy and still feel a little dry. Gently knead by hand five or six times to pick up any dry ingredients remaining in the bottom of the bowl and to create a loose ball.

Turn the dough out onto a lightly floured work surface and pat it into an 8-inch square, ¾ to 1 inch thick. Transfer the dough to the parchment-lined baking sheet, cover with plastic wrap, and chill for 20 minutes. Meanwhile, heat the oven to 425°F. Remove the dough from the refrigerator and trim about ¼ inch from each side to create a neat, sharp edge (a bench knife or a pastry scraper works well, or use a large chef's knife, being sure to cut straight down). Cut the dough into 9 even squares (about 2½ inches square) and spread them about 2 inches apart on the baking sheet. With a pastry brush or the back of a spoon, brush each biscuit with a thin layer of cream and sprinkle generously with sugar. Bake until the biscuits look a little dry and are mostly firm to the touch (they should spring back slightly when gently pressed), 18 to 20 minutes.

Meanwhile, prepare the strawberries: Toss the berries with 1 Tbs. sugar and taste. If they're still tart, sprinkle with another 1 to 2 Tbs. sugar. Let sit at room temperature until the sugar dissolves and the berries begin to release their juices, at least 30 minutes but no more than 2 hours.

Whip the cream: Pour the cream into a cold mixing bowl and beat with a hand mixer until it begins to thicken. Add the sugar and vanilla extract and, using a whisk, continue to beat by hand until the cream is softly whipped or until the whisk leaves distinct marks in the cream; it should be soft and billowy but still hold its shape.

Assemble the shortcakes: While the biscuits are still warm, split them in half horizontally with a serrated knife. For each serving, set the bottom half of a biscuit on a plate. Scoop about ½ cup of the berries and their juices over the biscuit. Add a generous dollop of whipped cream and cover with the top half of the biscuit. Top with a small dollop of cream. Garnish with some grated chocolate and a berry or two and serve.

Melons with Ginger Syrup

Serves four to six; yields about ⅓ cup syrup.

This dessert salad looks and tastes especially wonderful with a combination of melons, including cantaloupe, honeydew, Santa Claus, Persian, casaba, or seedless watermelon.

¼ cup sugar
¼ cup water
3½-inch-long piece fresh ginger (1 inch wide), peeled and very thinly sliced
8 cups mixed ¾-inch melon cubes (from 5 to 8 lb. melons)
Leaves from 5 sprigs mint (small leaves left whole; larger leaves sliced into thin strips)

Combine the sugar and water in a small saucepan. Bring to a simmer over medium heat, stirring occasionally until the sugar dissolves. Add the ginger and reduce the heat to low. Cook for 7 minutes to let the ginger infuse the syrup. Strain through a fine sieve, let cool, and refrigerate until completely chilled.

Just before serving, mix the melon cubes in a large serving bowl and pour on just enough of the ginger syrup to lightly coat the melons, about ¼ cup. Toss with the mint leaves.

Apricots with Moscato & Thyme Syrup

Serves four to six; yields 1 cup syrup.

Moscato can be expensive, but there are delicious, affordable examples, such as Sutter Home® Moscato, that work well in this recipe. A pluot is a cross between a plum and apricot.

2 to 3 cups Moscato or Moscato d'Asti (or any dessert wine made from Muscat grapes)
5 oz. dried apricots (15 to 20)
5 Tbs. sugar
4 sprigs fresh thyme; more for garnish
2 lb. fresh apricots or pluots (about 16 apricots or 7 medium pluots)

In a small saucepan, bring 2 cups of the wine to a boil. Remove from the heat and add the dried apricots. Cover the pan and let the apricots macerate in the wine for at least 8 hours or overnight.

Strain the wine from the macerated fruit into a measuring cup. You'll need a total of 1 cup wine; if you have less, supplement with more wine from the bottle. If you have more, discard the extra. Combine the 1 cup wine and the sugar in a small saucepan. Bring to a simmer over medium heat, stirring occasionally until the sugar dissolves. Add the thyme and reduce the heat to low. Cook for 7 minutes to let the thyme infuse the syrup. Strain through a fine sieve, let cool, and refrigerate until completely chilled.

Just before serving, cut the plumped dried apricots into quarters, slicing them lengthwise. Cut the fresh apricots or pluots in half, pit them, and slice each half into ½-inch-wide wedges. Put all the fruit in a large serving bowl. Pour on just enough of the Moscato syrup to lightly coat the fruit, about ⅓ cup. Garnish with fresh sprigs of thyme, if you like.

tip: For the most elegant fruit salads, pair related fruits: nectarines with peaches and apricots, strawberries with blueberries, cantaloupe with watermelon.

Infused syrups aren't just delicious drizzled over fruit. They add a nice zip to iced tea, lemonade, smoothies, or yogurt.

Pineapple "Carpaccio" with Mint Tea Syrup

Serves eight.

You'll have a bit of mint tea syrup left over, but it's easy to use up: A splash mixed into a glass of sparkling water makes a delicious drink.

1 cup water
1 Tbs. plus 1 tsp. (or 4 tea bags)
  good-quality mint-flavored
  green tea
½ cup sugar
1 tsp. honey
2 thin slices peeled fresh ginger
Grated zest of 1 lime
Juice of ½ lime (about 1½ Tbs.)
1 ripe pineapple
Fresh mint sprigs for garnish

In a small saucepan, bring the water to a boil. Put the tea in a Pyrex cup and pour the water over it; set aside to infuse for 15 minutes. Pour through a strainer, if needed, back into the saucepan, pressing on the solids to extract as much liquid as possible; discard the tea leaves or bags. Add the sugar, honey, ginger, lime zest, and lime juice to the pan. Cook over medium heat, stirring until the sugar dissolves. Bring to a boil, lower the heat, and simmer for 5 minutes. Set aside to cool. You should have about 1 cup of syrup. Strain and refrigerate until cold.

With a serrated knife, remove the top and a thin slice of the base from the pineapple. Stand the pineapple on either flat end and peel off the skin with the knife, being sure to remove the eyes. Slicing vertically from top to bottom, cut the pineapple as thinly as possible just until you reach the core. Be careful, the fruit is slippery. Slices may vary in shape; this is fine. Rotate the pineapple 180 degrees and slice as before until you reach the core. (Cut off the remaining sides and save for snacking.) Cover the slices with plastic wrap and refrigerate until ready to use.

To serve, arrange a few slices of the fruit in one layer on plates so the slices cover as much of the plate as possible. Drizzle a tablespoon or so of the mint tea syrup over the slices and garnish with a sprig of mint.

"Key" Lime Pie

Serves eight to ten; yields one 9-inch pie.

Although many versions of this pie are famously made with Key limes, which are smaller and quite flavorful, the pie is just as delicious made with well chosen "common" limes (which are known as Tahiti or Persian limes). Just be sure to choose limes that are fragrant and plump with smooth, medium-green skin.

FOR THE CRUST:
- 1½ cups unbleached all-purpose flour
- ½ tsp. table salt
- 6 Tbs. chilled unsalted butter, cubed
- 2 Tbs. chilled vegetable shortening, cubed
- 2½ to 3 Tbs. ice water

FOR THE FILLING:
- 2 14-oz. cans sweetened condensed milk
- 2 large egg yolks
- 1 cup fresh lime juice (from about 4 limes)
- 2 tsp. finely grated lime zest (from about 2 limes)

FOR THE GARNISH:
- 1 cup heavy cream
- 2 tsp. sugar
- 1 lime, zested into thin strips

Make the crust: Put the flour and salt in a food processor; pulse to combine. Add the butter cubes and pulse until they're the size of extra-large peas (about 10 quick pulses). Add the shortening and continue pulsing until the largest pieces of butter and shortening are the size of peas (10 to 15 more quick pulses). Sprinkle 2½ Tbs. of the water over the flour mixture and pulse a few times until the mixture just begins to come together. It should look rather crumbly, but if you press some between your fingers, it should hold together. (If it doesn't, sprinkle on another ½ Tbs. water and pulse a few more times.) Dump the crumbly mix onto a lightly floured surface and press the dough into a 1-inch-thick disk. Wrap in plastic and chill for 30 minutes.

On a lightly floured work surface, roll the dough into a round that's ⅛ inch thick and 12 to 13 inches in diameter. Drape the dough around the rolling pin and ease it into a 9-inch pie pan. With kitchen shears, trim the overhang to ½ inch. Fold the overhang under and crimp it to build up an edge. Prick the crust with a fork in several places. Cover with plastic and refrigerate for 30 minutes. Meanwhile, position an oven rack on the middle rung and heat the oven to 350°F.

Bake the crust: Grease one side of a sheet of foil with cooking spray, oil, or butter. Line the pie pan with the foil, greased side down, and fill it with pie weights or beans. Bake until the edges of the crust look dry and start to turn golden, 25 to 30 minutes. Carefully remove the foil and weights; continue baking until the entire crust is deeply golden brown, another 15 to 20 minutes. Let cool on a rack.

Make the filling: In a medium bowl, whisk the condensed milk, egg yolks, lime juice, and grated zest. Pour into the cooled pie crust and bake at 350°F until just set, about 30 minutes. The center may still be a bit jiggly. (Use an instant-read thermometer to double-check the doneness; the center of the pie should be at least 140°F.) Let the pie cool thoroughly on a rack and then cover with plastic and refrigerate to chill completely, at least 3 hours but no longer than a day.

To garnish and serve: Just before serving, whip the cream and sugar until stiff peaks form. Spread the cream on top of the pie, garnish with the strips of lime zest, and serve.

Raspberry & Blackberry Mousse

Yields 5 to 5½ cups; serves four to six.

This cool, luscious dessert is the perfect end to a summer dinner party. If you can't find ripe berries, don't use unripe, out-of-season fruit. Instead, look for individually quick frozen (IQF) berries, and use the same amounts.

12 oz. fresh raspberries, rinsed and drained
6 oz. fresh blackberries, rinsed and drained
¾ cup granulated sugar
1 tsp. fresh lemon juice
Pinch kosher salt
3 large eggs, separated
1¾ tsp. unflavored gelatin
Pinch cream of tartar
½ cup whipping cream

In a food processor, combine the raspberries, blackberries, ¼ cup of the sugar, the lemon juice, and the salt. Purée until smooth. Pass the purée through a fine sieve; discard the contents of the sieve. Set the purée aside.

Choose a medium stainless-steel bowl that can rest just inside a medium saucepan. Pour about 1 inch of water in the saucepan and bring to a boil. Choose a large bowl that's big enough for the medium bowl to fit inside it. Fill the large bowl with ice water; set aside.

Put the egg yolks, ¼ cup of the sugar, and ½ cup of the berry purée in the medium bowl. When the water in the saucepan boils, reduce the heat to a gentle simmer, and set the bowl with the berry mixture on the saucepan. Whisk until the mixture reaches 140°F on an instant-read thermometer. Turn off the heat but leave the bowl over the water and continue whisking for 3½ minutes. (If the temperature reaches 150°F, remove the bowl from the water, whisk until the temperature drops to 145°F, and then return the bowl to the water bath to continue whisking.) Remove the bowl from the saucepan, stir in the remaining purée, and set the medium bowl into the ice bath to cool. Don't pour the hot water out of the saucepan.

Pour ¼ cup cold water into a small heatproof custard cup; sprinkle the gelatin evenly over the water in the cup. Let sit for about 5 minutes. Set the custard cup with the gelatin in the saucepan with the hot water and stir the gelatin mixture until the gelatin melts and becomes translucent, about 2 minutes. Once the gelatin has melted, whisk it into the berry mixture. Whisk occasionally until the mixture cools to 50° to 55°F and thickens slightly.

In a dry, grease-free bowl, beat the egg whites with a hand mixer (be sure the beaters are dry and grease-free, too) at low speed until frothy; add the cream of tartar. Increase the speed to medium high. Beat until the whites turn opaque, begin to thicken, and look foamy, 1½ minutes. Gradually beat in the remaining ¼ cup sugar. Continue beating until the whites look thick and shiny (but not dry), resemble thickly whipped cream, and form medium peaks, about 3 minutes.

In a separate bowl (no need to clean the beaters this time), beat the cream until soft peaks form, about 2 minutes.

Whisk a couple of large spoonfuls of the beaten egg whites into the berry mixture to lighten it. Pour the ice and water out of the ice bath bowl; dry the bowl. Pour the lightened berry mixture into the cold bowl.

Scrape the remaining egg whites and cream on top and fold gently with a rubber spatula until just combined. Spoon the mousse into individual glasses, into a 6-cup bowl, or into individual soufflé dishes. Refrigerate, covered, until firm, at least 4 hours but no longer than 24 hours.

Folding in egg whites

The first step when folding egg whites into a heavier base is to lighten the base. This step sacrifices some of the air in the whites, but it ultimately makes it easier to fold in the rest of the whites.

1 Gently whisk or stir about one-third of the whipped egg whites into the base to lighten the mixture.

2 Gently drop the remaining whites on top. Pull the spatula toward you along the bottom of the bowl and then up the side to drag some of the base to the top. Gently flip the base onto the whites as you give the bowl a small turn with your other hand. Continue the circular motion of cutting down, dragging up, flipping, and turning until you no longer see streaks of egg white.

Lemon Bars

Yields sixteen 1½ -inch bars; 2½ cups lemon curd.

These bars feature an extra-tart, extra-thick layer of lemon curd over a rich, buttery shortbread crust. They'll last several days in the refrigerator in an airtight container but are best when fresh. The recipe can be doubled.

FOR THE SHORTBREAD:
- ¼ lb. (½ cup) unsalted butter, at room temperature
- 2 Tbs. granulated sugar
- 1 Tbs. confectioners' sugar
- ½ tsp. pure vanilla extract
- 2¼ oz. (½ cup) all-purpose flour
- 2½ oz. (⅔ cup) cake flour
- ¼ tsp. baking powder
- ¼ tsp. table salt

FOR THE LEMON CURD:
- 1 cup fresh lemon juice (from 4 to 6 lemons)
- 2 oz. (¼ cup) unsalted butter, cut into 2 pieces
- 2 Tbs. heavy cream
- 1 cup granulated sugar
- 4 large eggs
- 2 large egg yolks
- ¼ tsp. table salt
- ¼ tsp. pure vanilla extract

Make the shortbread: In a large bowl, cream the butter and both sugars with a hand-held mixer on medium speed (or mix by hand with a wooden spoon) until light and fluffy, about 5 minutes. Beat in the vanilla until thoroughly combined, scraping down the sides of the bowl.

In a medium bowl, sift together both flours, the baking powder, and the salt. With the mixer on low speed, slowly blend the dry ingredients into the wet ingredients, scraping down the sides, until the flour is completely blended and the dough is homogenous.

Scrape the dough from the bowl onto a sheet of plastic. Wrap well and press down to form a ½-inch-thick square. Refrigerate the dough until it's firm but still pliable, about 20 minutes. Heat the oven to 350°F. Prepare two sheets of parchment or waxed paper, each at least 11x11 inches. If using waxed paper, grease an 8x8-inch metal or glass baking pan with butter.

When the dough is firm, unwrap it and put it between the sheets of parchment or paper. Roll the dough to an approximate square, slightly larger than 8x8 inches and about ¼ inch thick. Remove the top sheet of parchment or paper, trim the dough with a dull knife to an 8x8-inch square, and, if using parchment, put it and the dough into an 8x8-inch baking pan. If using waxed paper, flip the dough into the greased pan and peel off the paper. Press the dough into the bottom of the pan, letting the excess parchment come up the sides (trim it to about 1 inch above the rim). The dough should be an even thickness all around but it needn't be perfectly smooth. Bake until the shortbread is light golden on top, 25 to 30 minutes; in a glass pan, look for a golden brown color on the bottom. Remove the pan from the oven, but keep the heat set to 350°F as you make the lemon curd.

Make the lemon curd: In a medium saucepan, heat the lemon juice, butter, and cream to just under a boil; the butter should be melted. Remove from the heat.

In a medium bowl, whisk the sugar, eggs, and yolks until combined. Whisk in a bit of the hot liquid and then gradually whisk in a bit more until it's all added. This technique, called tempering, heats the eggs slowly and gently so they don't curdle.

Pour the mixture back into the saucepan and heat on medium, stirring constantly with a wooden spoon, scraping the bottom and sides of the pan to keep the eggs from scrambling. Cook until the lemon curd coats the spoon thickly enough to leave a line when you draw your finger through, 5 to 8 minutes. Remove from the heat and strain through a fine sieve. Stir in the salt and vanilla.

To finish: Pour the curd over the baked shortbread and smooth it evenly with a spatula, if needed. Bake until the curd has set and jiggles like firm gelatin, 15 to 20 minutes. Let cool to room temperature. Gently tug on the parchment on all sides to loosen the bars from the pan. Lift them out and onto a cutting board and refrigerate until the curd has completely set, at least 4 hours. Trim the sides for a cleaner look and cut into 16 pieces.

5 Refreshing Granitas

Sangría Granita

Yields about 2 cups scraped granita; serves six to eight.

The wine's flavor comes through intensely in this granita, so it's best served in smaller portions.

¾ cup full-bodied red wine, such as Merlot or Cabernet
½ cup water
¼ cup plus 2 Tbs. granulated sugar
¼ cup fresh orange juice
2 Tbs. fresh lemon juice

Combine the wine, water, and sugar in a medium saucepan. Bring to a boil over medium heat. Boil for 1 minute. Remove the pan from the heat and stir in the orange juice and lemon juice. Let cool and then follow the 1-2-3 Freezing Method at far right.

Watermelon Granita

Yields about 8 cups scraped granita; serves sixteen.

Even more refreshing than a slice of watermelon on a hot summer day is a cool watermelon granita. A splash of lime juice heightens the flavor.

One 3-lb. seedless watermelon
¾ cup granulated sugar
1½ Tbs. fresh lime juice

Remove the rind from the watermelon and discard. Chop the flesh into 1½-inch pieces; you should have about 5 cups fruit. Purée the watermelon in a blender, in batches if necessary, until smooth. Strain through a fine sieve and discard the pulp; you should have 4 cups juice. Add the sugar and lime juice to the watermelon juice. Stir with a large spoon or whisk until the sugar has thoroughly dissolved. Follow the 1-2-3 Freezing Method at far right.

Granita flavors, clockwise from top: Sangría, Strawberry-Balsamic, Pink Lemonade, Mango-Lime, Watermelon.

Strawberry-Balsamic Granita

Yields about 6 cups scraped granita; serves twelve.

The balsamic vinegar adds an intriguing depth of flavor and is a natural partner to the strawberries.

10 oz. ripe strawberries (about 1 pt.), rinsed and cored
½ cup plus 1½ Tbs. granulated sugar
1½ cups water
1½ Tbs. high-quality balsamic vinegar

Cut each berry into quarters; you should have about 2 cups lightly packed fruit. In a food processor, combine the strawberries and sugar and process until smooth, about 1 minute. Transfer the purée to a medium bowl. Add the water and vinegar and stir well to combine. Follow the 1-2-3 Freezing Method at right.

Mango-Lime Granita

Yields about 8 cups scraped granita; serves sixteen.

Sweet, refreshing, and beautiful are the words that best describe this granita.

1½ ripe mangos (1½ lb. total), peeled
1 tsp. finely grated lime zest
2 cups water
¾ cup granulated sugar
1 Tbs. fresh lime juice

Cut the mango flesh away from the pit and chop it coarsely into 1-inch pieces; you should have 2 to 2½ cups packed fruit. In a food processor, combine the mango and lime zest. Process until completely smooth, 1 to 2 minutes, stopping to scrape down the sides with a rubber spatula as needed. Transfer the purée to a medium bowl and add the water, sugar, and lime juice. Stir with a large spoon or whisk until the sugar has thoroughly dissolved. Follow the 1-2-3 Freezing Method at right.

Pink Lemonade Granita

Yields about 4 cups scraped granita; serves eight.

Grenadine adds both color and flavor to this granita. Look for it in the supermarket with the cocktail mixers section.

1½ cups water
¾ cup plus 2 Tbs. granulated sugar
¾ cup fresh lemon juice (from 3 to 4 lemons)
2 tsp. grenadine

Combine the water, sugar, lemon juice, and grenadine in a medium bowl. Stir with a large spoon or whisk until the sugar has thoroughly dissolved, about 1 minute. Follow the 1-2-3 Freezing Method at right.

technique

1-2-3 granita freezing method

1 Pour the mixture from one of the recipes at left into a 9-inch-square shallow baking pan.

2 Put the pan in the freezer and stir every 30 minutes with a large dinner fork, being sure to scrape the ice crystals off the sides and into the middle of the pan, until the mixture is too frozen to stir, about 3 hours, depending on the individual recipe and on how cold your freezer is (some granitas can freeze in as little as 1 hour).

3 Cover the pan with plastic and freeze overnight.

When ready to serve the granita, place a fork at the top of the dish and pull it toward you in rows, moving from left to right and rotating the pan as well. Scrape up the shaved ice and fill your chilled glasses or bowls.

Strawberry Crisp
Serves eight.

This comforting crisp is reminiscent of buttered toast and strawberry jam. For the breadcrumbs, use firm-textured white bread or a white sourdough, removing the crusts and pulsing cubes of the bread in a food processor until you have large, irregular, coarse crumbs.

3 pt. small ripe fresh strawberries, hulled and halved
2½ cups coarse fresh white breadcrumbs
½ cup confectioners' sugar
½ tsp. finely grated lemon zest
¼ tsp. table salt
½ cup coarsely chopped hazelnuts
¼ cup unsalted butter, melted
3 Tbs. granulated sugar
Heavy cream or vanilla ice cream for serving (optional)

Position a rack in the middle of the oven and heat the oven to 375°F.

In a bowl, toss the strawberries with 1 cup of the breadcrumbs, the confectioners' sugar, lemon zest, and salt; scrape into an 8x8-inch Pyrex baking dish. In another bowl, toss the remaining 1½ cups breadcrumbs with the hazelnuts, melted butter, and granulated sugar; sprinkle evenly over the berries. Bake until the berries are bubbling, about 40 minutes. Let cool on a wire rack for about 10 minutes.

Spoon the warm crisp into bowls and top with a drizzle of heavy cream or a scoop of ice cream, if you like.

Gingery Plum Cake
Serves eight to ten.

Apricots or pluots can also work in this recipe.

FOR THE CAKE:
6 oz. (1⅓ cups) unbleached all-purpose flour; more for the pan
1 tsp. ground ginger
¾ tsp. baking powder
¼ tsp. baking soda
¼ tsp. table salt
3 oz. (6 tablespoons) unsalted butter, at room temperature; more for the pan
1 cup packed light brown sugar
2 large eggs
1 tsp. pure vanilla extract
⅔ cup (5½ ounces) sour cream

FOR THE TOPPING:
1 plum (or pluot or ripe apricot), halved, pitted, and cut into ⅛- to ¼-inch slices
2 tsp. finely grated fresh ginger
3 Tbs. firmly packed light brown sugar
1 Tbs. unbleached all-purpose flour
Whipped cream, for garnish (optional)

Make the cake: Position a rack in the center of the oven and heat the oven to 350°F. Lightly butter a 9x2-inch round cake pan. Line the bottom with a parchment circle cut to fit the pan and lightly flour the sides, tapping out the excess.

In a medium bowl, whisk the flour, ground ginger, baking powder, baking soda, and salt. In a stand mixer fitted with the paddle attachment (or with a hand mixer), beat the butter and sugar on medium-high until well blended and fluffy, about 3 minutes. Add the eggs, one at a time, beating on medium speed until just blended and adding the vanilla with the second egg. Using a wide rubber spatula, fold in half the dry ingredients, then the sour cream, and then the remaining dry ingredients. Scrape the batter into the prepared pan and spread evenly. Bake for 15 minutes.

Meanwhile, make the topping: Combine the sliced fruit and the grated ginger in a small bowl and toss until

the ginger is well distributed. Add the sugar and flour. Using a table fork, mix the ingredients to coat the fruit evenly. After the cake has baked for 15 minutes, scatter the topping evenly over the cake, working quickly. Don't worry about the fruit looking perfect—this is a rustic cake. Continue baking until a toothpick inserted in the center of the cake comes out clean, another 35 to 40 minutes.

Let the cake cool on a rack for 15 minutes. Run a knife around the inside edge of the pan. Using a dry dishtowel to protect your hands, lay a rack on top of the cake pan and, holding onto both pan and rack, invert the cake. Lift the pan from the cake. Peel away the parchment. Lay a flat serving plate on the bottom of the cake and flip the cake one more time so that the fruit is on top. Serve warm or at room temperature, with whipped cream if you like.

Strawberry & Champagne Terrine

Serves eight to ten.

This lovely terrine is made in a 6-cup loaf pan, but you can vary the look of it by using two or more smaller molds or mini loaf pans, or by alternating the Champagne and strawberry components in several layers in one pan. Just be sure that each layer is almost completely set before pouring on another. Serve the well-chilled terrine cut in thin slices.

FOR THE CHAMPAGNE LAYER:
¼ cup cold water
1 Tbs. powdered gelatin (about 1½ packets)
⅓ cup granulated sugar
1½ cups Champagne or sparkling wine
½ cup sliced strawberries

FOR THE STRAWBERRY LAYER:
1 Tbs. powdered gelatin (about 1½ packets)
2 Tbs. Champagne or sparkling wine
2 pt. strawberries, rinsed and hulled
2 tsp. fresh lemon juice
3 to 6 Tbs. granulated sugar

Sliced strawberries for garnish (optional)

Make the Champagne layer: Put the water in a small saucepan, sprinkle the gelatin on top, and leave to soften, about 3 minutes. Add the sugar and cook over medium-low heat, stirring to dissolve the sugar and melt the gelatin (don't let it boil). In a medium bowl, combine the gelatin mixture and Champagne. Set the bowl over ice and chill, stirring often, until it reaches the consistency of unbeaten egg whites. Carefully stir in the sliced strawberries.

Meanwhile, set a loaf pan in the refrigerator so that it's tilted at a 45-degree angle. (Use a wedge of cheese, sticks of butter, or something similar to prop up the pan.) Pour the Champagne mixture into the pan. Let sit until just set, about 2 hours.

For the strawberry layer: In a small saucepan, soften the gelatin in the 2 Tbs. Champagne, about 3 minutes. Set the pan over low heat and heat to dissolve the gelatin. In a food processor, purée the berries with the lemon juice, add the sugar to taste, and then strain the mixture through a fine sieve. Whisk the softened gelatin into the strawberry purée.

Once the Champagne layer has almost set, set the loaf pan on a level surface (preferably in the refrigerator so that it won't have to be moved) and carefully pour in the strawberry purée. Refrigerate for at least 6 hours but preferably overnight.

To unmold the terrine, cover a cutting board with waxed paper, dip the loaf pan quickly into hot water, and invert it onto the board. Slice the terrine into ½-inch portions; garnish with sliced fresh strawberries, if you like.

Italian Plum Cobbler

Serves six to eight.

Italian plums are great for cooking because they don't fall apart the way juicier ones usually do. If you can't find them, bigger Empress plums work well, as do apricots. You can also use a combination of plums and apricots.

FOR THE COBBLER DOUGH:
1 2/3 cups unbleached
   all-purpose flour
3 1/2 Tbs. sugar
1 1/2 Tbs. baking powder
1/8 tsp. table salt
6 Tbs. cold unsalted butter, cut
   into 1/2-inch cubes
2/3 cup plus 1 Tbs. heavy cream
1 tsp. turbinado sugar (also
   called raw sugar)

FOR THE FILLING:
2 1/4 lb. Italian prune plums, pitted
   and quartered (to yield 6 cups)
1/4 tsp. ground cinnamon
1/4 tsp. ground cardamom
1/4 cup sugar

**Crème fraîche or vanilla ice
cream for serving (optional)**

Make the cobbler dough: In a food processor or an electric mixer fitted with the paddle attachment, combine the flour, sugar, baking powder, and salt. Pulse or mix to combine. Add the butter and then pulse or mix until the mixture resembles fine crumbs. Add 2/3 cup of the cream and pulse until the dough just comes together, scraping down the paddle and bowl if necessary. Turn the dough onto a lightly floured surface and gently pat it together, incorporating any stray crumbs. Shape the dough into eight 2-inch balls. Set each ball on a baking sheet and flatten slightly. Refrigerate for at least 20 minutes but no longer than 2 hours.

Make the filling: Heat the oven to 350°F. In a large bowl, combine the plums, cinnamon, cardamom, and sugar; toss well. Spoon the fruit into a 2-qt. gratin dish or other shallow casserole dish (don't use a metal dish). Arrange the flattened dough balls on top of the fruit, leaving about 1 inch of space around each biscuit. Brush the biscuits with the remaining 1 Tbs. cream and sprinkle with the turbinado sugar. Bake on a baking sheet until the fruit is bubbling and the top is lightly browned, 40 to 45 minutes. Serve hot or warm, topped with crème fraîche or vanilla ice cream, if you like.

Strawberries with Balsamic Sabayon

Serves eight.

Serve fresh strawberries with this chilled creamy sabayon sauce enhanced with balsamic vinegar. The sauce will taste complex and delicious with a really good-quality aged balsamic, but it's wonderful as well when made with a more ordinary balsamic.

6 Tbs. sugar
4 egg yolks
2 Tbs. aged balsamic vinegar
**1½ cups heavy cream, whipped
   to medium-stiff peaks and
   refrigerated**
**1 pint fresh strawberries, rinsed
   if necessary and hulled**
**Crisp cookies for garnish
   (optional)**

Set aside a big bowl of ice. In a small stainless-steel bowl, whisk the sugar into the egg yolks until thoroughly combined and lightened in color. Set the bowl over a saucepan of simmering water and continue whisking the mixture until it thickens. The mixture is cooked when it's light in color and it trails off the whisk in ribbons. Don't overcook it. Remove the bowl from the heat and whisk in the balsamic vinegar. Set the bowl over the bowl of ice and continue whisking the sabayon until it's completely cooled, 5 to 10 minutes. The sabayon will stiffen as it cools. Very gently fold in the whipped cream and refrigerate the lightened sabayon for at least 2 hours before serving. It will hold overnight, but it's best served the day it's made.

Serve the sabayon draped over whole or sliced strawberries in a pretty glass dish with a garnish of crisp cookies, whole or crumbled, if you like.

Zabaglione with Summer Fruit

Serves six.

Marsala may be the traditional addition to zabaglione, but a spicy, floral Riesling pairs much better with plump and sweet ripe fruit. Look for an Alsatian-style dry or off-dry Riesling. Or try Champagne, Sauternes, or Vouvray, varying the amount of sugar to balance the sweetness of the wine.

4 large egg yolks
¼ cup sugar (or up to ⅓ cup if using a wine that isn't as sweet)
½ cup Riesling (see the note above)
½ tsp. unflavored powdered gelatin, softened in 1 Tbs. water (optional; see the note at right)
1 Tbs. boiling water
1 cup whipping cream
1 Tbs. Amaretto or brandy; more to taste
4 to 5 cups peeled, sliced summer fruit, like a mix of peaches, nectarines, and berries
⅓ cup crushed almond macaroons or biscotti (or 6 Amaretti di Saronno cookies, crumbled)

Fill a large bowl halfway with ice water. Set a large metal bowl on top of a pan of barely simmering water over medium-low heat (the water level should be about 2 inches below the bottom of the bowl). Put the yolks and sugar in the bowl and whisk vigorously until the yolks begin to thicken and lighten in color. Pour in the Riesling and continue whisking until the mixture is thick enough so that the whisk leaves a trail as it passes through the mixture. This may take 5 to 10 minutes, depending on the heat of the water. Remove from the heat and whisk for another minute or so.

In a small bowl, dissolve the softened gelatin in the boiling water. Slowly whisk this into the zabaglione. Set the custard bowl over the ice-water bath to cool while you whip the cream to stiff peaks. With a rubber spatula, fold the whipped cream and liqueur into the custard. Refrigerate for at least 4 hours but no more than 24 hours.

To serve, arrange the fruit in six parfait glasses or dessert bowls. Spoon the zabaglione over the fruit and garnish with the cookie crumbs.

Note: The gelatin prevents the zabaglione from separating in the refrigerator and lets you make the dessert up to a day ahead. If you plan to make the dessert the day you serve it, you can omit the gelatin, but be sure to chill the custard for 2 hours.

Silky Lemon Pudding

Serves four; yields about 3⅓ cups.

This simple pudding tastes both bright and comforting. Sample the pudding while it's still hot. If it's too tart for you, whisk in a tablespoon or so of sugar, but remember that chilling mutes flavors.

2¼ cups whole milk
½ cup sugar
½ cup packed light brown sugar
¼ cup cornstarch
4 large egg yolks
2 Tbs. lightly packed finely grated lemon zest
Pinch salt
½ cup fresh lemon juice
3 Tbs. unsalted butter, at room temperature
Whipped cream and candied violets for garnish (optional)

In a medium saucepan off the heat, whisk the milk, sugar, brown sugar, and cornstarch until smooth. Whisk in the egg yolks, lemon zest, and salt. Set over medium heat and cook, whisking frequently at first and constantly toward the end, until thickened and the whisk leaves a very defined trail in the pudding, 9 to 12 minutes.

Remove the pan from the heat, add the lemon juice and butter, and stir until incorporated. Pour through a coarse sieve into a large serving bowl or into four individual serving dishes. Let cool to room temperature. Refrigerate, loosely covered, until set and thoroughly chilled, at least 2 hours or up to two days. Serve chilled with whipped cream and candied violets, if you like.

Carrot Cake with Orange Cream Cheese Frosting

Serves twelve to fourteen.

This cake really comes into its own on its second day, when the flavors have mellowed to perfection.

FOR THE CAKE:
Olive oil for the pans
1 cup sugar
1 cup firmly packed light brown sugar
¾ cup olive oil
2 cups unbleached all-purpose flour, sifted
2 tsp. ground cinnamon
1 tsp. grated nutmeg, preferably freshly grated
2 Tbs. baking powder
½ tsp. table salt
1½ lb. carrots (8 to 10 medium), peeled and cut into 1-inch chunks
4 large eggs, at room temperature
2 tsp. pure vanilla extract
1 cup pecans, lightly toasted, cooled, and finely chopped by pulsing in a food processor
¼ cup dark rum

FOR THE FROSTING:
1 lb. cream cheese, somewhat softened
½ cup honey
1 Tbs. grated orange zest
½ cup heavy cream

Make the cake: Position a rack in the middle of the oven. Heat the oven to 350°F. Oil two 9x2-inch cake pans with olive oil, line the bottoms with parchment or waxed paper, and oil the paper.

Put the sugar, brown sugar, and olive oil in the bowl of a stand mixer and set aside. In a medium bowl, combine the flour, cinnamon, nutmeg, baking powder, and salt; mix well and set aside. In a food processor fitted with the metal blade, process the carrots until they're in tiny pieces, scraping down the sides of the bowl, about 25 seconds. Measure 3 cups of carrots and set aside. In a small bowl, lightly beat the eggs with a fork, stir in the vanilla, and set aside.

Beat the sugar mixture on low until well combined, scraping down the sides of the bowl once, 2 to 3 minutes (it will look like wet sand). Continuing on low speed, gradually mix in half the dry ingredients. Add the remaining dry ingredients in three or four additions, alternating with the egg mixture, and ending with the dry; scrape the bowl once or twice. Stir in the carrots, pecans, and rum, scraping the bowl once. Let the batter sit for 15 minutes.

Divide the batter between the cake pans (if you have a scale, weigh them to see if they're even) and bake until a toothpick inserted in the center of each comes out clean, 35 to 40 minutes. Let them cool in the pans on a rack for 15 minutes. Run a paring knife around the inside edge to release the cakes. With the help of a second rack, turn each pan over so the bottom faces up, remove the pan, and carefully peel off and discard the paper liner. Using the racks again, flip each layer over so the top faces up again. Let cool completely.

Make the frosting: When the layers are cool, put the cream cheese, honey, and orange zest in the bowl of a stand mixer and whip on high until smooth and light, 1 to 2 minutes, scraping the bowl. Add the cream and whip on medium, scraping the bowl, just until you see tracks from the whip or beaters, 1 to 2 minutes.

Frost the cake: Set one cake layer on a cardboard base or other support (like a removable tart pan bottom) and spread it evenly with about one-third of the frosting. Set the second layer on top and cover the top smoothly (or with little swirls) with about one-third more of the frosting. Coat the sides evenly with a very thin layer of frosting, and then use what remains to finish the sides with a second coat. Refrigerate the cake for several hours—this firms up the frosting and mellows the flavors—but give it some time at room temperature before serving to take off the chill.

Peach Cobbler with Star Anise

Serves eight.

To grind whole star anise, put the whole spice in a spice grinder or a coffee grinder dedicated to spices.

FOR THE PEACH FILLING:
Softened butter for the baking dish
½ cup packed light brown sugar
1 Tbs. cornstarch
Scant ¼ tsp. freshly ground star anise
Pinch table salt
3 lb. firm but ripe peaches (about 6 large), pitted
1 tsp. pure vanilla extract

FOR THE COBBLER TOPPING:
4½ oz. (1 cup) all-purpose flour
⅓ cup fine cornmeal
⅓ cup packed light brown sugar
1½ tsp. baking powder
¼ tsp. table salt
Pinch freshly ground star anise
2 oz. (¼ cup) cold unsalted butter, cut into ¾-inch pieces
6 Tbs. heavy cream
Lightly sweetened whipped cream for garnish (optional)

Make the filling: Position a rack in the middle of the oven and heat the oven to 375°F. Lightly butter a 10-cup baking dish (10x2-inch round or 9-inch square).

In a large bowl, mix the brown sugar, cornstarch, ground star anise, and salt until combined; break up any lumps.

Cut the peaches into 1-inch-wide wedges and cut each wedge in half crosswise. Add the peaches and vanilla to the dry ingredients and toss to coat evenly. Pour the fruit and its juices into the buttered baking dish, scraping the bowl of any sugar. Spread the fruit evenly.

Make the topping: In a food processor, combine the flour, cornmeal, brown sugar, baking powder, salt, and the pinch of ground star anise. Pulse briefly to blend. Add the cold butter pieces and pulse until they're the size of small peas. Pour the cream over the dough and pulse just until moist crumbs form.

Dump the dough onto a lightly floured work surface. Gather the dough and press it to create a square that's about 1 inch thick. Lightly flour the dough. Roll it out, flouring as needed, to a ½-inch-thick rectangle; it should measure about 5x9 inches. Cut the rectangle in half lengthwise, and cut each half into four pieces, each about 2½x2¼ inches.

Arrange the dough squares on top of the peaches, leaving spaces between each one. Bake until the filling is bubbling and the topping is nicely browned, about 40 minutes. The cobbler is best when served warm on the same day it's baked, preferably with a little lightly sweetened whipped cream on the side.

the twist

Star anise adds aromatic intrigue

With its unique flavor reminiscent of licorice, clove, and fennel seed, star anise goes beautifully with peaches. You can now find the star-shaped spice in supermarkets, but your best bets for freshness are Asian markets and mail-order spice houses.

Peach-Ginger Galette with Hazelnuts

Serves eight.

You can make the dough and the topping well ahead of assembling this rustic tart, but do serve it the day it's baked, preferably warm.

FOR THE GALETTE DOUGH:

2 cups unbleached all-purpose flour

3 Tbs. sugar

1 tsp. ground ginger

½ tsp. table salt

11 Tbs. very cold unsalted butter, cut into ½-inch pieces

⅓ cup very cold water

FOR THE TOPPING:

⅓ cup very coarsely chopped hazelnuts (with or without their skins)

1 Tbs. light brown sugar

1 tsp. unbleached all-purpose flour

1 Tbs. unsalted butter, melted

FOR THE FILLING:

3 Tbs. cornstarch

⅓ cup firmly packed light brown sugar

¼ tsp. table salt

2¼ lb. firm but ripe peaches (4 to 5 peaches), pitted and cut into ¾-inch wedges

2 tsp. minced fresh ginger

2 tsp. fresh lemon juice

2 Tbs. cream or milk

Vanilla ice cream or sweetened whipped cream for serving (optional)

Make the galette dough: Combine the flour, sugar, ground ginger, and salt in a food processor and pulse to combine. Scatter the chilled butter pieces around the bowl and pulse in 1-second bursts just until the mixture resembles coarse crumbs. Drizzle the water evenly over the crumbs and process just until the dough is moist but still extremely crumbly, about 5 seconds. Turn the dough onto a work surface and press it into a 6-inch disk. Wrap the disk in plastic and refrigerate until well chilled, at least 1 hour.

Make the topping: In a small bowl, combine the chopped hazelnuts, brown sugar, and flour with a fork until blended. Drizzle the melted butter evenly over the mixture and toss with the fork until combined.

Fill and bake the galette: Position a rack in the middle of the oven and heat the oven to 425°F. Line a rimmed baking sheet with parchment. Unwrap the galette dough and set it on a lightly floured work surface.

Roll out the dough, turning and lightly flouring it and the work surface as necessary, into a round that's ⅛ to ¼ inch thick and about 15 inches in diameter. Trim the excess dough to make a 14-inch round. Loosely roll the dough around the rolling pin and transfer it to the lined baking sheet. The dough will hang over the edges of the pan. Cover and refrigerate the dough.

Meanwhile, make the filling: In a large bowl, whisk the cornstarch, brown sugar, and salt until no lumps remain. Add the peach slices, minced ginger, and lemon juice. Toss until the peaches are well combined with the dry ingredients.

Assemble and bake: Remove the dough from the fridge. If it isn't pliable, let it warm up at room temperature for a few minutes. Give the peach filling a toss and pile it in the center of the dough, leaving a 3-inch border bare. Fold this border over the filling, pleating the dough as you go. Gently press the pleats to seal. Tuck in any peach slices that stick out. Brush the pleated border with the cream or milk and sprinkle the hazelnut topping on the border, pressing on the nuts so they stick.

Put the galette in the oven and immediately reduce the heat to 400°F. Bake until the crust is browned on the top and bottom, 45 to 50 minutes. Check the galette after about 30 minutes; if the nuts are darkening too much, cover very loosely with foil.

Serve warm or at room temperature with a scoop of vanilla ice cream or a dollop of lightly sweetened whipped cream, if you like.

Apricot-Raspberry Buckle

Serves eight to ten.

A buckle is a tender yellow cake with a fruit and streusel topping. This version features fresh apricots and raspberries both in the cake and on top.

FOR THE STREUSEL:
- ⅓ cup minus 1 Tbs. unbleached all-purpose flour
- ¼ cup sugar
- 1 tsp. ground cinnamon
- Pinch salt
- ¼ cup cold unsalted butter, cut into small pieces

FOR THE CAKE:
- 1⅓ cups unbleached all-purpose flour
- 1½ tsp. baking powder
- ½ tsp. table salt
- ¾ cup unsalted butter, softened at room temperature
- 1 cup sugar
- 1½ tsp. pure vanilla extract
- ¼ tsp. pure almond extract
- 3 large eggs
- ¾ lb. firm, ripe fresh apricots (about 4 large), halved, pitted, and cut into ¾-inch pieces (to yield 2 cups)
- 2 cups (about ½ lb.) fresh raspberries

Position a rack in the lower third of the oven and heat the oven to 375°F. Butter a 9-inch square baking pan.

Make the streusel: In a medium bowl, combine the flour, sugar, cinnamon, and salt. Add the cold butter and cut it in with a pastry blender or two table knives until the butter pieces resemble small peas. Refrigerate until needed.

Make the cake: Sift the flour, baking powder, and salt into a bowl and set aside. With an electric stand mixer (a hand mixer is fine, too), beat the butter with the paddle attachment on medium speed until smooth, about 1 minute. Add ¼ cup of the sugar and the vanilla and almond extracts. Beat for 1 minute on medium speed. Gradually add the remaining ¾ cup sugar while beating on medium speed. Turn off the mixer and use a rubber spatula to scrape the bowl and beater. Beat on medium-high speed until pale and slightly fluffy (the sugar will not be dissolved), about 3 minutes. Reduce the speed to medium and add the eggs, one at a time, mixing until the batter is smooth each time. Stop and scrape the bowl and the beater. On low speed, add the flour mixture and beat only until incorporated. Remove the bowl from the mixer and scrape the beater. The batter will be thick.

Add half of the apricots and half of the raspberries to the batter and fold them in gently with a large rubber spatula. Some of the raspberries will break, giving the batter an attractive pinkish cast. (When baked, the pink will disappear.) Spread the batter into the prepared pan and distribute the remaining fruit evenly on top.

Sprinkle the streusel over the fruit. Bake until the cake springs back in the center when lightly pressed and a toothpick comes out clean, 45 to 50 minutes. Let the cake cool in its pan on a rack. Serve warm or at room temperature.

Pear-Almond Gratin

Serves six.

Look for ginger preserves in the jelly section of a well-stocked supermarket. You can substitute apricot preserves for the ginger, if you like.

- ¼ cup plus 1 Tbs. sugar
- ¼ cup ginger preserves, at room temperature
- 1¼ tsp. finely grated orange zest
- Pinch salt
- ½ cup whole unblanched almonds
- ½ cup fresh white breadcrumbs
- 6 Tbs. cold unsalted butter, cut into cubes
- 1 Tbs. fresh lemon juice
- 2 lb. firm but ripe Bosc pears (about 4)
- ¾ cup light or heavy cream

Position a rack in the lower third of the oven and heat the oven to 400°F. Butter the bottom and sides of six 6-inch (8-oz.) gratin dishes (or one shallow 1½-qt. gratin dish or baking pan).

In a small bowl, combine 1 Tbs. of the sugar with the ginger preserves, orange zest, and salt. Stir well and set aside.

Put the almonds in a food processor and process until they're coarsely chopped. Add the breadcrumbs and the remaining ¼ cup sugar and pulse four or five times to combine. Add the butter cubes and pulse until the mixture barely comes together, about 30 seconds; it should be a chunky, crumbly mixture. (By hand: Coarsely chop the almonds and combine them with the breadcrumbs and sugar. Cut in the butter cubes with a pastry cutter or two knives until chunky and crumbly but combined.)

Put the lemon juice in a large bowl. Peel the pears, cut them in half lengthwise, and spoon out the core (a melon baller works well). Cut the pears lengthwise into ¼ inch slices, put them in the bowl, and toss gently with the lemon juice. Add the ginger mixture and toss again to coat.

Pour the pears and juices into the prepared gratin dishes and spread evenly. Scatter the almond mixture evenly on top.

Bake the gratins until the tops are browned, the juices are bubbling, and the pears are still intact but tender when pierced with a fork, 30 to 35 minutes for individual gratins (40 to 50 minutes for one large gratin). Let cool for 10 to 15 minutes before serving. Pass the cream separately in a pitcher for guests to drizzle over each serving.

Butter Pie Crust

Yields two 12-inch rounds, enough for one 9-inch double-crust pie.

8 oz. (1 cup) cold unsalted butter
9 oz. (2 cups) all-purpose unbleached
    flour
¼ cup granulated sugar
¼ tsp. table salt
¼ cup cold water

Cut the butter into ½-inch cubes. Combine the flour, sugar, and salt in the bowl of a stand mixer fitted with the paddle attachment (or in a large bowl, if mixing by hand). Mix for a second or two to blend the dry ingredients. Add the butter and then, with the mixer on low (or by hand with two knives or a pastry cutter), work the mixture until it's crumbly and the largest pieces of butter are no bigger than a pea (about ¼ inch). The butter should remain cold and firm. To test it, pick up some butter and pinch it between the thumbs and forefingers of both hands to form a little cube. If the butter holds together as a cube and your fingers are not greasy, then the butter is still cold enough. If your fingers look greasy, put the bowl in the fridge for

Double-Crust Jumble Berry Pie

Yields one 9-inch double-crust pie.

You can make this pie with only one type of berry, if you like, but it's nice to include a few strawberries as they add a nice floral-fruity lightness to the finished pie. The pie uses two types of thickeners—tapioca and cornstarch—to keep the texture of the filling somewhat firm and the juices contained around the fruit.

1 cup granulated sugar
2 Tbs. cornstarch
2 Tbs. quick-cooking tapioca
¼ tsp. table salt
6 cups washed and well-dried mix
   of blackberries, blueberries,
   raspberries, and quartered
   strawberries
1 Tbs. unsalted butter, cut into small
   pieces
1 recipe Butter Pie Crust (above right)

In a large bowl, mix the sugar, cornstarch, tapioca, and salt. Add the berries and toss with your hands until the berries are evenly coated.

Roll out the pie dough according to the directions in the recipe above right. Pile the berries into the dough-lined pie pan, sprinkling any remaining dry ingredients on top. Dot the surface with the butter and cover the berry mixture with the top crust. Make a strong double-edged seal by folding the top layer over the bottom one and then flute the edge, as shown in the photos at right.

Cut five or six slits in the top crust to let steam escape during cooking. Heat the oven to 400°F while you chill the pie in the refrigerator for 15 to 20 minutes.

Put the pie on a baking sheet to catch any drips, bake it in the hot oven for 15 minutes, and then reduce the temperature to 350°F. Continue baking until the crust is golden and the filling juices that are bubbling through the vents and edges are thick, glossy, and slow, another 50 to 60 minutes. For the best texture for serving, let the pice cool completely (it may take up to 5 hours), and then reheat slices or the whole pie just slightly before serving. (Cooling completely lets the filling juices firm up, while a quick reheat makes the pastry nice and flaky.) You can serve the pie while it's still warm, but the filling will be slightly liquid.

how to:

Fold for a good seal

Press the two layers of dough together (the top layer should extend farther than the bottom) and then fold the top crust over the bottom to get a thick, uniform edge.

15 minutes to firm up the butter before adding the water. As the mixer turns on low (or tossing with a fork if mixing by hand), sprinkle the cold water evenly over the flour and butter. Work the dough until it just pulls together as a shaggy mass.

Divide the dough; pat each half into a thick, flattened ball. Lightly flour a work surface. Tap one of the dough balls down with four or five taps of the rolling pan. Begin rolling from the center of your dough outward. Stop the pressure ¼ inch from the edge of the dough. Lift the dough and turn by a quarter; repeat the rolling until the dough is at least 12 inches in diameter. Reflour the work surface if the dough sticks.

Using a pot lid or a circle of cardboard as a template, trim the dough to form a 12-inch round. Fold the dough in half, slide both hands under the dough, and gently transfer it to the pie pan. Unfold and ease the dough into the bottom of the pie pan without stretching it.

Roll out the other dough ball in the same manner and cut a second 12-inch round for the top crust.

Flute for a pretty edge

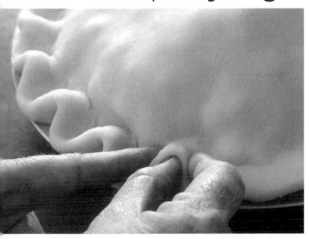

Lift up a section of dough and press down on either side to make a graceful vertical flute. The shape will settle down a bit during cooking but will still look nice.

Rhubarb-Ginger Fool
Yields 7 cups; serves six.

This dessert is called a fool because, well, almost anyone can make it. Just combine the stewed fruit with freshly whipped cream.

1½ to 2 lb. rhubarb, ends trimmed
1 to 1¼ cups granulated sugar
2 Tbs. chopped candied ginger
2 Tbs. freshly grated ginger
2 cups heavy cream

If the rhubarb stalks are more than 1 inch thick, cut them in half lengthwise. Cut the stalks into 1-inch-long pieces. In a stainless-steel pan with a tight-fitting lid, combine the rhubarb, sugar, candied ginger, and fresh ginger. (There's no need to add water; though it will look dry at first, the rhubarb will release enough water to cook without scorching.) Cover and cook over low heat until the rhubarb is tender and falling apart, about 30 minutes. Let cool and then refrigerate until well chilled.

Whip the cream until it holds soft peaks. Gently fold in the chilled rhubarb mixture until well combined. Spoon into serving glasses and chill until ready to serve.

Cranberry-Pear Tart in a Walnut Shortbread Crust

Yields one 9-inch tart; serves eight to twelve.

FOR THE CRUST:
1 large egg yolk
1 Tbs. half-and-half
½ tsp. pure vanilla extract
6¾ oz. (1½ cups) unbleached all-purpose flour
3 Tbs. granulated sugar
½ tsp. table salt
¼ lb. (½ cup) cold unsalted butter, cut into ½-inch dice
⅓ cup walnuts, toasted and finely chopped

FOR THE FILLING:
3 large ripe pears, such as Anjou or Bartlett
2 cups fresh cranberries, picked through and rinsed
1 Tbs. brandy
⅔ cup granulated sugar
2 tsp. unbleached all-purpose flour

½ tsp. ground cardamom
½ tsp. ground ginger
¼ tsp. ground cinnamon
⅛ tsp. ground allspice
⅛ tsp. table salt

FOR THE STREUSEL:
1¾ oz. (⅓ cup plus 1 Tbs.) unbleached all-purpose flour
¼ cup packed light brown sugar
⅛ tsp. table salt
1 oz. (2 Tbs.) unsalted butter, melted
¼ tsp. pure vanilla extract

Make the crust: Position a rack near the center of the oven and heat the oven to 400°F. In a small bowl, mix the egg yolk, half-and-half, and vanilla. Put the flour, sugar, and salt in a food processor; pulse until combined. Add the butter and pulse until the butter pieces are no longer visible. With the processor running, add the yolk mixture in a steady stream and then pulse until the moisture is fairly evenly dispersed, 10 to 20 seconds. Transfer the mixture to a bowl. Using your hands, mix in the chopped walnuts to distribute them evenly. The dough will be a mealy, crumbly mass.

Pour the crumb mixture into a 9½-inch round fluted tart pan with a removable bottom. Starting with the sides of the pan, firmly press the crumbs against the pan to create a crust about ¼ inch thick. Press the remaining crumbs evenly against the bottom of the pan. Prick the bottom of the crust all over with a fork and freeze for 10 minutes. Bake until the sides just begin to darken and the bottom is set, about 15 minutes. Transfer to a cooling rack. Reduce the oven temperature to 350°F.

Make the filling: Peel the pears, quarter them lengthwise, core, and cut crosswise into ¼-inch-thick slices.

In a food processor, coarsely chop the cranberries. In a medium bowl, mix the pears, cranberries, and brandy. In a small bowl, mix the sugar, flour, cardamom, ginger, cinnamon, allspice, and salt; add to the cranberry-pear mixture, tossing to combine. Spoon the filling into the par-baked crust, leveling the filling and packing it down slightly with the back of a spoon.

Make the streusel and bake: In a small bowl, mix the flour, brown sugar, and salt. Add the melted butter and vanilla. Combine with your fingers until the mixture begins to clump together in small pieces

when pressed. Sprinkle the streusel over the filling, breaking it into smaller pieces if necessary.

Bake at 350°F until the fruit is tender when pierced with a fork and the streusel and the edges of the crust are golden brown, about 50 minutes. If the tart begins to get overly brown at the edges, cover with foil. Let the tart cool on a rack until it's just barely warm before serving. The tart will keep, covered and at room temperature, for two to three days.

How to freeze cranberries

If you want to enjoy cranberry desserts (or quickbreads or muffins) year-round, your best bet is to freeze them yourself now while they're in season. (It's tough to find even frozen ones at the market in May.) Though they will last for about a month in the fridge, freezing will extend their life for much longer. Freeze cranberries in their original package or wash, dry, and pick them over before transferring them to a heavy-duty freezer bag. (This last option also allows you to portion the cranberries as you like.) There's no need to thaw the cranberries for baking; just rinse them under cold water in a colander and pat dry.

Cranberries' deep color and bright sweet-tart flavor don't diminish with heat, which makes them a favorite choice for bakers.

Cranberry Upside-Down Cake

Yields one 9-inch round cake; serves twelve.

This cake is best served warm and fresh.

½ lb. (1 cup) very soft unsalted butter; more for the pan
1 cup very firmly packed light brown sugar
¼ tsp. ground cinnamon
2 cups cranberries, fresh or frozen (thawed, rinsed, and dried), at room temperature
1 cup granulated sugar
1 large egg yolk, at room temperature
2 large eggs, at room temperature
⅔ cup sour cream, at room temperature
1 tsp. pure vanilla extract
½ tsp. table salt
7 oz. (1¾ cups) cake flour
1 tsp. baking powder
¼ tsp. baking soda

Position a rack in the lower third of the oven and heat the oven to 350°F. Lightly butter the bottom and sides of a 9-inch round cake pan with sides at least 2½ inches high.

Put 2 oz. (4 Tbs.) of the butter in the buttered pan. Put the pan in the oven until the butter melts, about 5 minutes. Remove the pan from the oven and stir in the brown sugar and cinnamon until well combined. Spread the brown sugar mixture evenly over the bottom of the pan and spread the cranberries evenly over the sugar.

Put the remaining 6 oz. (12 Tbs.) butter in a medium bowl. Using a wooden spoon, cream the butter with the granulated sugar and egg yolk until blended, about 20 seconds. Switch to a whisk and stir in the eggs one at a time. Whisk until the batter is smooth and the sugar begins to

dissolve, about 30 seconds. Whisk in the sour cream, vanilla, and salt. Sift the cake flour, baking powder, and baking soda directly onto the batter. Using the whisk, combine the ingredients until the mixture is smooth and free of lumps. Spread the batter evenly over the cranberry mixture in the cake pan.

Bake until the center of the cake springs back when gently touched and a skewer inserted in the center comes out with only moist crumbs clinging to it, 50 to 65 minutes. Set the pan on a rack to cool for 5 to 10 minutes (the cranberry syrup in the bottom of the pan will be too thick if you wait longer). Run a knife between the cake and sides of the pan. Invert the cake onto a serving plate and remove the pan. Let cool for at least another 15 minutes before serving.

Pear & Hazelnut Gratin
Serves six.

Look for ginger preserves in the jelly section of a well-stocked supermarket. You can substitute apricot preserves for the ginger if you like.

¼ cup plus 1 Tbs. granulated sugar
¼ cup ginger preserves, at room temperature
1¼ tsp. finely grated orange zest
Pinch salt
½ cup whole unblanched hazelnuts
½ cup fresh white breadcrumbs
6 Tbs. cold unsalted butter, cut into cubes
1 Tbs. fresh lemon juice
2 lb. firm-ripe Bosc pears (about 4)
¾ cup light or heavy cream

Position a rack in the lower third of the oven and heat the oven to 400°F. Butter the bottom and sides of six 6-inch (8-oz.) gratin dishes (or one shallow 1½-qt. gratin dish or baking pan).

In a small bowl, combine 1 Tbs. of the sugar with the ginger preserves, orange zest, and salt. Stir well.

Put the hazelnuts in a food processor and process until they're coarsely chopped. Add the breadcrumbs and the remaining ¼ cup sugar and pulse four or five times to combine. Add the butter cubes and pulse until the mixture barely comes together, about 30 seconds; it should be a chunky, crumbly mixture.

(If you don't have a food processor: Coarsely chop the hazelnuts and combine them with the breadcrumbs and sugar. Cut in the butter cubes with a pastry cutter or two knives until chunky and crumbly but combined.)

Put the lemon juice in a large bowl. Peel the pears, cut them in half lengthwise, and spoon out the core (a melon baller works well). Cut the pears lengthwise into ¼-inch slices, put them in the bowl, and toss gently with the lemon juice. Add the ginger mixture and toss again to coat.

Pour the pears and juices into the prepared gratin dishes and spread evenly. Scatter the hazelnut mixture evenly on top. Bake until the tops are browned, the juices are bubbling, and the pears are still intact but tender when pierced with a fork, 30 to 35 minutes for individual gratins (40 to 50 minutes for one large gratin). Let cool for 10 to 15 minutes before serving. Pass the cream separately for guests to drizzle over each serving.

Bosc, the best pear for baking

With its dense, grainy flesh and aromatic flavor, Boscs are the perfect pear for cooking and baking.

For cooking and baking, you want them "firm-ripe" or just at the beginning of the ripening window. Use fruit that yields only slightly when pressed near the stem.

Sweet Potato Spice Cake with Fresh Ginger & Pecan Streusel Topping

Yields one 9-inch square cake; serves sixteen.

One piece is never enough when it comes to this incredibly moist cake. The fresh ginger adds a vibrancy that other spice cakes can only dream of.

FOR THE TOPPING:
3 oz. (⅔ cup) unbleached all-purpose flour
½ cup very firmly packed light brown sugar
½ cup chopped toasted pecans
⅛ tsp. table salt
2 oz. (¼ cup) unsalted butter, melted; more as needed

FOR THE CAKE:
¾ cup vegetable oil; more for the pan
1½ cups very firmly packed light brown sugar
3 large eggs, at room temperature
1 cup baked, mashed sweet potato, at room temperature or slightly warmer (from about one 15-oz. sweet potato)
1 Tbs. molasses
1 Tbs. finely grated fresh ginger
¾ tsp. table salt
¼ tsp. ground cinnamon
¼ tsp. ground cardamom
⅛ tsp. freshly grated nutmeg or ¼ tsp. ground nutmeg
7½ oz. (1⅔ cups) unbleached all-purpose flour; more for the pan
1½ tsp. baking soda

Make the topping: In a small bowl, stir the flour, brown sugar, pecans, and salt. Drizzle the melted butter over the dry ingredients and stir until well combined. The streusel should feel clumpy, not sandy, when gently squeezed between your fingertips. If the streusel seems dry, add more melted butter.

Make the cake: Position a rack in the center of the oven and heat the oven to 350°F. Lightly oil and flour a 9-inch-square baking pan; tap out excess flour.

In a medium bowl, combine the oil, brown sugar, and eggs and, using a whisk, stir until the mixture is smooth and the sugar begins to dissolve, 30 to 60 seconds. If the sugar forms lumps, break them up with your fingers; a few tiny lumps are fine. Whisk in the sweet potato, molasses, grated ginger, salt, cinnamon, cardamom, and nutmeg. Sift the flour and baking soda directly onto the batter. Using a whisk or rubber spatula, combine the ingredients until well blended and almost smooth.

Pour the batter into the prepared pan, spreading it evenly with the spatula. Sprinkle the streusel evenly over the batter, creating small clumps as you go by squeezing the streusel between your fingers.

Bake until a skewer inserted in the center comes out with only moist crumbs clinging to it, about 45 minutes. Set the pan on a rack to cool for 15 minutes. Run a knife around the edge of the pan. Let cool until just warm and then cut into squares and serve from the pan, or wrap well in plastic. Store at room temperature for up to a week.

A baked sweet potato is the secret

Baked, mashed sweet potatoes not only add a toasty sweetness to this cake but also keep it moist. To bake a sweet potato, simply prick it all over and bake at 450°F until very tender, about 1 hour. When the potato is cool enough to handle, peel off the skin and smash the flesh in a bowl with a masher, or whisk until smooth.

Pumpkin in the can?

The recipe here calls for canned pumpkin as opposed to fresh. Why? Because pumpkin is one of the few foods that's actually better from a can. It's virtually impossible to get a purée from a sugar pumpkin at home that's as smooth, as consistently flavorful, and as dry as it is from that can in the supermarket. Look for labels that say "pure solid-pack pumpkin."

Spiced Pumpkin Cheesecake with a Gingersnap Crust

Serves sixteen.

This cheesecake is a luxurious twist on a traditional pumpkin pie.

FOR THE CRUST:
About 40 gingersnap wafers (to yield 2 cups cookie crumbs)
¼ cup packed light brown sugar
5 Tbs. unsalted butter, melted and cooled

FOR THE FILLING:
2 lb. (four 8-oz. packages) cream cheese, at room temperature
1⅓ cups packed light brown sugar
1 tsp. ground cinnamon
½ tsp. ground ginger
¼ tsp. ground allspice
¼ tsp. freshly grated nutmeg
¼ tsp. table salt
4 large eggs
2 large egg yolks
1 Tbs. pure vanilla extract
One 15-oz. can pure solid-pack pumpkin (not pumpkin pie filling)

Make the crust: Position a rack in the middle of the oven and heat the oven to 350°F. Pulse the cookies and brown sugar in a food processor until the crumbs are uniform. Transfer to a medium bowl and add the melted butter. Combine thoroughly, first with a spoon and then with your fingers, until the mixture is evenly moist, crumbly, and holds together when you squeeze a handful. Press evenly over the bottom and partway up the sides of a 9-inch springform pan. Chill for 5 minutes and then bake for 10 minutes. Let cool.

Make the filling: Heat a kettle of water. With an electric mixer or a wooden spoon, beat the cream cheese until smooth. In a separate bowl, whisk the brown sugar with the cinnamon, ginger, allspice, nutmeg, and salt; add this to the cream cheese. Beat until well blended, scraping the bowl as needed. Add the eggs and yolks one at a time, making sure each is thoroughly incorporated before adding the next, and scraping the bowl after each. Blend in the vanilla and pumpkin.

Scrape the batter into the cooled crust. The batter will come up past the crust and will fill the pan to the rim. Tap the pan gently once or twice on the counter to release any air bubbles. Set the pan in a larger baking dish (a roasting pan is good), and add enough hot water from the kettle to come about halfway up the sides of the springform pan.

Bake until the top of the cake looks deep golden and burnished and the center is set (the cake may just barely begin to crack), 1 hour 35 minutes to 1 hour 45 minutes. The cake will jiggle a little bit when tapped. The top may rise a bit but will settle as it cools.

Remove the cheesecake from the oven and run a thin-bladed knife between the crust and the pan sides (this will prevent the cake from breaking as it cools). Let the cheesecake cool to room temperature in the pan on a wire rack. Cover and chill overnight. Just before removing the cheesecake from the pan, gently run a knife around the pan's inside edge.

Vegetable Guide

If you've ever overindulged at a farmers' market, buying far more than you intended because everything looked so rapturously fresh and inviting, then this section is for you. When you don't need a recipe, but instead just want a little inspiration, you'll find it here, plus tips for buying, storing, and handling a dozen of our favorite spring and summer vegetables.

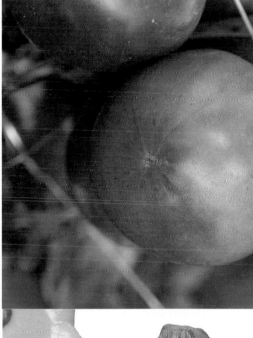

asparagus

Sweet, elegant asparagus. It just might be our favorite spring vegetable—so easy to prep (snap off the tough ends and you're done) and so many different ways to cook it (see the box at top right). Although it's available much of the year, asparagus is truly in season for only a few glorious weeks in April and May. During this time, even supermarket asparagus is likely to taste better than ever.

If you have a choice, choose thicker spears, which some people feel are more tender and sweeter than their thinner cousins. While green asparagus is a classic, these days you often have a choice of white or even purple asparagus. White varieties are mounded with soil to keep out sunlight; because the spears develop in darkness, they don't produce chlorophyll, so they never turn green. Their skin is slightly tougher, and their flavor is milder and doesn't seem as sweet. Purple asparagus, a relative newcomer, is an attractive alternative to green. But be forewarned: Unless you apply vinegar or lemon juice to the spears before cooking, they will discolor.

Asparagus pairs well with many foods, but some of its best flavor partners are lemon, orange, garlic, ginger, sesame oil, hard grated cheeses, eggs, mushrooms, and shellfish, particularly shrimp.

Judging freshness

Asparagus is commonly sold in bundles of about a pound, standing upright in a tray of water. Choose fresh-looking, firm spears with tight tips. Smell them first to be sure they don't give off an unpleasant odor (if they do, they're old). Check the cut ends of the stalks; they should be moist, not dried out. If dried ends are all that's available, cut about half an inch off the bottom when you get them home. To make sure they keep their freshness, stand asparagus bundles in about an inch of water in a jar or a shallow tray and keep them in the refrigerator. Cook the spears within two or three days.

Try different cooking methods

Boil or steam for pure, clean asparagus flavor. For boiling, use a wide, shallow pan filled with about 3 inches of water. For steaming, use a pasta pot with a perforated insert. Fill the pot so that about an inch of water fully enters the insert and stand the spears upright in the insert—this boils the thicker, tougher bases of the spears, while the rest only steams.

Grilling, sautéing, and roasting bring out a sweet nuttiness in asparagus. The simplest preparation is to just toss the spears with olive oil, a little salt, and pepper before putting them in a 400°F oven, a hot skillet, or on the grill. Cooking time depends on the thickness of the spears and how crowded your pan is, but when the spears are just tender (a knife will meet slight resistance), they're done.

Simple side dishes and more starring juicy, tender asparagus

For a zingy appetizer or side dish, sprinkle roasted or grilled asparagus with finely grated lemon zest and crushed toasted nuts (walnuts, pine nuts, or almonds would work well).

For an extra dash of flavor, drizzle roasted or grilled spears with Asian sesame oil, then sprinkle on a little salt and some lightly toasted sesame seeds (white, black, or a combination).

Dress up steamed asparagus simply and deliciously with a sesame-lemon mayonnaise. Add 3 Tbs. Asian sesame oil and 3 Tbs. fresh lemon juice to homemade or good-quality bottled mayonnaise. Drizzle over the asparagus or use the mayo as a dipping sauce.

Make a bright, flavorful pasta with asparagus and shrimp. Cut the spears into 1-inch pieces and blanch them briefly, then sauté the shrimp and asparagus with minced garlic and strips of sun-dried tomato. Finish with a little grated lemon zest and a squeeze of lemon juice and toss with bow ties or any small pasta shape.

Make a colorful niçoise-style composed salad with steamed, boiled, or roasted asparagus, strips of roasted red pepper, canned cannellini beans or chickpeas, hard-boiled eggs, black olives, and grilled or oil-packed tuna on a bed of butter or romaine lettuce. Scatter with some toasted pine nuts and drizzle with a lemon or red-wine-vinegar vinaigrette.

Make a pretty asparagus and orange salad. Boil asparagus spears until just tender. Make a vinaigrette with shallots, orange zest, and sherry vinegar and balsamic vinegars. Cut off the skin and pith from a couple of oranges and slice thinly. Toss the asparagus with the vinaigrette and plate with the orange slices.

For a quick and simple side dish to roast chicken, slice asparagus into ½-inch pieces and sauté in butter. Once it's tender, toss in parsley and grated Parmigiano.

Make an asparagus omelet by sautéing thinly sliced asparagus in butter. Pour beaten eggs with a little cream over the asparagus and cook until the egg is just set.

In the garden

Buy ready-to-plant asparagus roots, called crowns, in early spring, and cover them with moistened peat moss or soil until you're ready to put them in the ground. Dig a trench 6 inches deep, add some manure or compost to the bottom, and work it in. Create a mound of soil for each crown, spacing the mounds 12 to 18 inches apart. Place each crown on a mound with the pointed growing tip facing up. Refill the trench to the top, firming the soil as you go, and water well. The following spring, don't harvest any spears; the second spring, harvest only lightly. From the third spring on, you can harvest all the spears that come up.

bell peppers

High summer is the season for sweet, crunchy bell peppers. That's when these beautiful fruit (yes, they're technically fruit) are most abundant, most reasonably priced, and possibly even locally grown.

Bell peppers aren't the only variety of sweet pepper, but they're definitely the most famous (the term sweet pepper distinguishes it from the other main branch of the pepper family, the pungent chiles). And like most peppers, bells start out green before ripening to their mature color, which is most often red, yellow, or orange, although some varieties turn purple, pearl white, or chocolate brown. Green bell peppers are actually unripe, which explains their slightly bitter, less sweet flavor. If you prefer the sweeter, gentler flavor of ripe (red, yellow, or orange) bell peppers, you can often substitute them in recipes that call for green peppers.

Raw or cooked, fully ripe sweet peppers are delicious, but they're perhaps at their best when roasted. The sugars caramelize, and the softened flesh makes a pleasing addition to sauces, sandwiches, pastas, and much more. Raw peppers add a wonderfully sweet crunch to salads, or you can grill, sauté, or bake peppers to equally good effect. As for flavor partners, sweet peppers are very adaptable, pairing nicely with almost all other summer vegetables, with most herbs, and especially with pungent foods like black olives, capers, and anchovies.

Five weeknight ideas for fresh peppers

Bake a summer gratin with rings of sweet pepper and slices of summer squash and tomato. Season with salt, pepper, and fresh marjoram. Drizzle with olive oil and top with grated Parmigiano-Reggiano and a scattering of breadcrumbs. Bake in a moderate oven until the veggies are tender and lightly browned and the juices are bubbling.

Make a traditional ratatouille by sautéing chunks of red pepper, eggplant, tomato, zucchini, and onion in olive oil. Cook gently, covered, until all the vegetables are tender, and then stir in a big handful of torn or chopped basil. Finish with a squeeze of lemon juice.

Create an easy and delicious side dish, by combining slivered peppers and onions in a baking dish, drizzle with olive oil; season with salt and pepper, and tuck in several thyme sprigs. Roast until the vegetables are tender, limp, and darkened in places. Leftovers make a great topping for pizza or focaccia or a delicious addition to an omelet or sandwich.

Sauté a succotash of diced sweet pepper, diced onion, and fresh-cut corn kernels. Season with a little ground cumin, chopped oregano, and a drizzle of lime juice. Or use the same combination of vegetables for a festive-looking salsa, with the addition of chopped avocado.

Top grilled bread with diced roasted peppers, warmed goat cheese, chopped basil, and a drizzle of olive oil for a pretty bruschetta.

Cooking with roasted peppers

How to roast peppers

You can "roast" bell peppers in an oven, on a grill, over a gas flame, even in a fireplace, but all the methods aim for the same result: blackened skin that, once cool, peels easily away from the flesh, which has become soft and tender from the heat. My favorite method is under the broiler.

Position an oven rack to 6 to 7 inches below the broiler element and heat the broiler. Put the whole peppers on a baking sheet and broil until the skins are blistered and blackened, about 5 minutes. Turn carefully with tongs to expose an uncooked side and broil again until blackened. Repeat until the peppers are charred on all sides. Transfer them to a large bowl, cover the bowl with a dinner plate, and let the peppers steam for at least 15 to 20 minutes or until cool.

Working over the bowl to catch the juices, peel the skin off a pepper, pull out the stem and seed cluster, and separate the pepper into wide strips. Strip away any remaining seeds and trim off any white membrane. Layer the slices in a container and repeat with the remaining peppers. Strain the collected juices over the peppers. Cover and refrigerate for up to a week or freeze for several weeks.

For a pretty antipasto (above), arrange roasted peppers on a dish and sprinkle with chopped chives and parsley, minced garlic, capers, and perhaps chopped anchovies. Scatter more herbs over the top and drizzle with good olive oil.

For a sandwich with a kick, spread a wrap with horseradish mayonnaise, top with thin slices of grilled beef or lamb, thick slices of roasted pepper, and tender romaine lettuce leaves, and roll up. For entertaining, slice the wrap crosswise into wide wheels and secure with toothpicks.

For a hearty frittata, use roasted peppers, cooked diced potatoes, sautéed mushrooms and onions, and crumbled bacon as the base and top with grated cheese.

For a delicious soup, simmer roasted peppers with chicken broth, a chopped tomato, a pinch of saffron or a spoonful of grated fresh ginger, perhaps some grated orange zest, and salt and pepper. Purée in a blender, adjust the seasonings, and serve at room temperature or chilled for a sweet pepper version of gazpacho.

For a rich-tasting and vibrant pasta sauce, purée roasted peppers with sautéed onion and garlic, and then thin the sauce with broth and a bit of cream. Toss with cooked pasta and garnish with toasted pine nuts, grated Parmigiano Reggiano, and chopped tender herbs.

For a romesco-style sauce, purée a couple of roasted peppers with a handful of toasted almonds or hazelnuts, a dried chile soaked in hot water, a few cloves of garlic, plenty of paprika, a generous pinch of cayenne, a big splash of red-wine vinegar, and enough olive oil to create a pesto-like consistency. Use as a dipping sauce for raw vegetables, as a sauce for pasta or rice, or as a garnish for grilled vegetables or meat.

carrots

Carrots are like trusty old friends in the kitchen: supportive, low maintenance, and always there when you need them. They're often a background ingredient in braises, soups, and sautés, they keep well, and they're available year-round. Carrots are also an easy and satisfying snack, thanks to the deluge of "baby-cut" carrots in supermarkets. What sometimes gets forgotten is that carrots can be the feature attraction in many dishes, from soups and salads to purées and roasted vegetable combinations. Carrots take well to many different cooking methods; they can be boiled, steamed, braised, sautéed, glazed, stir-fried, roasted, and even grilled.

Finding the freshest carrots

Your best guarantee of freshness is to buy carrots in bunches, with their leafy green tops still attached. Even when they're very large, carrots with tops should still be tender, juicy, and full of good flavor. Look for firm roots and fresh, dark greens. Once you get them home, cut off the tops so they don't draw moisture from the roots. Instead of throwing away the tops, which are full of nutrition and flavor, try adding them to soups or chopping them and using in salads. When buying packaged carrots, look for plump, firm, fresh-looking roots with no sign of shaggy hair-like protrusions.

Baby-cut carrots, which are actually "adult" roots cut and trimmed to masquerade as sweet young things, have muscled in on full-size carrots' market share. These pre-peeled pieces are certainly convenient, since little or no prep is required, but that's the sole reason to buy them. Since they're already peeled, they lose moisture and flavor (and probably nutrients) faster than regular carrots.

There seems to be no correlation between flavor and size. Thick or thin, carrots can be tender, sweet, and crunchy, or tired and lackluster. One advantage to thicker carrots is that they're easier to peel and there's less waste.

Keeping carrots

Although carrots have good keeping qualities, they sacrifice sweetness and flavor to long storage. For that reason, aim to buy in quantities you'll use within a week or two.

Three styles of carrot salad

Raw or very lightly cooked carrots make great salads. Experiment with different cuts for raw carrots: tiny matchsticks, long curls made with a vegetable peeler, or shredded on a grater or mandoline. To help larger pieces of carrot better absorb a dressing, blanch them very briefly in boiling salted water first. Here are three differently cut and flavored carrot salads.

Shredded: Marinate shredded carrots and dried currants or raisins in fresh orange juice and a dash of sherry vinegar or balsamic vinegar. Garnish with toasted almonds.

Sliced: For a spicy North African carrot salad, simmer thick slices of carrots in salted water with a couple of bay leaves just until they lose their crunch. Drain, let dry, and toss with extra-virgin olive oil while still hot. Stir in a little harissa (hot chile paste) and chill. Arrange on a plate with chopped preserved lemon, slices of feta, and oil-cured black olives.

Julienned: Mix up a vibrant, spicy salad of julienned carrots seasoned with salt, sugar, a pinch of cayenne, and a good dousing of vinegar (white, cider, or malt). Toss with plenty of slivered fresh mint and basil and some thinly sliced fresh chile; garnish with a sprinkling of chopped toasted peanuts.

Sensational carrot sides

Make glazed carrots (shown above). Put cut-up carrots in a pan with butter, sugar, salt, and a small amount of water. Boil, with the lid slightly ajar, until the carrots are just tender. Uncover and let the liquid reduce to a syrup. Toss with fresh herbs.

Braise whole small carrots or long chunks in butter or olive oil, a little water or stock, and a bit of honey and Dijon mustard. Cook until tender and then let the liquid reduce to a syrupy, sweet-tangy glaze.

Roast carrots lightly coated in olive oil and seasoned with salt, pepper, cumin, and a pinch of cayenne in a medium-hot oven until tender and caramelized.

Make a mashed carrot purée by boiling carrots and perhaps parsnips and mashing as you would potatoes. Enrich the purée with butter or cream and season with a dash of nutmeg and ground ginger.

Fry up some spicy carrot fritters using a mixture of grated carrots and potatoes, chopped scallions, beaten eggs, a little cream, flour, salt, and crushed red pepper flakes.

24-karat flavor pairings
All of these taste delicious with carrots.

herbs	spices	fruits	accents
basil	cayenne	currants	ginger
bay leaf	cinnamon	fresh and dried hot chiles	honey
chervil	cloves		nuts
chives	coriander	lemon juice and zest	vinegar
cilantro	cumin		
mint	nutmeg	orange juice and zest	
parsley		raisins	
tarragon			
thyme			

corn

S weet corn is one of those vegetables that you simply shouldn't buy when it isn't in season and isn't locally grown. It's a long wait from the end of September to the following July, but it's worth it when you sink your teeth into an earful of plump kernels bursting with sweet, corny flavor.

The sugars in old-fashioned sweet corn varieties quickly turn to starch once the ears are picked, which puts the truth in the old line that you should pick the corn only once the kettle of water is at the boil. But plant breeding has led to sweeter corn varieties as well as corn that retains its sugars for longer after it's been harvested. The first improvement was the introduction of what the trade calls "sugar-enhanced" varieties. Then along came "super-sweet" corn varieties, whose smaller, crisper kernels are very much sweeter and stay so for even longer. Supersweet corn has its place: Its stay-crisp, non-creamy texture works well in salsas and relishes, but some people find that it delivers an overdose of sweet and not enough corny flavor. Of course, when you're buying corn, you often only have one choice of variety and it's frequently not labeled as anything but fresh corn. If you're buying at a local stand, the seller will likely be able to fill you in on the variety.

Despite all the genetic improvements, the main tricks to good corn eating are still to buy it as fresh as you can and to cook and eat it promptly. When choosing corn, look for ears with moist, fresh-looking husks. Don't worry about browning silks, which are the farmer's cue that the corn is ready to pick. Feel the ears to suss out how plump they are and whether the rows of kernels are fully formed. You can gently part the ends of the husks at the ear tip and take a peek at what's inside. As a matter of courtesy, it's best not to strip the ears and then not buy those you've disturbed.

Back home, don't shuck the corn until you're ready to use it. If you're not going to cook it all that day, stow the ears in the refrigerator, loosely wrapped in a dry plastic bag.

At the start of corn season, there's nothing better than boiled corn on the cob with butter and salt. But soon you'll be looking for ways to use corn in other dishes. It's a natural with most summer vegetables and herbs.

Off the cob, corn goes with nearly everything

Toss together a corn salsa with grilled corn (cut off the kernels after grilling), diced tomatoes, red onions, and roasted red peppers. Season with minced jalapeño and garlic, a touch of minced chipotle, and plenty of chopped cilantro. Moisten with olive oil and fresh lime juice.

Stir corn kernels into corn muffins or cornbread to punch up the corn flavor.

Make a rich, cheesy corn polenta by cooking coarse cornmeal in chicken broth, then stirring in ricotta and grated Parmigiano-Reggiano, corn kernels, and fresh thyme.

Make a southwestern-style sauté of diced onion, diced summer squash, diced sweet pepper, corn, minced garlic, and minced jalapeño, seasoned with a dash of cumin. Garnish with diced avocado and a squeeze of lime juice, or a scattering of grated smoked mozzarella or smoked Gouda. Use leftovers as a filling for tacos or quesadillas.

Build a pretty salad of thinly sliced cucumbers, beets, and red onion on a bed of butter lettuce. Scatter corn kernels and crumbled feta over all and dress with a lemony vinaigrette flavored with chopped dill.

Bake a savory tart filled with a mix of raw corn, sautéed sliced mushrooms, sautéed diced bell pepper and onion, and chopped blanched spinach, all bound with beaten eggs and a big spoonful of creamy ricotta or goat cheese.

Fresh kernels at the ready

Here's a simple way to preserve the sweetness of fresh corn and to keep corn kernels on hand for tossing into salads, side dishes, sautés, or other weeknight dishes. Cut the kernels off the cobs and blanch them in boiling water for 1 or 2 minutes. Drain, let cool, and store in a covered container in the fridge for up to five days. Or freeze the blanched kernels in a single layer on a baking sheet until hard, and then store in an airtight container in the freezer, where they'll keep for up to three months.

Cutting it off the cob

Cut the ear of corn in half crosswise. This gives you a flat surface (and means the kernels don't have as far to fall and won't bounce as much). Then stand a piece of corn on the cut end and slice down the length of the ear between the kernels and cob. Try to get as much of the kernel as you can, but don't cut too close to the cob or you'll have tough bits on the kernels. Rotate the cob and repeat until all the kernels are cut.

eggplant

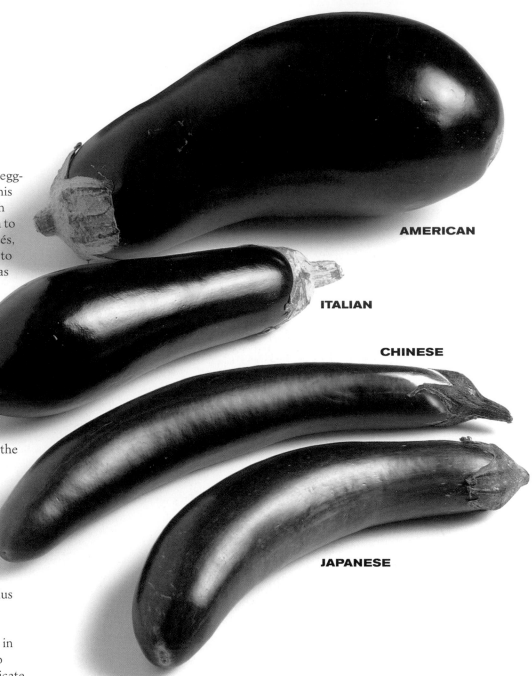

AMERICAN

ITALIAN

CHINESE

JAPANESE

With its firm curves and taut, shiny skin, eggplant can look quite voluptuous. But this late-summer vegetable can seduce with its earthy flavor as well. It's versatile enough to be used in soups, curries, stir-fries, and sautés, though perhaps the two most popular ways to cook it are roasting and grilling (see the ideas in the sidebars at far right).

You're probably most familiar with old-fashioned dark-purple globe eggplant, but that's only one small part of the eggplant family. Shapes range from the traditional oblong to teardrop to round, and colors can vary, too. Here's a rundown of the various types found in most grocery stores.

American or standard globe eggplant are the biggest, most common, and generally least expensive of all eggplant. They're teardrop-shaped and range in length from 6 to more than 10 inches. They tend to be less flavorful than other types, but they're useful for their high flesh-to-skin ratio, which makes for quick chopping into chunks for ratatouille, stews, and dips. Their wider diameter is a plus when slicing into cutlets.

Italian eggplant are similar in shape and color to American eggplant, but diminutive in size—only a few inches in diameter and 5 to 8 inches long. Italian eggplant are more delicate and sweeter than their larger cousins, and their smaller size makes them a good choice for stuffing, roasting, and broiling.

Chinese eggplant are easily identified by their pale violet skin and slender, cylindrical shape. They have the most delicate flavor of all the market varieties. Their even contours make them ideal for slicing, and because they cook quickly, they're good in stir-fries and-sautés.

Japanese eggplant are slightly smaller than Chinese eggplant and have the same dark purple skin as American varieties. Also quick-cooking but not so mild as Chinese eggplant, they're excellent for grilling and broiling, and they stand up to the assertive flavors of garlic, soy, and ginger.

Picking the best eggplant

Choose plump, firm eggplant with shiny skin that shows no sign of slackness; over-the-hill fruits are liable to be bitter. If you're growing eggplant, harvest them at any time after they size up and their skin turns shiny, but don't wait too long. Once the skin loses its gloss, an eggplant's quality deteriorates.

Eggplant on the grill...

To grill eggplant: Brush or spray eggplant slices lightly with oil and then grill over medium heat until deeply browned on both sides. If the flesh isn't completely tender, stack the eggplant slices, wrap them in foil, and let them steam to finish cooking.

For a savory side, brush eggplant slices with soy sauce, hot sauce, and Asian sesame oil before grilling. Sprinkle with sliced scallions and drizzle with soy sauce and rice vinegar.

Make a warm salad of grilled eggplant and onions with feta, spinach, and pine nuts. Drizzle with a red-wine vinaigrette.

Serve with a yogurt topping scented with coriander and mint to serve over warm or room-temperature grilled eggplant slices.

For a fresh take on ratatouille, grill chunky slices of eggplant, summer squash, bell peppers, and mushrooms. Toss with chopped tomatoes, olive oil, lemon juice, garlic, and basil.

Make a grilled caponata to spread on toasted country bread. Grill eggplant and onion slices as well as tomato halves. Chop coarsely and season with chopped olives, capers, olive oil, red-wine vinegar, chopped parsley, and a little sugar.

Use grilled eggplant in sandwiches, as a layer in a lasagna, or as a topping for pizza.

...and in the oven

To roast eggplant: Score the eggplant halves deeply, sprinkle with salt, and let rest for half an hour. Squeeze out the juice, brush with olive oil, and roast at 400°F, cut side down, until very tender. To roast slices, brush with olive oil, season with salt, and roast in a single layer until tender.

Roast halves on sprigs of thyme and serve with a lemon wedge or drizzle with vinaigrette, as shown above.

Make a dip like baba ghanouj from roasted eggplant halves or use the flesh as a base for a savory pasta sauce.

Make a summer vegetable gratin. Layer slices of roasted eggplant, summer squash, and tomato in an oiled baking dish. Season with salt and pepper, tuck in basil leaves, drizzle with olive oil, top with a sharp Italian cheese, and bake until tender.

For a zesty antipasto, marinate thinly sliced roasted eggplant. After roasting and cooling, toss with red-wine vinegar, slivers of garlic, basil leaves, and crushed red pepper flakes. Drizzle with olive oil and let sit for an hour. Serve on bread with a thin slice of tangy aged cheese.

Never undercook eggplant. The flesh should feel creamy and soft when fully cooked through.

Salt first for less oily eggplant

Eggplant soaks up oil like a sponge, but you can reduce its ability to absorb oil by salting the cut flesh and letting it sit for 30 minutes or more. Then drain, pat dry, and proceed with cooking.

fennel

With fennel, the bulb's the thing, but stalks are good for stock, and leaves make a pretty garnish.

Fennel has a split personality. Raw, it's got wonderful crunch and a cool flavor laced with anise. But when it's braised, roasted, fried, baked, or grilled, fennel reveals its other side: It gets soft—even silky—and its licorice flavor melts away to just a hint of its raw self.

There are two forms of edible fennel. One is strictly an herb whose leaves, stalks, and seeds are used as flavorings; the other—often called Florence fennel—is the vegetable we find in the market.

We refer to fennel "bulbs," but that swollen portion is really the thickened, succulent stem of the plant growing in tight layers above the ground. Fennel thrives in cool weather; its seasons are spring and fall, though as with many vegetables, it's usually available year-around. Grocers sometimes label fennel as anise, a misnomer.

Fennel is a natural partner for fish and shellfish, but it's also very good with pork, chicken, lamb, beef, and duck. It pairs well with onions, leeks, tomatoes, artichokes, and potatoes. As for seasonings, take a cue from fennel's region of origin, the Mediterranean. Olives and olive oil, lemon juice, balsamic vinegar, saffron, anchovies, and any anise-flavored liquor are good matches.

How to trim and cut fennel

To prep fennel, first trim off and discard the stalks and fully expanded leaves, or save them to use in stocks. If you want, save the dense, tight, baby leaves for mincing and garnishing the finished dish. If the outer layer of the bulb is in good shape and isn't too fibrous, you can use it; otherwise, discard it. Carefully trim off a thin slice of the root end, leaving the rest of the core intact to hold together wedges or vertical slices (see the photos at right). For diced or slivered fennel, cut the bulb lengthwise in half or quarters, and then cut away the dense inner core.

Wedges for braising or roasting

Fennel in the spotlight

Make a fennel gratin by layering blanched fennel slices in a gratin dish with tomato sauce or cream. Top either version with fresh breadcrumbs tossed with olive oil and grated Parmigiano-Reggiano and bake until tender and bubbly.

Broil blanched fennel wedges: Set them on a broiler tray, top with butter and grated Parmigiano, and broil until browned and bubbly.

Grill blanched wedges of fennel, drizzle with balsamic vinegar, and serve as a side dish or add to a pasta or salad.

Make a salad of thinly sliced fennel, arugula, apples, and shaved Parmigiano-Reggiano or Dry Jack cheese. Toss with an anchovy-spiked vinaigrette.

Top pizza with thin slivers of fennel slowly cooked in oil until caramelized. Or serve the slices as a side dish.

Fry thinly sliced fennel. Dip them in lightly whisked egg whites and dredge in seasoned flour or cornmeal before frying. Sprinkle with salt and lemon juice and eat while hot.

Fennel in a supporting role

In risotto, add diced fennel along with leeks or onions to the pot before adding the rice.

In mashed potatoes, boil fennel slices until tender, purée them, and then fold them in.

With whole fish, tuck thinly sliced fennel and lemon inside the fish before roasting or grilling.

For roasts, put fennel wedges in the roasting pan alongside chicken or pork, or set the meat on a bed of thinly sliced fennel.

In soup, simmer diced fennel with tomatoes for a flavorful base for fish chowder or vegetable soup. Or add fennel to leek and potato soup for another dimension of flavor.

In vinaigrette, add thinly sliced fennel to your favorite lemon-Dijon vinaigrette and let sit for 20 minutes so the fennel softens. Use to dress a salad or as a sauce for salmon.

For a side salad, simmer diced fennel with chickpeas and tomatoes. Drain, season with olive oil and lemon juice.

In the garden

Fennel likes spring and fall's shorter days and cooler temperatures. To prevent bolting in the long, hot days of summer, time spring fennel plantings to be mature by mid-June, before the summer solstice. In regions with long growing seasons, fall is an excellent time to grow fennel. If fennel does go to flower in your garden, let the seeds mature, harvest them when they've turned brown and dry, and use them in spice mixes to flavor meats, soups, pickles, and vinaigrettes.

Vertical slices for grilling or frying

Slivers or dice for sautés, soups, or risotto

Crosswise slices for salads

lettuce

Right about the time we're growing tired of winter salads, spring comes to the rescue with a wide array of tender and crisp lettuces. Because most lettuces love cool weather and are quick to grow, they're popular in farmers' markets starting in late March and heading through May and early June. Specialty grocers and natural-foods stores often have a good supply of spring lettuce, and even some supermarkets are now offering more than just the usual suspects like romaine and green leaf lettuce.

Experiment with different varieties

Whether you're scouting markets or planting your own (see the sidebar at far right), be adventurous. In addition to the common lettuces shown on this page, seek out heirloom varieties at farmers' markets. Try them alone, or make up your own mix of greens for salads.

When shopping for lettuce, look for heads or leafy rosettes that are dense and heavy for their size. Leaves should be unblemished. Avoid limp specimens or heads that have brown-edged leaves or hollow centers—this usually indicates poor handling after harvest. Skip soggy-looking heads with flaccid leaves that have been doused with too much water at the market to make them look perkier.

Keep lettuces in the crisper drawer of your refrigerator. This way, they'll enjoy high humidity and stay fresh a bit longer, but in any case, try to use them within a few days.

Leaf or cutting lettuce has an open, loose head and leaf shapes that range from notched and scalloped to frilly and ruffly. Colors run from bright green to cranberry and burgundy. Leaf lettuce is a good all-purpose choice for salads and sandwiches.

Romaine lettuce heads should feel heavy and tight. Romaine is crunchy, juicy, and sweet; the leaves stand up well to punchy dressings, and they're a great choice for main-dish salads with lots of ingredients. Because they stay crisp, romaine leaves are good in sandwiches, too.

Iceberg or crisphead lettuce deserves another chance after suffering from a few decades of disrepute. This thick, juicy-sweet lettuce may taste somewhat bland, but its crunchy texture is just right in Tex-Mex tacos, Chinese chicken salad, or cut into wedges and topped with blue cheese dressing.

Butterhead, Boston, or bibb lettuce, also called limestone lettuce, grows in softly folding heads known for their good flavor and buttery texture. Colors range from pale lime to a more medium green. The succulent leaves surround satiny delicate hearts; you'll find varieties both with loose open heads and with tighter heads. Try tossing bibb into a salad of toasted chopped walnuts, crumbled blue cheese, and sliced ripe pears.

Six good ideas for your next salad

Use nut oils in your dressing to complement a salad of mild-flavored lettuces like butter and loose-leaf varieties. Walnut and hazelnut oils are terrific (especially paired with sherry vinegar). Finish the salad with some aged goat cheese, a few shavings of Parmigiano-Reggiano, and some toasted nuts.

For a warm salad, try Batavian lettuces or baby romaine. Slice them thinly across the head, wash and dry, and then dress with a warm bacon and shallot vinaigrette. Or use as a base for a salad of warm potatoes and sausage.

Make composed dinner salads. Toss lettuces with your favorite vinaigrette and mound on dinner plates. On top, arrange cold sliced potatoes, leftover grilled meat or fish or good-quality canned tuna, hard-cooked eggs, cooked vegetables, sliced tomatoes, sautéed or raw mushrooms, or a combination. Drizzle with a vinaigrette and pass more at the table.

For an easy, pseudo-Caesar dressing, stir 1 chopped anchovy fillet, 1 minced garlic clove, 3 Tbs. extra-virgin olive oil, 1 Tbs. lemon juice, and about 2 Tbs. grated Parmigiano-Reggiano.

For a great weeknight spring salad use a mix of various lettuces—as many different colors and textures as you can muster—dressed with a little red-wine vinegar, olive oil, a bit of Dijon mustard, salt, and pepper. A blend of 1 Tbs. vinegar and 3 Tbs. oil is usually enough for three large or four modest servings of salad.

Make a bistro salad with a variety of loose-leaf and butter lettuces. Toss with a vinaigrette of sherry vinegar and hazelnut oil, salt, and pepper, and mound on plates. Top with rounds of warmed goat cheese and toasted hazelnuts.

Wash well to remove grit

Whether you grow your own lettuce or buy it, be sure to wash it well. Nothing ruins a salad like gritty greens. Swish the leaves in a large bowl of cool water, let them sit so the grit settles to the bottom, and then lift out the leaves. Repeat until no grit remains and then spin them dry.

In the garden

Salad greens are easy and quick to grow and don't take much space. You don't even need a garden; a windowbox or outdoor container works just fine. In spring, you can buy already-started lettuce plants, but you'll have more choice if you begin with seeds. You can start the seeds indoors with grow lights, or wait until the ground thaws and start your seeds outdoors.

If space is a concern, grow loose-leaf lettuces. Loose-leaf, or cutting lettuces, are more space-efficient than heading lettuces, which need about 8 inches of room in all directions. (Loose-leaf lettuces can be grown much closer together—even in a pot or windowsill.)

To start a loose-leaf lettuce patch, scratch the surface of the soil to roughen it slightly, then scatter seeds evenly over the surface, as if you were sprinkling salt. Sift a little more soil over the surface and water gently with a spray bottle.

Lettuce seeds should start germinating within a few days, and in three to four weeks, you'll be harvesting. To keep the harvest going as long as possible, don't cut the whole lettuce, but rather pick individual leaves from around the outside of each plant. Or you can cut an area of the planting with scissors, being careful to cut about 1 inch above the crown. If you pick this way, the lettuce will keep producing until hot weather finally causes the plant to bolt, at which point the leaves become unpalatably bitter.

peas

English peas, also called sweet peas, are creatures of cool weather—not cool enough to be cold, but not warm enough to be hot, either. In other words, spring—which means their appearance is brief in most places.

A bowl of freshly shucked peas, simmered briefly and then tossed with butter, is luxurious, and this is one of the very best ways to experience their unique sweetness and the engaging way they pop in your mouth. But if you're up for exploration, you'll find that fresh peas are wonderfully adaptable: They're equally suited to adding to risotto or pasta, puréeing for a soup, or, if you don't have very many, using as a garnish for vegetable ragoûts or sautés, salads, pastas, or stir-fries.

Fresh herbs are a natural with peas; even tender spring sage leaves with their minty overtones are pea-compatible. In fact, anything that's in season with peas is bound to partner with them well—especially spring onions, butter lettuce, leeks, sorrel, and new turnips.

Hurry peas home and cook them soon

Unless you grow sweet peas yourself, the farmers' market is the best source for good ones. Exposure to heat during long-distance travel can dry up their juices and turn their sugars to starch. Time does the same thing, which is why peas often don't look their best in the grocery store; they're days away from the field and tired from travel.

At the market, look for bright-green, moist-looking, medium-size pods. Pea pods should swell gently (rather than bulge) with their cargo. Too large and they're likely to be starchy; too small and chances are the peas nestled inside won't be much bigger than a small bead. If the pods look dried or yellowed or are beginning to shrivel in places, you can be pretty sure that the peas within will have lost their magic and are on their way to becoming starchy. Ask for a taste at the market—open up a pod and find out. A pea that's perfect will be sweet, moist, and crunchy.

Peas taste best when cooked as soon as possible after picking or purchasing, and they're done when their green color brightens, which usually takes about a minute in boiling water.

Enjoy sweet peas on their own...

A bowl of simply cooked fresh shucked peas tossed with sweet butter, sea salt, and freshly ground pepper is a wonderful thing. For even more flavor, try one of the ideas at right.

Try tossing briefly cooked peas with:

- Toasted sesame seeds, slivered scallions, cilantro, and a drizzle of Asian sesame oil (shown at left).

- Fresh butter with chopped chervil and chives, or chopped mint, tarragon, or lovage.

- A spoonful of fragrant olive oil with torn basil leaves or fresh sage, plus the blossoms.

- A few drops roasted peanut oil with freshly minced ginger and spring garlic.

...or in pasta or risotto

Add peas to curly egg noodles for a simple pasta: Soften shallots in butter, add dry white wine and reduce, then add broth and peas, cooking until tender. Stir in some crème fraîche and toss with hot pasta. Garnish with grated Parmigiano-Reggiano and fresh basil.

Add fresh peas to risotto toward the very end of cooking. When the peas are tender and the rice is done, stir in fresh mint, lemon juice and zest, along with some butter and a little grated Parmigiano.

In the garden

In that variable period between late winter and early spring, gardeners slyly ask one another, "Got your peas in yet?" It's a loaded question. Plant too early—when the soil is wet and under 45°F—and peas may rot in the ground. Plant too late and you lose precious time. One guideline is to plant peas six weeks before the last frost date. Soil should be well drained (raised beds are ideal). The classic planting method is a double row, 4 inches to 6 inches apart, with the peas spaced every inch or two. Harvest peas at least every two days, and to preserve their texture, pick them straight into ice water. Use two hands: one to hold the frond and one to pluck the pod. If you use one hand, you'll damage the plant.

Shucking peas

Peas seem to have been naturally designed for easy shucking, so the work goes fast. You can usually shuck a pound of peas, which yields about one cup of peas, in about ten minutes. So sit down and shuck away, opening up the pods with your thumbnail.

snap beans

A green bean goes by many names. Sometimes it's called a snap bean, because it can be broken or snapped to length. And sometimes it's called a string bean, since it used to have strings running down both sides. But happily, most green beans these days are stringless, and they aren't even necessarily green. Purple and yellow bean pods liven up the mix and the garden as well—although, sadly, purple beans change to green during cooking. These fresh edible pods come in different shapes, too: the standard round pods, the extra-thin French filet beans, and flat-pod Italian beans (also called Romano beans).

No matter what you call them, snap beans are delicious cooked many ways. They're terrific simply steamed or boiled, but they're also good braised, sautéed, roasted—even grilled. The elegantly thin filet bean is the classic type for steaming or boiling and serving whole. Broad Italian beans have great beany flavor and can also be cooked quickly when young, but the larger ones are ideal for braising, stewing, and roasting. Good flavor matches for all beans include cured pork (think bacon and pancetta); onion, shallots, and garlic; anchovies; lemon zest; dill, tarragon, mint, summer savory, or chervil.

Trim the stem, leave the tail

While it's always a good idea to trim the stem end of beans, it's not necessary to trim the thin, pointy end that looks like a tail unless it's especially tough. Leaving the tails on gives whole beans a more elegant look.

Trimming and cutting goes a lot faster if you gather a handful of beans in a neat bunch so their ends are aligned.

Five easy side dishes

Simmer up some southern-style beans. Cut green or flat-pod beans into 2-inch lengths and slowly simmer with diced onion, diced bacon, and freshly ground black pepper. Toward the end of cooking, taste and add a splash of cider or malt vinegar, and a bit of salt if necessary.

Make a succotash by cutting green beans into tiny pieces and blanching; sauté briefly with corn kernels in butter and add chives and a touch of cream.

Serve cooked beans with a tangy yogurt sauce flavored with mint, dill, or cardamom and spiked with a dash of cayenne.

Stir up a flavorful sauté of snap beans, slivered onion, sliced mushrooms, chopped garlic, olive oil, salt, and pepper. Add a dash of balsamic vinegar at the end.

Braise fully grown beans in savory stock. Brown the beans lightly in olive oil, season with salt and pepper, and then simmer, covered, in a little chicken stock until the beans are fully tender and the stock is reduced to a syrupy glaze.

Green beans in salads, risotto, and more

Compose a salade niçoise: Steam or boil whole filet or small green beans just until tender. Cover a platter with a bed of tender butter lettuce leaves and top with the cooked beans, tomato wedges, quartered hard-cooked eggs, and chunked cooked or canned tuna. Garnish with a scattering of whole black olives and anchovy fillets. Serve with a well-seasoned lemon–chive vinaigrette.

Add green beans to a warm potato salad made with small red-skinned potatoes. Toss with chopped shallots and a creamy mustard vinaigrette.

Add cooked beans to a crudité platter. They're delicious dunked into hummus, an herbed yogurt dip, a garlicky aïoli, or a pungent anchovy sauce.

Toss whole or cut cooked beans in a salad. A great combination is slivered endive leaves, green beans, and sliced red radishes in a mustardy vinaigrette.

Tuck cooked beans among slices of tomatoes and drizzle with olive oil for a simple, summery side dish.

Add short pieces of uncooked beans to risotto, or sauté them and add to a frittata.

In the garden

Snap beans come in both bush and pole varieties. Bush beans produce beans over about a three-week period; to have beans all summer, you'll need to make successive sowings. Pole beans, on the other hand, continue for many weeks once they start cropping, so you get a much bigger harvest from one planting. As the name implies, pole beans need support—a rough pole, a trellis, or a teepee.

Among round-pod beans, 'Kentucky Wonder', 'Blue Lake', and 'Kentucky Blue' are famous for flavor. 'Provider' is extra early. Yellow and purple beans are easier to spot than green ones, a big asset when harvesting.

spinach

Spinach might be the most versatile of all greens—it's delicious fresh in salads, or wilted as a simple side dish. It can be the main ingredient in a recipe, or a secondary ingredient to add color and flavor to a dish based on grains, meat, or another vegetable. And yes, it's good for you, too; spinach is high in antioxidants and extremely rich in vitamins A and C.

The freshest spinach isn't in a bag

Fresh, unpackaged spinach, whether loose or bunched, is often fresher and more flavorful than bagged spinach. It's also easier to see what you're getting, as sealed plastic bags can hide slimy spinach. At the market, you'll likely find varieties with smooth leaves (flat-leaf) and crinkled leaves (Savoy). Savoy spinach tends to be darker and less fragile than flat-leaf spinach. Fresh spinach leaves will often still be attached to their roots or "crowns." Choose the perkiest-looking bunches (with no rot or yellow leaves) and untie them as soon as you get them home. Before cooking, remove the crowns, trim any tough stems, and triple-wash the greens. The only thing worse than the crunch of grit in your teeth is the sound of it between your guests' teeth.

Both young ("baby") spinach and mature leaves (often Savoy) are sold packaged and washed. If using these, examine the bags for rot and check the packing dates. And don't count on pre-washed spinach being grit-free. It's good practice to wash it at least once, if not twice.

Start with a lot of spinach when cooking it; a pound of fresh leaves cooks down to about a cup.

Flavor pairings

Good partners for spinach are things that add richness or creaminess, or acidity or pungency. Cheese and eggs have a natural affinity to spinach, adding richness and smoothing its minerally flavor. Good choices include ricotta, goat cheese, mozzarella, Cheddar, Jack, feta, melting cheeses like Swiss, Emmental, and Gruyère, and hard grating cheeses like Parmigiano-Reggiano and Asiago. For seasonings, use lemon juice or vinegar for acidity, garlic for pungency, and nutmeg for a smooth, sweet note. Spinach is a perfect partner for shellfish and fish, and it goes well with most meats. Earthy vegetables like butternut squash work well with spinach, as do tomatoes, onions, and roasted red peppers.

Great ideas for using spinach...

The raw

For a warm spinach salad, heat some olive oil with a finely minced garlic clove or a sliced shallot, add lemon juice or sherry vinegar, salt and pepper. Drizzle over spinach and garnish with diced bacon or prosciutto fried until crisp.

Pair spinach with a balsamic vinaigrette to add both sweetness and acidity. Fancy up the salad with a garnish of toasted pine nuts and thin strips of sun-dried tomato, or with crumbled Gorgonzola and toasted pecans, or with rounds of goat cheese dredged in breadcrumbs and baked until soft and warm.

In sandwiches and wraps, use young, tender spinach leaves in place of lettuce.

Garnish with a spinach chiffonade. Cut the leaves as you would basil: Stack a few leaves, roll them into a cylinder, and cut crosswise into thin strips.

The cooked

Wilt spinach in hot olive oil with minced garlic, salt, and pepper. Add a dash of sherry or balsamic vinegar and toss with toasted hazelnuts and blue cheese (shown at right).

For a new take on quesadillas, add a few leaves of wilted spinach along with chopped scallion and pepper Jack cheese.

Top pizza with wilted spinach, caramelized onions, mozzarella, feta, or ricotta cheese, thin slices of plum tomato, and grated Parmigiano.

To make creamed spinach, stir cooked chopped spinach into a stock- or milk-based sauce thickened with a little flour and well seasoned with salt, pepper, nutmeg, and a dash of cayenne. Add a splash of cream at the end.

For a creamy spinach soup, sweat chopped onions in butter, add chopped spinach and wilt, add a little flour, stir, and add hot broth. Enrich with beaten egg yolks and cream. At the end, add a squeeze of lemon juice and a dash of nutmeg.

Fry up little fritters or pancakes of chopped wilted spinach (well drained) and chopped scallions, seasoned with salt, pepper, and nutmeg, and bound with a beaten egg and a little flour and cheese. Serve with a dab sour cream.

For a beautiful risotto, add chopped raw spinach when the rice is about halfway cooked.

In the garden

Spinach thrives in cool weather, but most varieties bolt when things heat up. For a long season of harvest, sow every ten days, starting in mid-spring and continuing as long as daytime temperatures are below 70°F. For early and late plantings, sow cold-resistant varieties, like 'Tyee' and 'Melody'. As temperatures climb, sow bolt-resistant types like 'Bloomsdale' or 'Teton'.

summer squash

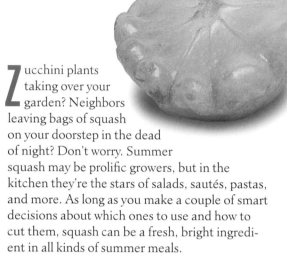

Zucchini plants taking over your garden? Neighbors leaving bags of squash on your doorstep in the dead of night? Don't worry. Summer squash may be prolific growers, but in the kitchen they're the stars of salads, sautés, pastas, and more. As long as you make a couple of smart decisions about which ones to use and how to cut them, squash can be a fresh, bright ingredient in all kinds of summer meals.

Whether you're choosing from the garden, the farmers' market, or the produce counter, pick small, firm squash, with a tight feel to them. Smaller squash are more tender because the skin is still thin and the seeds are unformed; they also contain less water than older squash.

After a gentle scrub under the faucet, the squash is ready to cut. There's no need to peel summer squash. Besides contributing color and nutrients, the skin helps the vegetable hold together better when cooked.

You can cut the squash into different shapes, depending on how you're using it. A medium dice (⅓ to ½ inch) is perfect for sautés, but for a more refined look, or to add to a dish during just the last few minutes of cooking, cut the squash into a small (¼-inch) dice. Round or half-moon slices are good for soups and gratins, and julienned squash works well for stir-fries and slaws. For layering in a lasagna and for frying, cut whole squash into thin, lengthwise slices. If you have a V-slicer or mandoline, you can make long zucchini strings, which are great tossed into soups or cooked lightly and coated with a dressing to serve as a side dish.

You'll see summer squash in all manner of shapes and colors at farmers' markets. Don't be shy about trying ones you haven't eaten before; you can swap one for the other in most dishes.

Bringing out the best in squash

Choose little squash. Their flesh is firm, not pithy, and it browns without turning to mush.

Wash squash well. To remove grit, rinse the squash well and wipe down the skin with a cloth or paper towel.

Don't move the squash much while cooking. This gives the exterior a chance to develop a deep golden color.

Serve cooked squash dishes immediately. Cooked squash softens as it sits, which isn't necessarily bad, but if left too long, it can get soggy.

Great meals from summer squash

For a quick gratin, layer thin slices of yellow and green pattypan squash and tomato in an oiled shallow baking dish. Season well with salt, pepper, and minced fresh herbs like basil, oregano, marjoram, and summer savory. Sprinkle with breadcrumbs and grated Parmigiano-Reggiano, drizzle with olive oil, and bake until golden.

Simmer a summer stew of zucchini, tomatoes, sweet onions, bell peppers, and corn or hominy. Season with cumin, fresh oregano, and chopped or puréed roasted mild chiles like poblanos. Garnish with sour cream and chopped fresh cilantro.

Make a colorful slaw by tossing blanched julienned squash, red and yellow bell peppers, and carrots with blanched baby green beans. Dress with a vinaigrette of olive oil, red-wine vinegar, and Dijon mustard.

Make a quick Asian-style soup by simmering chicken broth with a piece of lemongrass, a pinch of crushed red pepper flakes, and thinly sliced shiitakes. A few minutes before serving, add long strings of summer squash. Garnish with sliced scallions, cilantro, and lime juice.

Lighten a traditional lasagna by nestling blanched longthwise slices of zucchini on top of meat sauce, or use the slices as a layer with béchamel and cheese in a vegetarian lasagna.

Bake a savory tart: Fill a pastry shell with a mixture of ricotta cheese, beaten egg, grated zucchini, chopped parsley, and grated Parmigiano-Reggiano and Romano. Bake until set and golden brown. Delicious hot, warm, or cold.

For a simple sauté, heat olive oil, add diced zucchini, season with salt and pepper, and cook, tossing, until lightly browned but still firm. Off the heat, add some chopped fresh mint, basil, or thyme and a splash of lemon juice or white-wine vinegar.

For a side dish for grilled fish, briefly steam long strands or matchsticks of squash and toss with an Asian-flavored dressing that includes soy sauce, Asian sesame oil, sherry, grated ginger, and a bit of fresh lemon juice.

For a frittata, sauté diced or grated squash briefly with garlic and a little chopped onion. Add chopped basil and beaten eggs and bake until puffed.

Make a pretty salad from long, wide ribbons of tender raw squash tossed in a balsamic-Dijon vinaigrette. Use a vegetable peeler to make the ribbons.

For a vegetarian curry, sauté large dice or chunky slices of summer squash, onion, carrots, potato, bell pepper, and broccoli with red curry paste, and then simmer in coconut milk.

In the garden

Summer squash are easy to grow, although they do require some space. Once the weather and soil have warmed, plant seeds or young plants in a sunny area of the garden. Within a few weeks, you'll be harvesting. When the fruits are the size you want (check every day, as they grow quickly), cut—don't pull—them from the plant, using a small, sharp knife.

Squash plants produce separate male and female flowers. The male blossoms stand atop tall, thin stems; the female flowers are borne close to the plant, and often have baby fruits already formed below them. Either can be harvested, but if you pick female blossoms, you'll sacrifice potential squash.

Harvest squash blossoms early in the day, dip them in a bowl of cool water to rinse away dust, and then shake gently to dry. Pinch off the stamen in the center of each flower. Cut the yellow flowers crosswise into a chiffonade and use as a garnish or fry them whole, filled or not (goat cheese seasoned with fresh herbs is an easy filling). Twist the petal tips to close them, dip in an egg beaten with a little milk, roll in cornmeal, and fry until golden.

tomatoes

The flavor of a juicy, ripe tomato still warm from the sun is the essence of summer. And the chances of capturing that true vine-ripened flavor are always better the closer to your kitchen a tomato is grown. But if you can't grow your own, you're not out of luck; you can find home-grown quality at farmstands and farmers' markets in your area. Just don't expect to get it at the grocery store, where the varieties you'll find have been bred for the long haul, with qualities like thick skin and uniform shape often winning out over good flavor.

Beyond basil

Basil and tomatoes were made for each other, but just about all other herbs, especially chives, cilantro, dill, lovage, and savory are wonderful complements, too.

A galaxy of tomatoes

These are a few of the many types of tomatoes you might find at farmstands.

Plum: Also called a Roma or Italian tomato, this meaty, egg-shaped tomato can be red or yellow. It's good for cooking and canning because its water content is relatively low, and it yields lots of thick sauce.

Cherry: Red, orange, yellow, or green, this round bite-size tomato is about an inch or less in diameter. Red and yellow varieties have a more pronounced flavor. Use for salads, garnishes, quick sautés, and eating out of hand.

Pear: Also called "teardrop," this bite-size tomato has a shape that mirrors its two names. It can be yellow, red, or orange. It's slightly smaller and much milder than a cherry tomato, but its uses are the same.

Grape: Another bite-size tomato, this one is sweet and shaped like an elongated sphere (just like a grape). It's usually red or yellow and less than an inch in diameter. Use like cherry and pear tomatoes.

Slicer or globe: Ranging from golfball to baseball size, this generally juicy, flavorful tomato comes in all colors. A good tomato for slicing and for salads.

What to do with those ripe, juicy tomatoes

Slice them thickly, drizzle with olive oil, and sprinkle with salt. Serve as a side salad or layer between slices of crusty bread for a tomato sandwich.

For a beautiful salad platter, slice up different-colored tomatoes. Drizzle with a vinaigrette made with olive oil, balsamic vinegar, a spoonful of pesto, and salt and pepper. For a party, alternate the tomatoes with slices of fresh mozzarella, set out sliced toasted bread, and let guests build their own appetizers.

Make a variation on a BLT: bacon, arugula, tomato, and avocado. To gild the lily, spread on softened blue cheese or fresh goat cheese.

For an authentic bruschetta, grill or toast a slice of country bread, brush lightly with olive oil, and rub a peeled clove of garlic over the surface of the bread. Cut a medium-size ripe tomato in half horizontally and rub one half of the tomato onto the bread until the tomato flesh is thoroughly massaged into the toast. Top with basil.

Stir up a cool, tangy gazpacho from finely diced tomatoes, cucumbers, onion, and sweet peppers. Season with salt, pepper, minced garlic, and herbs. Add some minced jalapeño and lime juice or red-wine vinegar for spunk, and round out the flavors with a little olive oil. Refrigerate for at least an hour before serving.

Slow-roast beefsteak tomatoes. Cut the tops from tomatoes and gently squeeze out the juice and seeds. Set the tomatoes upright in a shallow baking dish, drizzle with olive oil, and season with minced garlic, salt, pepper, and minced herbs like rosemary, thyme, or parsley. Roast at 325°F until the tomatoes are soft and have collapsed. Serve as a savory side dish, or roast further until they're drier and use them as a topping for crostini or pizza.

Simmer up some fresh tomato soup. Sweat diced onion, celery, and fennel in a little oil. Add cut-up tomatoes and chicken, beef, or vegetable broth, cover, and simmer until tender. Pass the soup through a food mill (or blend and strain), and then reheat. Enrich with a bit of butter and stir in minced fresh chives, dill, or fennel leaf.

Use cherry tomatoes to brighten a bread salad—they hold up well. Combine halved cherry tomatoes with cucumbers, bell pepper and onion, all diced, and toss with well-seasoned vinaigrette. About 20 minutes before serving, add cubed day-old country bread or lightly toasted pita, torn into pieces, and toss well. Toss again just before serving.

Make a rich tomato sauce. Sweat diced onion, carrots, and celery in butter. Add cut-up tomatoes, salt, and pepper and simmer until soft enough to pass through a food mill. Reheat with a touch of cream, and then use it to top cheese-filled ravioli or tortellini.

Garnish grilled fish with a tiny dice of tomato. Gently seed tomatoes and dice the flesh into tiny, even cubes. Drizzle a tablespoon of dark green, fruity olive oil onto a warm dinner plate, strew a couple of tablespoons of tomato dice over the oil, and arrange a piece of grilled fish on top.

Beefsteak: This jumbo juicy tomato has an irregular pumpkin-like shape and comes in all colors. It's good cooked or raw (it has an intense tomatoey flavor) and, though messy, great for thick slices.

Green: There are two kinds—tomatoes that remain green when fully ripe, such as the tangy Zebras shown here; and red tomatoes picked before they ripen, which are quite tart and best used for frying, for broiling, and in relishes.

Heirloom: This name refers to any time-honored tomato variety grown from open-pollinated seeds. They may be sensitive to weather and disease, but their flavor can be exceptional.

Fresh Herb Guide

One of the easiest ways to make a dish feel fresh is to include abundant fresh herbs in its preparation. Even the simplest pasta dish (pasta with garlic and olive oil, for example) gets an enormous boost of flavor with the easy addition of chopped fresh parsley. (Try it and see for yourself.) Whether you have your own herb garden, a few plants in a windowsill, or you look to the market for your herbs, this guide will explain how to choose the right herb(s) for a dish, how to store and handle herbs, and how (and when) to use them in cooking.

Herb identification

BASIL Smooth, broad, bright-green leaves growing in pairs on a thick stem. Most common cooking variety: sweet basil. Other varieties: opal basil, Thai basil, lemon basil, cinnamon basil.

CHERVIL Fragile, lacy, pale-green leaves clustered in threes.

CHIVE Long, narrow, hollow, bright-green leaves; with edible pink bud clusters when in bloom.

CILANTRO Thin, rounded, toothed, bright-green leaves resembling flat-leaf parsley. Also called fresh coriander or Chinese parsley.

DILL Tender, feathery, blue-green fronds branching off a central stem.

OREGANO Small, oval, deep-green leaves with fine hairs. Most common cooking variety: Greek oregano. Other variety: Mexican oregano.

PARSLEY Vivid, green-toothed leaf clusters branching off a fibrous stem. Most common cooking varieties: Italian flat-leaf parsley and curly parsley.

ROSEMARY Glossy, needle-like leaves densely clustered along a central woody branch.

SAGE Numerous thick, soft, oblong, silvery-green leaves. Most common cooking variety: garden sage. Other varieties: purple sage, pineapple sage.

TARRAGON Large, shiny, toothed, dark-green leaves resembling its daisy relative. Most common cooking variety: French tarragon. Other varieties: Russian tarragon (not recommended).

THYME Clusters of tiny green leaves on a thin, woody stem. Most common variety for cooking: English thyme. Other varieties: lemon thyme, caraway thyme.

Flavors	Handling tips	What it's good in or with
Warm mint and clove with citrus and anise.	Leaves will blacken soon after chopping, so chop at the last minute. Use generously, adding toward the end of cooking.	A special affinity for tomatoes, fresh or cooked; the main flavor in classic pesto. Pair with Mediterranean and Asian ingredients. Also good in vegetable soups, butter sauces for white fish, and salads.
Delicate anise with the mild pepperiness of parsley.	Use liberally. Pick clusters of leaves or roughly chop sprigs. Add to dishes just before serving.	A gentle complement to delicately flavored dishes, including cream soups (especially carrot), shellfish, lean white fish, eggs, and spring vegetables.
Mild, fresh onion.	Use liberally. Finely chop or snip and add just before serving. Turns drab green when heated.	A mild alternative to raw onion. Pair with potatoes, eggs, cheese, and cream. Use to garnish soups, salads, and sautéed vegetables, or smear into softened butter for corn on the cob.
Tangy, with citrus notes.	Use liberally. Chop roughly or use sprigs and add just before serving. Flavor of leaves pales when heated.	Use as a cooling, zesty counterpoint to the spice in Asian, Latin American, and Indian dishes. Purée with garlic and oil, like a pesto, to serve with grilled shrimp or flank steak.
Mellow parsley, with warm spices.	Far less assertive than dill seed. Use liberally. Pick off whole fronds or roughly chop to add at the end of cooking or to use in cold dishes.	Associated with Scandinavian and Eastern European cooking. Add to potato salads, cucumbers, and deviled eggs, as well as potato or beet soups and dishes enriched with sour cream. Also great in biscuits.
Very assertive and peppery, with hint of pine.	Use judiciously; it can taste antiseptic. Chop roughly or finely and add early in cooking.	Pair the "pizza herb" with lemon and garlic to create Greek flavors. Accent red meats, roasted chicken, or hearty vegetables with it and use in zesty marinades and dressings for bold salads.
Subtle fresh celery and mild pepper.	Use generously. Chop leaves roughly or finely. Add toward the end of cooking or use uncooked. Keeps color well, so can be chopped ahead.	The star of Middle Eastern tabbouleh and Italian gremolata, this well-known garnish also adds vibrancy when added to dishes early in cooking. Use in bouquet garni for stocks, poaching liquids, and braises. Add leaves whole to salads for a fresh flavor.
Strong pine and fresh lemon.	Flavors can dominate; use judiciously. Use whole sprigs or roughly chop needles and add early in cooking or add finely chopped toward the end.	Excellent with grilled or roasted meats, particularly lamb, and roasted root vegetables. Team up with olive oil and garlic for marinades. Chop finely for use in breads and to top pizza. Infuse lemonade with a sprig.
Potent, savory, and earthy.	Can dominate and taste medicinal. Use judiciously. Chop roughly or cut into fine ribbons and add at beginning of cooking.	Think turkey stuffing. Pair with pork or veal or use to add an earthy quality to onions, winter squash, white beans, and root vegetable stews or gratins. Fry whole leaves in oil or butter to use as a tasty garnish.
Sweet and spicy licorice.	Flavors can dominate; use judiciously. Chop roughly or finely and add toward end of cooking.	Popular as an herbal vinegar for marinades and vinaigrettes. Use in French dishes such as béarnaise sauce and chicken with tarragon, but also a great partner for lobster, eggs, and spring vegetables.
Subtle pine and lemon, and spice.	Versatile, but can overwhelm delicate foods. Use liberally but carefully. Add whole sprigs or chopped leaves at any stage of cooking.	Adds depth of flavor to meats, seafood, and vegetables. Use to fully flavor stocks, sauces, and soups. Rounds out flavor in a classic shallot vinaigrette. Add sprigs to slow-roasted tomatoes, braises, and pasta sauces.

Refresh Your Spice Rack

Let's face it. Most spice racks, including my own, are in serious need of an overhaul. Here's why: With spices, freshness is everything, and with the passing of time, a spice's flavor irreversibly fades.

Tony Hill, the author of The Contemporary Encyclopedia of Herbs & Spices, explained it to me this way: "Picture the flavor of a fresh spice as having a hundred notes. After a couple of months, you lose ten flavor notes off the top and ten off the bottom. Over time, the notes keep dropping off, and eventually only the middle twenty or so notes remain."

That means even if you dump copious amounts of an over-the-hill spice into a recipe, you'll never recapture the full flavor profile of the fresh spice. You can, however, almost instantly transform your spice rack by replacing everything more than six months old. And while you're at it, why not improve and expand your collection by trying new varieties and taking a fresh look at under-appreciated essentials? You might also want to consider buying more whole spices to grind yourself, as the flavors in whole spices keep longer than ground. Finally, when you get your spices home, protect them from light and heat, which hasten flavor loss, by storing them in a cool drawer or cabinet.

An easy way to boost flavors: replace spices more than six months old and add some new spices to the mix

1 Brown or white cumin
Whole seeds and ground: This spice is the signature flavor of Mexican and Indian cuisines, as well as American-style chili.

2 Turkish bay leaves
Whole: Their savory flavor enhances slow-cooked stocks, stews, and tomato sauces.

3 Coriander
Whole seeds and ground: This spice adds a lemony pop of flavor to rubs, marinades, pickles, and curries.

13 Fleur de sel
This delicate, flaky, French salt is a delicious and elegant way to finish a dish.

12 Dried chiles
Whole, flakes, or ground: Use ancho, pasilla, or guajillo chiles for flavor. Use cayenne for its clean, sharp heat.

11 Sweet Hungarian paprika *Ground:* If you make barbecue rubs, this spice is a must-have.

10 Fennel seeds
Whole: This licoricey-sweet, earthy flavor is essential in Italian sausages and delicious in tomato sauce and in rubs for seafood, pork, lamb, and beef.

9 Cassia cinnamon
Sticks and ground: Whole sticks are great for infusing sweet flavor into stews and braises; use ground cinnamon in baking recipes.

8 Cloves
Whole and ground: The sweet, peppery warmth of cloves goes as well with salty ham and hearty stews as it does with sweet apple and pear desserts.

4 Pimentón de la Vera *Ground:* Use this smoked Spanish paprika to add a smoky flavor to any dish without firing up the grill.

5 Green cardamom
Whole pods or seeds: This sweet, peppery flavor is equally at home in Indian curries, spiced tea (chai), and fruit desserts.

6 Tellicherry peppercorns
Whole: Look for large black or reddish-black peppercorns, and always grind them yourself.

7 Nutmeg
Whole: Grate this aromatic spice into everything from cookie doughs to cream sauces for pasta.

Freezing & Thawing 101

The words "fresh" and "frozen" are often viewed as mutually exclusive. Yet for keeping foods tasting fresh, a freezer is often your best ally. Freezing is also a way for people who can't get to the market every day (which means most of us) to easily create fresh-feeling meals any night of the week.

My own freezer holds everything I need—frozen tortillas and breads, an assortment of vegetables and meats—to make tasty meals within minutes of arriving home from work. And when time is on my side, I know I'll have chopped herbs, homemade stock, berries, pastry dough, and many other ingredients on hand to prepare more elaborate dishes.

How does the freezer make all this possible? Well, when you freeze food, a couple of important things happen. First, the pathogens that cause foodborne illness can't grow, which makes food-safety experts like me jump for joy. In fact, as long as food remains frozen, it's as safe as the day it was put in the freezer. (It's thawing that invites trouble, but we'll get to that later.) Second, freezing also preserves food's quality by slowing down the microbes and chemical reactions that degrade food. But some of these reactions do continue during frozen storage, so eventually, the flavor, color, and texture deteriorate to the point that the food just isn't appealing, even if it's still technically safe to eat.

How to freeze for freshest flavor and safety

It might seem like the only role you play in freezing is finding space in the freezer, but actually there's a lot you can do to streamline the freezing process and to keep your food in optimum condition.

Faster is better. The packaged frozen foods you see at the supermarket were most likely "flash frozen" in a super-cold industrial freezer. The faster food freezes, the better—because freezing is a bit injurious to food. As the water in food freezes, ice crystals form and rupture cell walls. Rapid freezing keeps the ice crystals tiny and reduces the time for cells to leak fluids, which is good for the food's quality. Large ice crystals can

damage meat or produce, leading to texture and moisture loss when the food is thawed.

Your home freezer can't mimic the efficacy of an industrial freezer that freezes food in minutes and stores it well below 0°F. But you can still get decent results at home by using the tactics in the box at right.

Freezing isn't forever. Commercially frozen foods often have a "best if used by" date, which makes inventory control easy. But what about all the food you've frozen yourself: Can you eat that chili from 2001?

I don't think there's a simple answer. Storage guidelines, like those listed far right, give wide estimates because they depend on many variables: How fresh was the food when it was fro-

zen? How quickly did it freeze? What was the storage temperature, and was it consistent? How will the food ultimately be used? And, perhaps most important, how discriminating is your palate? For the sake of flavor, I'd probably make a new batch of chili before consuming vintage 2001, but some people wouldn't give it a second thought.

Use the kitchen refrigerator's freezer for fast turnover only. There are two reasons for this. The temperature inside fluctuates over a broad range because it's opened often, and also because the self-defrost feature includes programmed heating and cooling to melt frost before it builds up.

Those temperature fluctuations cause microscopic melting

> ## Q: Is it OK to refreeze food that's been thawed?
>
> A: Food can be safely refrozen within 48 hours of thawing if the thawing took place in the refrigerator or in cold water and the temperature of the thawed food has remained below 40°F. But the food's quality might suffer because fluids that seep from cells during refreezing and subsequent thawing can adversely affect texture and flavor.

and refreezing in foods, which encourages ice-crystal growth. Over time, this harms the food's texture. And as water moves from one area in the food to another, the surface of the food dries out—a condition known as freezer burn. Water migration can also create visible ice crystals. If you've kept ice cream for longer than a couple of weeks, you know what I mean.

So for long-term frozen storage (up to 12 months) stash food in a stand-alone freezer that won't be opened often and doesn't have a defrost feature.

Thawing foods safely

There's one thing I don't like about frozen food: thawing it. From a food-safety perspective, that's when you court trouble. As food thaws, the outer surface warms up first. Cells that were damaged during freezing release nutrients and moisture. And in some foods, this can create ideal conditions for pathogens to grow and multiply.

Thaw food at the temperature you plan to store it. Baked goods, breads, cakes, and cookies can be safely thawed and stored at room temperature. But meat, prepared entrées, fruits and vege-

tables, and raw dough should be thawed and stored in the refrigerator to minimize pathogen activity. Just like slow freezing, slow thawing can lead to moisture loss, but food safety always trumps quality.

Admittedly, doing things the right way can try one's patience. To safely hasten thawing, seal the frozen item in a leakproof container or plastic bag and immerse it in cold tap water. (Check the water every half an hour to be sure it remains cold.) Once thawed, refrigerate the food and use it soon. Thawed frozen food spoils as fast as, or faster than, its never-frozen counterpart because cells ruptured during freezing and thawing release nutrients for microbes to consume.

If you're in a real hurry to put something on the table, you can use your microwave's defrost feature to thaw food you plan to prepare and eat right away.

Or, better yet, skip thawing entirely. Some frozen foods, such as vegetables, can go straight from the freezer to the stove. And you might try putting frozen fruit right into the blender for a quick—not to mention pleasingly cold—smoothie.

To freeze— or not to freeze?

Foods that freeze well

Red meat: 4 to 12 months

Poultry: 9 to 12 months

Seafood: 3 to 6 months

Raw bacon: 1 to 2 months

Some casseroles: 1 to 4 months

Soup, stew, and stock: 2 to 4 months

Cooked legumes: 4 to 6 months

Whole berries: 8 to 12 months

Peeled ripe bananas: 2 to 4 weeks

Blanched vegetables: 2 to 12 months, depending on the vegetable

Bread: 6 to 8 months

Pie dough: 6 to 8 weeks

Nuts: 6 to 12 months

Butter: 6 to 9 months

Egg whites: 12 months

Flour: 6 to 12 months

Foods that don't freeze well

High-moisture vegetables like lettuce, celery, and cabbage become watery.

Cream and custard fillings separate.

Meringue toughens.

Milk undergoes flavor changes.

Sour cream and yogurt separate.

Heavy cream won't whip after being frozen.

Tip: Stick labels on the foods you freeze. Write the item's name (sometimes chili and meat sauce are hard to tell apart) and the date. Use the guidelines at left to help calculate a "use-by" date.

Help your freezer do its job

- **Set the freezer to 0°F or lower and monitor the temperature with a freezer thermometer (available at supermarkets and hardware stores).**
- **Try to place foods on the freezer's floor or near the walls.**

- **Don't overload the freezer with too much unfrozen food at once. And once food is frozen, keep the items stacked closely together. Freezers are most energy efficient when full. If your freezer is looking empty, consider freezing jugs or containers of water.**

- **Store food in containers that provide a barrier to air and moisture. Well-sealed plastic freezer containers work, as do heavy-duty plastic freezer bags or wrap, freezer paper, or heavy-duty foil.**

- **Many foods expand upon freezing, so don't overfill containers, but at the same time don't leave too much air space.**
- **Arrange unfrozen packages in a single layer, slightly separated from one another, so they freeze faster.**

- **Small items freeze faster, so freeze food portions you normally use in recipes: one or two cups of stock, a cup of sliced bananas, a tablespoon of tomato paste.**

Equivalency Charts

Oven Temperatures

Gas Mark	°F	°C
½	250	120
1	275	140
2	300	150
3	325	165
4	350	180
5	375	190
6	400	200
7	425	220
8	450	230
9	475	240
10	500	260
Broil	550	290

Liquid/Dry Measures

U.S.	Metric
¼ teaspoon	1.25 milliliters
½ teaspoon	2.5 milliliters
1 teaspoon	5 milliliters
1 tablespoon (3 teaspoons)	15 milliliters
1 fluid ounce (2 tablespoons)	30 milliliters
¼ cup	60 milliliters
⅓ cup	80 milliliters
½ cup	120 milliliters
1 cup	240 milliliters
1 pint (2 cups)	480 milliliters
1 quart (4 cups; 32 ounces)	960 milliliters
1 gallon (4 quarts)	3.84 liters
1 ounce (by weight)	28 grams
1 pound	454 grams
2.2 pounds	1 kilogram

Contributors

Bruce Aidells is the author of *Bruce Aidells's Complete Book of Pork* and *The Complete Meat Cookbook*. He also founded Aidells Sausage Company.

Amy Albert was a senior editor for *Fine Cooking*. She is now a senior associate editor at *Bon Appetit* magazine.

Pam Anderson is a contributing editor to *Fine Cooking* and the author of several books, including *Perfect Recipes for Having People Over*.

Jennifer Armentrout is a graduate of The Culinary Institute of America. She is *Fine Cooking's* Test Kitchen Manager and senior food editor.

Ben Baker is chef and co-owner of Magnolia Grill in Durham, North Carolina.

Jessica Bard is a culinary instructor, cookbook author, and food stylist. She teaches hands-on cooking classes at Warren Kitchen and Cutlery in Rhinebeck, New York.

Karen Barker is the pastry chef and co-owner of the award-winning Magnolia Grill restaurant in Durham, North Carolina and the author of *Sweet Stuff: Karen Barker's American Desserts*.

Lidia Bastianich is an award-winning chef and the co-owner of Felidia, Becco, and Del Posto in New York City.

Kay Baumhefner lives and teaches cooking in Petaluma, California.

Peter Berley is the author of *Fresh Food Fast* and award-winning *Modern Vegetable Kitchen*.

Paul Bertolli is a writer, artisan food producer and award-winning chef in the San Francisco Bay area of California.

Mark Bliss is executive chef of Silo Elevated Cuisine in San Antonio, Texas.

David Bonom is a chef, recipe developer and contributor to *Cooking Light* magazine.

Julianna Grimes Bottcher is a food writer and recipe developer.

Flo Braker is a renowned pastry chef and author of *The Simple Art of Perfect Baking* and the IACP award-winning cookbook *Sweet Miniatures*.

Ethel Brennan is a writer and food stylist from San Francisco, California.

Georgeanne Brennan is an award-winning cookbook author who lives in Northern California.

Becky Campbell is a tropical fruit expert and lives in Homestead, Florida.

Joanne Chang is pastry chef and owner of Flour Bakery & Cafe in Boston, Massachusetts.

Gary A. Coley trained at Dumas Père school for chefs in Glenview, Illinois. After running Wicklein's and Cornelia's of Chicago, he left the restaurant industry; he is currently a private chef in Atlanta, Georgia.

Jesse Cool, a restaurateur for over 25 years, is owner of CoolEatz Restaurants and Catering in Central California.

Leona Dalavai grills tandoori chicken with her family.

Regan Daley is the author of *In the Sweet Kitchen,* 2001's IACP Cookbook of the Year. She lives in Toronto, Canada.

Natalie Danford is a writer and editor living in New York City.

Erica DeMane is a food writer specializing in Italian cooking, whose books include *Pasta Improvvisata* and *The Flavors of Southern Italy*.

Tasha DeSerio is a former cook at Chez Panisse restaurant and café and is now the co-owner of Olive Green Catering in Berkeley, California. She also teaches cooking and writes about food.

Bill Devin was an exporter of Spanish products and resided in Tarragona, Spain.

Abigail Johnson Dodge is the author of *The Weekend Baker* and a contributing editor to *Fine Cooking*. She was the founding director of the *Fine Cooking* test kitchen.

Beth Dooley is a food writer and critic. **Lucia Watson** is an award-winning chef and restaurateur. They both authored *Savoring the Seasons of the Northern Heartland* and reside in Minneapolis, Minnesota.

Maryellen Driscoll is a contributing editor of *Fine Cooking* magazine.

Stephen Durfee is a pastry chef and instructor at The Culinary Institute of America at Greystone, California.

Ali Edwards is one of the founding farmers of Dirty Girl Produce and runs The Green Table, an organic catering company, both in Santa Cruz, California.

Allison Ehri is a food stylist and recipe tester for *Fine Cooking* magazine.

Josh Eisen teaches and writes about wine and food and lives in New York City.

Eve Felder is an associate dean and instructor at The Culinary Institute of America.

Claudia Fleming is a James Beard Award winner and former pastry chef of Gramercy Tavern in New York City. She and her husband, Gerry Hayden, currently run The North Fork Table and Inn in Southold, New York.

Janet Fletcher is a staff food writer for The San Francisco Chronicle.

Jean-Louis Gerin is chef-owner of Jean-Louis in Greenwich, Connecticut and was named Best Chef of the Northeast by the James Beard Foundation in 2006.

Joyce Goldstein is the former chef-owner of the famed Square One restaurant in San Francisco; she currently teaches and writes about cooking.

Aliza Green is a cookbook author, journalist and chef. She lives in Philadelphia, Pennsylvania.

Gordon Hamersley is chef-owner of Hamersley's Bistro in Boston, Massachusetts.

Lisa Hanauer is a former chef-restaurateur who now writes about food and teaches preschool. She lives in Oakland, California.

Linda J. Harris, Ph.D. is Associate Director of the Western Institute for Food Safety and Security and is a Specialist in Cooperative Extension at the Food Science and Technology program at the University of California-Davis.

Sam Hayward co-owns Fore Street, an award-winning restaurant, and Scales, a seafood restaurant and fish market in Portland, Maine.

Peter Hoffman is owner and chef of Savoy and Back Forty in New York City.

Martha Holmberg is the former editor in chief of *Fine Cooking*. She is currently the food editor at *The Oregonian* newspaper in Portland, Oregon, and a free-lance food writer.

Scott Howell is chef-owner of Nana's restaurant in Durham, North Carolina.

Irit Ishai is founder and head pastry chef of Sugar, Butter, Flour, a bakery in Sunnyvale, California.

Arlene Jacobs is a New York city-based restaurant consultant, freelance recipe developer, cooking instructor, and food writer.

Sarah Jay is a contributing editor of *Fine Cooking* magazine.

Steve Johnson is chef-owner of Rendezvous in Central Square, Cambridge, Massachusetts.

Elizabeth Karmel is the author of *Pizza on the Grill* (published by Taunton) and *Taming the Flame: Secrets for Hot and-Quick Grilling and Low-and-Slow BBQ*.

Eva Katz is a recipe developer and food writer who lives in Jamaica Plain, Massachusetts.

Hubert Keller is chef-owner of several restaurants including Fleur de Lys in Las Vegas, Nevada and San Francisco, California.

Ris Lacoste has been a professional award-winning chef for nearly 25 years, including 10 years as the executive chef at 1789 Restaurant in Washington, D.C.

David Lebovitz is the author of many cookbooks, including the best-selling title *Room for Dessert*. He teaches cooking lessons around the world and resides in Paris, France.

Seen Lippert is a chef who graduated from the Culinary Institute of America and cooked at Chez Panisse for over 10 years. She currently lives in Greenwich, Connecticut.

Ruth Lively is a food and garden writer; she is the former editor of *Fine Gardening* magazine.

Lori Longbotham is a New York City-based food writer, cookbook author, and recipe developer.

Rita Maas is a food photographer and lives in New York City.

Deborah Madison is a freelance food writer and an author of many vegetarian cookbooks including *Local Flavors*, winner of a James Beard Award. She lives in Galisteo, New Mexico.

Domenica Marchetti is a food writer and author of *The Glorious Soups and Stews of Italy*. She lives in Alexandria, Virginia.

Kimberly Y. Masibay trained as a pastry chef in Germany and studied journalism at Columbia University before becoming a senior editor at *Fine Cooking*. She is now a freelance food writer.

Jennifer McLagan is a food stylist, food journalist and regular contributor to *Fine Cooking* magazine. She lives in Toronto, Canada.

Perla Meyers teaches cooking at workshops around the country and has cooked in restaurants throughout Italy, France, and Spain.

Susie Middleton was *Fine Cooking*'s editor; she is now *Fine Cooking*'s editor at large as well as a food writer and cookbook author.

Jean-Pierre Moulle has spent over twenty years as head chef at Chez Panisse in Berkeley, California.

Jan Newberry is the Food and Wine Editor of *San Francisco* magazine.

David Page & Barbara Shinn own Shinn Estate Vineyards, a winery and bed and breakfast in Mattituck, New York.

Greg Patent is an award-winning baker and cookbook author. He lives in Missoula, Montana.

Caprial Pence and her husband, John, are co-owners and executive chefs of Caprial's Westmoreland Kitchen in Portland, Oregon. They also star in the cooking show Caprial and John's Kitchen: Cooking for Family and Friends.

Leslie Glover Pendleton, a former editor of *Gourmet* magazine, is a food writer, recipe developer, and cookbook author. She lives in Hartford, Connecticut.

Steve Petusevsky is a graduate of the Culinary Institute of America in Hyde Park, New York. A food journalist and cookbook author, he is currently a culinary instructor and teaches classes at many retail markets and cooking schools nationally.

James Peyton is a food writer and expert in Mexican cooking.

Mai Pham is a cookbook author, food writer, culinary instructor and the chef-owner of Lemon Grass Restaurant in Sacramento, California.

Odessa Piper is a sustainable farming expert and is the founder of L'Etoile Restaurant in Madison, Wisconsin. She currently resides in Maryland.

Nicole Plue is the pastry chef at Julia's Kitchen at COPIA in Napa, California.

Debra Ponzek is chef-owner of Aux Delices restaurants and caterers in Riverside, Greenwich and Darien, Connecticut.

Steve Raichlen is the author of the best-selling *The Barbecue Bible* and television host of *Barbecue University* and *Primal Grill*.

Nicole Rees is a food scientist, cookbook author, and baker based in Portland, Oregon. She co-wrote the revised edition of *Understanding Baking,* as well as its companion recipe book, *The Baker's Manual*.

Leslie Revsin was a successful chef, restaurateur and cookbook author.

Rick Rodgers is the author of over 30 cookbooks, including the best-sellers *Thanksgiving 101* and *Fondue*.

Tony Rosenfeld is a contributing editor to *Fine Cooking* and the author of Taunton's *150 Things to Make with Roast Chicken*.

Pascal Sauton, named Oregon's Top Seafood Chef in 2006, is chef/owner of Carafe Bistro in Portland, Oregon.

Chris Schlesinger is a chef and cookbook author, whose books include *The Thrill of the Grill*.

Regina Schrambling is a freelance food writer and popular blogger (www.gastropoda.com).

Katherine Eastman Seeley is a pastry chef and food writer.

Maria Helm Sinskey is the culinary director and executive chef at Robert Sinskey Vineyards and the author of *The Vineyard Kitchen: Menus Inspired by the Seasons*.

Ana Sortun, awarded Best Chef: Northeast in 2005 by the James Beard Foundation, is chef/owner of Oleana in Cambridge, Massachusetts.

Stu Stein is a chef and the author of *The Sustainable Kitchen*.

Molly Stevens is a contributing editor to *Fine Cooking*. She won the IACP Cooking Teacher of the Year award in 2006; her book *All About Braising* won the James Beard and International Association of Culinary Professionals awards.

Kathleen Stewart runs the Downtown Bakery and Creamery in Healdsburg, California.

Craig Stoll is chef and co-owner of Delfina in San Francisco, California.

Alan Tangren, a food writer, was a pastry chef at Chez Panisse and co-wrote *Chez Panisse Fruit* with Alice Waters.

Alan Tardi is a restaurant consultant and freelance writer who spends his time in New York City and Italy.

Fred Thompson is a food writer, food stylist and culinary developer. He is author of four cookbooks including *Grillin' with Gas* which will be released in May 2009. Thompson lives in Raleigh, North Carolina, and New York City.

Jerry Traunfeld is the former executive chef of The Herbfarm in Woodinville, Washington, and author of *The Herbfarm Cookbook*.

Norman Van Aken is chef-owner of Norman's New World Cuisine in Coral Gables and Orlando, Florida.

Carolyn Weil, a baker and baking instructor, is an author and avid contributor to *Fine Cooking* magazine.

Joanne Weir is a cooking teacher, cookbook author, and star of the PBS show *Joanne Weir's Cooking Class*.

Nancy Wiese, with this recipe, was a finalist in *Fine Cooking* magazine's America's Best Home Cook Contest of 2004. She lives in Plano, Texas.

Clifford Wright, an expert in Mediterranean cuisine, is a successful food writer, author and cooking teacher living in Texas.

Patricia Yeo, a famed chef, is the author of *Cooking from A to Z* and *Everyday Asian*.

Su-Mei Yu is the chef-owner of two San Diego restaurants, Saffron Thai Chicken and Saffron Noodles and Sate.

Daphne Zepos is owner of the Essex Street Cheese Company in Long Island City, New York.

Photo Credits

Steve Aitken: p. 225 (right)

Amy Albert: p. 83, 132-133, 138, 139, 184 (left), 208 (peas), 209 (tomatoes), 224 (left), 232 (top)

Todd Bryant: p. 116-117

Grey Crawford: p. 99

Mark Ferri: p. 100, 118, 120, 173

Ben Fink: p. 58, 66, 72, 107 (right), 115, 154

Boyd Hagen: p. 160 (left), 221 (top), 227, 231

Brian Hagiwara: p. 96

Gentl & Hyers: p. 20

Martha Holmberg: p. 6 (bottom), 21, 175 (right), 200 (bottom), 201 (bottom)

Saxon Holt: p. 223

Steve Hunter: p. 85, 158-159, 234 (all except top left)

Sarah Jay: p. 18-19, 26 (top), 33, 150, 171 (left), 174-175, 178 (top photos),215,

Susan Kahn: p. 211

Ruth Lively: p. 114, 229 (bottom)

Rita Maas: p. 27, 88-89, 102 (bottom), 191 (right), 193

Maura McEvoy: p. 152

Scott Phillips: p. 2, 4, 5, 6 (top), 7, 8 (left and below), 10, 11, 12, 13, 14, 15, 16, 23, 24, 25, 26 (bottom), 28, 29, 30, 31, 34, 35, 36, 39, 40, 41, 42, 43, 44, 46, 47, 49, 51, 52 (top), 53, 54, 55, 56, 59, 60, 61, 62, 63, 64, 67, 68, 69, 70, 71, 74, 76, 77, 78, 79, 81, 87, 90 (bottom), 91, 92, 93, 94, 95, 97, 98, 101, 102 (top), 103, 104, 106, 107 (left), 108, 109, 110, 113, 119, 121, 122, 123, 124, 125, 128, 129, 130, 131, 133, 134, 135, 136, 137, 140, 141, 142, 143, 144 (bottom), 145, 147, 148, 149, 151, 153, 155, 156, 157 (top), 158 (left), 159 (right), 160 (right), 161, 162, 163, 165, 166, 167, 168, 169, 170, 171 (right), 172, 174 (left), 176, 177, 178 (bottom), 179, 181, 182, 183, 184-185, 186, 187, 188, 189, 190, 191 (left), 192, 194 (bottom), 195, 196, 197, 198, 199, 200 (top), 202, 203, 204, 205, 206, 207, 208 (except peas), 209 (except tomatoes), 210, 212, 213, 214, 216, 217, 218, 219, 220, 221 (bottom photos), 222, 224 (right), 225 (left), 226, 228, 229 (top), 230, 232 (bottom photos), 233, 234 (top left), 238, 240, 242, 246

Alan Richardson: p. 9 (right), 80

France Ruffenach: p. 38, 50, 144 (top), 194 (top)

Judi Rutz: p. 82, 90 (top)

Ellen Silverman: p. 45, 112, 116 (left)

Joanne Smart: p. 32

Mark Thomas: p. 8-9, 52 (bottom), 65, 84-85, 105, 126, 157 (bottom), 164, 201 (top)